Political Persuasion and Attitude Change

Political Persuasion and Attitude Change

Edited by Diana C. Mutz,
Paul M. Sniderman,
and Richard A. Brody

Ann Arbor
THE UNIVERSITY OF MICHIGAN PRESS

Copyright © by the University of Michigan 1996
All rights reserved
Published in the United States of America by
The University of Michigan Press
Manufactured in the United States of America
⊗ Printed on acid-free paper

1999   1998   1997   1996   4   3   2   1

A CIP catalog record for this book is available from the British Library.

Library of Congress Cataloging-in-Publication Data

Political persuasion and attitude change / edited by Diana C. Mutz,
    Paul M. Sniderman, and Richard A. Brody.
        p.   cm.
    ISBN 0-472-09555-2 (hardcover : alk. paper). — ISBN 0-472-06555-6
    (pbk. : alk. paper)
    1. Mass media—Political aspects.   2. Persuasion (Rhetoric)
3. Attitude change.   4. Public opinion.   I. Mutz, Diana Carole.
II. Sniderman, Paul M.   III. Brody, Richard A.
P95.8.P645   1996
302.23—dc20   96-10248
                                                              CIP

Contents

CHAPTER 1

Political Persuasion: The Birth of a Field of Study

Diana C. Mutz, Paul M. Sniderman,
and Richard A. Brody

As a field of study, political persuasion has a long lineage but a brief history. On the one side, it is easy—and fitting—to point to classical studies, by scholars of propaganda analysis, public opinion, and marketing research, all calling attention to the new dynamics of democratic politics created by the simultaneous rise of mass media and public institutions for mass literacy. As Walter Lippmann (1937) explained, "A new situation has arisen throughout the world, created by the spread of literacy among the people and the miraculous improvement of the means of communication. Always the opinions of relatively small publics have been a prime force in political life, but now, for the first time in history, we are confronted nearly everywhere by mass opinion as the final determinant of political and economic action." On the other side, even today, despite all the notable studies that have been accomplished, it is difficult to point to a body of cumulative studies establishing who can be talked out of what political positions and how. It is, accordingly, the twofold purpose of this book to make the case for the systematic study of political persuasion, separate from and comparable in importance to the study of voting and public opinion, and to contribute, from a variety of angles and drawing on a number of independent research programs, to this new field of study.

Politics, at its core, is about persuasion. It hinges not just on whether citizens at any one moment in time tend to favor one side of an issue over another, but on the numbers of them that can be brought, when push comes to shove, from one side to the other or, indeed, induced to leave the sidelines in order to take a side. Politics is about turning minorities of today into majorities of tomorrow, and the risk as well as the strength of democratically contested politics lies precisely in its openness to change.

Persuasion is ubiquitous in the political process; it is also the central aim of political interaction. It is literally the stuff of politics: Whether the object is to deter nuclear attack, cajole an obdurate legislator, win over a Supreme

Court justice, hold a supporter in place, or nudge a voter in a favorable direction, the end is *persuasion*.

Democracy, in particular, is distinguished as a form of governance by the extent of persuasion relative to coercion. Yet, the study of public opinion and political psychology has concentrated on the statics, rather than the dynamics, of political preferences. It is not our intention to suggest that there has been a complete dearth of interest in the issue of change. On the contrary, one can point to quite a few distinguished studies, some of which we shall say a word about in a moment. It is instead our aim to underline that, in the study of politics as elsewhere, method tends to drive substantive focus at least as much as substantive focus shapes method.

The cross-sectional general population survey has been far and away the principal vehicle for the study of public opinion and politics. It has proven to be a tool of exceptional value, but the very size of the benefits it has conferred has tended to obscure the size of the costs it also has imposed. Most fundamentally, the objective of a cross-sectional public opinion survey is to offer a portrait of public opinion in one specific slice of time, and the inevitable consequence for the systematic study of public opinion has been a focus on the statics, not the dynamics, of political preferences.

Different research designs—most notably panel samples, which involve interviewing and then reinterviewing the same individual at two or more points in time—have been deployed from time to time. Yet, in an irony worth acknowledgement, the study of change has been put to use in precisely the substantive context where it has been least useful—namely, the study of voting. From the classic studies of Lazarsfeld and his colleagues at Columbia to those of Converse and his colleagues at Michigan, the lesson that panel studies have taught is the overpowering stability of partisan loyalties both between and during election campaigns (e.g., Lazarsfeld, Berelson, and Gaudet 1944; Berelson, Lazarsfeld, and McPhee 1954; Converse 1962, 1970). Panel studies of political attitudes over extended periods of time fixed attention on two patterns of public opinion at opposing extremes. At one pole, attitudes that were integrally tied up with electoral choices—above all, partisanship—although not set absolutely in cement, proved to be over-whelmingly fixed even over relatively extended periods of voters' lives. At the opposite pole, attitudes toward a miscellany of nonelectoral issues seemed so variable, either over time or in response to apparently trivial changes in question wording, as to call into question the presumption that a genuine attitude had been there in the first place (Converse 1964; Zaller 1992). From either direction, there seemed little point to studying systematically the conditions under which ordinary citizens could be persuaded to take one rather than another position on an array of issues: political attitudes either changed so little that they could hardly be said to change at all or changed so much that it could hardly be said that they were attitudes at all.

Panel studies have thrown light on the dynamics of political attitudes, and longitudinal studies focusing on time series generated by the repetition of cross-sectional opinion surveys with fixed questionnaire content have thrown still more.[1] But whether panel or repeated cross section, this stream of studies has been confined to the study of the natural fluctuation of political preferences, providing a record of what preferences have changed, by how much, and when. As useful as a record of the natural variation of political preferences over an extended period of time is, it is doubly limited as a basis for understanding change. It is limited, in the first instance, because it illuminates only obliquely the actual processes of change at the individual level. Partly, this is because what is systematically measured is change in response, not the stimulus that evoked it, and there are, unavoidably, huge constraints on inference from naturally occurring covariation of any appreciable degree of complexity. Actual political-historical events are complex, simultaneously involving multiple aspects of change, and only through experimental randomization can these analytically distinguishable aspects be causally unconfounded to determine which aspects are prepotent and which are not.

Restricting analysis to the study of naturally occurring change is confining in a second way as well. The objective must be to understand how processes of change, in general, and political persuasion, in particular, work, and this requires, as a moment's reflection will make plain, observing not only how people responded to the play of forces in any given historical circumstance, but also how they respond when put in different circumstances and exposed either to different forces or to similar ones in a different mix. It is just this competence of catching hold of behavior in circumstances more varied than those that actually occurred, but not merely hypothetical, that sets experimentation apart.

Experimentation is not a necessary condition for the study of change. The studies of political persuasion presented in this volume clearly demonstrate otherwise.[2] Researchers have capitalized on combining a wide variety of methodological approaches so that rigorous designs can be synthesized with findings that are generalizable to real-world political settings. Indeed, research on political persuasion is characterized by an unusual degree of methodological pluralism. Likewise, the chapters in this volume reflect a wide range of methodological approaches. In many chapters, survey data are combined with experimental studies to circumvent the shortcomings of each. For example, in chapter 3, Miller and Krosnick use both approaches in an attempt to resolve inconsistencies between experimental and survey studies in identifying who is most susceptible to persuasion under what conditions. In chapter

7, Sigelman and Rosenblatt highlight the contributions of methodological pluralism to understanding the power of presidents to persuade mass opinion. In still other chapters, traditional panel studies, longitudinal designs, and cross-sectional surveys are combined with laboratory experiments, personal interviews, and quasi-experimental designs. What we are arguing, then, is this: experimentation is not a necessary condition for any individual study of change, but having experimentation as part of the mix of methodological approaches is a necessary condition for launching political persuasion as a systematic field of study.[3]

But what does it mean to speak of the study of political persuasion as a distinctive field of study? Why use the term *political persuasion* at all? Why not just speak of studies of persuasion that happen to concentrate on opinions about public issues? Isn't the study of the conditions under which political preferences can be modified merely a derivative subfield of the study of attitude change *tout court?* And even if the particular examples are taken from the realm of politics, aren't the fundamental ideas and systematic principles in fact the work of social psychologists, with political scientists assigned the secondary role of applying them to the particular field of public affairs?

We do not wish to leave the impression that we place a low value on the study of attitude change as it has developed in other disciplines and, above all, in social psychology. On the contrary: for originality, breadth of interest, imagination in operationalization, fertility in application, rigor of argument, and sheer intellectual flair, the social psychological study of attitude change has no counterpart of which we are aware. And yet we see a case for political persuasion as an autonomous field of research, responsive to intellectual and methodological advancements outside itself but developing on its own lines, guided by the need to address its own distinctive problems.

A variety of considerations serve to highlight the uniqueness of political persuasion. For one, questions of politics stand out, because just insofar as they are considered to be political matters, it is socially acceptable for people to take different positions on them. Of course, people can have a very short fuse with others who disagree with them about political issues, but differences of opinion about public affairs have a legitimacy that is distinctive. Indeed, they have both the encouragement and the protection of an array of political and social institutions, of which the First Amendment has become the most conspicuous.

Moreover, it is legitimate not only for citizens to disagree about public affairs, but also for each to try to persuade the other to change his or her mind. As a democratic polity, we have not merely permitted but institutionalized argument about public issues and personalities. Political discourse across lines of difference is essential to most conceptions of a democratic public sphere (e.g., Habermas 1964). It is important precisely because it creates opportunities for political persuasion to occur.

Arguments about political issues, precisely because they are so well practiced, tend to be well scripted: people can get the point, recognize the broader argument being made, notwithstanding the unevenness of their interest in politics and the thinness of their understanding of abstract political ideas. A symbolic phrase or two—a reference here or there to the "welfare mess," to mention only one example—can call to mind a whole line of argument. The general public is fairly adept at making out the political bottom line of arguments over public affairs directed at them. Ordinary citizens, despite the fitfulness of their attention to politics, are also not bad at the political fingerprints on these arguments: they are capable of recognizing whether particular arguments come from political quarters with which they are broadly sympathetic or those they cannot abide.

A quite different argument for the distinctiveness of political persuasion as a field of research comes from the intrinsic properties of mass politics. Political views tend to be less involving just insofar as politics characteristically fails to involve the deepest interests of most citizens. For this very reason, political attitudes tend to be based on notoriously low levels of information. Furthermore, in politics, unlike many other areas of life, persuasive messages tend to be communicated not directly but indirectly, often through mass mediated channels. The fact that this form of communication is public and simultaneously reaches many people has important implications for the persuasion process. Moreover, studies of political persuasion inevitably require taking into account the persuasive efforts of political elites as well as the mass media and mass public.

Although psychological studies have been extremely useful in understanding who is most susceptible to persuasive attempts, it is often unclear how these findings translate to a range of political contexts. To presume that political attitudes are altered in the same way as attitudes toward products or personal matters ignores the uniqueness of the political context. Even within the realm of political contexts, there is tremendous variability from one election to another, from one kind of issue to another, and from one social environment to another.

To date, most models of the political persuasion process have not taken these factors into account. The early source-message-receiver model emphasized "who says what to whom, with what effect," but did not systematically study the context in which persuasion occurred. Even the far more complex communication/persuasion matrix developed by McGuire is, in his words, "a theory of persons" (McGuire 1981).

In his now classic formulation, Lewin (1936) described attitudes as a function of both people and circumstances. However, variability across people initially received the bulk of research attention. Since that time, one of the most important contributions that social psychology has made to understanding human behavior is an appreciation of the power and subtlety of situational influences on attitudes and behaviors, "that manipulations of the immediate social situation can overwhelm in importance the type of individual differences in personal traits or dispositions that people normally think of as being determinative of social behavior" (Nisbett and Ross 1991).

The implications of this generalization have yet to be fully heeded in studies of political persuasion and attitude change. More often than not, our topics of study and the methods we employ fail to take into systematic account the power of situations to influence political attitudes. This is particularly unfortunate in studies of political persuasion, because the fluidity of circumstances is precisely what gives politics its dynamic quality. After all, basic characteristics of individuals—their level of education, for example, or their overall outlook on politics, or even the level of their interest in politics—tend to be stable over time. In contrast, the features of their circumstances are transient, changing as one situation gives way to another. In the political realm in particular, "situations" are ever changing; as the ebb and flow of public debate varies from day to day, the political environment in which people find themselves is changed.

Our goal in *Political Persuasion and Attitude Change* is to highlight a variety of substantive areas in the study of political attitude change, but to do so in a way that better mirrors the intricate world of political persuasion by systematically incorporating aspects of persons and their political environments. In this chapter, we begin by situating these contemporary research efforts in the broader context of research on political persuasion.

In the early 1900s, research on political persuasion flourished under the guise of propaganda analysis, public opinion research, social psychology, and marketing research. This emphasis emerged out of a general consensus that persuasion had become increasingly important as a result of major societal changes. The United States' involvement in two world wars early in this century fueled tremendous levels of interest in public opinion and attitude change.

But today, despite the rich history of research in psychology and in studies of voting behavior, the parameters of political persuasion remain elusive. One important reason for our limited knowledge is the early emphasis on the role of personal traits and individual predispositions in conditioning responses to political persuasion. Studies oriented around the source-message-receiver model focused on identifying empirical regularities that held across situations—for example, how persuasive impact is related to the age, gender, or attractiveness of a source; which message characteristics (negative versus positive appeals, fast versus slow delivery) enhance persuasion; and which demographic or personality traits contribute to greater persuasibility (e.g., Hovland, Janis, and Kelley 1953).

The first phase of research in political psychology also was marked by a shared enthusiasm for using personality and the early life experiences shaping it to explain political attitudes and behaviors (McGuire 1993). The focus on personality emphasized attitude stability over an individual's lifetime (e.g., Adorno 1950). Sometimes long-term changes in political attitudes were argued to result from the slow evolution of personality types (e.g., Riesman 1950), but the emphasis was still on relative stability, particularly within the range of short-term political conflicts. In studies of voting behavior, this same enthusiasm manifested itself in the concept of party identification as a stable personal predisposition acquired early in life (see Chaffee and Hochheimer 1982).

Methodological considerations further contributed to the emphasis on individual traits and predispositions. One of the key legacies of the wartime emphasis on the persuasive influence of mass media was an experimental approach to the study of persuasive effects (Czitrom 1982). Studies of the "Why We Fight" series of army orientation films illustrated this new emphasis on rigorously controlled laboratory experiments oriented toward identifying individual psychological variables conditioning the persuasion process. While increasing the methodological rigor of many studies, the experimental approach to persuasion often separated research from its social contexts, be they political or otherwise. The interpersonal social context was considered extremely important in early survey research on political attitudes (e.g., Katz and Lazarsfeld 1955). But when the dominant research mode shifted away from community-based studies to large national surveys, context did not fare well. The national scope of these projects often made it difficult to locate respondents in a particular political and social milieu. And perhaps more importantly, the findings of very little persuasion in the early studies of presidential elections were assumed to generalize to future elections. The focus of research became attitude stability or the lack thereof, rather than the sources of change in political views.

In addition to multimethod approaches, this collection of studies reflects important innovations in the study of political persuasion. The contributors to this volume have used a variety of methods that give concrete form to our proposed model by explicitly incorporating context into their studies. For example, Diamond and Cobb suggest a new way of using the traditional survey instrument that better represents people's attitudes as a range of possible responses or positions. Mondak, Mutz, and Huckfeldt take advantage of a unique data collection design that samples not only potential targets of persuasion, but also their immediate social contexts. Still other contributors such as Kuklinski and Hurley use hybrid survey-experiments. By using the survey interview as an opportunity to vary systematically the situational pressures respondents face, the survey is transformed from a passive to an interactive process, and one that better imitates the range of situations in which real-world political opinions are expressed.

Precisely because political persuasion has resisted formulaic simplification, its study requires sophisticated methodological approaches. Some persuasive considerations have more impact on some persons than on others; some opinions are more subject to modification than others; and both are more readily modifiable in some situations than in others. Characterizing the contexts in which political persuasion occurs is inevitably complex. To date there is precious little evidence specifying who can be talked out of what beliefs, and under what conditions. The studies in this volume reflect this complexity in that characteristics of the political environment are not studied in isolation from one another; instead, they emphasize interactions between characteristics of persons and their political environments.

In *Political Persuasion and Attitude Change* we present an array of empirical studies developing this framework both substantively and methodologically. The contributors to this volume review a wide range of topics dealing with political persuasion. These include purposeful attempts by political elites to persuade mass public opinion, effects that flow from journalists' discretion in the selection of news stories, and influence that flows between people in the course of their interpersonal interactions. Since the authors are major figures in research on each of the respective areas they review, they also are able to contribute their latest findings and new insights into research on these topics.

The three sections of the book center on the three major agents of political persuasion. Part 1 is entitled "Mass Media and Political Persuasion," and it reviews several major areas of research on mass media's influence on political attitudes, including research on priming effects, the impact of political advertising, and the capacity for news coverage to change public opinion. In chapter 2, John Zaller begins this section with a broad statement of the problems involved in studying mass media's impact on political attitudes. In "The Myth of Massive Media Impact Revived: New Support for a Discredited Idea," Zaller argues that large media effects are seldom detected, not because such effects do not exist, but rather because the conditions necessary for detecting such effects are infrequent. In addition to good measurement of key variables, these conditions include large variations in the flow of communication reaching the public and an imbalance between the flow of messages promoting opposing sides. He concludes that media effects on mass opinion are both very large and very common; these effects are simply difficult to observe because large changes in media content are infrequent and difficult to predict, and because stable flows of competing communications effectively cancel one another out in terms of their net effects.

In illustrating these points, Zaller extends his earlier work on conditional relationships between exposure to political communication and attitude change. Using election data and attitudes toward a variety of public issues, he demonstrates how "exposure gaps" generated by differences in the intensity of various campaigns combine to form a "crossover effect," whereby those most susceptible to persuasion are those least informed in some contexts, while it is the more informed who may be moved in other contexts.

In chapter 3, Joanne Miller and Jon Krosnick review and add new evidence to the burgeoning research on the priming hypothesis, a major area of media effects research. The authors provide a detailed account of research on the priming hypothesis as an important form of mass political persuasion. In addition to synthesizing the literature bearing on the extent to which news media alter the standards the public uses in evaluating political figures, they pay particular attention to who is most susceptible to priming effects. Miller and Krosnick find that the role of political involvement in susceptibility to persuasion is particularly complex, with multiple components predicting quite different outcomes. For example, high levels of exposure and attention to political news weaken priming effects, while high levels of knowledge facilitate greater priming effects. Thus, a prime candidate for priming would be a highly knowledgeable person who, nonetheless, faces a situation in which he or she has little time to attend to political news.

The last chapter in part 1 departs from this emphasis on the effects of the news media and addresses political advertising as yet another form of mass mediated persuasive communication. In "The Craft of Political Advertising: A Progress Report" Stephen Ansolabehere and Shanto Iyengar review their extensive research program on the persuasive power of political advertising. Using laboratory experiments, they isolate individual components of political advertisements and tease apart interactions between multiple factors influencing the persuasion process. At the same time, they note that political advertising does not occur in a vacuum and, therefore, methodological accommodations need to be made in order to systematically incorporate the effects of the political context in which advertisements occur.

Part 2 focuses on persuasion by political elites. These three chapters illustrate substantive and methodological problems in past research on the persuasive efforts of political elites, while simultaneously breaking new ground in our understanding of why elites succeed or fail in influencing public opinion. The section begins with an exploration of the impact of political elites on the interpretation of persuasive messages. In chapter 5, James Kuklinski and Norman Hurley use an experimental design to demonstrate the powerful effects that merely changing the source of a given message has on the interpretation of messages. Moreover, these interpretations vary by characteristics of the receiver in interaction with characteristics of the source of the message. For example, black citizens interpreted a message advocating black self-reliance very differently depending on whether it was purported to have been stated by Jesse Jackson, Clarence Thomas, Edward Kennedy, or George Bush. In "It's a Matter of Interpretation," Kuklinski and Hurley conclude based on evidence of these strong source effects that what seems like random attitude change on the part of the mass public may not be random at all.

In the second chapter of this section, Kathleen McGraw and Clark Hubbard review research on "account giving" as a strategy of elite persuasion, that is, the efforts of political elites to control public opinion by accounting for their behavior in strategic ways in order to persuade their constituents that they are deserving of continued support. In addition to reviewing work on account giving as a form of political persuasion, chapter 6 emphasizes the kinds of personal characteristics that make the explanations offered by political elites compelling forms of political persuasion.

In chapter 7, Lee Sigelman and Alan Rosenblatt discuss the most prominent forum for elite persuasion of mass opinion: the presidency. The authors review work on the president's ability to persuade the public with an emphasis on the necessity of methodological innovation to improve the validity of evidence pertaining to presidential powers of persuasion. The relatively small sample of presidents and the problems involved in distinguishing changes in opinion that occur for other reasons make this a particularly difficult persuasion context for establishing both internal and external validity.

Political persuasion is clearly not a simple, mechanistic process whereby one agent puts forth a persuasive message and its audience automatically falls prey; people play an important role in their own persuasion. Thus, Part 3 of this book focuses on the tremendously important yet often overlooked role that individuals play in their own persuasion. Given the large amount of potentially persuasive information that people encounter, they inevitably weigh some considerations more than others and are more easily persuaded in some contexts than in others. The four chapters composing the section on "Individual Control of the Political Persuasion Process" directly address individual susceptibility and resistance to persuasion.

In chapter 8, Dennis Chong proposes a general theory of the process by which people select among the many considerations upon which they might rely in making up their minds about where they stand on a given issue. He examines political attitudes as a function of frames of reference that are sampled from the political environment. Since an individual cannot bring to bear all of the considerations surrounding a given issue when offering an opinion, he or she must sample from a reservoir of considerations that are available for use in evaluating an issue. Since this frame of reference for viewing a given political issue can change based on the availability of various considerations and the conclusion toward which various considerations point, so too may his or her attitude.

Chong's model sheds light on attitude instability, survey response effects, and the process of attitude change. It suggests that some attitude instability may result from situational variation rather than unreliable measurement or randomly expressed pseudoattitudes. Moreover, if individual attitudes are expected to vary across situations, then it makes little sense to use consistency of attitudes within individuals as the sine qua non of "real" attitudes.

In chapter 9, Gregory Diamond and Michael Cobb propose a theory of attitude measurement that takes into account the fact that people may not have policy choices that can be accurately described by some optimally preferred point on an attitude scale. For most people in most situations, distinguishing between the precisely right response and the sufficiently right response is hardly worthwhile given their low levels of interest in politics and the costs of acquiring and analyzing new information. The authors conceptualize individual attitudes as ranges of possibilities rather than as single point estimates. Using latitude theory drawn from the work of Sherif and Hovland (1961), they measure attitudes as ranges of acceptance and rejection rather than as point estimates. In so doing, they question the very essence of what it means to be persuaded. For example, when attitudes are measured as optimal point placements, as is traditionally the case, persuasion is an act of conversion from one point on a line to another. When attitudes are conceptualized instead as ranges of acceptance, rejection, and noncommitment, persuasion also includes the widening or narrowing of these ranges. Thus, from the perspective of political elites, "the battle is not to convince citizens that one's policy is right, but simply that it is not unreasonable." Political actors may further their policy preferences not only by changing people's minds, but also by widening their latitudes of noncommitment. Diamond and Cobb's approach, like Chong's in the preceding chapter, suggests that although individuals may not have long-lasting, consistent opinions on many issues of the day, their opinions still matter and are not entirely at the mercy of political elites.

In the third chapter of this section, Jeffery Mondak, Diana Mutz, and Robert Huckfeldt explore the process by which individuals come to rely on some social contexts over others in making their political judgments. Social context clearly matters in forming political attitudes, but given that individuals are embedded in multiple social contexts, how do they sort through the often conflicting information that they receive when taking social context into account? Many political judgments occur across multiple social contexts. It is one thing to argue that context influences political attitudes, but quite another to determine which of the many "contexts" in which people live are important for a given political attitude. After reviewing evidence on how a variety of different economic contexts influences vote choice, the authors add new evidence bearing on the role of the neighborhood social context.

The last chapter of the book also concludes with an emphasis on the importance of context in political persuasion. "Time of Vote Decision and Openness to Persuasion" revisits one of the most persistent puzzles in research on political persuasion, the paradoxical relationship between exposure to political messages and susceptibility to persuasion. In their classic study of the 1940 presidential election, Lazarsfeld, Berelson, and Gaudet (1948) argued that the very same characteristics that lead people to expose themselves to political messages also insulate them from potential influence. In particular, the "last-minute deciders" who make up their minds during the course of the presidential campaign are generally uninterested in politics and highly unlikely to expose themselves to political messages. In chapter 11, Steven Chaffee and Rajiv Rimal explore the window of opportunity during which potential voters are open to being persuaded. Based on a review of past research and on new evidence from the 1992 elections, they conclude that time of voter decision is not a stable personal trait as has long been assumed. Instead, it is something that varies for individuals according to characteristics of the political context surrounding a given election.

Although persuasive skills have always been a valued asset (Lasswell, Lerner, and Speier 1979–81), there are few eras in human history in which persuasion has been as important a force as in the current mass media age (McGuire 1985). Collectively, these chapters exemplify the vitality of the newly emerged discipline focusing specifically on political persuasion. In one sense the studies described in this volume are part of a long lineage of research focusing on factors that bring about change in political attitudes. But they also mark the beginning of a more programmatic agenda of research and a formal field of study, one that is explicitly political in orientation and focused specifically on change, rather than the stability of political attitudes.

Volume upon volume has been written about political leadership, but scant attention has been paid to when and under what conditions people will follow. Whether those leaders are elected officials, network news anchors, or ordinary citizens, persuasion is the mechanism by which they exercise political leadership. The study of who follows under what conditions is of sufficient importance and distinctiveness substantively that a field of study is long overdue.

The quantity and quality of political persuasion is a core issue in evaluating the health of democratic systems of government. Although persuasion may be carried out in forums as seemingly disparate as the Lincoln-Douglas debates and 30-second television advertisements, the underlying principles are the same. Moreover, the study of political persuasion concerns itself with the most fundamental issue: the vitality of public debate as it is carried out through the constant clamor of politics, the pull and tug of persuasive arguments. With this volume, we hope to mark the beginning of an equally vital field of research.

NOTES

1. See, for example, Page and Jones 1979; Stimson 1992.
2. See also, for example, Brody 1991.
3. It is important to observe that the character of experimentation itself has changed through the introduction of computer-assisted interviewing. Instead of being confined to the simplicities and rigidities of the classic split-ballot design, experiments of a high degree of complexity can be embedded in a public opinion interview in a way that is invisible to the respondent and effortless for the interviewer (see, e.g., Piazza and Sniderman 1989; Kinder and Palfrey 1993).

REFERENCES

Adorno, T. W. 1950. *The authoritarian personality.* New York: Harper.

Berelson, B., P. F. Lazarsfeld, and W. McPhee. 1954. *Voting.* Chicago: University of Chicago Press.

Brody, Richard A. 1991. *Assessing the president: The media, elite opinion, and public support.* Stanford: Stanford University Press.

Chaffee, S. H., and J. L. Hochheimer. 1982. The beginnings of political communication research in the United States. In *The media revolution in America and Western Europe,* ed. E. M. Rogers and F. Balle, 263–83. Norwood: Ablex.

Converse, P. E. 1962. Information flow and the stability of partisan attitudes. *Public Opinion Quarterly* 26: 578–99.

Converse, P. E. 1970. Attitudes and non-attitudes: Continuation of a dialogue. In *The quantitative analysis of social problems,* ed. E. R. Tufte, 168–89. Reading, Mass.: Addison-Wesley.

Converse, P. E. 1964. The nature of belief systems in mass publics. In *Ideology and discontent,* ed. D. E. Apter, 206–61. New York: Free Press.

Czitrom, D. J. 1982. *Media and the American mind from Morse to McLuhan.* Chapel Hill: University of North Carolina Press.

Habermas, J. 1964. *The public sphere.* Translated by S. Lennox and F. Lennox, *New German Critique* 3 (1974).

Hovland, C. I., I. L. Janis, and H. H. Kelley. 1953. *Communication and persuasion.* New Haven: Yale University Press.

Katz, E., and P. F. Lazarsfeld. *Personal influence.* Glencoe, Ill.: Free Press.

Kinder, D. R., and T. R. Palfrey, eds. 1993. *Experimental foundations of political science.* Ann Arbor: University of Michigan Press.

Lasswell, H. D., D. Lerner, and H. Speier, eds. 1979–81. *Propaganda and communication in world history.* Vols. 1–3. Honolulu: University of Hawaii Press.

Lazarsfeld, P. F., B. Berelson, and H. Gaudet. 1944. *The people's choice: How the voter makes up his mind in a presidential campaign.* New York: Duell, Sloan and Pearce.

Lewin, K. 1936. *A dynamic theory of personality.* New York: McGraw-Hill.

Lippmann, W. 1937. Editorial foreword. *Public Opinion Quarterly* 1.

McGuire, W. J. 1981. Theoretical foundations of campaigns. Chap. 2 in *Public communication campaigns,* ed. R. E. Rice and W. J. Paisley. Beverly Hills: Sage.

McGuire, W. J. 1985. Attitudes and attitude change. In *The handbook of social psychology,* 3d ed., ed. G. Lindzey and E. Aronson. New York: Random House.

McGuire, W. J. 1993. The poly-psy relationship: Three phases of a long affair. Chap. 2 in *Explorations in political psychology,* ed. S. Iyengar and W. J. McGuire. Durham: Duke University Press.

Page, Benjamin I., and Calvin Jones. 1979. Reciprocal effects of policy preferences, party loyalties, and the vote. *American Political Science Review* 73:1071–89.

Piazza, T., P. M. Sniderman, and P. E. Tetlock. 1989. Analysis of the dynamics of political reasoning: A general-purpose computer-assisted methodology. In *Political analysis,* Vol.1, ed. J. A. Stimson, 99–120. Ann Arbor: University of Michigan Press.

Riesman, D. 1950. *The lonely crowd.* New Haven: Yale University Press.

Stimson, James A. 1992. *Public opinion in America: Mood, cycles, and swings.* Boulder, Colo.: Westview Press.

Zaller, J. R. 1992. *The nature and origins of mass opinion.* New York: Cambridge University Press.

Part 1.
Mass Media and
Political Persuasion

CHAPTER 2

The Myth of Massive Media Impact Revived: New Support for a Discredited Idea

John Zaller

The mass media have been a source of great frustration to social scientists. On one hand, citizens in modern democracies routinely develop opinions about political events and personalities far beyond their direct experience. It is hard to imagine where many of these opinions come from if not from the mass media. And yet it has proven maddeningly difficult to demonstrate that the mass media actually produce powerful effects on opinion. The scholarly consensus of the 1940s and 1950s, cast in canonical form in Joseph Klapper's essay *The Effects of Mass Communication,* was that the media tend to have "minimal effects." As recently as 1986, William McGuire began a review essay on "The Myth of Massive Media Impacts" as follows:

> That myths can persist despite conflicting evidence is illustrated by the robustness of the belief that television and other mass media have sizable impacts on the public's thoughts, feelings, and actions, even though most empirical studies indicate small to negligible effects.

Echoing this view in a recent study of presidential elections, Finkel (1993, 1) wrote that exposure to the media had "negligible consequences for the electoral outcome." He did find evidence of media effects, but he reported that

> The findings here . . . indicate that the changes produced by the media . . . served mainly to strengthen the probability that the individual will vote in accord with his or her initial predispositions. (19)

Some recent research does find important media effects, but researchers have remained circumspect in their claims, often emphasizing subtle and arguably second-order aspects of media influence rather than direct persuasive effects. Typical is research on priming and agenda setting. The central argu-

17

ment in this literature is that media influence consists more in telling people what to think about than in telling them what to think. Other studies, like that of Finkel, contend that media exposure reinforces preexisting opinion rather than changes opinion.

No empirical research has gone so far as to argue that the direct persuasive impact of mass communication is, in general, large. "Not so minimal" is perhaps the best characterization of the current consensus among quantitative researchers on the size of media effects. Words like *massive* are used only in denial.

Against this backdrop of scholarly reticence, the present chapter argues for a complete break with the old "minimal effects" tradition. It maintains that, at least in the domain of political communication, the true magnitude of the persuasive effect of mass communication is closer to "massive" than to "small to negligible" and that the frequency of such effects is "often." Exactly as common intuition would suggest, mass communication is a powerful instrument for shaping the attitudes of the citizens who are exposed to it, and it exercises this power on an essentially continuous basis.

The very large media effects that, as I claim, are all around us are obviously somewhat difficult to observe, since many carefully designed studies have failed to detect them. But this, by itself, is no embarrassment to my thesis. Other scientific disciplines have long since learned that the ease or difficulty of observing a phenomenon has little to do with its magnitude or ultimate importance. Scientists routinely struggle for years or decades to establish what are eventually taken to be basic truths. What matters in the end is whether, under appropriate circumstances, a putative effect can be made to stand out clearly against whatever background noise may also be present.[1]

In light of this, the obligation of someone wishing to establish the thesis of very large media effects is (1) to state clearly a theoretical model capable of capturing media effects, (2) to specify the conditions under which the model applies, (3) to demonstrate that large effects can be observed when the appropriate conditions are met, and (4) to explain why, if these conditions arise only intermittently, it is reasonable to generalize from these special situations to others in which effects, though still present, are harder to observe. These are the goals of this chapter.

The empirical conditions under which very large media effects can be observed may be simply stated:

1. Good measurement of key variables, especially individual-level variation in reception of communication from the mass media.
2. Good variance in key independent variables, especially the content of the mass communication to which individuals are exposed.

These conditions are obviously mild. Few would expect to observe large effects in the absence of well-measured variation in key independent variables.

Meeting the conditions in the context of studies of mass communication is, nonetheless, trickier than it may seem. Take first the measurement condition. The key individual-level variable in studies of media impact is reception of communication, which most researchers measure by means of people's self-reports of media use (e.g., "How many days in the past week did you watch the news on television?"). This seems a justifiable measurement strategy: Such questions have obvious face validity as measures of exposure to mass communication, and they typically form statistically reliable scales. Yet, notwithstanding this, these types of questions perform poorly as indicators of news reception, leading, as we shall see shortly, to systematic underestimation of media effects.

The variance condition is also problematic. Difficulty arises from the fact that the flow of political communication in the United States on many (and perhaps most) important matters is relatively stable over time—locked into fixed patterns that reflect underlying divisions of power, partisanship, and societal inertia. For example, partisan and ideological disagreement on the desirability of activist government has been stuck in the same rut since the 1930s, and as a result, the flow of communication on this issue seems, at least on casual observation, to have been roughly constant, in terms of both overall volume and net directional thrust, for about five decades.

Few researchers, I suspect, would deny the existence of stable communication flows on major political issues, but many fail to recognize one of its major consequences: inadequate variation in the media inputs to mass opinion for ready detection of media effects, even if such effects are massively present. When media inputs to mass opinion do vary sharply, mass opinion is highly responsive, as I shall show in this chapter.

Once the nature of the measurement problem is appreciated, it is easy to design surveys that carry adequate measures of news reception (though many surveys still fail to do so). It is more difficult to get such surveys into the field in a context in which there is adequate variance in the flow of mass communication. Communication flows do sometimes change sharply, but when and on what issues change will occur is, in most cases, hard to forecast.[2] In consequence, there are relatively few data sets in which it is possible to demonstrate much in the way of large media effects. There are, however, enough good data sets to make clear that very large media effects do occur when appropriate conditions have been met.

In addition to these empirical requisites for detecting large media effects, a theoretical condition must be met. The researcher must use a statistical model capable of capturing, in an incisive way, the effects of crosscutting communication. The critical issue here is that if, as they do, the mass media routinely carry competing political messages, members of the public who are heavily exposed to one message tend to be heavily exposed to its opposites as well. Each message, as we shall see, has its effects, but the effects tend to be mutually canceling in ways that produce the illusion of modest impact.

Simple linear models—that is, models that assume that more exposure leads in additive linear fashion to more media influence—are of little use in disentangling the effects of crosscutting communication. Yet these are the kinds of models that overwhelmingly predominate in the study of mass communication.[3] An entirely different class of model is needed, and a principal purpose of this chapter is to further develop and popularize this type of model.[4]

This chapter is organized in five parts, as follows. The first demonstrates the inadequacy of the most commonly used measure of news reception, and in so doing it lays the intuitive foundation for the more substantive arguments to follow. The second section introduces a simple static model of the effects of two competing messages and applies it to the case of voting in congressional elections. The third section develops a dynamic version of this model and applies it to opinion data from the contest between Walter Mondale and Gary Hart for the Democratic presidential nomination in 1984. In both congressional elections and the 1984 nomination contest, there are very large swings in media coverage, thus making it possible to demonstrate very large media effects. In the fourth section, I turn to cases in which the flow of communication is relatively stable, as is more typical in the United States. Here I show that a generalization of the model used in earlier sections can explain the patterns of mass opinion that these stable communication flows produce. The fifth section recaps the chapter and suggests the conclusions that follow from it.

In writing this chapter, I have worked hard to maintain accessibility to the widest possible audience.[5] As part of this effort, I have relegated all nonessential technical material to appendixes and expressed most of what remains in graphical form. A few of the graphs may seem intimidating at first glance, but none is more difficult to read than a train schedule. Having severely cut back the amount and difficulty of the technical matter, I assume that readers will pay attention to what remains and so have relied on graphs to carry the main argument of the chapter. Readers who go lightly over the graphs, or skip them and attend only to text, will fail to grasp the chapter's main points. (Figures 3, 5, 7, 8, 14, and 15 constitute the intellectual core of the chapter.)

There are two other preliminary points. The first concerns the nature of the mass communication that, as I claim, influences public opinion. By mass communication I mean any communication that reaches large segments of the public via the mass media, namely, radio, TV, newspapers, or the postal system. Distinctions among types of message (factual versus interpretive), sources of messages (reporter versus public official), and types of media (print versus electronic) are important for many purposes, but I do not explore them. The analysis here is spare and, so far as I am able to make it so, entirely general.

The other preliminary point is the relationship of this chapter to my previous work on attitude change (Zaller 1992). Whereas my previous work most often relied on models of a single communication flow, even where opposing messages were admittedly present, this chapter relies exclusively on multimessage models. The mathematical forms of the new models are similar to those of older ones, but the new models are more realistic, powerful, and simple. Also, whereas my earlier work emphasized the role of political elites—mainly politicians and journalists—in shaping mass opinion, the present chapter is framed in terms of the effects of mass communication. This difference is to some extent stylistic, since politicians and journalists communicate to the public mainly through the mass media, but it serves the purpose of bringing the earlier work into contact with an important and quite different intellectual tradition, that of communication studies. Finally, some parts of this chapter, especially in the fourth section on probable frequency of very large media effects, mainly recapitulate prior work. I include this material because it will be unfamiliar to many readers but is necessary to the generalizations I seek to establish here.

Measurement Issues

Exactly What Do We Want to Measure and Why?

Part of the legacy of Carl Hovland's pioneering work in the 1940s and 1950s is widespread recognition of the importance of disaggregating the persuasion process into a series of discrete steps, each of which may have its own mediators. Consideration of the first three steps in this process is a useful point of departure for this chapter.

The first of Hovland's steps is exposure to a persuasive message, where *exposure* may involve only physical proximity to a message, as in the case of someone who is present in a room in which radio news is plainly audible but who is too distracted to listen. *Reception,* the second step in the chain, involves actually "getting" or "taking in" or "cognizing" the given message. The third step is *yielding* to, or *accepting,* a given message, a step that can normally take place only after reception has occurred.

If, as Hovland claimed and most researchers agree, persuasion takes place in such a sequence of discrete steps, researchers ought to use concepts and measures that are tailored as closely as possible to the particular step in the process they are studying. What this means in the present case is that, since we will be interested in *yielding* to mass communication as our dependent variable, we should use as our independent variable the concept that is closest to yielding in the chain of persuasion, namely, *reception* of communication.

Suppose, by way of illustrating this point, that a researcher wanted to know the effect of a particular medicine on recovery from a disease. The researcher might examine the correlation between prescription of the medicine by a doctor and recovery from the disease, or perhaps the correlation between getting the medicine from the pharmacist and recovery. But the most reliable estimate of the influence of the treatment would be the correlation between actually taking the medicine and recovery. The argument for using reception as the principal independent variable in studies of mass persuasion (i.e., yielding) is essentially the same.

In light of these general concerns, let us now consider how the reception of mass communication can best be measured in the context of naturalistic (i.e., nonlaboratory) studies of political persuasion.

The first point to make is that researchers rarely make any effort to measure reception of particular pieces of persuasive communication. Rather, they attempt to measure general propensity for reception of news and public affairs information, or what I shall refer to as "habitual news reception." The three most commonly used measures of habitual news reception are self-reported levels of media use, level of political knowledge and awareness, and education.

Of these, media use is closest to being a pure exposure variable. It directly taps frequency of contact with various media, independently of how much communication actually gets picked up. To whatever extent there is slippage between exposure to and reception of mass communication—and the slippage appears to be considerable (Neuman, Just, and Crigler 1992)— media use is an inappropriate measure of news reception.

By contrast, political knowledge or awareness, as measured by simple tests of objective political information, is almost purely a measure of propensity for reception of the news, in that it directly taps information, such as the name of the Speaker of the House of Representatives, that the vast majority of citizens will have acquired (if they have acquired it at all) from the mass media. Because there is a naturally close relationship between exposure to and reception of mass communication, media use and political awareness will be correlated, but owing to the slippage between exposure and reception, they will not be the same thing.

Education, finally, taps elements of both exposure and reception. Better-educated people are more likely to expose themselves to the mass media; they are also, as Neuman, Crigler, and Just (1992) showed, more likely to receive the messages they encounter there. Because it is conceptually mixed, education is closer to being a measure of reception than is self-reported media use.

These considerations suggest that, in most naturalistic studies, general political awareness as measured by simple tests of political knowledge should be the most acute mediator of persuasion effects (i.e., yielding to communication), and that self-reports of media exposure should be relatively less useful.[6]

We shall see in the next few pages that political awareness is, in fact, the most empirically powerful mediator of the persuasive impact of mass communication. My aim in this section has been to show that persuasion effects obtained from awareness measures are, from the standpoint of the most widely shared framework in communication research, also the most theoretically pertinent.

"Reception Gaps"

A fundamental assumption in communication research is that media influence is likely to be, all else equal, proportional to the amount of communication received from the mass media.[7] I share this assumption—as far as it goes. But what happens when the media carry opposing messages, as in partisan election campaigns or cases of controversial issues? In such cases, citizens who receive the most communication from one point of view may receive just as much from the other. What effects, if any, might this competing communication be expected to have on those who receive it?

Since, as I have indicated, it is extremely common for the mass media to carry competing political communications, this problem is as important as it is difficult. Its neglect by media researchers is, I believe, a principal reason that studies of the effects of mass communication often turn up anemic or even null findings even when large media effects are present.

In cases in which the intensities of the opposing messages are exactly equal, their tendency to cancel one another may make it practically impossible to observe a dynamic effect on opinion (i.e., attitude change). But if the intensities of the opposing messages differ—if, that is, one message is repeated more often or in more places or with greater salience than the other— then it should be possible to locate individuals who have gotten one message but not the other. These non-cross-pressured individuals, as I shall attempt to show, provide invaluable leverage for discerning the true effects of mass communication.

The first problem is how to locate individuals who have received only one of two competing messages. Figure 1, which shows data on the diffusion of two dramatic news stories through the population, suggests how this can be done. The solid line in the left panel shows the proportion of citizens at each level of habitual news reception—where habitual news reception has been

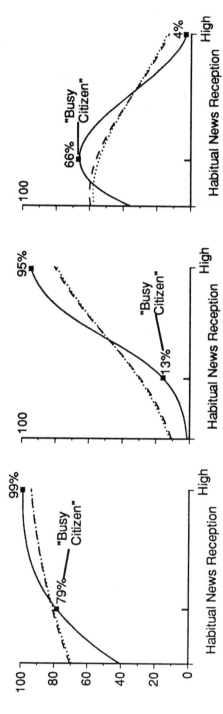

Fig. 1. Patterns of news diffusion, as captured by three measures of habitual news reception: political awareness (————), level of media use (— · —), and education (· · · · ·). (Data from 1989 NES Pilot Survey.)

measured by tests of political knowledge and awareness—who learned about the crash of a DC-10 airliner in a cornfield at the time of a 1989 survey, an occurrence that received extremely heavy coverage in the mass media. (Ignore for the moment the dotted and dashed lines in figure 1; they will be discussed in a moment.) As can be seen, higher levels of habitual news reception are associated with steadily higher chances of receiving news of this particular event. For example, the graph shows that someone at the top level of habitual news reception has nearly a 100 percent chance of receiving news of the DC-10 crash; meanwhile, a hypothetical "busy citizen" has a 79 percent chance of receiving the DC-10 story.

The solid line in the center panel of figure 1 shows the proportion who learned of a second major news event, the resignation of House Speaker Jim Wright. This was a story that received extensive, though less visually arresting, coverage at the time of the same survey. Thus, for example, the center graph shows that someone at the highest level of news reception only has about a 95 percent chance of receiving this less arresting story, and the same hypothetical "busy citizen" who had a 79 percent chance of getting news of the DC-10 crash has a 13 percent chance of getting news of the Wright resignation.

Who, then, are the people most likely to have received one of these stories but not the other? The solid line in the right panel of figure 1 provides a clear answer to this question by showing the *difference* in reception rates of the two stories for individuals at each level of habitual news reception—a difference that I shall refer to as the "reception gap." The line showing the reception gap has been calculated by simple subtraction of the two reception curves previously discussed: For example, the reception gap for the hypothetical "busy citizen" is 66 percent, because 79 percent reception for the first story minus 13 percent reception for the second leaves a gap of 66 percentage points. Similarly, the reception gap for someone at the top level of habitual news reception is about 4 percent ($99 - 95 = 4$).

The key point in figure 1 is that the reception gap for these two stories is largest among citizens who score in the middle range of habitual news reception. Hence, if the DC-10 and Wright stories were competing persuasive messages that said, respectively, "believe X" and "don't believe X," we would expect to find the largest number of converts to X among people in the middle range of habitual news reception, because they would be the ones most likely to receive the first message but not the second.

Reception gaps like this one are actually quite common. To anticipate a later argument, imagine that the data in figure 1 involve the diffusion of campaign messages about an incumbent and a challenger in a contested House election. The reception of messages about the incumbent might resemble the pattern for the more intense or salient of the two stories, the DC-10 crash, while the reception of messages about the challenger might resemble the pattern for the less salient story, the Wright resignation. Given this, we would expect to find the largest number of pro-incumbent converts among voters who fall in the middle ranges of habitual news reception, since they would be the ones most likely to receive the incumbent's message and not the challenger's one.

Before testing this and similar notions, I return briefly to the measurement issue.

Measurement of News Reception

Figure 1 actually contains three parallel sets of results. The solid line in each panel shows the effect of political awareness, as measured by knowledge tests, on reception of the DC-10 and Wright stories. The dashed line shows the effect of a respondent's level of self-reported media use, and the dotted line shows the effect of education on news reception.

As can be seen, the political awareness measure is by far the strongest performer of the three. When, in the left panel, awareness is used to measure propensity for reception of the DC-10 story, reception rises from a minima of about 41 percent among the least habitually attentive to a maxima of 99 percent among the most aware, a difference of 58 points. But when self-reported media use is employed to measure propensity for reception, the rise is from 71 percent to 94 percent, a difference of 23 points. And when education is used, the rise is from about 70 percent to 94 percent.

Are differences of this magnitude across measures important for analyzing the effects of competing political messages? Clearly so. In the right panel, the "reception gap" between the DC-10 and Wright stories—and, by implication, any persuasion effects that might depend on the reception gap—takes entirely different forms, depending on how news reception has been measured. When measured by means of education or self-reported media use, the gap appears to be moderate in size and negatively associated with individual differences in news reception; but when it is measured by means of political awareness items, the reception gap is both larger and nonmonotonically associated with differences in news reception.

Without going into detail that is available elsewhere, let me summarize by saying that results in figure 1 are representative of many others. Across 19 news stories like the DC-10 crash and the Wright resignation, the bivariate unstandardized logit coefficient for the regression of news reception on political awareness was, on average, more than 50 percent larger than that obtained from a scale of media use or from education (Price and Zaller 1993). These results were obtained despite the fact that the media use scale contained more items than the awareness scale (25 versus 9) and had a higher level of scale reliability (alpha .84 versus .82).

Many researchers will be surprised that a highly reliable media use scale is not good enough to detect an effect that, by another measure of habitual media use, appears quite distinct.[8] But the example I have given is anything but an isolated case, as we shall see.

Effects of Reception Gaps in House Elections

Incumbent members of the House of Representatives who seek reelection can expect not only to retain the loyalty of most voters of their own party, but also to attract many "defectors" from the other party. In recent elections, opposition party voters have defected to House incumbents at rates above 50 percent in some races (Jacobson 1992).

Defections to House incumbents afford an unusually rich opportunity for the study of mass persuasion, for three reasons: First, most voters, including most who call themselves independents, retain a substantial degree of loyalty to one of the parties (Keith et al. 1988); hence, decisions to cross party lines to vote for the House incumbent are decisions that really do require persuasion—persuasion that, owing to the enormous size of contemporary congressional districts, must invariably involve heavy doses of mass communication. Second, the National Election Studies (NES) survey organization has conducted high-quality surveys in 100 to 150 House races in each election year since 1958, with most studies carrying sufficient items for an adequate or even excellent measure of political awareness. Thus, data from House elections satisfy the first of the empirical conditions I specified for observing large media effects. Third, House races range from very-low-intensity, almost pro forma contests in which the incumbent runs nearly unopposed, to very-high-intensity contests in which both sides compete fiercely. Hence, the second of the two empirical conditions for observing large media effects—a large amount of variance in the media inputs to opinion—is also satisfied.

My aim in this analysis, then, will be to show how the opposing communication flows generated by incumbent and challenger campaigns persuade opposition party voters either to vote loyally for the challenger of their own party or to defect to the incumbent of the other party.

The initial expectations for this analysis have been set in the preceding sections: Given that the intensity of incumbent campaigns is on average much greater than the intensity of challenger campaigns (Jacobson 1992), we expect to find a nonmonotonic relationship between news reception and defection to the incumbent, as sketched in the righthand panel in figure 1.

This basic expectation, as I have shown in previous work, is handsomely

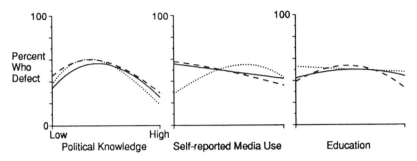

Fig. 2. Defections to incumbent in 1986 (———),1988 (-----), and 1990 (·····) House elections. Estimates based on coefficents in table A2. (Data from National Election Studies.)

met for the set of off-year elections between 1958 and 1990 (excluding elections in close proximity to reapportionment, in which incumbency status is ambiguous). Some of the evidence is displayed in figure 2, which shows parallel data from three elections and for three measures of habitual news reception—political awareness, as measured by knowledge items; media exposure, as measured by self-reports of media use; and education. As can be seen, the expected nonmonotonic pattern of defection is sharpest and most consistent when political awareness is used as the indicator of news reception; the media use and education variables generate modest evidence of nonmonotonicity in one case and none at all in the other two.[9] (Technical information concerning these data is contained in appendix B.)

These results strongly confirm the importance of high-quality measurement in the study of the effects of mass communication. Weak measurement produces results that are not merely weaker than they ought to be, but qualitatively different in their implications for the nature of media influence.[10]

This conclusion is qualified by the fact that, in contrast to the tests reported in figure 1, the knowledge scales used in these tests are more reliable than their competitors, particularly media use.[11] The qualification, however, is a relatively minor one. For one thing, these are the best measures of habitual media use that can be built in these NES surveys—and hence the ones that wind up being used by scholars who uncritically assume that a variable labeled "media use" is always a better measure of news reception than a variable labeled "political knowledge and awareness." Second, more reliable measures of media use do not necessarily produce more reliable results, as shown by the analysis in figure 1. Hence, the main point of the comparison stands: that scholars who try to assess communication effects with a measure of self-reported media use are likely to obtain results that are systematically weaker than they ought to be and to risk finding nothing at all, even when important effects are actually present.

A Static Two-Message Model
of Communication Effects

Varieties of Reception Gaps and Their Consequences

It is no accident that the reception gap for the DC-10 and Wright stories, as shown in figure 1, has roughly the same shape as the pattern of vote defection to House incumbents, as shown in figure 2. It is no accident because, for presentational purposes, I chose the two cases to be as much alike as possible.

Yet reception gaps may take many different shapes and forms, depending on the intensities of the opposing communication flows that generate them. In order to exploit the full potential of the reception gap model I am proposing, as well as to rule out alternative explanations for patterns like those shown in figure 2 (see Converse 1962; McGuire 1968), it is necessary to demonstrate that the reception gap model can accommodate a wider range of cases than examined so far.

This section takes up that task. The first part develops expectations for how reception gaps—and by extension, patterns of media influence—ought in theory to vary as the intensities of opposing communication flows vary. This exercise closely resembles the earlier analysis of the reception gap between the DC-10 and Wright stories, with two differences: First, I use invented data to *simulate* the diffusion of communication rather than, as in the earlier analysis, real data; second, I simulate reception gaps for many hypothetical messages rather than just two. The greater flexibility of this sort of simulation makes it possible to develop clear theoretical expectations concerning the effects of opposing communication flows. The second part of the section then shows that the theoretical expectations developed by means of the simulations are matched by actual data.

I begin, then, with simulation of the diffusion of four sets of hypothetical campaign messages and the reception gaps they create. This simulation, shown in figure 3, is the single most important piece of my argument concerning the nature of media influence. It is therefore essential that all readers, whether math phobic or not, become thoroughly comfortable with it.

Look first at the top row, which shows hypothetical patterns of reception of campaign messages from a House incumbent on the top left, from a House challenger in the top middle, and the resulting reception gap on the top right.[12] As in the earlier analysis, the reception gap has been calculated by

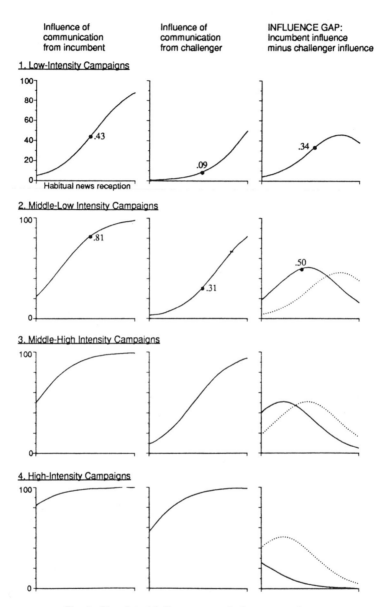

Fig. 3. Simulated influence gaps in four campaigns.

simple subtraction of the two reception curves. (Readers are urged to verify this point by subtracting the numbers shown on the figure.)

Now focus on the second row of figure 3, where both the incumbent and challenger campaign messages have both become more intense, or louder, than they were in the top row. (In saying that one message is more intense than another, I mean that it has been repeated with greater frequency or salience or vividness in the media, so that comparably attentive citizens are more likely to receive it.) Thus, for example, a moderately attentive voter in the second row has a .81 probability of receiving the message from the incumbent campaign, while the same type of voter in the first row has a .43 probability of receiving the incumbent's message. Similarly, voters in the second row have a higher chance of receiving the challenger message than do comparably attentive voters in the first row. The reception gap for these two more intense messages is shown as the solid line in the right panel of the second row; for visual reference, the reception gap from the less intense campaign in the top row is repeated as a dotted line.

The key point to notice is how reception gap changes as the competing messages become more intense. As can be seen, the gap shifts to the left, so that instead of being centered over voters who are well above average in habitual news reception, it is now centered over voters who are below average.

This shift in the location of the reception gap (as can be seen by comparing the solid and dotted lines) implies a corresponding shift in the expected pattern of defections to the incumbent. In the more intense campaign of the second row, there are fewer defections to the incumbent among the most attentive voters (more of whom will be held in line by the more intense campaign of the challenger), but more defections to the incumbent among less attentive voters (more of whom will be won over by the intensified incumbent campaign). I refer to this pattern of crosscutting effects—whereby middle-attentive citizens change in the direction of the louder message and highly attentive ones change in the direction of the second message—as the "cross-over effect." The crossover effect, or something visually close to it, is expected to occur whenever, as in this simulation, two opposing messages both increase in intensity. Although the conditions necessary to generate crossover effects are not especially common, they are important for the unusually clear light they shed on the dynamics of media influence; hence, I will place considerable emphasis on crossover effects as my argument develops.

Let us turn now to the third row of figure 3, in which both the incumbent campaign and the challenger campaign have gained yet another increment of intensity. As can be seen in the right panel of the third row, increases in campaign intensity cause the reception gap to shift farther to the left, so that now it is centered over voters who score near (but not quite at) the bottom of

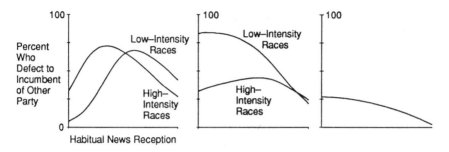

Fig. 4. Defections to incumbent party in U.S. national elections. (Data based on results shown in Zaller 1992, table 10.6.)

the scale of habitual news reception. Finally, in the fourth row of figure 3, both campaigns have become so intense that the reception gap has almost disappeared. The small gap that still exists is centered over the very least attentive voters, so that the reception gap becomes steadily smaller as habitual attentiveness to the media increases. Note that crossover effects are apparent in row 3 only.

These curves are, as indicated at the outset, an elaborate set of theoretical expectations about how reception gaps—and, by implication, patterns of defection to an incumbent—may be expected to vary across campaigns that vary in the intensities of the opposing messages.

In a previous publication, I presented data that bear on these expectations. The data involve patterns of defections to incumbents in several types of elections, which may be rank-ordered by level of campaign intensity as follows:

> Low-intensity House elections
> High-intensity House elections
> Low-intensity Senate elections
> High-intensity Senate elections
> 1984 Presidential election

If these elections vary in campaign intensity from low to high in the order listed, then the pattern of defections to incumbents ought to conform to the theoretical expectations developed in figure 3. In fact, they do. As shown in figure 4, defections in these elections are a quite reasonable approximation to those shown in the right column of figure 3. Defections in the low-intensity races (i.e., House elections) have the same pattern as the defection gap in the top right of figure 3, while defections in the highest-intensity case (the presidential election) have the same pattern as in the bottom right of figure 3.

Middle intensity cases (Senate elections) conform to the middle pattern in figure 3.

The data in figure 4 were, however, generated by conspicuously ad hoc modeling procedures and by coefficients lacking in statistical robustness. In light of these shortcomings, one purpose of this chapter is to replicate the pattern of effects in figure 4 with an appropriate model and a wider range of cases.

An appropriate model is especially important. Until it has been shown that a model embodying a particular set of principles fits a set of data, one cannot be certain that the principles have any relevance for the data. Hence, in the next section, I show how a model embodying the principles of the foregoing analysis can be applied to a wide range of House election data. This section, though no more difficult than what has come before, is somewhat dry, so I have made it possible for nontechnical readers to skip to the next section without loss of continuity to the overall argument.

A Statistical Model of the Effects of Competing Campaign Messages

The fundamental assumption will remain that people are influenced by mass communication in proportion to the amount of it they receive. When, as in the case of contested House elections, the media carry competing messages, voters will be pulled, all else equal, in the direction of the campaign from which they have received more communication. Hence, the voters most likely to be swayed by mass communication will not be those who receive the largest overall amount of communication, but the ones for whom the reception gap between competing messages is greatest.

As in previous analysis, I will endeavor to understand reception gaps by understanding the separate communication flows that create them. It is necessary, however, to add a major new element to the argument: the notion that people may refuse to "accept" or "yield to" some of the communication they receive. In the case of the DC-10 and Wright stories, yielding was not a concern, since the majority of people believe ostensibly neutral news reports when they receive them; in the case of House elections, however, citizens have values and predispositions that prevent them from passively yielding to the messages they receive.

We must, then, switch from modeling simple "reception" of communication to modeling "reception plus acceptance"—which is to say, we must begin to model the "persuasive influence" of communication. This change, though conceptually fundamental, does not greatly change the flavor of the argument. In the case of House elections, I have simply added the assumption that, all else equal, individuals with stronger attachments to one of the parties will be less likely to accept (or "yield to") the communication they receive from politicians of the other party. The model for "influence by the incumbent campaign" thus becomes

$$\text{Influence}_{INC} = f(\text{intensity}_{INC}, \text{ habitual news reception, party attachment})$$

where the f refers to an additive mathematical function by which the three variables are "added together" to estimate the persuasive effect of communication from the incumbent campaign. Similarly, the persuasive impact of the challenger's campaign can be described as

$$\text{Influence}_{CHL} = f(\text{intensity}_{CHL}, \text{ habitual news reception, party attachment})$$

These additive influence models, whose details I leave to appendix C, are standard fare in communication and voting research. The departure here—and it is a major one—is that there are two of them, one for each candidate's campaign.

The next step, therefore, is to combine the two influence models into an overall model of net influence. To do this, I proceed as follows: I first conceive each candidate's campaign as one grand message that either reaches and persuades a voter or else fails to do so. Influence, thus, becomes an all-or-nothing dichotomy—it either occurs or it doesn't. Given this, and continuing to focus on voter defection to House incumbents, there are four logically distinct possibilities for what can happen: Voters may be influenced by both campaigns, by neither campaign, by only the challenger campaign, or by only the incumbent campaign. If the voter is influenced by neither campaign or by the challenger campaign alone, the probability of defecting to the incumbent will be essentially zero. If a voter has been reached and influenced by both campaigns, the influences will tend to be mutually canceling, thus again leaving the voter unmoved.[13] Finally, if the voter has been influenced by the incumbent campaign but not the challenger campaign, the probability of defection will be relatively high.

In view of all this, I will model the probability that a partisan will defect to the incumbent of the other party as

$$\text{Pr.(Defect)} = \text{Probability of being influenced by the incumbent campaign } and \text{ not being influenced by the challenger campaign}$$

$$= [\text{Pr.(Influence}_{INC})] \times [1 - \text{Pr.(Influence}_{CHL})]$$

$$= (1 + \exp [-b_0 - b_1 * \text{Reception} - b_2 * \text{Party}$$
$$- b_3 * \text{Intensity}_{INC}])^{-1}$$
$$\times \{1 - [1 + \exp (-b_{00} - b_{11} * \text{Reception}$$
$$+ b_{22} * \text{Party} - b_{33} * \text{Intensity}_{CHL})]^{-1}\} \qquad (1)$$

In plain language, the claim here is that probability of defection equals probability of being influenced by the incumbent's message *and* not being influenced by the challenger's, where influence depends in each case on habitual news receptivity, campaign intensity, and party attachment.

A key technical feature of the model is use of the logistic form to specify the two influence subfunctions. This feature is justified by the notion that the influence is a dichotomous variable, as indicated. (Logistic functions vary between a minimum of 0 and a maximum of 1, which enables them to capture the probabilistic nature of dichotomous concepts.) A perhaps more appealing justification is that the gradual flattening out that occurs as outputs from logistic functions approach 1 reflects diminishing marginal effects from news reception. Under this interpretation, influence depends on the relative amount of reception of each message, with defection most likely to occur when a person has more exposure to one message than the other.[14]

Three Tests of the Model

The model developed in the previous section has been applied to voting data from the 1966, 1978, and 1986 House elections.[15] The form of the model and the variables included in it are the same in each case.

The results, which are shown visually in figure 5 and in statistical form in appendix C, provide strong support for the model. On the visual side, the results give a clear and orderly illustration of the full range of media effects suggested in the simulation in figure 3. Most tellingly, they demonstrate the existence of crossover effects, whereby, as described earlier, increases in the intensities of the two opposing communication flows cause middle-attentive voters to change in the direction of the louder campaign message and highly attentive voters to change in the direction of the other campaign. On the statistical side, all the key coefficients in all three election years achieve high levels of statistical significance. (Technical details of the estimation procedure may be found in appendix C.)

Note that overall defection rates to incumbents are higher in the 1978 and 1986 elections than in 1966. Unfortunately, this increase is partly artifactual. In 1978, the NES survey changed its vote question in a way that led to an overreport of support for incumbents.[16] But the increase in defection rates is

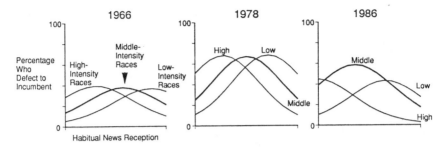

Fig. 5. The effect of campaign intensity on patterns of defection to House incumbents. Based on coefficients in table A3. (Data from CPS/NES Election Studies.)

also partly real. Incumbent vote margins—as measured by election returns rather than surveys—grew during the 1960s and perhaps early 1970s (Alford and Brady 1993). The reasons are still not completely clear, but the most likely explanation is that incumbents became increasingly able to wage "continuous campaigns" for election, and to monopolize the resources necessary to do so. To judge from the pattern of campaign effects in figure 5 and from other data, the intensified campaigns of incumbents bore fruit mainly among voters in the middle and lower ranges of political awareness—that is, among voters who paid too little attention to politics to pick up the lower intensity communications of the 1960s but are able to pick up the higher intensity communications of the present.[17]

Conclusions

We are now in a position to draw some important conclusions. The first is that very large campaign effects—effects of mass communication—do occur. Defection probabilities in figures 2, 4, and 5 range from about 70 percent to close to zero, depending on the configuration of campaign communication in a particular race and how much attention individual voters pay to it. It is hard to imagine that campaign effects in competitive elections could ever be, in practice, much larger than this.

But although large effects occur, it is also easy to see how they might fail to become evident. Any variant of a simple linear model would fail to detect and disentangle the variety of patterns that occur, because effects, even when large, do not conform to a simple straight-line pattern. Even an appropriate nonlinear model might yield unimpressive results if applied within a narrow empirical context, such as presidential elections alone or Senate elections alone.[18] In the set of House, Senate, and presidential elections, only House elections contain sufficient variance in the key independent variables—the intensities of the opposing communication flows—to meet the variance condition necessary for the detection of very large media effects.

These points are hard to overstate. As I have noted, communication effects are typically evaluated by means of linear models, and these models are typically applied to only a single case of mass persuasion at a time, often cases, such as presidential elections, in which the opposing campaigns are evenly balanced and hence mutually canceling. These limitations, in conjunction with the equally typical failure to use an adequate measure of reception of mass communication, virtually guarantee systematic underestimation of media impacts.

One other point needs to be made. At first glance, the data in figure 4 suggest that communication effects are largest in House campaigns, because that is where the variance attributable to differences in news reception is greatest. But this impression is misleading. Effects seem largest in House elections only because the opposing messages are least evenly matched in that context, thus permitting the louder message to generate effects without much impediment. Conversely, effects seem smallest in presidential elections only because the competing messages in this case, which are extremely intense and generate far more mass learning than in House elections, are most evenly matched and hence largely cancel out.

This analysis suggests that it is a serious mistake for scholars to conflate mutually canceling effects with nonexistent or only "minimal" effects. Just as the effects produced by the heaves of opposing behemoths in an evenly matched tug-of-war are not minimal, so the forces exerted by political campaigns in high-intensity Senate and presidential races are not minimal. Effects can be very great, even when, as in a tug-of-war, they function simply to cancel out the efforts of the other side.

Some may be tempted to read my disagreement with the existing scholarly consensus on "minimal effects" as merely terminological, as follows: My claims about very large media effects refer to *total media effects,* whether they net out to near zero (as in presidential elections) or show a net imbalance in favor of one side (as in House elections). The existing literature, by contrast, seems to refer primarily to *net media effects,* which are often close to zero, as even my data from Senate and presidential elections show. So it might all be just a matter of which aspect of reality one wishes to draw attention to.

I believe, however, that my disagreement with the existing consensus runs deeper. This consensus sees the media as relatively incapable of pushing citizens around, as if people are either too savvy, or too insulated from mass communication, to let that happen. I see the media as extremely capable of pushing citizens around, and I maintain that the effects of the pushing around are hard to see only because the media often push in opposite directions.

This disagreement is closely related to another, even more profound issue: Is American politics generally stable because it is founded on the rock of a stable public opinion, which largely resists fads, passions, and excitements of the kind the nation's constitutional framers feared (see Page and Shapiro 1992)? Or is it stable because—and only to the extent that—elite and media politics tend to be stable?

In light of such questions, I see it as essential for theories of media influence to attribute importance to the entire configuration of causes and effects that operate in a given situation, whatever their net balance.

A Dynamic Two-Message Model

If wide variance in the intensities of competing messages is the sine qua non of effective communication studies, then presidential primary elections ought to be another locus of exciting research on media effects—as, indeed, they have been (see McClure and Patterson 1974; Patterson 1980; Brady and Johnston 1987; Bartels 1988). It is not quite true, as Andy Warhol said of American life in general, that every candidate gets to be famous for 15 minutes, but many candidates have been able to claim such fleeting fame, progressing from nonentity to charismatic leader to has-been in the course of a few short weeks of intense media coverage.

In some of these cases, media coverage takes a quite distinctive form: It begins with a modest flow of mostly positive messages as reporters "discover" the new candidate. As the candidate then "takes off" in the public opinion polls, the flow of both positive and negative messages increases, as reporters undertake both to explain the candidate's "better-than-expected" success and to scrutinize more seriously the candidate's credentials for office.

This pattern of increasing positive and increasing negative coverage is precisely what was simulated in figure 3. In this section, I examine two presidential campaigns that generated this pattern of rising positive and negative coverage—those of Gary Hart in 1984 and Ross Perot in the spring of 1992 (i.e., before the general election). The aim is to provide further evidence for, and a more rigorous test of, the model of media effects that was simulated in figure 3. I begin with a brief review of the Hart and Perot campaigns.

Gary Hart and Ross Perot

For the first six weeks of the 1984 nomination contest, Gary Hart ran far back in the pack of presidential hopefuls, garnering little media attention or mass

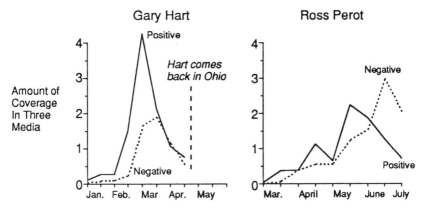

Fig. 6. Press coverage of Gary Hart and Ross Perot. (Data from Hunt and Zaller 1995.)

enthusiasm. Neither he nor any of the other candidates, including the initially popular John Glenn, seemed capable of catching Walter "Fritz" Mondale, the presumptive Democratic nominee. "Can Anyone Stop Fritz?" was the way *Newsweek* summarized the race in the headline of its January cover story on the contest.

As Glenn's campaign faltered, Hart began to establish himself as the most likely alternative to Mondale. In the first real contest of the season—the Iowa caucus elections in the third week in February—Mondale finished, as expected, in first place. But Hart finished ahead of Glenn, thereby achieving status as a top-tier candidate. Hart went on, in perhaps the biggest political surprise of the decade, to trounce Mondale in the New Hampshire primary the following week. The resulting tide of positive publicity for Hart so undermined Mondale's support that he came close to quitting the race. Hart's picture graced the covers of the newsweeklies, network television provided near saturation coverage of his every activity, and his name became an overnight household word. But although Hart's coverage was mostly positive, the media also made him the butt of jokes about his name and his age, and they played up the lack of specificity of the "new ideas" that Hart claimed were fueling his campaign. When Hart finally suffered a major defeat (in Illinois in late March), his coverage turned predominantly negative and he sank in the polls.

Hart's media coverage in the initial months of the race is summarized in the left panel of figure 6. These media data are based on content analysis of network TV news, the *New York Times,* and *Time* and *Newsweek.*[19] As can be seen, the volume of both positive and negative coverage of Hart increased

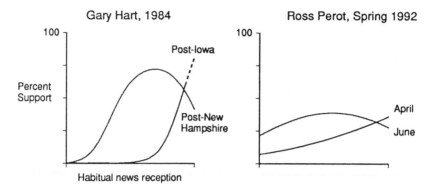

Fig. 7. Patterns of support for Gary Hart and Ross Perot. Hart support based on all Democrats; Perot support based on all poll respondents. Data are summaries of simple logistic regressions. Technical details in text and appendix D. (Data from NES Continuous Monitoring Survey: April 20–23 *New York Times* survey; June 3–7 *Washington Post* survey. All are available through ICPSR.)

sharply in late February and early March, then turned negative and declined in overall volume. We shall examine the effects of this coverage on public opinion shortly.

Press coverage of Ross Perot's 1992 run for the presidency was, despite the multiple unorthodoxies of his campaign, quite similar in certain respects to that of Hart. Coverage began in March, about a month after Perot's fabled announcement of his candidacy on the Larry King show, with a modest flow of generally positive messages. Early coverage noted Perot's prickliness but laid more stress on his colorful background, can-do mentality, and appealing political style. This coverage, as argued elsewhere (Hunt and Zaller 1995), was far more important to Perot's rise in the polls in April and May than the direct effects of his appearances on talk shows, which reached too small an audience to have much direct effect. As Perot gained momentum, the press provided more positive coverage, but also more negative coverage, until, as in the case of Hart, the negative coverage outstripped the positive and Perot began to fall in the polls. Data summarizing this coverage are also shown in figure 6.

What effect did this coverage have on public opinion? Figure 7 shows patterns of public support for Hart and Perot at two comparable points—the takeoff of each candidate's campaign, when coverage was low in volume and mainly positive in tone, and the peak of each candidate's campaign, when coverage was much higher in volume and also less one-sidedly positive. For Hart, the peak was the three-week window that included the New Hampshire and "Super Tuesday" primaries; the latter referring to the day on which eight states held primaries. For Perot the peak was early June, when he was running ahead of both George Bush and Bill Clinton in polls asking citizens who they would vote for "if the election were today." The curves indicating public support for the two candidates are summaries of the raw data based on simple logit regressions (technical details are given in appendix D).

As can be seen in figure 7, the patterns of public support for Hart and Perot are consistent with expectations developed for such cases in figure 3. Early in each campaign, support was concentrated among those most capable of picking up low-intensity communication, namely, those high on habitual news reception. Later in the campaign, middle-attentive people became more supportive of Hart and Perot as a result of the high-intensity positive messages that then began to reach them, and highly attentive people became (it appears) less supportive in response to the lower-intensity negative messages that were, at that point in the campaign, still able to reach only them.

The Hart and Perot patterns are obviously not identical. It would be surprising if they were: Hart was competing against a fellow Democrat in the Democratic primaries, while Perot was competing against the leaders of both the Democratic and Republican parties in a race involving the whole electorate. Identical correspondence cannot be expected in such different cases. What can be expected is that a broadly similar stimulus (increases in the intensity of two messages, where the initially louder message remains the louder one) will produce markedly different effects among people who pay more attention to public affairs (and hence get both messages) than among people who pay less attention (and get only the louder message). And that expectation appears to be met.

Or is it? Although it is not obvious from figure 7, the data used in this analysis are exceedingly frail. In the Hart case, the NES survey interviewed only 34 Democrats in the critical week after the Iowa caucuses and before the New Hampshire primary, thus making it extremely difficult to tell what exactly Hart's support was, especially at the highest level of habitual news reception. (The dashed line in figure 7 is an extrapolation into a region in which there are no cases.) In the Perot case, there were abundant interviews at both time points, but the measure of habitual news reception was poor (consisting most importantly of a four-point education variable; see appendix D). Weak reception measures tend, as we saw in figures 1 and 2, to flatten even sharply curvilinear relationships. Thus, although the data do conform in both cases to the theoretical expectation of crosscutting media effects, the data themselves are so noisy that it is hard to be sure what is really going on.

The appropriate response to such situations is to bring in more data and a more powerful model. In the next section I do both. Using data from the NES Continuous Monitoring Survey, I examine a longer and more varied segment of the Hart-Mondale contest, and I present a model capable of fitting the more complex pattern of back-and-forth opinion change that occurs in this period.

A Dynamic Two-Message Model of Media Effects

In modeling the effects of the competing pro-Hart and pro-Mondale communications, my central assumption will continue to be that influence gaps—whereby individuals receive and accept messages from one campaign but not from the other—are the key to understanding media effects. But in contrast to the case of congressional elections, in which one could safely assume that influence gaps always ran more or less in favor of one candidate (the incumbent), the assumption here must be that influence gaps may favor either candidate at any point. That is, within every phase of the campaign, there may be many citizens who get only a pro-Mondale message and others who get only a pro-Hart one, as well as citizens who get both or neither.

The model will focus on candidate support across pairs of adjacent time periods. Indexing these time periods as t and $t + 1$, support for Mondale within each time period can be written as

Mondale support at Time $(t+1)$ = Mondale support at Time(t)

+ Time(t) nonsupporters of

Mondale who experience a

pro-Mondale influence gap

− Time(t) Mondale supporters

who experience a pro-Hart

influence gap

A parallel model of support for Hart within each time period is also required. It can be written as

Hart support at Time $(t+1)$ = Hart support at Time(t)

+ Time(t) nonsupporters of Hart

who experience a pro-Hart

influence gap

− Time(t) Hart supporters who

experience a pro-Mondale

influence gap

Within each time period, influence gaps will be modeled as a function of two variables: (1) The society-level flow of pro-Hart and pro-Mondale communications, and (2) individual differences in habitual attention to this coverage. The mathematical form of the influence gap functions is identical to that used in equation 1 and is shown in appendix E.

In addition to Mondale, Hart, and Glenn, the 1984 Democratic nomination contest included Jesse Jackson and a host of lesser lights. All attracted some support at various points. To keep the modeling task manageable, I restrict attention to a three-way contest among Mondale, Hart, and "no preference," the latter being an especially popular response option in the early weeks of the contest and among less involved individuals. I also restrict attention to self-described Democrats or Democratic leaners, who are the only people whose preferences between Hart and Mondale have any clear meaning.

Following my initial discussion, the campaign has been divided into four distinct phases: the pre-Iowa period in which Mondale dominated; the Iowa caucuses and related events, in which Hart established himself as Mondale's chief competitor; the New Hampshire primary and its aftermath, in which Hart dominated; and the low point in Hart's campaign, which was after a string of primary losses and just before his big comeback victory in the Ohio primary.

Having created the four time periods to correspond with natural phases of the campaign, I will assume that patterns of media coverage are roughly constant *within* each period, so that the important differences in coverage occur *across* time periods. This is a major simplifying assumption but, as I argue in appendix D, not an especially problematic one.

To measure media content, I used campaign coverage by *Time* and *Newsweek* magazine. Each paragraph in each story on the campaign was rated as pro-Hart, pro-Mondale, anti-Hart, anti-Mondale, or neutral. The coding rule was extremely simple: Was the given paragraph "good press" or "bad press" for the candidate? References to other candidates were not counted, except insofar as they explicitly referred to Hart or Mondale (e.g., a Jesse Jackson criticism of Mondale would be counted as pro-Hart). Pro-Hart and anti-Mondale paragraphs were combined into a single pro-Hart paragraph count, and an overall pro-Mondale paragraph count was created in the same way.[20] The paragraph counts have been aggregated over the four time periods, as shown in table 1.[21]

These media content data are obviously crude. Differences in the intrinsic appeal or persuasiveness of different paragraphs are entirely neglected, as are idiosyncrasies in when the newsmagazines chose to run feature stories. About the only thing that can be said in favor of the media data is that they are in quantitative form and hence usable for testing a model.

Remaining details of modeling and variable construction are relegated to appendixes D and E. I urge all readers at least to glance at appendix E, which gives a full statement of the influence gap model. The complexity of the model makes a substantively important point that the field of mass communication (and, in generic form, behavioral social science as a whole) has only begun to grasp: *Even when the process of media influence is assumed to conform to the simplest possible principle—that media influence increases with the amount of mass communication received—the model logically implied by that principle is quite complicated.* It is thus no surprise that, in 50 years of research, simple linear models of media influence have generally performed weakly.

The results of the modeling are shown in figure 8, which depicts estimated levels of support for Hart and Mondale in the four time periods. Let us look first at support for each candidate in the early phase of the campaign, as shown in the left panels of figure 8. This first time period covers the time in January and early February in which media coverage was light and favorable to Mondale, as shown in table 1. Mondale at this point also enjoyed the accumulated benefits of media coverage of himself as Jimmy Carter's well-respected vice president and senior spokesperson for the Democratic party during Ronald Reagan's first term. The point to notice here is that the effect of habitual news reception is to induce greater support for the candidate one-sidedly favored by press coverage at that point in the campaign. Yet Mondale's support flattens out at the highest level of news reception. This is because, at that high level of attentiveness, a few citizens were able to pick up Hart's countervailing message and thereby develop a preference for the Colorado senator.

I turn now to the second time period, a brief window in which results from the Iowa caucuses dominated the campaign. News coverage, though still relatively light, became more favorable to Hart at this point (table 1). The

TABLE 1.   Media Coverage of the 1984 Hart and Mondale Campaigns in *Time* and *Newsweek*

	Pre-Iowa Caucuses	Iowa Caucuses	New Hampshire to Super Tuesday	Post–Super Tuesday
Weekly rate of pro-Mondale paragraphs	11.6	18	81	22.0
Weekly rate of pro-Hart paragraphs	3.4	15	37	36.2
Number of weeks in period	5.0	2	3	5.0

Note: See text for further information about content coding. Dates of the four periods, which are based on when the magazines were actually published rather than their nominal cover dates, are January 16 to February 13; February 20 and 27; March 5 through March 19; and March 26 through April 23.

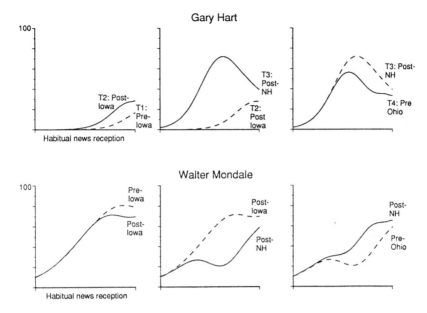

Fig. 8. Support for Gary Hart and Walter Mondale in four phases of the campaign. Based on modeling procedures described in appendixes D and E. (Data from NES Continuous Monitoring Study.)

result, as figure 8 shows, is that Hart makes gains among the small group of politically attentive voters who can pick up low-intensity communication and that Mondale suffers corresponding losses among people in the same group. But most citizens—people in the middle and lower ranges of habitual attentiveness to politics—changed their preferences little in this period, because campaign coverage was insufficiently intense to reach them.

I turn now to the third time period, the three-week interval containing the most important events of the campaign, the New Hampshire primary and Super Tuesday. Campaign coverage in this period was both heavy and heavily slanted toward Hart, who reaped a huge coverage bonus for his unexpected victory over Mondale in New Hampshire and his strong showing on Super Tuesday. Yet despite Hart's news advantage, Mondale managed to get a respectable volume of good press (table 1). The net effect of this coverage, as can be seen in figure 8, was a large gain in public support for Hart—but a gain that was concentrated among citizens in the middle range of news receptivity, where the reception gap in favor of the louder message is normally greatest.

Note that, in this set of estimates, there is no crossover effect between the Iowa caucuses and the New Hampshire primary. In view of the appearance of a such an effect in the raw data in figure 7, this is a disappointment. But the disappointment carries no large implications, for two reasons.

The first is the thinness of the data. In the week after Iowa, the NES survey drew, as noted earlier, just 34 Democrats, including few at moderately high levels of news reception and none at the top level. Hence it is no surprise that, despite the great theoretical importance of what happens among cases at relatively high levels of news reception, the model made little effort, in a statistical sense, to thread the regression line through them.

Second, even if this is a case of "almost" rather than actual crossover, it remains clear that the dynamics driving it are the same as those outlined in figure 3. It is clear, that is, that different segments of the public responded differently to post–New Hampshire coverage of the campaign, depending on whether they were, by virtue of their habitual news reception, likely to receive both, neither, or only the louder of the competing campaign messages. Whether the configuration of post–New Hampshire messages was such as to produce a crossover is interesting but not important; what matters is whether the process envisioned by the model applies—which, as should be apparent, it does.

I turn now to the nadir of Hart's campaign, a period in which he was defeated in a series of primary contests and received mixed but mostly negative coverage (table 1). As in the previous phase of the campaign, the most highly attentive voters tended to receive both positive and negative messages concerning Hart, and so to remain relatively unchanged in their preferences. Such change as occurred was centered mainly among the moderately attentive, who were the people most likely to receive only the louder message of the period, which was now the pro-Mondale message. A comparison of these estimates with the raw data shows that, as in the case of the "almost crossover effect," the model underpredicts the raw data but does accurately pick up the main trend of the period. (Raw data are not shown here, but see Zaller 1992, 255.)

A final point is that the model makes explicit estimates of "no preference" responses, as shown in figure 9. Less attentive and moderately attentive respondents are, throughout the campaign, most likely to lack a preference, but there is a notable decline in no-preference responses in the aftermath of the heavily covered New Hampshire primary. Most of those forming preferences at that time became, as would be expected, Hart supporters. What is perhaps most impressive about figure 9, however, is how many citizens never paid enough attention to public affairs to form preferences at all, even at the time of the massively covered New Hampshire primary.

These results add up to a quite solid performance by the model. Although containing only two variables (news reception and media content), it is able to correctly predict 67.4 percent of the cases (as against 46.7 percent for the null model). More importantly, it offers a substantively coherent explanation of a

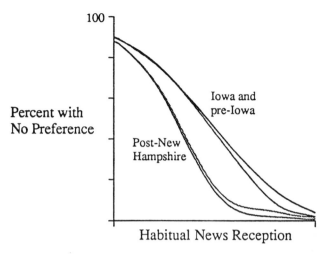

Fig. 9. Changing pattern of "no preference" in Hart-Mondale contest. Based on modeling procedures described in appendixes D and E. (Data from NES Continuous Monitoring Study.)

complex pattern of change among three nominal response categories. The model does systematically underpredict the raw data, but when one takes into account the limitations of these data—small sample size, a relatively weak measure of habitual news reception, and crude media content analysis—it is hard to maintain that even an ideal model could perform very much better.[22]

The conclusions one reaches from this analysis are the same as were reached from the previous analysis of congressional elections, except that they are based here on a more challenging data set and a more powerful model of media effects: The first conclusion is that very large media effects do occur. In the case of Mondale, estimated support in the initial period ran from about 10 percent among the least attentive Democrats to more than 80 percent among highly attentive Democrats. In the case of Hart, support rose from essentially nothing to more than 70 percent, depending on habitual news reception and the pattern of media coverage. The second conclusion is that media effects, though large and systematic, cannot be captured by any simple linear function of news reception. Rather, a model capable of capturing the nonlinear and interactive effects of competing communication is necessary.

The Probable Frequency of Very Large Media Effects

The foregoing analyses have demonstrated that very large media effects do occur. The logical next question is how often they occur. The answer, as I shall now argue, is often.

To establish this contention, it is necessary to distinguish sharply between *actual frequency* of large media effects and frequency of *detection* of such effects. Clearly, the frequency of detection of large media effects is low. But the reason for this situation may have nothing to do with actual frequency. It may have to do only with the conditions necessary for detection.

It must be reiterated, in this connection, that in order to demonstrate very large media effects in the previous sections, I had to examine cases in which there were large swings in media coverage: the difference between a low-key, almost pro forma House race and a presidential election, and the difference between Hart's scant coverage when he was a political nonentity in January and his extravagant coverage in the wake of his surprise victory in New Hampshire.

Such swings do not routinely occur in all domains of political life. Yet unless there is large variation in the stimuli to which people are exposed, it will be impossible to detect large *net* effects of media coverage, and this will be so even when, to invoke the tug-of-war metaphor again, the actual *total* influence of opposing forces is continuously great. For example, the odds are against detecting large net media effects—that is, swings of 30 or 40 points in public opinion traceable to changes in the content of mass communication—in the context of presidential elections, because the flow of opposing communications is likely to remain, except for short interludes, fairly evenly balanced (though see Johnston, Blais, Brady, and Crete 1992).

The difficulty in detecting large net media effects, then, is that for many and perhaps most matters of importance—high-visibility elections, chronic political issues, basic social conflicts—the media keep up a more-or-less stable flow of competing messages that makes it all but impossible to detect the extent to which citizens are responsive, in a dynamic sense, to the flow of political communication.

Citizen response to stable communication flows may nonetheless generate distinctive patterns of opinion holding. My aim in the next section is to use the theoretical machinery developed so far as a basis for figuring out what these patterns may be expected to look like. Before doing so, however, I must digress to consider the role of political values in the communication process.

Political Values and Mass Communication

My analysis so far has been framed in terms of the relative intensity of opposing communication flows. Individual differences in propensity to yield to communication, as determined by political values and partisan attachments, have been acknowledged but not emphasized. For example, in the case of House elections, I confined analysis within one partisan group, namely, outparty voters deciding whether to defect from their party to that of the incumbent.[23] The intent has been to show, with as little extraneous theoretical machinery as possible, the very large effects that differences in communication flow can generate independently of other factors.

With this aim now largely satisfied, I can broaden the analysis to take account of the effects of partisan biases in information processing—biases that are, as would be expected, very large. Doing so will complicate the analysis, but it will not require any alteration of basic theoretical principles.

I begin with a definition: By political values I refer to any individual-level trait, demographic characteristic, or ideological predisposition that might affect yielding to mass communication, given reception of it. Party attachment, liberal or conservative ideology, religion, ethnicity, and gender can all be used as indicators of value differences.

One can imagine two models of how values might affect yielding to persuasive messages. In the first model, individuals think for themselves about each message and its implications for their values. Thus, a committed American nationalist might, in scrutinizing communication urging American involvement in an overseas war, ponder whether the war would truly advance American interests. In the second model, individuals do not attempt to think for themselves about the communication they receive. Rather, they attend (whether consciously or not) to the elite and ideological sources of the messages, using this information as a cue for accepting or rejecting the messages.

My analysis will, for reasons well stated by McGuire (1968), adhere to the second model.[24] Summarizing the evidence on the importance of "source" factors in persuasive communication, he wrote that the message "receiver"

> can be regarded as a lazy organism who tries to master the message contents only when it is absolutely necessary to make a decision. When the purported source is clearly positively or negatively valenced, he uses this information as a cue to accept or reject the message's conclusions without really absorbing the arguments used.

There is, however, a crucial difference between source effects as they occur in laboratory experiments of the kind summarized by McGuire and source effects as they occur in mass media settings: In laboratory settings, the advocates of persuasive messages are so closely linked to the positions they espouse that even a sleepwalker would notice the connection; in the real world, these linkages are easy to miss. Partly this is because journalists do not routinely repeat which leaders advocate which policies every time they do a story about the policy, and partly it is because many citizens pay too little attention to pick up the cues that are available.

Take as an example the war in Vietnam. During the 1972 presidential election, George McGovern ran on a platform of immediate withdrawal of

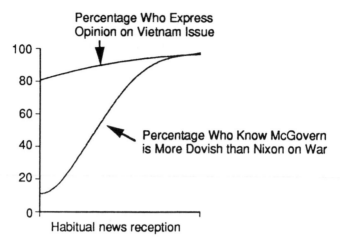

Fig. 10. The difffusion of source information concerning Vietnam War. (Data from 1972 National Election Studies.)

American forces from Vietnam, while his opponent, Richard Nixon, ran on a platform of gradually reduced American involvement so as to achieve "peace with honor." Their policy difference was, by the standards of American presidential politics, both very clear and very large. Yet, as figure 10 indicates, tens of millions of American failed to notice. To be sure, nearly 100 percent of politically knowledgeable Americans absorbed the information that McGovern was more in favor of immediate withdrawal than Nixon was, but among citizens in the middle ranges of political awareness, only about 50 percent acquired this information, and among the least aware citizens, only 10 percent did so.[25]

Examples like these, which could be multiplied many times, mark the existence of sharp limits to the incidence of source effects in the domain of mass communication, at least in the United States. And if, as I have maintained, source information is necessary for citizens to recognize the implications of their partisan and ideological values, there must also be sharp limits to value effects—especially among citizens who are relatively inattentive to public affairs and hence fail to pick up most source information.

Modeling the Effects of Stable Communication Flows

The question now is how to incorporate source and value effects, to the extent that they occur, into a model of competing political communication. Following in the spirit of the models already developed, I assume (1) that citizens get information about the elite advocates of policies—which I have elsewhere called "cueing information"—in the same place they get most other public affairs information, that is, from the mass media; (2) that they get this advocacy information in proportion to their habitual propensity for news reception in general; and (3) that the advocacy information, once acquired, acts as one of the competing messages in the process of mass persuasion.

The third point requires some elaboration. Recall that, in our earlier analyses, citizens could receive and accept either of two competing messages. If they received and accepted only one message, they were converted to its position; but if they received and accepted both messages, no conversion occurred. It thus appeared that acceptance of one message functioned to neutralize the other.

I will assume that source information acts to neutralize persuasive communication in the same way, with this key difference: Its neutralizing effect interacts with the values of the message receiver, such that only messages from antagonistic sources are neutralized. Thus, liberals refuse to accept conservative messages if they possess the source information necessary to recognize them as such, and conservatives do the same with respect to liberal messages. But liberals and conservatives (or Democrats and Republicans) who do not possess source information are unable to tell which messages are inconsistent with their values, and so often they end up accepting messages that they would reject if better informed.

For each major issue, then, we must recognize as many as four types of communication: a substantive message urging a position on an issue, a substantive message urging the opposite position, and two messages carrying source information. For an issue like the Vietnam War, examples of the two substantive messages might be "This war is necessary to defeat communism" and "This war is a useless quagmire." A source message might be "All pro-war arguments come from conservatives who are too uptight about communism and shouldn't be believed" or, perhaps more simply, "That's a disreputable conservative [or liberal] argument; don't believe it!"

I make one further assumption: that substantive messages tend to be more frequent and salient than source messages—that is, more intense. As a result, people are more likely to be persuaded to form opinions on issues than they are to be aware of the ideological and partisan implications of the messages they accept. (Figure 10, which shows the percent of people who had opinions on the Vietnam War as well as the percent knowing the positions of Nixon and McGovern, indicates that this assumption is very plausible.)

Let us now try to figure out what patterns of opinion holding we should expect to observe in a populace in which mass persuasion operates on these principles.

I deal first with a simple but important type of case: one in which the media carry a stable stream of substantive messages and source information that overwhelmingly support some general policy. In this type of situation, there is no way for communication to be neutralized. The result is that the greater a person's propensity for habitual news reception, the greater the likelihood of being influenced in the direction of the predominant message.

An example of this type of case is the Persian Gulf crisis and war. When President Bush decided in August 1990 to "draw a line in the sand" by sending U.S. troops to the Persian Gulf, he was vocally supported by many members of Congress who rushed back from their summer recess to issue statements in Washington supporting him. According to *Congressional Quarterly,* not one member of Congress issued a statement opposing the decision to send troops, nor did the media carry other information suggesting that it was a mistake to send troops into what clearly was a potential battleground (see Bennett and Paletz 1994). Even in the congressional debate on whether to authorize the president to use force against Iraq—a separate and highly contentious matter—there were scarcely any congressional voices arguing that it had been a mistake to commit U.S. forces to the gulf. The main opposition argument was only that it would be a mistake to go to war until economic sanctions and diplomacy had run their course.

Given this stable and largely one-sided flow of political communication, the guiding assumption of this chapter—that media influence increases monotonically with the amount of mass communication received—implies that there should be a positive relationship between habitual news reception and support for policies advocated by the mainstream media.

To test this expectation, we need survey items that embody the position of the mainstream position. Two good choices are available. The first, a fairly standard survey item, asks whether the United States did the "right thing" in sending troops to the Persian Gulf. A second question asks:

> Which of the following do you think we should do now in the Persian Gulf?
> —Pull out U.S. forces entirely
> —Try harder to find a diplomatic solution
> —Tighten the economic embargo
> —Take tougher military action

Since multiple answers to this question were accepted, people could, for example, say that the United States should pull out its troops *and* work harder to find a diplomatic solution. In analyzing these answers, I counted any response or combination of responses that did *not* include the "pull out" option as indicating support for the basic U.S. policy of military confrontation with Iraq.

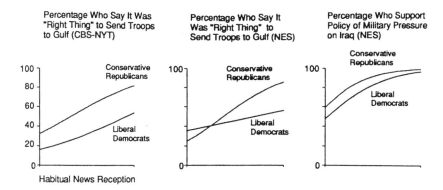

Fig. 11. Effects of party and media exposure on "mainstream" issues in Gulf Crisis. (Data from CBS News–*New York Times* surveys, January 11–13, and 1990 National Election Studies; adapted from Zaller 1994.)

The data obtained from these two questions are presented in figure 11. They show, as expected, that higher levels of habitual news reception are consistently associated with higher levels of support for the consensual media and elite policy. This association holds within the public as a whole as well as within separate partisan and ideological groups. It holds even within separate racial and gender groupings (data not shown). Although people do differ in their propensity to support a policy of military assertiveness, the effect of habitual news reception within each group is to induce greater support for this policy.[26]

Note that the persuasion effects shown in figure 11—if that is what they are—are very large. As a separate analysis shows, 23 percent of those in the lowest reception group in the NES study said the United States was right to send troops, as against 57 percent who said the United States should have stayed out. In the highest reception group, by contrast, 76 percent favored this policy, as against 24 percent who favored staying out—a gain of some 53 percentage points for the mainstream position.[27] The size of this effect is, quite simply, the difference between a populace that mainly opposes a policy and one that mainly supports it.

Having now considered a case in which a media and elite consensus supports one side of an issue, I turn now to a second, probably more common type of case, one in which the mass media carry roughly balanced streams of *opposing* substantive and source messages and, further, carry these messages in a steady fashion over a long period of time. How might we expect public opinion to respond to this pattern of communication?

Let us consider first the likely effect of news reception on opinion within one partisan group, say, liberals. And let us start with the most politically attentive liberals. Such people will tend to receive all substantive and source messages. This will lead them to reject conservative messages while accepting those tagged as liberal, and this, in turn, will lead them to express liberal opinions with high reliability.

Next take the case of citizens who are liberal and inattentive to politics. They receive essentially no source messages, since, as we saw in figure 10, advocacy information rarely reaches the chronically inattentive. Such people may receive some opposing substantive messages—for example, "Support our troops," "This war is a disaster"— but these messages will have, for the less aware, no discernible links to liberal values. Hence these liberals will wind up yielding to whatever message they encounter most often or most recently, which, under my stylized assumption that the opposing substantive messages are equally intense, is equivalent to flipping a coin. Hence, less aware liberals end up supporting the liberal position about half the time.

Finally, consider the intermediate case, namely, liberals who are moderately attentive to politics. Some, but not all, will receive source messages from the media. This will enable them, taken as a group, to support the liberal position more often than chance but still not at the high level of reliability of the most politically aware liberals.

Altogether, then, the expectation is that, among liberals, increases in habitual news reception will be associated with steady *increases* in support for the liberal position.

By parallel logic, the same argument can be made for conservatives: With increases in habitual news reception, they may be expected to become steadily more supportive of the conservative position. Thus, the overall effect of habitual news reception for a case in which the media carry a steady stream of ideologically balanced communication is to drive liberals and conservatives into increasingly polarized opposition to one another.

It is straightforward but not particularly illuminating to cast this verbal argument into a mathematical model and show formally that it is logically coherent. It is more pertinent to examine some empirical cases that roughly fit the assumptions underlying the argument.

The case of the Gulf War can again furnish examples. As just indicated, mainstream liberal and conservative elites largely agreed on a generic policy of deploying U.S. troops to the Persian Gulf region, but they disagreed on many specifics of how and whether those forces should be used against Iraq. Above all, mainstream elites disagreed among themselves on Bush's basic policy of threatening to start a war, and then actually starting one, upon expiration of a United Nations deadline for Iraq to withdraw from Kuwait.

As can be seen in figure 12, public opinion on policies over which

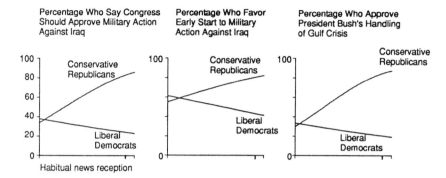

Fig. 12. Effects of party and media exposure on partisan issues. (Data from CBS News–*New York Times* surveys, January 11–13; adapted from Zaller 1994.)

partisan elites disagreed—whether Congress should authorize the initiation of military action against Iraq; whether the United States should attack when the UN deadline expires; Bush's overall handling of the crisis—conforms to the expected polarization pattern. Higher levels of habitual news reception induce conservatives and Republicans toward greater support for administration policies, but have just the opposite effect on liberals and Democrats.

There are numerous cases in which the patterns of mass opinion shown in figures 11 and 12 can be found. These cases involve, besides foreign policy, such issues as welfare, civil liberties, and racial policy (see Zaller 1992, figure 6.5).

The real question is not how frequent these patterns are, for they are frequent enough to sustain the general point of this chapter. The real question is what should be made of them. In particular, is it reasonable to regard them as effects of the diffusion of competing liberal and conservative communication flows? If so, my argument that very large media effects occur with regularity would be established.

The reason for regarding the data in figures 11 and 12 as evidence of media effects is that, as I have just argued, the mainstream and polarization patterns are exactly the patterns one would expect to observe in the presence of communication flows that are either one-sided or competitive and that carry source information that is less salient than substantive information.

But this argument is essentially a dynamic argument applied to static, or cross-sectional, data. The case for large media effects would be stronger if it could be shown that the stable communication flows supposedly responsible for the mainstream and polarization effects change at least occasionally, and that when they do change, public opinion responds in the theoretically expected manner.

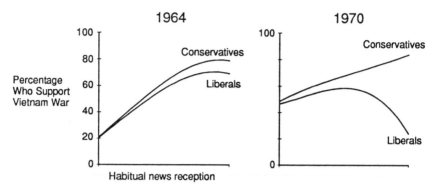

Fig. 13. Support for the Vietnam War in 1964 and 1970. Estimated patterns of war support are based on coefficients and modeling procedures
described in Zaller 1991. (Data from 1964 and 1970 CPS surveys.)

As noted at the start of this chapter, there are few cases in which dramatic
changes in communication flow occur in conjunction with surveys capable of
registering the effects of the change on mass opinion. One such case is the
Vietnam War, an issue that I have extensively investigated elsewhere (Zaller
1992, chap. 9). I will now briefly recap the results of this work: The flow of
mass communication evolved from consensual elite and media support for the
war in 1964 to opposing and roughly evenly balanced messages and source
cues in 1970.[28] As this change occurred, public opinion evolved from a
standard mainstream pattern, in which habitual news reception was associated
with support for the war, to a standard polarization pattern, in which habitual
news reception was associated with a polarization between liberals and conservatives. These data are shown in figure 13.

The most revealing evidence of the effect of mass communication comes
from the period between 1964 and 1966. In this period, the intensity of pro-
war communication, as measured by counts of stories in *Time* and *Newsweek*
magazines, increased markedly, while at the same time, the intensity of antiwar communication, which hardly existed in 1964, also became greater
(Zaller 1992, fig. 10.1).

This pattern of communication flows—in which the intensity of both pro
and con communication flows becomes greater—is the same pattern that
tends to generate the crossover pattern of media effects (see figures 3 and 6).
As figure 14 shows, it generated a crossover pattern of opinion change during
the Vietnam War as well. That is, between 1964 and 1966, middle-aware
liberals became more supportive of the war, a response to the pro-war message that, for the first time, developed sufficient intensity to reach them. Since

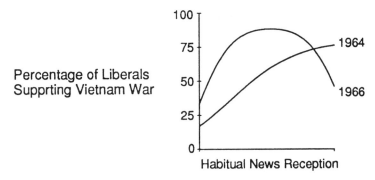

Percentage of Liberals
Supprting Vietnam War

Fig. 14. Patterns of support for Vietnam War among liberals in 1964 and 1966. (Data adapted from Zaller 1992, chap. 9.)

moderately attentive people are, for reasons just explained, often ignorant of the ideological coloration of the communication they receive, the fact that pro-war communication was increasingly associated with conservativism did not prevent moderately aware liberals from yielding to it.

In this same time period, highly aware liberals, who had heavily supported the war in 1964, began to *reduce* their support for it. The reason is that, by 1966, they were beginning to pick up antiwar communication that had been almost nonexistent in 1964 but that was by 1966 developing sufficient intensity to reach highly attentive persons.

No crossover effect, I should add, was observed among conservatives in this period—nor should one have been. The increase in pro-war communication generated more support for the war among middle-aware conservatives, just as it did among middle-aware liberals. But the increase in antiwar communication had no effect on highly aware conservatives, who became, if anything, slightly more supportive of the war between 1964 and 1966 (data not shown). This was a reflection of the fact that antiwar messages were, owing to the ideological coloration of war critics both on the street and in the U.S. Congress, unambiguously tagged as liberal, which then led highly aware conservatives to reject them.

In fact, as figure 13 indicates, there was as much support for the Vietnam War in 1970 among highly aware conservatives as there had been in 1964. Such doggedness in the face of extremely frustrating real-world outcomes is explained by the fact that highly aware conservatives received a consistent set of pro-war messages and cues from people they respected; this communication led them to believe, in spite of everything in the so-called liberal press of the era, that it was important for the United States to persist in trying to contain communism. Sophisticated conservatives, in other words, were not so much doggedly resisting bad news as choosing between competing views of the world offered them in the media. Any indication of independent thought among highly aware conservatives—or, for that matter, among highly aware liberals—is entirely absent from figures 13 and 14. What we glimpse instead is a highly regular response to a particular pattern of communication.

Taken together, this is a powerful set of results: Changes in the pattern of mass communication—including both substantive information and source information—had two theoretically revealing effects on mass opinion: (1) the generation of a crossover effect at the point, early in the war, when both pro-war and antiwar communication flows were both increasing in intensity, and (2) the transformation of the mainstream pattern of mass opinion of 1964 into the polarization pattern of 1970 and thereafter.

The conclusion to be drawn from these results, I contend, is that the mainstream and polarization patterns of mass opinion represent neither a natural nor a static configuration of opinion, but rather a response to the particular pattern of communication conveyed to the public by the mass media. If, as is typically the case, the response of mass opinion remains stable over long periods of time, it is because the media inputs to opinion, including the structure of partisan cues, are more stable for most issues than they were for the issue of Vietnam.

When I advanced this argument at a recent academic symposium, a member of the audience noted, correctly, that my case depends rather heavily on the existence of crossover effects and that it seemed to him, in view of the infrequency of these effects, that I might be making too much of them. This objection reflects the kind of thinking that I believe the field of mass communication needs to break with. The critically important question about crossover effects should not be how often they occur, but whether they occur in the situations in which they would be theoretically expected to occur, and if so, whether my analysis of their cause is correct.

If I might be permitted a somewhat grandiose analogy to the physical sciences, I would recall the well-known case in which scientists wanting to test Einstein's theory of relativity traveled to a Pacific island to see whether, as theoretically predicted, light would appear to curve as it traveled past the eclipsed sun. The appropriate response to their discovery that light did, indeed, appear to curve was not to say, "Yes, but eclipses are very rare." It was, rather, to be thankful for rare but illuminating events.

Changes in the partisan structure of elite cues on major issues are, like eclipses, inherently rare events. Large changes in the thrust of media coverage in the absence of changes in the positions of partisan elites may (except in certain electoral contexts) be nearly as rare. But there is no reason to believe that rare events cannot be as illuminating about the nature of reality as common ones can. Hence, my contention is that, although crossover effects are admittedly uncommon, there is good reason, in light of the larger system of theoretical and empirical observations made in this chapter, to believe that the communication effects illuminated by the crossover pattern are anything but rare.

Conclusions

This chapter has developed three related models of the effects of mass communication. The first model was tailored to a situation is which there is one dominant and one secondary communication flow and was applied to the case of incumbent voting in House elections, where these conditions hold. The second model was fitted to a case in which there are two opposing messages of variable intensity over time and was applied to the seesaw contest between Gary Hart and Walter Mondale for the 1984 Democratic nomination. The third was tailored to cases in which a flow of opposing messages is both roughly balanced and stable over time and was applied to a number of issues fitting these conditions.

Each model begins with the standard assumption that influence from mass communication increases monotonically with the amount of communication received. Each leads to the theoretical expectation that the net pattern of influence produced by competing communication flows can take dramatically different forms, depending on the relative intensities of the opposing communication flows. Finally, each model is supported by evidence of very large media effects.

The reasons that previous researchers have been unable to detect the very large media effects that, as I have argued, commonly occur are two:

Failure to meet the prerequisites of most successful scientific enterprises, namely, good measurement of variables that actually do vary. As I have explained, there are very understandable reasons for this failure.

Failure to develop sufficiently incisive models of the effects of competing communication. Almost all work has involved essentially linear models that are, as should now be clear, incapable of capturing many of the mass persuasion effects that may plausibly occur.

I do not pretend that this short chapter has definitively established the thesis that very large media effects are commonplace. One main reason is that my use of evidence has been selective, consisting of a handful of examples culled from nearly half a century of public opinion data. Such selectivity, as I have argued, is not only warranted but essential for fair-minded assessment of the question of media effects, but even so, it will take a broader range of evidence than I have presented here to establish my thesis.

The warrant for some of my empirical claims is also in doubt. For example, I have provided no empirical substantiation for the claim that the flow of competing communication is more stable over time on most issues than it was for Vietnam, which I have claimed to be unusual. The basis of the claim is simply impressionistic. Also, for all my emphasis on sharp measurement of individual differences in news reception, my measurements of media content have been very crude. Finally, in the strongest part of my argument— the statistical models of competing communication flows—I was forced to rely at a key juncture on a somewhat strange assumption, namely, that media influence occurs in a dichotomous rather than continuous fashion.[29]

The contribution of this chapter to establishing the thesis of very large media effects must therefore lie more in the realm of plausibility than of conclusive demonstration. It must lie, more specifically, in three, somewhat narrower, achievements:

> Showing that the standard assumption of media research—that, all else equal, media influence increases monotonically with the amount of communication received from the media—has theoretical implications that are a great deal more complicated than can be captured in the types of models that predominate in communication research.
> Demonstrating that these theoretical implications can be confirmed under appropriate empirical conditions.
> Demonstrating, in particular, that very large media effects do occur.

This contribution is, I hope, sufficient to convince my professional peers that, in spite of 50 years of mostly null or modest results from research on the effects of mass communication, it is still possible that very large media persuasion effects are lurking all around us, waiting to be brought more fully to light by more appropriate measures, models, and theoretical perspectives.

APPENDIX

These appendixes have been written to encourage replication of the empirical findings in this chapter as class exercises by students in introductory seminars in mass communication and applied statistics. All of the SPSSx code used in the analysis in this chapter is available upon request for ready use by interested scholars or students.

Appendix A: News Diffusion in 1989 NES Pilot Study

Appendix A describes the analysis for the comparative performance of self-reported media use, political awareness, and education in predicting reception of two news stories.

Between July 6 and August 1, 1989, the National Election Studies conducted a pilot study of new survey content. Subjects were 614 individuals from the 1988 NES election study. The pilot included a wide range of items measuring exposure to the mass media and a series of queries about recent news stories. The latter were intended for use in validating the performance of alternative media exposure items (see Price and Zaller 1993).

The two news items used in this analysis were the resignation of Jim Wright and the crash of a DC-10 airliner. Respondents were first asked if they had noticed any stories about the event, and then a more specific follow-up, as follows:

> Have you read or heard any news articles about the resignation of Congressman Jim Wright? Do you happen to recall why he resigned?
>
> Have you seen or heard any stories about a major airline disaster? What exactly happened?

Respondents who could supply any sort of specific information in response to the second query were counted as having received the story. Correct answers in the Wright case could be as rudimentary as "scandal" or "under attack" (codes 2 through 9 on V7450 counted as correct, or 1; 0 and 99 as missing; else as incorrect, or 0); correct answers in the DC-10 case could be as simple as "plane crashed" (same scoring as for Wright item).

Media exposure was measured by means of 17 items from the 1988 NES study and the first wave of the pilot study. Because the ranges of the items varied, the scale was built from the factor scores of a principal components analysis of the items; alpha reliability of the scale was .87.

In scoring these and similar items in this study, I followed a uniform set of conventions, the most important of which was that no missing data were permitted. If respondents weren't sure how much or whether they used a certain kind of medium, or if they reported themselves unsure of the answer, they were given the lowest score on that measure, indicating either no exposure or lack of information. The one exception to this rule is education, where missing cases were coded to the status of high school graduate.

Items from the 1988 NES study contributing to overall level of news exposure were: days watch TV (v202); days read newspaper (v204); attention to the presidential campaign on TV (v203), in newspapers (v209), in magazines (v211), on radio (v213). From the July wave of the 1989 pilot study, the following items were also used: days watch TV news (v7356); attention to politics in TV news (v7357); days read newspaper (v7360); attention to politics in newspaper (v7361); days in week watch morning news like *Today* (v7437), local TV news (v7438), network TV news (v7439); read news magazines for news (v7444, codes 2, 3); how often read stories about local politics (v7445), national politics (v7447), international affairs (v7448). The alpha reliability of the scale is .87.

The scale of political knowledge and awareness was constructed from 17 dichotomous items, all measured in the 1988 NES survey. For the 614 respondents of the pilot survey, this scale had a mean of 8.86, a standard deviation of 4.61, and an alpha reliability of .88. The first 10 items were direct information tests: knowledge of the job or office held by seven nationally prominent politicians (e.g., Ted Kennedy, Jim Wright, William Rehnquist; v5827 to v5833); which party controls House and Senate (v5834, v5835); which party is more conservative (v5656). Respondents received one point each for ability to recognize and rate Robert Dole and Mario Cuomo (v226, v227; 997, 998, 999 = 0, else = 1). The remaining four items involved correct relative location of a pair of politicians or groups on seven-point scales, as follows: Dukakis to the left of Bush on ideology (v418, v419), government services (v606, v607), and defense (v610, v611); Democrats to the left of Republicans on ideology (v421, v422), job guarantees (v627, v628), and cooperation with Russia (v712, v713). To receive credit for a correct answer, respondents were required to recognize a distance of two or more scale points between the groups.[30] Education was measured as years in school (v1005, v1007); master's degrees were counted as 18 years and more advanced degrees as 20.

The two dependent variables (reception of DC-10 and Wright stories) were run in separate bivariate logit regressions against media use, education, and political awareness, with the results shown in table A-1. See Zaller (1992, 105) for the conventions used in creating graphical representations of these results, as shown in figure 1. These graphing conventions have been used throughout this chapter.

Appendix B: Voting in the 1986, 1988, and 1990 House Elections

Appendix B describes analysis of the comparative performance of self-reported media use, political awareness, and education in explaining defection to the incumbent in contested House elections in 1986, 1988, and 1990. I first describe models, then results, then measures.

The model used to estimate the effect of media exposure on probability of defection to the incumbent is an entirely straightforward verbalization of the argument made in the text. The model is based on the subtraction of two logit functions of

TABLE A-1. Coefficients for News Diffusion

	DC-10	Wright
Intercept	2.43	−0.44
Political awareness	1.44	1.95
(standardized)	(.31)	(.18)
Intercept	1.86	−0.26
Level of media use	0.51	0.97
(standardized)	(.28)	(.13)
Intercept	1.82	−0.25
Education	0.52	0.92
(years in school, standardized)	(.23)	(.14)
N of cases	152	611

Source: 1989 NES Pilot Study.
Note: Estimation is ML logit. Standard errors appear in parentheses.

individual differences in media exposure—abbreviated below as *Media*—to capture the "exposure gap" between competing campaign messages, as follows:

Prob.(defection) = Prob.(reception and acceptance of incumbent

communication)

− Prob.(reception and acceptance of challenger

communication)

$$= f_1(\text{Media}) - f_2(\text{Media})$$
$$= (1 + \exp[-b_0 - b_1 * \text{Media}])^{-1}$$
$$- (1 + \exp[-b_2 - b_1 * \text{Media}])^{-1} \qquad \text{(B-1)}$$

This model was estimated for three different measures of *Media*—namely, self-reported media use, political awareness, and education—in each of the three elections. Results are shown in table A-2.

The 1986 scale of political knowledge and awareness was constructed from 14 dichotomous items. For the 2,176 respondents in the 1986 NES survey, this scale had a mean of 6.03, a standard deviation of 3.71, and an alpha reliability of .85. The first eight items were simple information tests: knowledge of the offices held by six prominent politicians, plus party control of Congress before and after the election (v343 to v350). There were two recognition tests, Robert Dole and Gary Hart (v140, v143). Respondents also got one point each for placing Democrats two or more points to the

TABLE A-2. Coefficients for Defection to Incumbent in 1986, 1988, and 1990 House Elections

	1986	1988	1990
Intercept (b_0)	1.26	1.68	1.67
Political awareness	1.03	0.97	1.05
(standardized)	(.38)	(.42)	(.45)
Intercept (b_2)	−1.35	−1.11	−1.18
Intercept (b_0)	13.8	2.20	0.74
Level of media use	0.13	0.30	.77
(standardized)	(1.7)	(.69)	(.51)
Intercept (b_2)	−0.02	−0.45	−1.74
Intercept (b_0)	1.05	0.87	11.3
Years in school	0.35	0.69	0.05
(standardized)	(.57)	(.36)	(6.19)
Intercept (b_2)	−1.14	−1.47	−.03
N of cases	241	267	163

Source: National Election Studies.
Note: Estimation is ML logit. Standard errors appear in parentheses.

left of the Republicans on ideology (v393, v394), defense spending (v412, v413), U.S. involvement in Central America (v435, v436), and government services (v455, v456). Coding was as described in appendix A.

The 1986 media use scale was built by means of factor scores from a principal components analysis of five items; the alpha reliability was .67. The items were attention to the campaign on radio (v61), in newspapers (v63), and in TV news (v65); also days per week reading a newspaper (v70) and watching national TV news (v71).

The 1988 scale of political awareness is the same as described in appendix A for the 1989 pilot study, except that variable numbers and descriptive statistics are different. For the 2,040 respondents in the 1988 NES survey, this scale had a mean of 7.92, a standard deviation of 4.83, and an alpha reliability of .89.

The 1988 media use scale was built from a principal components analysis and includes the six media use items from the 1988 study that were described in appendix A. The alpha reliability of this scale is .67.

The 1990 scale of political awareness was constructed from 16 dichotomous items. For the 2,000 respondents in the 1990 NES survey, this scale had a mean of 6.54, a standard deviation of 3.61, and an alpha reliability of .83. The first 10 items were simple information tests: knowledge of the offices held by seven prominent politicians (v395 to v401), party control of Congress (v402, v403), and which party more conservative (v350).[31] Respondents received one point each for ability to recognize and rate Mikhail Gorbachev and Mario Cuomo (v135, v136; 997, 998, 999 = 0, else = 1). Respondents also got one point each for placing Democrats two or more points to the left of the Republicans on ideology (v413, v414), defense spending (v443, v444), aid to blacks (v450, v451), and government services (v456, v457).

The 1990 media use scale was built by means of factor scores from a principal components analysis of five items; the alpha reliability was .74. The items were attention to the campaign in the newspaper (v64) and on TV (v67), watching news programs about the campaign (v66), and number of days reading a newspaper (v71) and watching TV news (v72).

The dependent variable in the analysis is "defection to the incumbent." This variable was measured only in contested House races involving an incumbent and only for voters who expressed some degree of attachment (strong, weak, or lean) to the party opposite that of the incumbent.[32]

Appendix C: Estimation of the Effects of Campaign Intensity on House Voting

The most difficult part of estimating equation 1 in the text is measuring the intensities of the opposing communication flows. Ideally, we would like to have measures of the amount and directional thrust of all news reports and paid advertisements in each congressional race. This, however, is not feasible—probably not in any election cycle and certainly not in elections held as long ago as the 1960s. Viable proxy variables are, however, available. In the 1978 NES study, which is the best of the CPS/NES midterm studies, all respondents were asked:

How many newspaper articles did you read about the campaign for the U.S. House of Representatives in your district—would you say a good many, several, or just one or two?

Since scores on this variable varied greatly across districts, the average response within each district can be taken as a partial measure of the amount of news coverage of that district's race. It is partial only because it conveys no information about how much coverage went to the incumbent and how much to the challenger.

Another measure of campaign intensity is the amount of money each candidate spent on the race. Spending has obvious appeal as a measure of campaign intensity, but it also has problems. One is that a given dollar expenditure will buy much more communication in some districts than in others, depending on media market structure. Another is that incumbents spend their largest sums when they are on the verge of losing (typically because of scandal or an unusually strong opponent rather than lack of spending) and trying to reverse the inevitable. This makes it appear that high spending by an incumbent increases the chances that the incumbent will lose—which it does not.

I have attempted to correct the shortcomings of the two measures by combining them into a joint measure of communication flow, as indicated by the following variable definitions and operationalizations:

News = District average of response to question about news articles read

Incspend = Log of reported spending by incumbent

Chalspend = Log of reported spending by challenger

$Intensity_{Inc.}$ = Amount of incumbent communication

= News X \IF(Incspend, Incspend + Chalspend)

$Intensity_{Chal.}$ = Amount of challenger communication

= News X \IF(Chalspend, Incspend + Chalspend)

These measures weight news coverage by the relative vigor of the incumbent and challenger campaigns, as determined by each's spending. The assumption in doing so is that journalists cover candidates in rough proportion to their spending, as suggested by Westlye (1988). At the same time, the measures assume that the efficiency of campaign spending is proportional to the amount of news that, by virtue of media market structure, gets through to voters in a district.

In the 1978 study, campaign intensity was measured in the manner just described. In the 1986 study, the measure of news coverage was not available, so I tried to measure the overall amount of communication that gets through to voters in another way: as the district average of the level of candidate name recall and name recognition (i.e., the sum of the two variables, both scored 0–1). District means were calculated separately for challenger and incumbent, then weighted by spending in the manner just described. In the 1966 study, the only available indicators of communication flow were average levels of incumbent and challenger name recall. Hence district averages of these variables were used to measure the amount of communication by each candidate that got through to voters in a given race.[33]

The results of estimating the model in equation 1 on these variables are shown in table A-3. I will discuss results for the unconstrained model first, as shown in the first, third, and fifth columns of the table. Note first that, although only three of six news reception coefficients are statistically significant at the .05 level, all six have correct signs and similar magnitudes. The probability of getting the sign right by chance alone is $.5^6$, or .016. Also, the mean of these six coefficients is 1.21 with a standard error of .15; this yields a t-ratio of 7.9 (df = 5), which indicates p $<<$ .01.[34] Hence there is no question about the statistical significance of this set of six coefficients.

TABLE A-3.   Coefficients for House Voting Models

| | Incumbent subfunction | | | | | |
	1966		1978		1986	
Intercept	−0.57	−0.31	1.93	1.94	1.57	1.74
Habitual news reception	0.82	1.06	1.09	1.56	1.28	1.13
(standardized)	(.54)	(.45)	(.60)	(.34)	(1.04)	(.37)
Party attachment	−0.13	−0.80	−1.85	−1.25	−0.25	−1.30
(1 if strong identifier,						
else 0)	(1.21)	(.41)	(.73)	(.36)	(1.33)	(.37)
Incumbent campaign						
intensity	0.41	0.65	1.30	0.71	0.74	0.80
(standardized)	(.32)	(.25)	(.57)	(.23)	(.55)	(.24)
	Challenger subfunction					
Intercept	−2.88	−1.88	−2.72	−2.27	−1.77	−1.72
Habitual news reception	1.08	a	1.91	a	1.07	a
	(1.14)		(.74)		(.61)	
Party attachment	−2.10	a	−0.76	a	−1.84	a
	(1.55)		(.71)		(.65)	
Challenger campaign						
intensity	1.00	a	0.71	a	0.83	a
	(.77)		(.31)		(.36)	
N of cases	199		279		237	

Source: CPS/NES election studies.

Note: Model is equation 1 from text. Estimation is by the maximum likelihood technique described in Zaller (1992, 149–50). Standard errors for parameter estimates are shown in parentheses. None of the constraints indicated in the table resulted in a significant increase in residual variation.

aConstrained to equal corresponding coefficient in incumbent subfunction.

In converting these coefficients into the graphical estimates in figure 5, I used scores corresponding to the 5th, 50th, and 95th percentile on the campaign intensity measures to represent low-, middle-, and high-intensity elections.[35]

Similarly, although only three of six coefficients measuring campaign intensity are individually significant at the .05 level, all six have correct signs and roughly similar magnitudes. The average of the six coefficients is .83 with a standard error of .12, for a *t*-ratio of 6.77. Hence, again, there is no question concerning statistical significance.

The standard errors reported in table A-3 reflect the effects of opposing biases. On one hand, the SE's are calculated on the assumption that individual observations (i.e., survey respondents) are independently drawn, which they are not; rather, observations are clustered in a few dozen districts (and often in a few neighborhoods of these districts) in which all individuals experience the same campaign. The effect of this clustering would lead to estimates of standard errors that are smaller than the true standard errors. On the other hand, the district-level measures of campaign intensity are based on district samples that are generally small and also (except in 1978) highly variable in size across districts, thus introducing large and unequal amounts of measurement error across cases. The effect of such error is to make the reported standard errors larger than the true standard errors. (Consistent with this latter point, *t*-ratios from the 1978 study, in which congressional districts were sampled so as to be self-representing, are larger than in either 1966 or 1986, when such sampling was not used.)

I emphasize that none of these problems leads to biased parameter estimates; they affect only the efficiency of parameter estimates and the magnitudes of the standard errors. I also note that neither I nor, so far as I know, anyone else knows how to make statistical corrections for these kinds of problems in a model such as equation 1. In these circumstances, the best indicator of statistical precision is stability across multiple independent tests of the model; happily, the evidence of such stability, as described in the previous paragraph, is strong enough to effectively rule out the possibility that the model is capturing only chance variability.

There is, however, some year-to-year variability in the magnitudes of the unconstrained estimates, and it seems likely that this is due to purely chance factors, such as which districts (i.e., clusters of respondents) and kinds of districts get tough races in a particular year. Chance error is likely to be especially great in light of the fact that the model is estimated on relatively small data sets in which the dependent variable is a 0–1 dichotomy, and that most of the action in the model occurs near the polar extremes of the intersection of two roughly normally distributed variables: district-level campaign intensity and individual-level habitual news reception. To gain control over this chance variability, I reestimated the model with three constraints. The first required habitual news reception to be as strongly correlated with reception of incumbent messages as challenger messages; the second required strength of party attachment to have (with a sign change) the same effect on acceptance of incumbent messages as on acceptance of challenger messages; the third required both challenger and incumbent messages to be, on average, equally potent at each level of measured intensity. Though only the first of these assumptions could plausibly be made a priori, none is inherently implausible. The constrained estimates are shown in columns two, four, and six of table A-3.

Because these estimates are more stable across years, and because the constraints caused nothing close to a statistically significant reduction in explanatory power in any of the years (though the f-tests are subject to the biases noted earlier), I consider them more valid estimates of the true effects of campaign communication than the unconstrained estimates and used them to create the graphical estimates in figure 5.

The pseudo r-squares for the three constrained models are 8.8 percent, 18.6 percent, and 20.0 percent in 1966, 1978, and 1986. Given that the dependent variable is a dichotomy, these are repectable values. (The difference between 1966 and the other two years is due in significant part to the difference in the skew of the dependent variable.) The argument for the model is not, however, that it explains a particularly large amount of variance. The argument, rather, is that it reveals the dynamics of communication flow. These dynamics, as explained in the text, imply very large media effects, even when, owing to the cancellation of opposing messages, observable effects are not large.

But could the independent variables included in the influence gap model do just as well in simpler model? The answer is no. The pseudo r-squares from a logistic regression model containing the same variables and number of parameters are 5.6 percent, 14.1 percent, and 17.1 percent, respectively. On a paired difference of means test, these r-squares are less than from the first set at $p < .05$ (df $= 2$, $t = 5.87$, two-tailed). Thus, there is statistically significant evidence that the influence gap model outperforms a standard null model.

Although there is, as I have maintained, little doubt of the statistical significance of the results obtained from the three election studies I have examined, there remains the question of whether these studies are representative of the larger set of CPS/NES studies from 1958 to 1992.

I have tested the simple model reported in table A-2 for all of the off-year data sets between 1958 and 1990, along with three on-year elections, 1972, 1980, and 1988. I have found support for the model in all the studies I have examined, but support is stronger in some studies than others. The factors associated with stronger results are (1) stronger measures of political awareness, (2) midterm rather than presidential election years (perhaps because presidential coattails affect defection rates independently of the intensity of the congressional campaigns), and (3) elections not associated with reapportionment (probably because reapportionment disrupts the flow of incumbent communication, thereby undermining a model of vote defection to the incumbent). The three elections selected for intensive study in this chapter rank high on each of these criteria and so are not representative of all election years. I believe, however, that the criteria for selection are reasonable, and I stress that there is support for the model in all studies examined, especially in the three conducted since 1986, when the NES began to carry a strong measure of political awareness (see figure 2).

The measure of awareness in the 1966 study is a grab bag of what was available, a total of six dichotomous items and three scales, as follows: names of up to four Supreme Court justices, each scored 0–1 from v167 (someone who got four or more names correct would receive 1s on four 0–1 variables; someone who got three names correct would receive 1s on three 0–1 variables, etc.); party control of Congress (v100, v101); interviewer rating of respondent's information (v242, scored 1 to 5);

follow public affairs (v64, scored 1–4); years of education. The scale was constructed from the factor scores of a principal components analysis and has an alpha reliability of .83. The 1978 measure is the same as described in Zaller (1992), except that missing data have been handled in the simpler manner described previously and the purged v43 has been eliminated, also for the sake of simplicity. The 1986 awareness measure is the same as described previously.

Appendix D: Estimation of the Hart-Mondale Model

Several practical adjustments had to be made in developing and estimating the model. First, when the NES survey began in mid-January, Mondale support was already above 40 percent in national surveys, while Hart's was negligible. Mondale's initial support was the result of previous media coverage. To capture this baseline level of Mondale support, I added a simple logistic term to the model that included a news reception variable and an intercept, where the intercept was intended to capture the effect of communication up to that point.

In specifying the four time periods, I sought, as explained earlier, to isolate periods in which the balance of opposing communication flows was stable. Having done this, I assumed in estimating the model that all respondents, whether interviewed early or late in a given period, were exposed to the same coverage. The alternative— estimating a model in which each day constitutes its own period—is theoretically straightforward but practically infeasible. Taking account of day of interview within each period was feasible, but paid no dividend that was worth the extra parameters. The fit of the model was, however, slightly improved by weighting the media exposure counts to reflect aggregate levels of exposure, as described in a note.[36]

The four time periods do not have equal numbers of cases in them. To prevent the ML estimator from attaching greater importance to periods in which there were more cases, I weighted the estimation by the inverse of the number of cases in each period, as shown in appendix E. The time periods are (1) prior to Iowa caucuses, beginning of study on January 11 through February 15; (2) Hart rise in week following Iowa caucuses, February 22 through February 28 (omitting February 16 through 21 as a transitional period); (3) period of New Hampshire primary and Super Tuesday, February 29 through March 20; and (4) April 9 through April 23 (low point of Hart campaign).

Appendix E gives in the form of SPSSx code the full model used in estimation of the Hart-Mondale contest.

Results obtained from estimating the model are shown in table A-4, with coefficients keyed to the model statement in appendix E. These results are almost completely lacking in intuitive meaning. Note, however, that the coefficients for the two variables in the model, news reception and media content, are highly statistically significant (the *t*-ratios are 2.40 and 3.59).

The 1984 Continuous Monitoring Survey contained no direct tests of political information. It did, however, contain a large assortment of items, and from these I pieced together a passable measure of political awareness. The items, scored as 29 0–1 dummies, are as follows: eight items testing recognition of political figures ("As I read

TABLE A-4. Coefficients for Model of Hart-Mondale Contest

Baseline function:	
Intercept (b_0)	0.46
Habitual news reception (a_0)	1.04
(standardized)	(.30)
Media influence function:	
Intercept (b_1)	−4.36
Habitual news recpetion (a_1)	1.97
	(.82)
Media content (b_2)	0.113
(see table 1 and note 35 for values)	(.032)

Source: 1984 NES Continuous Monitoring Survey.
Note: Coefficients keyed to model in appendix E. Standard errors appear in parentheses. Measures described in appendix D. $N = 359$. Percent of cases correctly predicted is 67 percent, compared to a null model of 47 percent.

each name, please tell me when I come to a person you have never heard of . . ."), v205 to v208, v210 to v213 (items used only if they had no time dependency); ability to rate political figures on feeling thermometer, v219 to v221, v224, v225, v228, v232; correct placement of Ronald Reagan, Walter Mondale, and Jesse Jackson on ideology scales, v614, v622, v626; correct placement of Reagan on defense spending, domestic spending scales, v805, v876 (one point for getting correct direction, an additional point for indicating that Reagan favored large changes); attention to the campaign, v407 (up to four points); follow government, v146 (up to three points). The later two variables were converted to a set of Guttmanized 0–1 items; for example, a respondent scoring in the highest of five categories, as in v407, would get a point on each of four 0–1 dummies; a respondent scoring in the second highest category would get a point on each of three 0–1 dummies, etc.). The 29 dummy variables were combined into a scale by means of factor scores from a principal components analysis. The alpha reliability is .85.

In the April 20–23 *New York Times*-CBS News survey and in the June 3–7 *Washington Post*-ABC News survey, the measure of news reception was built additively from education, ability to assess the ideological inclinations of Bush and Clinton, willingness to rate a leading political figure, and willingness to offer opinions (rather than "don't knows") on a selection of issues. The two scales are, I believe, as comparable as measures built from different data sets can reasonably be.

From the *Times* survey, education is measured as a four-point scale, the ideological rating items are Q. 24 and Q. 27, the rating item involves Jerry Brown (Q. 6), and the opinionation items involve Q. 32a–38, 50–65, 80. From the *Post* survey, education is measured as a four-point scale (by collapsing a six-point scale to be comparable to the *Times* equivalent), the ideological rating items are Q. 26 and 27, the rating item involves Dan Quayle (Q. 20d), and the opinionation items are Q. 35a–d, 36–44, 908.

Up to five "no opinion" responses, on a scale of 0 to 5, were taken as indicators of lack of awareness in each study.

The ideological rating items in the *Post* survey required some adaptation. The questions asked whether a candidate was too liberal, too conservative, or just about right. These were converted to awareness tests as follows: ratings of Bush as about right or too conservative, and of Clinton as about right or too liberal were accepted as correct, except from self-described strong liberals/conservatives, whose answers were also accepted as correct if they rated Clinton as too conservative or Bush as too liberal, as appropriate. In both surveys, the ideological awareness items were double-weighted.

The alpha reliabilities of these scales do not look good: They are .56 for the *Times* scale and .44 for the *Post* scale. However, these values are obviously misleading, since education, the principal component of all for scales, is highly reliable, and since the additional items, despite their low correlations with education, do add to its explanatory power. The reliabilities are reported only for the sake of convention.

The Hart and Perot support scores in figure 7 were modeled by means of logistic regressions in which the independent variables were news reception and news reception squared. The coefficient for squared term was statistically significant and negative in both time 2 models, but was not significantly negative in either time 1 model. In fact, the reception-squared coefficient in the time 1 model for Hart was positive. This suggested an overfit of the data in a very small data set ($n = 34$); the visual effect of this unexpectedly positive coefficient, moreover, was to make the crossover effect in the Hart case look implausibly large in a region in which there were no actual cases. For these reasons, I omitted the squared term from the final analysis of the Hart time 1 data.

Appendix E: The Hart-Mondale Model

The variables used in the model are

INFO, which is a standardized political awareness variable;
period, referring to the four time periods of the study;
wt, a weight indicating the number of cases in each time period, scaled so as to sum to 1.0;
mondmed, pro-Mondale media count in a given period, as shown in table 1 and weighted as described in note 36;
hartmed, pro-Hart media count in a given period; and
hart, mondale, dk are 0–1 variables indicating support for Hart, Mondale, or no preference.

The form of the estimator, at the bottom of the program, is the ML routine suggested to me by Doug Rivers and explained in Zaller (1992, appendix to chap. 7). The SPSSx code for the model, with some bracketed asides, is as follows:

recode period (1 = .276)(2 = .094)(3 = .29)(4 = .34) into wt [*values refer to proportion of cases in each period*]

```
compute var0= 0
model parms a0=1 a1=2 b0=.80 b1=-4 b2=.10
compute f1=1/(1+exp(-b1-a1*INFO-b2*hartmed1))
compute f2=1/(1+exp(-b1-a1*INFO-b2*hartmed2))
compute f3=1/(1+exp(-b1-a1*INFO-b2*hartmed3))
compute f4=1/(1+exp(-b1-a1*INFO-b2*hartmed4))
compute f5=1/(1+exp(-b1-a1*INFO-b2*mondmed1))
compute f6=1/(1+exp(-b1-a1*INFO-b2*mondmed2))
compute f7=1/(1+exp(-b1-a1*INFO-b2*mondmed3))
compute f8=1/(1+exp(-b1-a1*INFO-b2*mondmed4))
compute ht0=0 [baseline support for Hart, assumed to be 0]
compute mt0=(1/(1+exp(-b0-a0 *INFO))) [estimated baseline support for Mondale]
compute ht1=ht0+f1*(1-f5)*(1-ht0) -f5*(1-f1)*ht0
compute mt1=mt0+f5*(1-f1)*(1-mt0)-f1*(1-f5)*mt0
compute ht2=ht1+f2*(1-f6)*(1-ht1) -f6*(1-f2)*ht1
compute mt2=mt1+f6*(1-f2)*(1-mt1)-f2*(1-f6)*mt1
compute ht3=ht2+f3*(1-f7)*(1-ht2) -f7*(1-f3)*ht2
compute mt3=mt2+f7*(1-f3)*(1-mt2)-f3*(1-f7)*mt2
compute ht4=ht3+f4*(1-f8)*(1-ht3) -f8*(1-f4)*ht3
compute mt4=mt3+f8*(1-f4)*(1-mt3)-f4*(1-f8)*mt3
compute hp=(p1*ht1+p2*ht2+p3*ht3+p4*ht4)
compute mp=(p1*mt1+p2*mt2+p3*mt3+p4*mt4)
compute nc=1-mp-hp
compute pred=((-lg10(hp)*hart1-lg10(mp)*mondale1-lg10(nc)*dk)**.5)/w t
nlr var0 with INFO p1 p2 p3 p4 hartmed1 to mondmed4 mondale1 dk hart1 wt
```

NOTES

This chapter was written while on a sabbatical leave supported by the Guggenheim Foundation and the Center for Advanced Study in the Behavioral Sciences. I remain grateful to Chris Achen, Phil Converse, Herb McClosky, and, perhaps most importantly, William McGuire for starting me down the road that led to this chapter. I also thank Ken Bollen, Barbara Geddes, Darcy Geddes, and Vince Price for incisive comments on earlier drafts. A grant to the author from the National Science Foundation facilitated the collection of data for the chapter. The chapter also makes use of data collected by the National Election Studies under a grant from the National Science Foundation and made available by the Interuniversity Consortium for Social and Political Research at the University of Michigan.

1. For example, the capacity of celestial bodies to bend light, a truly massive effect, can be observed only under highly stringent conditions. Likewise, much of the current understanding of cell biology is based on observations of a relatively small number of organisms chosen for study because their simplicity makes them, in contrast to the vast majority of organisms to which results are generalized, easily susceptible to manipulation and study.

2. One area in which one can count on change is news on presidential job performance. This predictable variability, along with regular measurement of public opinion on presidential performance, makes this an ideal case for examining media effects, as Brody (1991) has demonstrated.

3. Logit, probit, LISERL, and structural equation models are among those that are linear in their basic structure.

4. I should add that McGuire (1986) explicitly recognizes the possible importance of each of the three problems I have mentioned (two empirical conditions and one theoretical one), along with more than a dozen others. However, he also discounts the likely importance as explanations for the weak media impacts commonly observed.

5. I thank Darcy Geddes, a twelfth grader with no love of math but much interest in politics, for helping me in this endeavor.

6. This rule does not hold in cases in which different media carry different messages, for which it is necessary to have good measures of both exposure to particular media and general propensity to receive the information to which one is exposed (Bartels 1993). In this study and in most other studies of mass communication, however, no such media differences are investigated.

7. Any study that enters "media exposure" as an independent variable in a regression to explain either opinion or opinion change has implicitly assumed that media influence is proportional to the amount of information received from the media. Strictly speaking, the assumption to be used in this chapter is slightly weaker: that there is a monotonically positive relationship between reception and influence.

8. Differences in the performance of the two scales may seem at first glance like the standard effects of differences in scale reliability and, as such, correctable by standard statistical techniques. The problem, however, is not so simple. For one thing, the reliabilities of the awareness and media use scales are very similar, so correcting for measurement error, if it were possible to do so, would not much affect the difference in their performance. But more importantly, no one has yet figured out how to correct for scale reliability in models that include complex interaction effects, as plausibly specified models of media effects need to do. It is therefore necessary to deal with the ubiquitous problem of measurement error at the stage of data collection, by including a measure of political awareness in one's surveys, rather than at the data analysis stage, where it is not presently feasible to do so.

9. Patterns vary somewhat across time, with more defections in the later period; also, the nonmonotonicity is more pronounced in some election years than in others. But in most elections, the voters most likely to defect to the incumbent are voters who fall somewhere in the midranges of habitual propensity for news reception (Zaller 1993).

10. The importance of strong measurement is, I suspect, especially acute in cases, like the ones under examination, in which the researcher needs to identify not a *linear path* of influence generated by the *additive effects* of reinforcing messages, but a *nonmonotonic region* of influence generated by the *subtraction of crosscutting effects*.

11. The awareness scales in the three studies had 14 to 16 items each and alpha reliabilities of .83 to .89, whereas the media use scales have 5 or 6 items and reliabilities of .67 to .73.

12. The curves in figure 3 were generated from a simple logistic function, with values as follows: The news reception variable ran continuously from -2 to $+2$, with a coefficient of 1.25. The intercepts for the four incumbent messages were $-.50$, 1.25, 2.5, and 4; for the four challenger messages the intercepts were -2.5, -1, .25, and 2.75.

13. In preliminary work on model specification, I estimated the probability of defection for voters influenced by both campaigns. This probability turned out to be quite low, about .04, and did not approach statistical significance. Hence the assumption of no defections, as made in the text, appears empirically plausible.

14. Technical note: In other work (Zaller 1987, 1989) I model attitude change as:

$$Pr.(change) = Pr.(Reception) \times Pr.(Acceptance/Reception)$$
$$= (1 + \exp[-b_0 - b_1*Awareness])^{-1}$$
$$\times \{1 - [1 + \exp(-b_2 - b_3*Awareness + b_4*Party)]^{-1}\}$$

Thus, attitude change is modeled as the probability of "receiving and accepting a single message"; the "influence gap" model in this chapter models attitude change as the "probability of receiving and accepting a first message" times "the probability of not receiving and accepting a second message"—with no separate acceptance function and partly different variables in the model. Thus, the new "two-message" model loses the ability to capture the separate effects of awareness on "reception" and "acceptance," as emphasized by McGuire (1968). Elsewhere, I make a great effort to understand exactly why awareness appears to affect acceptance. My conclusion is that, although it plays several roles, awareness is most important for its association with reception of secondary or "countervalent" messages that inhibit acceptance of the primary message. In this chapter, I emphasize the second message much more than in earlier work, but do so at the expense of other effects awareness may have on acceptance. Some may find this cost disturbing. But in preliminary work, I investigated models having separate acceptance subfunctions and found them superfluous. Versions of such models are used in Zaller (1992, chap. 9), but it is possible that a simpler model would have worked as well. For discussion of these theoretical issues, see Zaller (1992), pp. 118–22, 245–46, 285–87.

My use of logistic functions in this chapter, on the grounds that they imply "diminishing marginal returns from reception," may be, in effect, a way of incorporating a mild resistance effect from high political awareness without having to use a separate subfunction to get it. In limited empirical exploration, I found that simply logging the two influence functions—which is an alternative way of implementing diminishing marginal effects—works less well than logistic functions.

15. See appendix C for discussion of other election years.

16. See Gow and Eubank (1984), Wright (1993), and Jacobson and Rivers (1993).

17. Between 1958 and 1966, and again between 1966 and 1972, there were significant increases in pro-incumbent voting, and these increases were concentrated among voters falling in the low to middle ranges of political awareness (data not shown). I stress these findings, which are untainted by changes in question wording, because

Jacobson and Rivers (1993) show that the change in question wording, when it came in 1978, generated overreported support for incumbents mainly among less educated voters.

18. It is possible that there is more going on in Senate elections than appears in figure 4. Unfortunately, poor measurement makes it very hard to tell, since the 1988 and 1990 NES Senate election studies carried no political knowledge items, and the 1992 study carried only two.

19. Separate indices of positive and negative coverage were built for each of the three types of medium, standardized and combined into the overall measures shown in figure 6. Coding of the TV data was based on the indices published by the Vanderbilt archives; coding of the *New York Times* was based on the *Index to the Times;* coding of the newsmagazines was based on the magazines themselves. The intercoder reliability of the coding was about .9; alpha scale reliability based on interindex correlations was about .8. Further details of the coding of these data, as well as further analysis, are available in Hunt and Zaller (1995), from which these data are excerpted.

20. In the first time period, when Glenn was Mondale's primary opponent, anti-Mondale paragraphs were not counted as pro-Hart, since Hart was not their most likely beneficiary.

21. All coding was done by one person, Mark Hunt, who was unaware of the uses to which the coded data would be put. On a related project, the intercoder reliability of Hunt's judgments, aggregated at the level of weekly summaries, was .96.

22. The two most important limitations in model specification—failure to include a separate acceptance function (see note 13) and treating the data as if they came from periods of homogeneous media coverage—do not, so far as I could tell, contribute to the model's underfitting of the data.

23. I did control for strength of party attachment in table A3 but partialed its effect out of my graphical analysis.

24. See, however, note 25.

25. Respondents were counted as recognizing that McGovern was more in favor of immediate withdrawal if they placed him one or more points to the left of Nixon on the NES 7-point "Vietnam Action" scale. Political awareness in this figure is measured by tests of political knowledge.

26. Data are shown in Zaller (1994), figure 4. The fact that groups differ in their support for the war shows, incidentally, that values can have effects that are independent of source cues. These group effects, however, operate alongside, rather than in place of, the source effects that I emphasize in the text. See text associated with note 23.

27. A useful baseline for assessing the impact of media coverage of the Gulf crisis is a 1988 poll that found that only 18 percent of the public was willing to send troops to protect the Saudis from invasion by Iran (Mueller 1994, 49). Yet support for sending U.S. troops to protect the Saudis from Iraq ran as high as 80 percent in polls taken in the first weeks of the Gulf crisis.

28. To give one indication of the strength of the initial elite support, the Senate vote on the Gulf of Tonkin resolution, which authorized use of force against North Viet-

nam, was 88–2, while in the House of Representatives it was 388–0. By 1970, of course, Congress was deeply divided on the war. See Zaller (1992, chap. 9) for evidence on the parallel evolution of press coverage.

29. This assumption justifies my use of logit functions as the cornerstone of my models; linear and exponential functions, as implied by the notion of media influence as a continuous and open-ended process, do not seem to work well. See also note 14 and associated text.

30. For the Dukakis-Bush comparison on ideology, the following SPSSx code was used:

```
recode v418 v419 (8 9 0=sysmis)
if v419 gt (v418 + 1) duklib = 1
recode duklib (sysmis=0)
```

31. For v399, respondents were given full credit for saying either that Margaret Thatcher was prime minister of Britain or that she had just resigned, even though the former answer was incorrect.

32. For 1990, SPSSx code to create the measure of defection is

```
recode v320 (0 1 2=1)(4 5 6=−1) into pid/v58 (12 21=1) into contested
if contested eq 1 and pid eq 1 and v288 eq 35 defect=0
if contested eq 1 and pid eq 1 and v288 eq 34 defect=1
if contested eq 1 and pid eq −1 and v288 eq 33 defect=1
if contested eq 1 and pid eq −1 and v288 eq 36 defect=0
```

33. Other details of the construction of the measures of campaign intensity are as follows: Because name recall and number of news articles read depend on individual-level differences in political awareness as well as district-level differences in communication flow, I purged the individual-level recall and news coverage variables of the effects of awareness before creating the district means. Also, because name recall is itself a determinant of voting behavior, and because some districts are represented by only a few individuals, I calculated the district means in the case of the 1966 and 1986 studies on the basis of in-party voters and nonvoters—that is, persons other than those whose vote decisions I was attempting to model. Because news coverage (independent of directional thrust) is not a determinant of vote choice, this correction procedure was not employed in the 1978 study.

34. The standard deviation of the six coefficients is .374; to get the standard error, one divides this number by the square root of the number of cases, which is 6. The key assumption in this test is that each of the six coefficients represents an independent estimate of the true parameter for "the effect of campaign information." Within each year the estimates are not independent, but the covariance is slightly negative, so the bias of the test is conservative.

35. The exception was 1986, when scores for the 5th and 50th percentile of challenger campaign intensity were nearly the same (low) number; hence in this case, I simulated a middle intensity race as one at the 70th percentile.

36. If, for example, a period was three weeks long, then one-third of the sample saw only one-third of the coverage before being interviewed, one-third saw two-thirds of it, and one-third saw all—for an aggregate weight of $.33 \times .33 + .33 \times .67 + .33 \times 1 = .67$. Weights derived in this way and applied to the four media counts in table 1 were .6, 1, .67, and .80. In the final period, in which a two-week interval of respondents was interviewed following five weeks of media content, the weight was calculated as $.5 \times .8 + .5 \times 1 = .9$. The statistical estimates are nearly the same if these weights are omitted; I include them because they improve the visual fit of the data by a just noticeable amount.

REFERENCES

Alford, John R., and David W. Brady. 1993. Personal and partisan advantage in U.S. congressional elections, 1846–1990. In *Congress reconsidered,* ed. Lawrence C. Dodd and Bruce I. Oppenheimer. Washington, D.C.: CQ Press.

Bartels, Larry. 1988. *The dynamics of presidential primaries.* Princeton: Princeton University Press.

Bartels, Larry. 1993. Messages received: The political impact of media exposure. *American Political Science Review* 87:267–85.

Bennett, W. Lance, and David Paletz. 1994. *Taken by storm.* Chicago: University of Chicago Press.

Brady, Henry, and Richard Johnston. 1987. What's the primary message: Horse race or issue journalism? In *Media and momentum,* ed. Gary Orren and Nelson W. Polsby, 127–86. New York: Chatham.

Brody, Richard. 1991. *Assessing the president. S*tanford: Stanford University Press.

Converse, Philip. 1962. Information flow and the stability of partisan attitudes. *Public Opinion Quarterly* 26:578–99.

Finkel, Steven. 1993. Re-examining the "minimal effects" model in recent presidential campaigns. *Journal of Politics* 55:1–21.

Gow, David, and Robert Eubank. 1984. The pro-incumbent bias in the 1978 and 1980 national election study. *American Journal of Political Science* 27:224–30.

Hunt, Mark, and John Zaller. 1995. The rise and fall of candidate Perot: The outsider vs. the system. Part 2 of a two-part article, *Political Communication* 12:97–123.

Jacobson, Gary C. 1992. *The politics of congressional elections.* 3d ed. New York: HarperCollins.

Jacobson, Gary, and Douglas Rivers. 1993. Explaining the overreport of vote for incumbents in the national election studies. Paper given at annual meeting of the Western Political Science Association, Pasadena, California.

Johnston, Richard, Andre Blais, Henry Brady, and Jean Crete. 1992. *Letting the people decide.* Stanford: Stanford University Press.

Keith, Bruce, Elizabeth Orr, David Magleby, Candace Nelson, Raymond Wolfinger, and Mark Westlye. 1988. *The myth of the independent voter.* Berkeley: University of California Press.

McClure, Robert, and Tom Patterson. 1974. *The unseeing eye.* New York: Putnam.

McGuire, William. 1969. The nature of attitudes and attitude change. In *Handbook of social psychology,* 2d ed., vol. 3, ed. Gardner Lindzey and Elliott Aronson. Reading, Mass.: Addison-Wesley.

McGuire, William. 1986. The myth of massive media impact: Savagings and salvagings. *Public Communication and Behavior* 1:173–257.

Mueller, John. 1993. *Policy and opinion in the Gulf War.* Chicago: University of Chicago Press.

Neuman, W. Russell, Marion Just, and Ann Crigler. 1992. *Common knowledge.* Chicago: University of Chicago Press.

Page, Benjamin, and Robert Shapiro. 1992. *The rational public.* Chicago: University of Chicago Press.

Patterson, Thomas. 1980. *Mass media election.* New York: Praeger.

Price, Vincent, and John Zaller. 1993. Who gets the news: Measuring individual differences in likelihood of news reception. *Public Opinion Quarterly* 57:133–64.

Wright, Gerald. 1993. Errors in measuring vote choice in the national election studies. *American Journal of Political Science* 37:224–30.

Zaller, John. 1987. The diffusion of political attitudes. *Journal of Personality and Social Psychology* 53:821–33.

Zaller, John. 1989. Bringing Converse back in: Information flow in political campaigns. *Political Analysis* 1:181–234.

Zaller, John. 1991. Information, values and opinion. *American Political Science Review* 85:1215–38.

Zaller, John. 1992. *The nature and origins of mass opinion.* New York: Cambridge University Press.

Zaller, John. 1994. Elite leadership of mass opinion: New evidence from the Gulf War. In *Taken by storm,* ed. Lance Bennett and David Paletz. Chicago: University of Chicago Press.

CHAPTER 3

News Media Impact on the Ingredients of Presidential Evaluations: A Program of Research on the Priming Hypothesis

Joanne M. Miller and Jon A. Krosnick

Since the 1920s, social scientists in the United States have been concerned with the effects of the mass media on citizens' attitudes and behaviors. Initially, the fear that the news media could be a powerful propaganda tool led researchers to explore the persuasive impact of media messages (Roberts and Maccoby 1985). However, in 1960, Klapper reviewed the existing body of available research and concluded that the media do not in fact persuade individuals to change their attitudes but rather simply reinforce attitudes already in place. Support for this conclusion comes from investigations undertaken during World War II as part of a U.S. Army attempt to indoctrinate new draftees (Hovland, Lumsdaine, and Sheffield 1949), studies of presidential debates (Katz and Feldman 1962; Sears and Chaffee 1979), studies of the television series "Roots" (Hur and Robinson 1978; Ball-Rokeach, Grube, and Rokeach 1981) and more (e.g., Patterson and McClure 1976).

The psychological process of interest in this research, persuasion, presumably occurs when individuals decide to change an attitude in response to a message advocating a particular position or point of view. This can occur either because an individual finds the arguments contained in the message to be compelling or because the source of the message is viewed as credible (e.g., because of his or her expertise or attractiveness). In general, such attitude change is rare because preexisting attitudes guide individuals' exposure to and interpretation of media messages. Specifically, people are usually exposed only to attitude-consistent media messages (see Sears and Freedman 1965; Frey 1986), and attitude-inconsistent messages are typically interpreted and recalled in ways that reinforce rather than challenge existing attitudes (see, e.g., Cooper and Jahoda 1947; Lord, Ross, and Lepper 1979; Roberts 1985). Furthermore, attitudes changed as a result of perceiving the source of the message to be credible or attractive are unstable and as a result do not persist over time (Petty and Cacioppo 1986).

However, much research challenges the assumption that the media have no effects at all, by showing that they can influence attitudes by more subtle mechanisms (see, e.g., MacKuen 1981). Even as early as the 1920s, Lippmann (1920, 1922, 1925) proposed that the news media may affect public opinion by focusing attention on some national problems and political issues while ignoring others. This idea has come to be known as the agenda-setting hypothesis: media coverage of an issue increases the national importance that Americans ascribe to it (see, e.g., Kosicki 1993; McCombs 1993). A great deal of evidence offers support for this hypothesis, from longitudinal analyses matching survey data to content analyses of media coverage (e.g., Behr and Iyengar 1985), and from laboratory experiments that systematically manipulated media exposure (Iyengar and Kinder 1987).

Building on the notion of agenda-setting, Iyengar, Kinder, Peters, and Krosnick (1984) proposed another hypothesis regarding subtle media impact, this time on assessments of presidential performance. Such evaluations have important political implications. A president's power in Washington depends partly on how favorably he is evaluated by the nation, because popular presidents tend to have things their way with Congress (Neustadt 1960; Rivers and Rose 1981).

If the media do, indeed, shape what individuals consider important, they may also alter the bases of judgments about presidential performance. More specifically, by focusing on some issues and not others, the news may determine the standards by which a president's performance is evaluated and may, as a result, provoke surges and declines in presidential popularity. If this notion, dubbed the priming hypothesis, is correct, then it identifies a subtle mechanism by which the media alter the conduct of public policy-making.

In this chapter, we will describe a program of research on the priming notion. First, we will describe the five hypotheses that form the core of this work. Then we will review two laboratory tests of these hypotheses and two survey studies of them. Finally, we will highlight the implications of our findings for future research. As will become apparent, our original ideas regarding priming were quite straightforward and were largely empirically supported. But as we progressed through our investigations, our results began to paint an increasingly complex picture of how the media shape presidential approval.

Priming

The notion of priming is based upon psychological research showing that when people make decisions, they rarely take into consideration the entire array of available relevant evidence. Rather, because of the cognitive burdens imposed by a complete and comprehensive information search and integration process, people tend to "satisfice" rather than "optimize" (see Simon 1957; Simon and Stedry 1968). That is, they often derive their decisions from limited subsets of the available information pool so as to make satisfactory judgments without expending a great deal of effort.

According to the theory of priming, satisficing occurs in political decision making just as it does for other sorts of judgments. When Americans are asked to evaluate the job performance of their president, an optimal assessment might entail gauging the president's performance in a wide array of policy domains and integrating those domain-specific judgments into an overall summary. More likely, according to the theory of priming, would be a satisficing approach: assessing presidential performance in only a small sample of policy domains.

Which particular pieces of information get used, according to the priming hypothesis, may be those that come to mind quickly and automatically for an individual—those that are most accessible (Higgins and King 1981; Wyer and Hartwick 1980; see also Zaller and Feldman 1992). And the accessibilities of various policy domains are in turn presumed to be determined importantly by news media coverage. Issues that have been the subject of extensive attention on television and radio and in newspapers may be particularly likely to come to citizens' minds shortly thereafter and thereby enjoy enhanced impact on presidential evaluations. In contrast, topics that have been addressed only minimally in the news media are presumably rarely primed and are therefore likely to play little if any role in presidential assessment processes. Hence, by calling attention to some matters while ignoring others, news media may alter the standards by which the president is evaluated.

This notion of priming proposes quite a different mechanism by which the media may affect attitudes than the traditional persuasion approach presumes. Whereas persuasion focuses on media messages advocating particular positions, priming can be provoked simply by a news story devoting attention to an issue without advocating a position. And whereas persuasion is thought to result from effortful decision making about a message's likely veracity, priming presumably occurs as a result of automatic and effortless processes of spreading activation in people's minds.

The Gradient Hypotheses

In order to understand precisely what attitudes will be primed by what stimuli, it is useful to think of a person's stable of political attitudes as structured in memory within an associative network (Anderson 1983; Collins and Loftus 1975). In such a network, political attitudes can be thought of as nodes, each one having some inherent strength. The strength of a node is presumed to be a function of prior activation of it (see, e.g., Anderson 1983). The more one has thought about an attitude in the past, the stronger its node will be.

Within this representational structure, nodes are linked to one another. For instance, a person's attitude toward affirmative action may be linked to his or her attitude toward school integration. Such linkages evolve when the attitudes are thought about simultaneously and when one attitude is perceived to imply, support, or contradict the other (Judd and Downing 1990; Judd et al. 1991). Attitudes that are not conceptually related in some way are unlikely to become linked.

When a specific attitude is called to mind, activation of its node will spread to other attitudes to which it is linked. The stronger the activated node, the more spreading activation would be expected. Consequently, we would expect that priming induced by a news story would occur mostly for attitudes that are directly relevant to the story. For example, news stories about President Clinton's economic plan would presumably activate attitudes about economic performance most strongly. However, we might also observe spreading activation to, say, attitudes about health care policies, because they have economic implications. Thus, there might be a gradient of priming effects, decreasing in strength as attitudes become more and more remote from those being directly activated by a story.

At the same time, as media attention to certain issues enhances their impact, other issues are likely to see their impact diminished, for two reasons. First, people have neither the ability nor the motivation to comprehensively incorporate every potentially relevant issue into their presidential evaluations. As some issues are brought into the foreground of people's thinking by the news media, others will be pushed into the cognitive background. Second, because television news broadcasts are limited in length and newspaper front pages are of a fixed size, they can only focus on a small set of issues on any given day. Therefore, when the media devote attention to certain issues, they must of necessity devote less discussion to others. Consequently, priming is likely to be hydraulic in nature: increases in the impact of some issues should be accompanied by decreases in the impact of other, unrelated issues.

However, simply priming attitudes does not mean they will have enhanced impact on all political judgments. Rather, the impact of accessible attitudes may be great or negligible depending on their perceived relevance to the judgment at hand. Information regarding a person's intelligence may be largely ignored when evaluating that same person's honesty, for example (Hamilton and Fallot 1974). Therefore, increasing the accessibility of some information will influence only those judgments to which the information is relevant, and only to that degree.

When studying presidential evaluations, it is useful to distinguish among three types of judgments: evaluations of the president's general performance, competence, and integrity. Information made accessible by news coverage that is deemed highly relevant for one may be regarded as largely irrelevant for another. Because our research focused on news media coverage of national problems, the accessibility of news stories should have the greatest impact on judgments of the president's overall job performance. Such judgments, after all, are presumably just weighted averages of how well the president is doing on specific national issues. Inducing people to concentrate on one of these issues should therefore substantially influence its relative impact on judgments of how well the president is performing overall.

The standards used in judging competence should also be influenced, but not as much, because Americans no doubt recognize that performance on any one issue reflects the president's competence imperfectly. Even the most competent president cannot advance his agenda on every issue successfully. Performance is determined in part by forces beyond a president's control, including the economy, the Congress, other countries, and many more. Therefore, citizens probably assess presidential competence partly from domain-specific performance, but more weakly than when they make overall performance assessments. Good outcomes constitute good performance, regardless of whether a president deserves complete credit for them or not.

Judgments of a president's integrity should be affected even less than competence, because performance-diagnostic events seem even less informative with regard to this trait. However, some issues directly implicate a president's integrity (e.g., the Iran-Contra affair), and priming may affect integrity assessments more powerfully in such cases.

Thus, the gradient hypothesis has two parts. The first, which we shall call the target gradient hypothesis, addresses which attitudes have their accessibilities altered as a result of priming and by how much. The second, which we shall call the consequence gradient hypothesis, addresses which overall presidential evaluations are altered and to what degree.

The Dosage and Knowledge Hypotheses

The final hypotheses we tested addressed which citizens are influenced most by the news media. We presumed that the magnitude of impact of the news media on any particular individual is determined by two regulatory factors: dosage and resistance. By dosage, we mean the amount of media coverage on an issue that enters a person's short-term or working memory (see, e.g., Estes 1988). The greater one's dosage of media content, the more one should be influenced by it. And presumably, dosage is a joint function of the amount of news to which an individual is exposed and the amount of attention he or she pays to it.

Holding dosage constant, the more knowledge about politics one has, the more resistant one should be, because knowledge helps one to withstand influence. Individuals who have a lot of knowledge about politics presumably have relatively crystallized calculi by which they make evaluations of a president's performance. Because these people are practiced at making such judgments, the weights they give to various pieces of information may become established and justified by knowledge about particular issues and politics in general. Consequently, knowledgeable people may be especially resistant to temporary increases in accessibility of one or another policy domain. Individuals with little knowledge, on the other hand, are presumably not practiced at making presidential performance evaluations and probably do not have crystallized formulas for making such judgments. Therefore, they should be highly responsive to increases in accessibility of policy domains emphasized by the media.[1]

Overview

The two experimental studies (Iyengar et al. 1984) and two survey studies (Krosnick and Kinder 1990; Krosnick and Brannon 1993) we will describe tested all these hypotheses. We expected the media to influence only those aspects of public opinion that were directly implicated by a story and that the priming effect would be moderated by the relevance of the news stories to the judgment being made. In addition, we hypothesized that media impact would be greatest on people with the highest levels of exposure and attention and the lowest levels of knowledge about politics.

Laboratory Study 1: Energy Policy

Both of our laboratory studies were conducted while Jimmy Carter was president. The first study tested the basic priming hypothesis as well as the consequence gradient and dosage hypotheses. Yale undergraduates viewed one of three 40-minute sets of network television news stories. The sets of stories varied levels of exposure to energy stories. Some subjects viewed a set of stories that included six about energy, totaling 16 minutes (high exposure condition), others viewed three energy stories, totaling 8.5 minutes (intermediate exposure condition), while others viewed no energy stories (no exposure condition).[2] The energy stories were distributed evenly throughout the set, surrounded by stories about other contemporary problems.

After viewing one of the three sets of news stories, subjects completed a questionnaire that assessed (a) judgments of President Carter's performance in each of eight specific areas, including "implementing a national energy policy"; (b) judgments of Carter's overall performance; and (c) judgments of his competence and integrity.

As expected, the effect of energy performance on ratings of Carter's overall performance was significantly larger in the intermediate and high exposure conditions than in the no exposure condition (see table 1). Thus, individuals who watched news stories that emphasized energy policy weighed their attitudes toward Carter's energy policy performance more heavily in their evaluations of Carter's overall performance than did those who watched no such stories. Contrary to the dosage hypothesis, however, no differences appeared between subjects in the intermediate and high exposure conditions, which suggests that even moderate amounts of activation are sufficient to maximize priming.

Consistent with the consequence gradient hypothesis, priming of energy performance ratings had more influence on evaluations of Carter's overall job performance than on judgments of his competence and integrity evaluations (see table 1). However, this gap was bigger than we expected: in fact, the impact of the news stories on the latter two judgments was negligible. Thus, the energy stories made attitudes about Carter's energy performance more accessible and thereby enhanced their influence on overall evaluations of his job performance, but they did not alter competence or integrity judgments.

Thus, the results of study 1 were consistent with both the priming and gradient hypotheses, though not the dosage hypothesis. To explore the generalizability of these findings to other issues and subject populations and to examine the role of political knowledge, we conducted a second laboratory study.

Laboratory Study 2: Energy, Defense, and Inflation

Subjects in our second study were adult residents of New Haven, Connecticut. As in study 1, these individuals viewed a set of 12 television news stories lasting again approximately 40 minutes. The amount of exposure to stories about three target issues (energy, defense, and inflation) was varied across individuals. Subjects in the high exposure condition saw six stories about

TABLE 1.   Impact of Energy Performance Ratings on Overall Evaluations of President Carter in Study 1

	Condition	
Overall Evaluation	No Coverage	Some Coverage
General performance	.10	.27**
Competence	.15	.19
Integrity	.00	.06
N	21	73

Source: Iyengar, Kinder, Peters, and Krosnick (1984).
Note: Table entries are unstandardized regression coefficients.
**$p < .01$.

either energy, defense, or inflation. Subjects in the intermediate exposure condition saw three stories about one of these issues. And some subjects saw no stories about each issue. After viewing the news stories, subjects completed the same basic measures as in study 1. In addition, subjects answered nine political knowledge questions, three on each issue (energy, defense, and inflation).

As expected, subjects who viewed news stories on a target issue weighed President Carter's performance on that issue more heavily in deriving overall performance evaluations than did subjects who saw no stories on that issue (see table 2). Thus, exposure strengthened the relation between evaluations of Carter's performance on the specific issue and evaluations of his overall performance. Again, as in study 1, no differences appeared between subjects in the intermediate and high exposure conditions, which reinforces the notion that even moderate dosages can maximize priming.

Consistent with the consequence gradient hypothesis, judgments of Carter's competence and integrity were less influenced by the television story content manipulations. In fact, as table 2 illustrates, these latter effects were almost always nonexistent. Finally, as anticipated, subjects who were less knowledgeable about an issue were consistently more influenced by the priming manipulation than were more knowledgeable subjects (see table 3).

In sum, study 2 replicated the results of study 1 with a more heterogeneous sample of subjects. In addition, the results of study 2 were consistent with the hypothesis that political knowledge constitutes a basis for resisting priming effects.

The Iran-Contra Study

Next, we moved outside of the laboratory to evaluate how well these hypotheses explain presidential evaluations as they evolve naturally among represen-

TABLE 2.   Impact of Problem Performance Ratings on Overall Evaluations of President Carter in Study 2

Overall Evaluation	Energy		Defense		Inflation	
	No Coverage	Some Coverage	No Coverage	Some Coverage	No Coverage	Some Coverage
General performance	0.43***	0.51***	0.37***	0.52***	0.65***	0.71***
Competence	0.17	0.13	0.17**	0.33***	0.28***	0.28**
Integrity	0.14*	0.19*	0.17**	0.03	0.24**	0.15
N	92	48	94	46	94	46

Source: Iyengar, Kinder, Peters, and Krosnick 1984.

Note: Table entries are unstandardized regression coefficients.

$*p < .05$; $**p < .01$; $***p < .001$.

TABLE 3. **Changes in the Impact of Problem
Performance Ratings on Overall Ratings Due to News
Media Coverage by Level of Political Knowledge**

Issue	Low Knowledge	High Knowledge
Energy	0.19	0.06
Inflation	0.16	0.05
Defense	0.15	0.10

Source: Iyengar, Kinder, Peters, and Krosnick 1984.
Note: Table entries are unstandardized regression coefficients.

tative samples of adults. Our first such attempt focused on the Iran-Contra scandal (Krosnick and Kinder 1990).

The Iran-Contra drama was ignited on November 25, 1986, when Attorney General Edwin Meese announced to a national television audience that funds obtained from the secret sale of weapons to Iran had been channeled to the Contras fighting to overthrow the Sandinista government in Nicaragua. In the months following this revelation, the news media were virtually consumed with the scandal. Along with this media attention came a major decline in President Ronald Reagan's approval ratings. The media's focus on the Iran-Contra disclosure, as per the priming hypothesis, should have enhanced the impact of attitudes toward U.S. policy in Central America on the public's views of President Reagan. Because citizens' attitudes toward U.S. intervention in Central America during this time were quite negative, Reagan's approval ratings would be expected to decline as a result, just as they did (Krosnick and Kinder 1990).

In order to test the priming hypothesis in this context, we analyzed data from the 1986 National Election Study. In late 1986, face-to-face interviews were conducted with a national probability sample of more than 2,000 U.S. adults, 1,086 of whom completed Form A of the questionnaire. This form included elaborate assessments of views of President Reagan as well as a battery of foreign affairs questions and standard questions about the campaign, the candidates, parties, national problems, policy attitudes, and demographics.

To test the priming hypothesis, we estimated regression equations predicting Reagan's overall performance from attitudes toward U.S. aid to the Contras and involvement in Central America, U.S. involvement in the affairs of other countries in general, or what we call *isolationism,* U.S. strength in the world, the health of the national economy, and federal aid to blacks. Such an equation was estimated once for respondents who were interviewed before the November 25 revelation (the prerevelation group) and again for those who were interviewed after that date (the postrevelation group).

As anticipated, attitudes toward aid to the Contras and involvement in

Central America were more important determinants of overall performance evaluations in the postrevelation group than in the prerevelation group (see table 4). Consistent with the target gradient hypothesis, a slightly smaller priming effect appeared for general views about isolationism, the predictor most closely related to U.S. involvement with the Contras in Central America. Essentially no priming effects appeared for the even more distant predictors of U.S. strength and assessments of the U.S. economy. And, in fact, a *negative* effect appeared for aid to blacks: attitudes on this issue had *less* impact after the revelation than before. This finding is consistent with the idea that priming may be hydraulic in nature: as some problems come into the foreground, others are forced into the background.

The results were also consistent with the consequence gradient hypothesis, though the effect was a bit different than we saw in the laboratory studies (see table 5). The principal priming effect on Contras–Central America attitudes was just as apparent in judgments of Reagan's competence and integrity as in judgments of his overall job performance. This is not surprising, given that the Iran-Contra affair raised questions about Reagan's competence and integrity explicitly. However, the priming effect on isolationism attitudes was weaker for competence and integrity judgments than for overall performance evaluations, as was the negative effect we saw for attitudes regarding aid to blacks.

Finally, as expected, the Iran-Contra revelation had a substantial priming effect on people who knew relatively little about politics and was less effective among more knowledgeable people (see table 6). Specifically, the principal priming effect on Contras–Central America attitudes and the negative effect

TABLE 4.   Estimates of the Impact of Policy Attitudes on Assessments of President Reagan's Performance before and after the Iran-Contra Revelation

Opinion Domain	Unstandardized Regression Coefficients		Difference	Significance of Difference[a]
	Prerevelation Group	Postrevelation Group		
Contras–Central America	.18*	.29*	.11	.17
Isolationism	.02	.10*	.08	.02
U.S. strength	.14*	.15*	.01	.45
Economic assessments	.33*	.35*	.02	.36
Aid to blacks	.22*	.00	− .22	.05
N	607	296		

Source: Krosnick and Kinder 1990.

[a]Entries in this column are one-tailed *p*s.

p < .05 (one-tailed)

on aid toward blacks attitudes were both strong among low-knowledge respondents and were reduced to nonsignificance among respondents high in knowledge. Interestingly, the priming effect on isolationism attitudes appears to have been a bit stronger among the more knowledgeable respondents. This may reflect the fact that such individuals were more likely to have such general attitudes and to see them as linked to more specific attitudes on intervention in particular regions of the world. Thus, it seems, less knowledgeable citizens were primed on those aspects most directly related to the content of the news coverage, whereas more knowledgeable individuals were influenced at a more abstract level.

The Gulf Crisis Study

Just as the news media's focus on the Iran-Contra scandal altered the standards by which U.S. citizens evaluated President Reagan, media attention to the Persian Gulf War in 1991 may have affected evaluations of President Bush. In October 1990, before the war began, Bush's approval ratings were moderate at best. However, after gradual massing of allied troops in the

TABLE 5. Impact of Policy Attitudes on Assessments of President Reagan's Character before and after the Iran-Contra Revelation

Opinion Domain	Unstandardized Regression Coefficients		Difference	Significance of Difference[a]
	Prerevelation Group	Postrevelation Group		
Assessing Reagan's Competence				
Contras–Central America	.09**	.20**	.11	.15
Isolationism	.04**	.09**	.05	.04
U.S. strength	.12**	.06*	−.06	.06
Economic assessments	.10**	.07	−.03	.07
Aid to blacks	.14**	.12**	−.02	.41
N	632	304		
Assessing Reagan's Integrity				
Contras–Central America	.03	.12**	.09	.14
Isolationism	.05**	.06**	.01	.21
U.S. strength	.07**	.07**	.00	.47
Economic assessments	.13**	.13**	.00	.39
Aid to blacks	.05*	.04	−.01	.28
N	629	303		

Source: Krosnick and Kinder 1990.

[a]Entries in this column are one-tailed ps.

*$p < .10$ (one-tailed).

**$p < .05$ (one-tailed).

Middle East and U.S.-initiated air attacks on Iraq beginning in mid-January 1991, the news media became obsessed with these events and provided nearly nonstop coverage of them for weeks. Interestingly, at the same time, Bush's approval ratings increased to a high of 90 percent (see Krosnick and Brannon 1993).

According to the theory of priming, the dramatic shift in news coverage at the onset of the war and continued focusing on the crisis for months after the war may have led individuals to weigh attitudes toward Bush's Persian Gulf performance more heavily when they evaluated his overall performance. Because most individuals approved of Bush's Persian Gulf decisions, this could partially explain the increase in his approval ratings beginning in mid-January.

We tested this possibility using data from the 1990–1991 National Election Panel Study of the Political Consequences of War. For this survey, a nationally representative sample of 1,385 U.S. adults was interviewed in late fall 1990, before the major events of the war and the dramatic increase in media attention to the Gulf crisis. These individuals were reinterviewed in summer 1991, long after the military strike was completed. During both the

TABLE 6. Impact of Policy Attitudes on Assessments of President Reagan's Performance before and after the Iran-Contra Revelation, Separately for Respondents High and Low in Political Knowledge

| | Unstandardized Regression Coefficients | | | |
Opinion Domain	Prerevelation Group	Postrevelation Group	Difference	Significance of Difference[a]
Low-Knowledge Respondents				
Contras–Central America	.12*	.35*	.23	.06
Isolationism	.01	.08*	.07	.09
U.S. strength	.14*	.18*	.04	.32
Economic assessments	.29*	.39*	.10	.19
Aid to blacks	.20*	.03	.17	.05
N	383	191		
High-Knowledge Respondents				
Contras–Central America	.22*	.28*	.06	.43
Isolationism	.06	.20*	.14	.05
U.S. strength	.16*	.06	.10	.29
Economic assessments	.39*	.41*	.02	.41
Aid to blacks	.20*	.07	.13	.37
N	222	105		

Source: Krosnick and Kinder 1990.

[a]Entries in this column are one-tailed *p*s.

p < .05 (one-tailed).

pre- and postwar surveys, respondents were asked questions gauging evaluations of President Bush's overall job performance and his handling of the Gulf crisis, foreign affairs generally, and the domestic economy. To estimate priming, we computed regression equations predicting the first of these attitudes with the latter three.

Consistent with the priming hypothesis, the impact of Bush's Persian Gulf crisis performance on his overall evaluations increased after the war (see table 7). And consistent with the target gradient hypothesis, the impact of foreign policy performance and domestic economic performance did not change significantly. Thus, it seems that, for the nation as a whole, news media attention to the war increased the weight people attached to Bush's handling of the Gulf crisis in deriving their overall performance evaluations without shifting the impact of some other ingredients.

This latter finding is interesting, partly because it is conceivable that focusing the American people's attention on this conflict overseas might have increased attention to other political attitudes as well. That is, when a war occurs and news coverage of it is intense, it may stimulate thinking about related issues on which the conduct of the war has effects. At the very least, because the Gulf War involved complex coordination of efforts by many countries worldwide, Americans might have become more attentive to and concerned about U.S. relations with these various other countries. Instead, consistent with the experimental studies, our results suggest that no such widening of attention occurred.

TABLE 7. Impact of Domain-Specific Evaluations on Overall Evaluations of Bush's Performance before and after the Gulf War

Performance Domain	Unstandardized Regression Coefficient		Pre-Post Difference	Significance of Difference[a]
	Prewar	Postwar		
Gulf crisis	.21***	.30***	.09	.00
	(.02)	(.02)		
Foreign relations	.22***	.21***	−.01	.38
	(.02)	(.02)		
Economy	.26***	.27***	.01	.48
	(.02)	(.02)		
Number of cases	1090	1090		

Source: Krosnick and Brannon 1993.
[a]Entries in this column are one-tailed *p*s.
***$p < .001$

To test the knowledge hypothesis as we had in previous studies, we initially used respondents' answers to a nine-question political knowledge quiz to separate them into relatively more and less knowledgeable groups. And as expected, the priming effect was especially pronounced among the less knowledgeable individuals. Contrary to the dosage hypothesis, though, priming was stronger for people who were less exposed to and less attentive to the news media.[3]

When we examined the effects of knowledge, exposure, and attention simultaneously in a multivariate analysis, these latter two variables' effects stayed the same. Priming was more pronounced among individuals who were less exposed and who paid less attention to the media. However, the effect of knowledge on priming was precisely the opposite of what we expected. Priming was stronger, not weaker, as knowledge increased (see Krosnick and Brannon 1993 for the details of this analysis).

Given that these findings were quite surprising, we returned to the Iran-Contra data and conducted the same multivariate analysis using measures of knowledge, exposure, and attention. And, again, priming was greatest for individuals who were less exposed and paid less attention to the media. However, there was no effect of knowledge on priming in the Iran-Contra study.

Discussion

So where does this leave us? First, across all four studies, we have seen consistent evidence of priming, just as our hypothesis led us to expect. Furthermore, both the target and consequence gradient hypotheses were sustained, lending support to the associative network model of spreading activation. However, our findings regarding exposure, attention, and knowledge were quite surprising. We turn now to possible explanations of these findings.

Exposure and Attention

In our laboratory studies, we found no effects of increased dosage from some stories on a topic to many, which suggests that priming can be maximized with just a few stories when measurements are taken immediately after exposure. But when a delay is involved, as in our survey studies, weaker priming effects appeared among the most exposed and attentive.

We can see at least three possible explanations for this result. Consider first the Gulf War. The primary message of the news media during the Gulf War was the conduct and progress of the war itself. It was usually the lead story on television and on the front page of newspapers. In addition, peripheral war-related stories reported on the types of weapons being used, tales about local heroes, accounts of government relations with the press, and more. People who were only minimally exposed and attentive to the news media probably absorbed these main messages about the war and little else.

In contrast, highly exposed and attentive individuals certainly absorbed the war messages, but these people probably absorbed more peripheral stories as well, on topics completely unrelated to the war (e.g., crime, unemployment, and inflation). Consequently, the priming impact of the principal message may have been diluted by the many other knowledge domains that were also made accessible. This might explain why priming effects of a principal story theme (such as the Gulf War) were strongest among individuals lower in exposure and attention. Needless to say, at absolute zero levels of exposure or attention, no priming at all should occur. But such low levels were probably exceedingly rare among Americans during the Gulf War. Likewise, because the Iran-Contra affair dominated the media only a short time before presidential evaluations were assessed, it was probably primed even among minimally exposed and minimally attentive people. For highly exposed and attentive people, stories of the Iran-Contra affair probably were diluted by other stories, as in the case of the Gulf War.

This sort of dilution might also have occurred at a point in time much later than encoding, via retroactive interference. People who are especially interested in politics and who absorb lots of information about a particular primed issue no doubt continue to attend closely to political news after the priming event has occurred. Consequently, as the media's attention to matters other than the primed issue increases subsequently, these highly attentive individuals fill their minds with this new information, which would interfere with the cognitive effects of the initial priming. Thus, greater attention and exposure may yield more absorbing of information about the primed problem, but also of information about a range of other political matters. Thus, priming effects for these people may be relatively short-lived, because they are quickly overcome by subsequent increases in the accessibility of new issues and problems.

Another possible explanation for the attention result involves awareness of priming manipulations. Recent studies suggest that such manipulations may have the greatest impact when they occur without people paying much attention to them (Lombardi, Higgins, and Bargh 1987; Strack et al. 1993; see also Berkowitz and Troccoli 1990). When people attend closely to and are aware of the potential impact of context on their judgments, they correct for it. In our case, highly attentive viewers may therefore have said to themselves, "I know the news media have paid a lot of attention to inflation lately, but I don't want that to cause me to place too much weight on inflation in deriving my presidential performance evaluation. So I'll reduce its weight a bit." This could explain why weaker priming effects appeared among the most attentive citizens.

There is one other possible explanation for the attention and exposure findings as well (see Hastie and Park 1986; Lodge, McGraw, and Stroh 1989). People who are highly attentive and exposed to the flow of political news are likely to think a great deal about political affairs. This extensive thought may lead them to form a set of general political evaluations (e.g., regarding a president's overall job performance) stored in memory and to continually update them as new relevant information is acquired. Therefore, if asked by a pollster to report an assessment of a president's performance, these individuals need only retrieve and report these previously formed evaluations. Such judgments have a great deal of inertia, because they are based on large sets of previously acquired information, so new pieces of information have only small impact on them. Consequently, recent news media content might have relatively little effect on highly attentive and exposed citizens.

In contrast, citizens low in attention and exposure are unlikely to have such general political evaluations stored in memory. They will most likely have to respond to an inquiring pollster by recalling whatever they can about presidential performance and deriving an overall evaluation on the spot. As the priming hypothesis suggests, instead of drawing upon expansive arrays of performance domains, these individuals are most likely to consider only the small handfuls of performance domains that come to mind most easily. Thus, lower levels of exposure and attention would again be associated with the greatest priming effects because a memory-based judgment strategy would be employed.

Knowledge

In our two laboratory studies, we found low knowledge respondents to be more susceptible to priming. But when we controlled for exposure and attention, higher knowledge was found to facilitate priming in the Gulf War Study, whereas no knowledge effect was present in the Iran-Contra Study. One possible explanation for this discrepancy goes as follows. In the laboratory studies, presidential evaluations were assessed immediately after exposure, and knowledge was presumably positively associated with resistance. Therefore, priming was stronger among the least knowledgeable (see the top line in figure 1).

But in the Gulf War Study, presidential evaluations were measured long after the media exposure of interest. The news media content would only affect these evaluations if it was stored in people's memories and could be retrieved at the time of judgment. Thus, factors that enhance the likelihood of

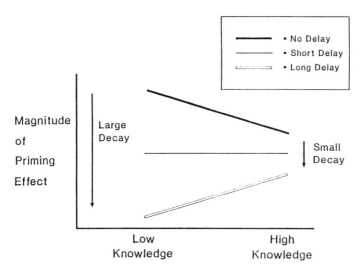

Fig. 1. Effect of political knowledge and delay on the magnitude of priming.

storage and retrieval should enhance media priming effects, and political knowledge may be one such factor.

In general, the more schematically organized knowledge one has about a domain, the more efficiently and effectively one can make sense of new information, find an appropriate place to incorporate it into one's memory, and retrieve it sometime later (see Fiske and Taylor 1991, 121–32). The more knowledge one has about politics, the more quickly and easily one can make sense of a news story, and the more efficiently one can store it in and retrieve it from an elaborate and organized mental filing system. Therefore, when there is a delay between media exposure and attitude assessment, as in the Gulf War Study, knowledge might facilitate priming by facilitating retention over time.

The bottom line in figure 1 illustrates how the resistance and retention functions of knowledge might combine with one another. When presidential evaluations are measured a significant period of time after media exposure, the priming effect decays a great deal among low-knowledge individuals (shown on the left side), whereas it decays only a small amount among high-knowledge people (shown on the right side). Consequently, after a delay, the priming effect that remains is stronger among the latter individuals than among the former, even though the opposite was true immediately after exposure.

In the Iran-Contra Study, presidential evaluations were assessed after a relatively short delay of days or weeks. After this moderate delay, there could be no effect of knowledge on the strength of the priming effect, as the middle line of figure 1 illustrates.

Directions for Future Research

The research we have outlined suggests a number of useful directions for future research. First, the speculations we have offered can all be tested in future laboratory experiments manipulating dilution, awareness, delay, and other factors. In addition, future work might attempt to test the mechanism of priming explicitly. Although it has been widely assumed that the relevant mechanism is accessibility, its mediational role has never been documented. One could expose individuals to news stories on a particular political issue and assess impact on the accessibility of attitudes on that issue directly (see, e.g., Fazio and Williams 1986). One could also see whether increased accessibility is responsible for any increased impact of the issue on presidential evaluations.

Although accessibility may turn out to be the sole mediator of priming, it is also possible that agenda setting mediates priming. That is, increased accessibility of an issue may increase the likelihood that people will view that issue as nationally important. And that belief in national importance may cause increased weight to be attached to the issue in presidential evaluations. This, too, can be tested in future studies.

Coda

If accessibility mediates priming, our results imply a rather unflattering view of the American public. Indeed, they would hark back to the first phase of media research, in which citizens were viewed as passive recipients of "hypodermic" injections from the media. And if people *are* simply victims of the architecture of their minds, then the attitudes they express toward presidential performance should probably not play the central role in policy-making that they do.

NOTES

1. Our conceptions of dosage and resistance are a bit different from treatments of similar concepts by others. For example, although we view political knowledge simply as a basis for resistance, Zaller (1987, 1992, chap. 2 in this book) views knowledge as a measure of political *awareness,* which he defines as the confluence of high exposure to political information, high attention to that information, and good understanding of it, yielding high levels of absorption (see Zaller 1992, 21). We believe that exposure and attention can be conceptualized as distinct from the amount of knowledge a person

has stored in memory, that these various constructs can be effectively measured separately, and that understanding their effects may require multivariate statistical analyses using all of such measures simultaneously. In such analyses, we treat knowledge as a measure of just that: the amount of political information a person has stored in memory.

2. We did not measure attention in either of the two laboratory studies, so we could not control for it.

3. In this study, we combined respondents' answers to questions about their frequency of watching television news in general, watching television news about the 1990 elections, reading newspapers in general, and reading newspaper stories about the 1990 elections to yield an index of general exposure to the news media. Attention was assessed using answers to a question regarding how much attention respondents had paid to news about the Gulf War.

REFERENCES

Anderson, John R. 1983. *The architecture of cognition.* Cambridge: Harvard University Press.

Ball-Rokeach, S. J., J. W. Grube, and M. Rokeach. 1981. "Roots: The next generation"—Who watched and with what effect? *Public Opinion Quarterly* 45:58–68.

Behr, Roy L., and Shanto Iyengar. 1985. Television news, real-world cues, and changes in the public agenda. *Public Opinion Quarterly* 49:38–57.

Berkowitz, Leonard, and Bartholomeu T. Troccoli. 1990. Feelings, direction of attention, and expressed evaluations of others. *Cognition and Emotion* 4:305–25.

Collins, A. M., and E. F. Loftus. 1975. A spreading activation theory of semantic processing. *Psychological Review* 82:407–28.

Cooper, E., and E. Jahoda. 1947. The evasion of propaganda: How prejudiced people respond to anti-prejudice propaganda. *Journal of Psychology* 23:15–25.

Estes, W. K. 1988. Human learning and memory. In *Steven's handbook of experimental psychology,* ed. R. C. Atkinson, R. J. Herrinstein, G. Lindzey, and R. D. Luce. New York: Wiley.

Fazio, Russell H., and L. J. Williams. 1986. Attitude accessibility as a moderator of the attitude-perception and attitude-behavior relations: An investigation of the 1984 presidential election. *Journal of Personality and Social Psychology* 51:505–14.

Fiske, Susan T., and Shelley E. Taylor. 1991. *Social cognition.* New York: McGraw-Hill.

Frey, D. 1986. Recent research on selective exposure to information. In *Advances in experimental social psychology,* ed. Leonard Berkowitz. San Diego, Calif.: Academic Press.

Hamilton, D. L., and R. D. Fallot. 1974. Information salience as a weighting factor in impression formation. *Journal of Personality and Social Psychology* 30:444–48.

Hastie, Reid, and Bernadette Park. 1986. The relationship between memory and judgment depends on whether the judgment task is memory-based or on-line. *Psychological Review* 93:258–68.

Higgins, E. Tory, and G. King. 1981. Accessibility of social constructs: Information-processing consequences of individual and contextual variability. In *Personality, cognition, and social interaction*, ed. Nancy Cantor and John Kihlstrom. Hillsdale, N.J.: Erlbaum.

Hovland, C. I., A. A. Lumsdaine, and F. D. Sheffield. 1949. *Experiments on mass communication*. Princeton, N.J.: Princeton University Press.

Hur, K. K., and J. P. Robinson. 1978. The social impact of "Roots." *Journalism Quarterly* 55:19–24.

Iyengar, Shanto, and Donald R. Kinder. 1987. *News that matters*. Chicago: University of Chicago Press.

Iyengar, Shanto, Donald R. Kinder, Mark D. Peters, and Jon A. Krosnick. 1984. The evening news and presidential evaluations. *Journal of Personality and Social Psychology* 46:778–87.

Judd, Charles M., and James W. Downing. 1990. Political expertise and the development of attitude consistency. *Social Cognition* 8:104–24.

Judd, Charles M., Roger A. Drake, James W. Downing, and Jon A. Krosnick. 1991. Some dynamic properties of attitude structures: Context-induced response facilitation and polarization. *Journal of Personality and Social Psychology* 60:193–202.

Katz, E., and J. J. Feldman. 1962. "The debates in the light of research: A survey of surveys. In *The great debates*, ed. S. Kraus. Bloomington: Indiana University Press.

Klapper, Joseph. 1960. *The effects of mass communications*. New York: Free Press.

Kosicki, Gerald M. 1993. Problems and opportunities in agenda-setting research. *Journal of Communication* 43:100–127.

Krosnick, Jon A., and Laura A. Brannon. 1993. The impact of the Gulf War on the ingredients of presidential evaluations: Multidimensional effects of political involvement. *American Political Science Review* 87:963–75.

Krosnick, Jon A., and Donald R. Kinder. 1990. Altering the foundations of support for the president through priming. *American Political Science Review* 84:497–512.

Lippmann, Walter. 1920. *Liberty and the news*. New York: Harcourt Brace Jovanovich.

Lippmann, Walter. 1922. *Public opinion*. New York: Macmillan.

Lippmann, Walter. 1925. *The phantom public*. New York: Harcourt Brace Jovanovich.

Lodge, Milton, Kathleen McGraw, and Patrick Stroh. 1989. An impression-driven model of candidate evaluation. *American Political Science Review* 83:399–419.

Lombardi, Wendy J., E. Tory Higgins, and John A. Bargh. 1987. The role of consciousness in priming effects on categorization: Assimilation versus contrast as a function of awareness of the priming task. *Personality and Social Psychology Bulletin* 13:411–29.

Lord, C. G., L. Ross, and M. R. Lepper. 1979. Biases assimilation and attitude polarization: The effects of prior theories on subsequently considered evidence. *Journal of Personality and Social Psychology* 37:2098–109.

MacKuen, Michael B. 1981. Social communication and the mass policy agenda. In

More than news: Media power in public affairs, ed. M. B. MacKuen and S. L. Coombs. Beverly Hills, Calif.: Sage.

McCombs, Maxwell E. 1993. The evolution of agenda-setting research: Twenty-five years in the marketplace of ideas. *Journal of Communication* 43:58–67.

Neustadt, R. E. 1960. *Presidential power.* New York: Wiley.

Patterson, T., and R. McClure. 1976. *The unseeing eye: The myth of television power in national elections.* New York: G. P. Putnam.

Petty, Richard E., and John T. Cacioppo. 1986. The elaboration likelihood model of persuasion. In *Advances in experimental social psychology,* ed. Leonard Berkowitz. San Diego, Calif.: Sage.

Rivers, D., and N. Rose. 1981. Passing the president's program. Paper delivered at the annual meeting of the Mid-West Political Science Association, April, Chicago.

Roberts, Donald F., and Nathan Maccoby. 1985. Effects of mass communication. In *Handbook of social psychology,* ed. Gardner Lindzey and Elliot Aronson. New York: Random House.

Roberts, J. V. 1985. The attitude-memory relationship after 40 years: A meta-analysis of the literature. *Basic and Applied Social Psychology* 6:221–41.

Sears, David O., and S. H. Chaffee. 1979. Uses and effects of the 1976 debates: An overview of empirical studies. In *The great debates,* ed. S. Kraus. Bloomington: Indiana University Press.

Sears, David O., and J. T. Freedman. 1965. Effects of expected familiarity with arguments upon opinion change and selective exposure. *Journal of Personality and Social Psychology* 2:420–26.

Simon, Herbert A. 1957. *Models of man.* New York: Wiley.

Simon, Herbert A., and A. C. Stedry. 1968. Psychology and economics. In *Handbook of Social Psychology,* ed. Gardner Lindzey and Elliot Aronson. Reading, Mass.: Addison-Wesley.

Strack, Fritz, Norbert Schwarz, Herbert Bless, Almut Kubler, and Michaela Wanke. 1993. Awareness of the influence as a determinant of assimilation versus contrast. *European Journal of Social Psychology* 23:53–62.

Wyer, Robert S., and J. Hartwick. 1980. The role of information retrieval and conditional inference processes in belief formation and change. In *Advances in experimental social psychology,* ed. Leonard Berkowitz. New York: Academic Press.

Zaller, John R. 1987. Diffusion of political attitudes. *Journal of Personality and Social Psychology* 53:821–33.

Zaller, John R. 1992. *The nature and origins of mass opinion.* New York: Cambridge University Press.

Zaller, John R., and Stanley Feldman. 1992. A simple theory of the survey response: Answering questions versus revealing preferences. *American Journal of Political Science* 36:579–616.

CHAPTER 4

The Craft of Political Advertising: A Progress Report

Stephen Ansolabehere and Shanto Iyengar

The voice of the people is but an echo. The output of the echo chamber bears an inevitable and invariable resemblance to the input. As candidates and parties clamor for attention and vie for popular support, the people's verdict can be no more than a selective reflection from among the alternatives and outlooks presented to them. Even the most discriminating popular judgment can reflect only ambiguity, uncertainty, or even foolishness if those are the qualities of the input into the echo chamber.

—V. O. Key, *The Responsible Electorate*

V. O. Key's depiction of the American electorate seems as apt now as it did 30 years ago, with one important caveat. Today, information pours into political campaigns primarily through televised advertising.[1] Candidates for federal office spend more on broadcast advertising than on any other campaign activity (Fritz and Morris 1992), and citizens find advertising to be more informative than newspapers and television news programs (Patterson and McClure 1976; Kern 1989).

Most observers view the rise of televised political advertising with considerable alarm. Journalists, elected officials, and even some consultants argue that Madison Avenue's flash and slogans have eclipsed serious political discussion. Instead, the argument goes, the messages that candidates pack into 30-second spots are superficial, deceptive, and increasingly nasty. Campaigns offer citizens little hard information with which to make a reasoned choice, and the information that voters do acquire is slanted and negative. Not surprisingly, the dissonance that goes into the echo chamber also comes out. Contemporary campaigns reportedly leave voters disaffected from our political process. Many of them simply stay home, others express their anger at the polls (Bode 1989; Broder 1989; Jamieson 1991; Neale 1991).

Are American campaigns as bad as all that? Simply put, we don't really know. There is little systematic evidence on the contribution of campaign messages (and specifically of advertising) to election outcomes. In *The Re-*

sponsible Electorate, V. O. Key complained that observers at the time knew very little about what voters saw and heard in the months leading up to the election (111). Certainly, political scientists and practitioners have made great strides in survey research over the last three decades. We now have a time series of National Election Studies spanning nearly two generations, as well as numerous other academic surveys. We can also learn from the more than 200 media polls conducted throughout the presidential campaigns. However, we still know little about what voters actually see and hear and about how that information affects their voting behavior.

Several interesting histories of political advertising have been written (for instance, Diamond and Bates 1992), but only recently have scholars attempted to document systematically the nature, use, and impact of campaign advertising. This chapter describes current research on the general effectiveness of advertising, the role of advertising content and valence, and the importance of context. We do not give a comprehensive review of the literature on advertising. For instance, we ignore the vast literature on affect, emotion, and advertising (see Kosterman 1991). Rather we outline a research agenda for the study of political advertising. As priorities, we recommend that researchers (1) focus on questions of issue content, tone, and context of political advertising, (2) emphasize the behavioral consequences of political advertising, (3) make greater use of and improvements in experiments, and (4) collect accurate data on how much is spent on advertising and what concerns are emphasized in the campaigns.

This chapter is organized in two parts. First, we review the different methods used to study political advertising and establish research guidelines for studying the causal effects of advertising on voting behavior. Second, we briefly discuss research findings on each of these topics and point out avenues for further inquiry.

Research Methods

The study of political advertising must both describe what voters see and hear in campaigns and measure the effects of political advertising on viewers. Research on both goals is still in its nascency.

Several projects, most notably the Political Advertising Archive at the University of Oklahoma, have made great strides toward simply documenting what candidates show and say in their political commercials. The Oklahoma Archive, overseen by Lynda Kaid and her associates, contains more than 5,000 commercials from gubernatorial, congressional, and presidential candidates. The collection is most complete for the most recent years. Several other projects categorize and analyze the content of several types of ads (Johnson-Cartee and Copeland 1991; Kern 1989; Shyles 1986). While all these efforts describe the ads that candidates aired, they do not document the frequency with which particular ads were broadcast. Additional data on media buys are needed to measure how many people were exposed to each commercial and the relative importance of that message in the overall campaign of the candidate. To date no comprehensive data on media buys has been collected.[2] This last sort of data is essential if researchers wish to measure the aggregate effect of advertising on electoral outcomes.

Given the limitations of aggregate data on advertising usage, researchers wishing to estimate the effects of political advertising have concentrated on doing so with survey data or with experiments. Indeed, this is one area of political science characterized by significant use of controlled experiments. Scholars have promoted experimentation as an efficient way to study social phenomena: experiments permit researchers to draw causal inferences and contribute to the rapid accumulation of knowledge in the discipline at large (Hovland 1959; Campbell and Stanley 1963; Achen 1987). In the case of political advertising, however, there has been little accumulation of knowledge. Many experiments have found significant effects of political advertising on what viewers know and how they think. However, if political scientists believe anything about political advertising, it is that campaign commercials have minimal or no effect on election outcomes.

There are two reasons for the belief that advertising is of minimal importance. First, survey research, which has a stronger intellectual tradition and thus more credibility in political science, is hard pressed to uncover either attitudinal or behavioral effects. In the 1970s Thomas Patterson and Robert McClure (1973, 1976) set out to measure the effects of campaign advertising. Their surveys showed significant evidence that the public learned about the candidates' issue positions from advertisements, but no evidence that the particular advertisements persuaded people to vote for a candidate. More recent survey work by Mark Westlye (1991), Charles Franklin (1991), Gary Jacobson (1990) and others uses more subtle measures of campaign exposure and more sophisticated statistical techniques, but once again comes up empty-handed.

The fundamental problem with most survey research is the inability to determine with accuracy who has seen and who has not seen a specific advertisement. Surveys must rely on self-reports or recall of a particular advertisement to measure exposure to advertising. Such measures are notoriously unreliable and bias survey findings away from finding any effects. Experimental research (which controls who sees an ad and who does not) tends to find that only half of those exposed to a commercial embedded in a television program can remember seeing a political ad just half an hour after seeing the ad (Ansolabehere and Iyengar 1993a). The implication for survey research is obvious. Large numbers of people who are classified as not seeing a commercial are in fact exposed to the commercial. Since those misclassified as not seeing an ad (roughly half of the actual number exposed) will in fact have been influenced,[3] the difference in the dependent variable between those who remembered seeing an ad and those who did not will be smaller than the difference between those who actually saw the ad and those who did not. Self-reported recall will, thus, understate the magnitude of the effect of the advertisement, and the degree of underestimation is likely to be large.

Recent scholarship that examines errors in survey data corroborates this argument based on experimental findings. Closer examination of survey data finds internal evidence of the unreliability of self-reported media exposure (Price and Zaller 1993). Once the data are adjusted for measurement error there is a noticeable effect of campaign messages (Bartels 1993). These statistical corrections however, rely on assumptions that are themselves subject to criticism. Only controlled experiments can avoid those objections.

The second reason for the belief that advertising is of minimal importance is that political scientists have tended to ignore the findings of experimental research on advertising. The fault does not lie entirely in our intellectual tradition, which is heavily invested in survey research. Rather, it is hard to infer the electoral effects from most experiments involving political commercials.

Most experimenters ignore political behavior. Instead, they typically focus on a particular psychological theory, taking their dependent variable to be some measure of attitudes toward the candidates. Very little of the existing experimental work examines the effects of advertisements on turnout and voting preference, and none show how psychological factors translate into behavior. (See surveys of the massive psychological literature by Kaid [1981] and Kosterman [1991] for more details.) While psychological inquiries may ultimately unlock the key to political advertising, political scientists and communications scholars do not know even the magnitude of change in behavior that is ultimately at stake.

In addition, experimental standards in this field are extremely lax. The stimuli (i.e., the treatment ads) in most experiments confound several factors, such as issue content and tone, making it hard to infer which factor is responsible for the effect of the advertisements. Many experiments use contrived materials, such as hypothetical candidates or advertisements from past elections or elections in other states. It is doubtful that such treatments elicit genuine responses, since viewers ultimately cannot vote for those candidates on election day. Moreover, experimental participants are very unrepresentative of the general population. Typically experiments use college sophomores, who, to quote Hovland (1959), are not "real people." Finally, almost all experiments involve small numbers of subjects. In our own readings, the typical experiment employs about 150 subjects, though some researchers have used as few as 15 people. With such small sample sizes one needs to find enormous effects in order to detect statistically significant results. Because of these constraints, a considerable leap of faith is usually required for generalizing experimental results to the real world.

The remedies for these problems lie in better experimental design. Limits on aggregate data and inherent difficulties with surveys mean that those methods will likely not yield reliable results. Some experiments suffer from idiosyncratic problems, such as lack of control or contrast groups. We ignore these problems and instead focus on three shortcomings common to almost all experimentation on political advertising.

Stimuli

The basic tension in all social science experimental research is between the experimenter's control over the materials, which is necessary to draw causal inferences, and the realism of the treatments, which dictates the external validity of the results.

Let us first consider the more fundamental matter of control. Without adequate control over experimental materials, an experiment loses its validity. The typical experiment uses political commercials that were actually shown by the candidates in a race. The problem with using such stimuli is that many factors are confounded. Say, for instance, that the researchers show a negative advertisement to one group of people and a positive advertisement to another group (see Kaid and Boydston 1987; Johnson-Cartee and Copeland 1991). The difficulty with drawing causal inferences from this design is that the two groups saw advertisements that differed in many ways, such as visuals and music, not only in the one respect about which the researcher wished to draw an inference.

The only way to exert strict control over the materials is to create treatment advertisements that are identical in all respects except for the factor to be examined. Garramone (1985) is a good example. She wished to determine whether there was a difference between the reactions to attack ads that were sponsored by a candidate and attack ads sponsored by an independent organization, such as the National Conservative Political Action Committee. Stimuli consisted of two versions of the same advertisement. In version one the tag at the end of the advertisement read in bold letters "Sponsored by Candidate X"; in the other version the tag read "Sponsored by the National Conservative Political Action Committee." In all other respects the treatments were identical. (As noted subsequently, Garramone found that the negative ad hurt the candidate who attacked when he was identified as the sponsor, but it did not affect his ratings when NCPAC was the sponsor.) Our own research consists of multiple replications of the following design. Stimuli consist of advertisements that have the same video track, but different voice tracks. The scripts for the voice tracks were identical in all respects except for changes in 10 to 15 words that dictated the experimental manipulation (e.g., negative v. positive, choice of issue, the sponsoring candidate). (For examples, see Ansolabehere and Iyengar 1991a; Ansolabehere and Iyengar 1993a; Ansolabehere, Iyengar, Simon, and Valentino 1993.)

While control is essential to experimentation, an experiment is useful and interesting to the extent that it can be tied to actual political behavior. A valid criticism of controlled advertising experiments is that they often involve a great many fictions. Some use fake candidates, whom the subjects could never vote for and likely have no interest in learning about.[4] In addition, the production quality of the advertisements is sometimes sufficiently low that the reality of the treatment is lost. Concerned about the realism of their manipulations, many researchers use actual campaign advertisements from out-of-state campaigns or from previous elections. This attempt to improve realism comes at the expense of experimental control. Ironically, studies that use actual campaign advertisements introduce a potentially more damaging fiction. The experimenters are essentially asking the subjects to form opinions about candidates for whom they could never vote. It seems doubtful that subjects would be as attentive to such commercials as they would be to commercials from races that currently affect them.

Actually, the best way to prevent confounding effects and to maintain realism is to exert *greater* control over the experimental materials. In order to have such control, the experimenters must create advertisements that are identical in all respects except one—for example, the negativity of the ad. In order to maintain realism, experimental stimuli must be credible in content and professionally produced. The video, the voice track, the sound track, and the editing must all be of the same quality across treatments, and they must be the same quality as the typical political advertisement.

Even though survey and content analysis are poor methods for testing the effects of campaign advertisements, they are extremely useful in developing experimental stimuli. Surveys can be used to select issues that can fruitfully be experimented with, to determine on which issues the public views a candidate or party to be strong, and to measure the candidates' credibility. As will be discussed, all these are crucial to interpreting the effects of particular advertisements. Careful examination of actual campaign advertisements can provide researchers with endless ideas with which to work and even templates for fake commercials.

Realism must be enhanced in other ways as well. To guard against Hawthorne effects, subjects should not be aware of the intentions of the experimenters in advance. Subjects should view the treatment videos in a comfortable setting, not a sterile room or classroom that forces people to concentrate on the materials before them. Lastly, the stimuli should be shown in their natural setting, during the commercial break in a television show.

Subjects

The typical experiment involves a fairly small sample size. How many subjects must participate in order for experimenters to observe significant effects? We can estimate the minimum sample size using previous research results. In our own work we found that the effect of exposure to an ad versus no ad on vote intentions was .077 with a standard deviation of .745. To have less than a 20 percent chance of a false positive and less than a 5 percent chance of a false negative requires 253 subjects, with a one-sided hypothesis, and 374 subjects, with a two-sided hypothesis. Many researchers, however, do not fully exploit the technique since they typically use samples half the size required to have statistical confidence in results.

Further difficulties arise with sample selection. While random assignment of subjects to treatments ensures that estimated effects are unbiased, randomization does not guarantee that the findings generalize the population at large. For this a random sample is ideal. Since participation in media experiments means that the subjects must come to a laboratory, random samples are not usually possible. In the worst case, experimenters use college students. This seriously limits generalizability of results. Eighteen- to twenty-year-olds have decidedly different television viewing habits and political opinions and behaviors than do older cohorts. To get more representative samples, many researchers recruit subjects from a variety of places—civics organizations, shopping malls, office buildings, and even lists of registered voters. Though not random, careful selective recruitment often produces demographically representative samples.

Replications

Concerns about the generalizability of results suggests that experimenters should replicate their results internally and externally. Internal replication repeats the same basic design, with perhaps slight variations in the materials on a different sample of subjects. Most papers present multiple internal replications of a given experimental design. External replications involve reconstructing the basic experimental setup with quasi-experimental or observational data. For example, Ansolabehere, Iyengar, Simon, and Valentino (1993) estimated the effect of negative versus positive advertising on intentions to turnout. Then, using data from 34 Senate campaigns in 1992, they estimated the effect of negative versus positive campaigns on statewide turnout rates. The results were nearly identical. External replications are rare in this field but extremely important since they represent direct generalizations from the experiment to the real world.

The Electoral Effects of Political Advertising

Minimal Effects

The most nagging puzzle in the study of campaigns generally and political advertising in particular is whether campaign messages exert any influence on electoral behavior. Consultants and commentators cite a long list of political advertisements that apparently produced significant shifts in voting preferences or reversed the momentum of a political campaign (Germond and Witcover 1989; Jamieson 1991; Rosenstiel 1993). Most political scientists, however, question whether campaign messages such as advertisements exert any influence on voting decisions. Forty years of survey research have repeatedly found that the effects of campaigning are negligible compared to circumstantial factors such as the state of the economy, party, and incumbency (see Berelson et al. 1954; Campbell et al. 1960; Patterson and McClure 1973; Tufte 1978; Fiorina 1981; Rosenstone 1983; Hibbs 1987). Survey research that specifically attempts to measure the effects of campaign advertisements reaches the same conclusion: there is no statistical evidence from surveys that campaign advertisements are persuasive (Patterson and McClure 1973; Patterson and McClure 1976; Garramone 1984).

The argument that campaign advertising has only minimal effects on elections is difficult to reconcile with candidates' actual behavior. All serious campaigns invest heavily in advertising. What is more, as noted earlier, surveys likely understate the magnitude of the effect of campaign advertisements.

What evidence is there that the effect of televised campaign advertisements is more than minimal? Rejection of the minimal consequences verdict would require that researchers observe differences in voting intentions between those people exposed to a typical political advertisement and a control group (e.g., those exposed to a nonpolitical commercial). Looking specifically at voting intentions, Ansolabehere and Iyengar (1993a) find that exposure to a political advertisement increased the lead of the candidate who sponsored the advertisement by 7.7 percentage points (plus or minus 4.0 points with 95 percent confidence). This finding is based on six carefully controlled replications of the same basic experimental design that involved more than 2,000 subjects and used different candidates and different advertisements across replications.

The magnitude of these experimental findings reveals a further reason why survey researchers have been unable to detect significant effects. The effects of airing a single advertisement to a population are too small to detect except with very large surveys. Using the estimated means and standard deviations from Ansolabehere and Iyengar (1993a), we can calculate the minimum sample size needed to detect significant effects while guarding against false positives. If half of the public is exposed to an advertisement, then a sample of 1,013 people is needed for a survey to detect a significant effect at the .05 level with a one-sided test. A two-sided test requires at least 1,498 respondents. None of the advertising surveys comes close to the necessary sample size: Garramone (1984) sampled 500 people; Patterson and McClure (1976) interviewed 700 people.

Content

Political commentators have long complained about the superficiality of campaign advertising. To many, the very format of spot advertising does violence to serious political debate. How is it possible to engage any important question in just three and a half minutes (i.e., with six or seven 30-second spots)? This charge is hard to address in any meaningful or scientific way. While many reform proposals contain incentives for candidates to use debates or lengthier format,[5] like Perot's half-hour segments, it is not obvious that political advertising should be curtailed. However sparse the messages, candidates are able to reach many more people with television than was ever possible with newspapers, trains, rallies, or other campaign gimmicks (U.S. House 1991). In addition, survey-based research suggests that the public does indeed extract considerable substantive information from televised spots (Patterson and McClure 1976). Finally, voters do not have to be perfectly informed in order to make a reasoned choice (Sniderman, Brody, and Tetlock 1992).

Most criticisms of advertising content, though, focus not on the format but on the information that candidates pack into 30-second spots. Several important studies have documented the history (Diamond and Bates 1992); the character and rhetoric (Kern 1989); and the strategies of political advertising (Schwartz 1972; Jamieson 1992). The main contrast drawn by this literature is between *issue* and *image* spots, or, to use the product advertising jargon, the *hard sell* and the *soft sell*.

The hard sell sticks with the facts, just the facts. The idea behind this form of advertising is that voting is a very deliberative process. Citizens need to know who is running, what they want to do once in office, how credible those promises are, and the consequences of those promises. The typical ad in this genre features the candidate speaking directly to the audience, outlining his or her political accomplishments and policy positions. Sometimes the candidate's voice is dubbed over striking pictures; rarely is music used. In 1992, Bill Clinton's messages outlined his plan to create eight million new jobs over the next four years.

The soft sell plays on passions. Voting is assumed to be more emotional than rational. The thrust of the soft sell is not issues and policies, but images of the candidates and the myths of local cultures. A typical soft sell may feature the candidate surrounded by his or her family, spectacular pictures of the candidate's state, and uplifting music. The aims of such commercials are to make viewers feel good about a politician (or bad about his or her opponent), but not to convey information about what the candidate will do if elected. In 1984, Ronald Reagan ran on the slogan that after four years of his governance it was once again "Morning in America."

It is perhaps best to think of the issue-image distinction as a continuum. Some issues, such as abortion and race, tap emotions as much as rational calculation. Similarly, many symbols signal to the voters information about where the candidate likely stands on a variety of issues. An advertisement featuring the candidate saluting the American flag and watching patriotically a military parade may signal support for a stronger military, more defense spending, and more U.S. military intervention abroad.

Traditionally, political advertisers have used the hard sell. For example, Patterson and McClure's (1973) analysis of advertising in the 1972 presidential election found that nearly 70 percent of all the ads dealt exclusively or chiefly with issues. In the 1980s, the advertising message changed. Although use of issues predominated, content analysis of actual political spots reveals that candidates increasingly use symbols and emphasize their own image rather than issue positions (Shyles 1984).

Is issue advertising more informative or more persuasive than image advertising? Only a handful of survey and experimental studies examine the effectiveness of these different sorts of advertising. A cursory review of the findings reveals no consensus on the effectiveness of symbolic and substantive appeals. Patterson and McClure (1976) concluded from their survey data that "advertising image-making is wasted effort" (111). People judge candidates based on "what they say, not how they say it." Pfau and Burgoon's (1988) field experiments echoed the general conclusions of Patterson and McClure. They concluded that image ads are more effective at the start of a campaign but quickly lose their punch. Throughout much of the campaign they examined, Pfau and Burgoon found issue ads to be more persuasive. On the other hand, experiments by Geiger and Reeves (1991) and Garramone (1983) found image advertising to be a superior way of packaging political candidates.

These contradictory results are the product of more than methodology. Rather, the distinction between issue and image (or hard- and soft-sell) advertising is too crude. The knowledge that voters have (or infer from party labels, gender, race, etc.) conditions how they evaluate the claims made in political advertisements and whether the advertisement is ultimately persuasive. Bill Clinton's draft and sex scandals damaged his reputation as an honest politician; George Bush's approval of the 1990 Tax Act ruined his credibility on taxes. In addition, on most issues the parties have long-standing reputations from which voters infer the likelihood that a candidate makes good on a promise.

Candidate credibility, then, should be viewed as a separate dimension of advertising content. Voters must infer from the content of an advertisement not only whether they like a candidate (for reasons of either policy or passion) but whether they want that candidate to represent them. Credibility includes questions of trust, competence, and past performance. These may be either general or specific to a given question. For example, voters trusted George Bush in general in 1992, just not on taxes or the economy.

The importance of candidate credibility suggests three ways that the content of campaign commercials may matter. First, candidates can build their general reputations as good representatives or leaders using ads that focus on performance and integrity. As discussed earlier, this sort of appeal can be quite persuasive.

Second, candidates tend to be more persuasive on issues on which they or their parties are credible representatives. Similarly, they should avoid issues on which they have no credibility. Research on public opinion finds that parties "own" particular issues (Petrocik 1991). For example, Republicans are viewed as tough on crime, Democrats as defenders of working-class jobs. Ansolabehere and Iyengar (1991a) found no evidence of Republican issue ownership on the issue of crime in the 1990 California gubernatorial election (i.e., Feinstein and Wilson were equally persuasive using crime ads), but they did find some evidence of issue ownership on crime, unemployment, and "women's" issues in the 1992 California Senate elections (Ansolabehere and Iyengar 1993b).

Third, advertisements can prime viewers to think in terms of particular issues. Like newscasts (Iyengar and Kinder 1985), advertisements can elevate the importance of an issue in the voters' minds. If the candidate or party is viewed as better on that issue than the opposition, then priming the public will work to the sponsoring candidate's advantage. For example, by advertising on so-called women's issues (e.g., abortion, sexual harassment, breast cancer research), female candidates can increase the importance of those issues in the minds of all voters (including men) and thereby increase the support for women candidates (Ansolabehere, Iyengar, and Valentino 1993).

In sum, the traditional distinction between issues and images is inadequate to characterize which ads work. The importance of issue and image advertising depends significantly on the candidates' and parties' credibility on particular messages. Candidates try to improve their overall credibility by broadcasting commercials on their performance in office or their integrity. On issues where they have strong reputations, candidates can be directly persuasive or they can prime viewers to think about certain issues that will benefit all members of their party, not just themselves. The strongest evidence is that candidates can capitalize on an issue on which they are credible.

Tone

Over the last decade, consultants and campaign managers have increasingly turned to "attack" or "negative" ads, commercials in which candidates or their surrogates assail their opponents' abilities, experience, and integrity rather than promote themselves and their own record, issue positions, or ideas. Traditionally, such attacks were used late in the campaigns or by desperate candidates seeking any edge. Now, roughly half of the political ads aired attack the opposition, and many campaigns have become completely negative (Guskind and Hagstrom 1988).[6]

The nasty tone of current political campaigns is widely thought to generate serious political externalities. Citizens allegedly become disaffected from conventional politics and are less likely to vote. The bitterness of campaigns continues long after the election, creating greater animosity between the parties within the legislature and greater problems disciplining members to vote on controversial issues (Crocker 1989).

In their defense, many campaign consultants and managers claim that attack advertisements are more memorable, more informative, and more persuasive than positive advertising.[7] But even the practitioners disagree about the effectiveness of negative ads. Democratic pollster Mark Mellman argued that "if you're filling empty heads, it's a lot easier to do it with negatives" (Guskind and Hagstrom 1988, 2782). A report of the Republican Congressional Campaign Committee, however, concluded that attacking is a "high-risk" strategy, since "it must walk the fine line between making its point and turning the voter off" (Sabato 1981, 166).

Is there in fact a "negativity bias" in advertising that causes the electoral benefits of attacking to exceed the benefits of promoting one's own cause? Are there side effects of lower turnout, less efficacy, and greater cynicism?

On the question of turnout, the overwhelming evidence is that negative ads demobilize the electorate, and positive ads can stimulate people to vote. Copeland and Johnston-Cartee's (1990) survey research in the southeastern United States found that individuals who accepted negative appeals exhibited lower levels of political efficacy and political participation. In a study of five experiments involving more than 1,700 subjects, Ansolabehere, Iyengar, Simon, and Valentino (1993) demonstrate the causal connections between negative advertising, alienation, and lower turnout.[8] In that study, intentions to vote were 5 percentage points lower (significant at the .01 level) among viewers who saw negative versions of a political advertisement. Subjects exposed to advertising were also more cynical about the political process in general. These effects were not mediated by party (e.g., partisans were not stimulated to vote when a candidate of their party attacked).

On the persuasiveness of negative advertising, researchers find strong but conflicting evidence. Kaid and Boydston (1987) measured differences between pre- and post-test on attitudes toward the candidates in reaction to 5 negative test ads. They found significant changes in attitudes. However, since there was neither a control group nor a contrast group (who saw positive ads), we cannot tell if the effect is due to seeing an ad or to seeing a negative ad. Garramone (1984) tried to get at this contrast using a local survey of residents in the East Lansing, Michigan, area. She found a strong backlash: Ratings of the targeted candidate were reduced by attack advertising, but so were ratings of the source. In an experiment in which college classes as a group viewed experimental ads from two fictitious Senate candidates, Garramone et al. (1990) found that negative advertisements produced stronger issue discrimination than positive ads, but they did not test for effects on preferences. Copeland and Johnson-Cartee's (1990) experiment using actual campaign ads from California's 1986 campaign shown to students at a southeastern university found no evidence of a backlash.

Part of the reason for these conflicting findings may be methodological. The surveys relied on self-reported recall, which, as we have noted, is extremely unreliable. The experiments either lacked proper controls or involved unrealistic treatments, asking viewers to form opinions about elections in which they could not vote (out-of-state Senate races) or about candidates who did not exist.

Even after correcting these methodological objections, results are mixed: Negative advertising is sometimes shown to be more persuasive than positive advertising and is sometimes shown to be less persuasive. Ansolabehere and Iyengar (1993e) found evidence of a strong backlash against candidates who attacked in their experimental study of the 1992 California primary, but they also found evidence that negative messages were more effective than positive ones in the 1992 California general election. Importantly, the candidates were the same in both sets of experiments, so idiosyncratic factors associated with the personalities cannot generate this reversal. The authors offered circumstantial evidence that the electorate was the key. Democrats and Republicans do not like to see intraparty strife and punish candidates who initiate such fights.

The best experimental evidence, then, echoes the opinions expressed by consultants. Negative advertising tends to alienate voters generally, producing lower turnout and lower efficacy. Sometimes this effect also manifests itself as a backlash against the attacking candidate, though at other times attacks boost a candidate's support more than positive messages do. Understanding when viewers will find attack ads more persuasive than positive ads and when they will punish the attacking candidate is the key to understanding the effectiveness of negative advertising.

Context

So far we have discussed research that attempts to examine the effects of particular aspects of campaign advertisements in isolation. Advertising, however, does not occur in a vacuum. In the real world, viewers see advertisements from competing candidates and news stories about important public policy issues or different aspects of the campaign. The effectiveness of a candidate's advertising may ultimately depend on other candidates' messages and on the flow of information coming from sources that the candidates do not control.

The noisy world of political campaigns presents campaign managers with two problems. First, how should one anticipate or respond to opposition advertising properly? Second, how can the campaign attract news coverage (also called "free media") or direct the attention of reporters to issues and questions favorable to the candidate?

Campaign consultants need only worry about opponents' advertising messages to the extent that the effectiveness of an advertisement depends on the presence of competing messages. If candidates' messages work independently, then the effect of advertising on electoral results is chiefly a function of the relative volume of the campaigns. If, on the other hand, advertising is interdependent, then candidates must calculate the proper response to competing messages.

The interdependency between candidates' messages has received the most discussion in terms of negative campaigning. When a candidate is attacked, she or he may defend against the charges, counterattack on the same issue or on an issue that voters care about more deeply, assail the opponent's character or integrity, or ignore the attack altogether. The conventional wisdom among consultants is that the first three options can work if handled properly, but the last is a prescription for failure.

To test for the interactive effects of campaign advertisements, Ansolabehere and Iyengar (1991b, 1993d) developed a "paired experimental design" in which subjects were shown two political advertisements, one from each candidate in a race, in the context of a local newscast. The commercials either promoted the sponsor of the ad or attacked the opponent, and the treatments consisted of all possible permutations (candidate 1 positive and candidate 2 positive, 1 positive and 2 negative, 1 negative and 2 positive, and both negative).[9] In two of three experiments of this form, the authors found significant interactive effects of the tone of the candidates' ads on respondents' voting intentions. Specifically, the best response of the candidates in these studies was to answer a negative message with a positive one, contrary to the received wisdom.

Michael Pfau and Henry Kenski (1990) offered a psychological explanation as to why this might be true: inoculation and reinforcement. By answering an attack with a direct refutation, candidates give viewers arguments to counter the message of attack advertisements. Viewers tend to find direct responses more persuasive than counterattacks, and direct refutation insulates the candidate from further attacks. Pfau and Kenski confirmed their argument in experiments conducted in 1986 and 1988. The effects of attack ads were muted when subjects were shown contrary materials before the ad was shown (inoculation) or after the ad was shown (reinforcement).

How important these strategic effects are is still a matter of speculation. These strategic considerations may be enlightening for consultants wishing to control the damage caused by a heat-seeking commercial, but the main job of most campaigns has to be getting their own message across to the voters.

That task is complicated by the constant flow of newspaper and television news coverage of important issues. As with campaign advertisements, news stories can elevate the importance of certain issues in the voters' minds. Candidates certainly try to influence reporters by issuing press releases and holding press conferences on specific problems. However, the tide of stories about crime, the economy, foreign affairs, and so on is impossible to stem. Candidates must either hope for good news on issues that they own, or they can try to use advertising to ride the wave of favorable news coverage.

News stories, then, can operate through two mechanisms: "issue ownership," discussed earlier, or "riding the wave," which is a variant of priming. Ansolabehere and Iyengar (1993b) found evidence (albeit statistically weak) that stories about crime, unemployment, and women's issues redounded to the benefit of Republicans, Democrats, and women, respectively.

Evidence of "riding the wave" is weaker still. Schleuder, McCombs, and Wanta (1991) conducted four separate experiments on the effects of priming by the news of campaign advertising. In all four cases, the authors found that those people primed by a news story were significantly more likely to remember the content of an advertisement than those who were not primed. Ansolabehere and Iyengar (1993b) detected a similar priming effect that produced shifts in voting intentions on women's issues in 1992. Specifically, a story about the "year of the woman" in politics significantly increased the weight that subjects accorded to the abortion issue when evaluating women candidates, but it did not change the weight given to the issue when subjects evaluated male candidates. Based on these findings, it would seem that the news certainly matters but that candidates typically cannot use advertising to make additional gains from favorable news. (It is not known if an advertisement can offset the effects of an unfavorable news story.)

Candidates can rarely anticipate the ebb and flow of routine news. This is not the case with campaign news. In their attempt to attain neutrality and objectivity, reporters end up merely echoing the candidates' own messages. Stories about debates, rallies, survey results, and other features of the campaign may, in turn, influence public opinion of the candidates. This sort of feedback is especially controversial when newspapers and television news cover political advertisements.

Following the 1988 election, commentators generally deplored the mindless search for sound bites and staged photo opportunities, the orchestration of news by political consultants, and, perhaps most important, the frequency with which television news programs uncritically replayed misleading political advertisements (Dennis et al. 1992; Germond and Witcover 1988; Jamieson 1992). Distinguished journalists including David Broder (1990) and Ken Bode (1992) suggested that the press should evaluate the content and truth of campaign advertisements on a regular basis and condemn those ads that distorted or blurred the record. A new genre of campaign journalism, called the "adwatch," was born.

Who benefits from coverage that is critical of campaign advertising? Two separate studies have investigated this question and reached the same conclusion: adwatch journalism backfires. Ansolabehere and Iyengar (1993) and Kern et al. (1993) report findings from several experiments, all showing that the candidate whose advertising is criticized in an adwatch receives a boost in support. Neither investigation can determine why this occurs, but several possibilities deserve further attention. It may be the case that by replaying the ads, the adwatch unintentionally reinforces the candidate's message. Alternatively, adwatches may elicit sympathy for a candidate whose ad is criticized by a "biased" and "hostile" press.

Conclusions

Political advertising has long been viewed as anathema to democratic politics. Candidates must cram their message into 30 brief seconds. What candidates can say in that time allegedly lacks depth or force of reason. And more often than not, candidates assail their opponents, leaving many viewers cynical about politics and unhappy with the choices.

Popular opinions about campaign advertising contrast starkly to the received wisdom among scholars that campaign messages have minimal effects on election outcomes. To most political scientists, criticism of campaigning and calls for reform are blown way out of proportion to the observed effects, which, if any, seem small.

Recent academic research paints a different picture of campaign advertising. Contrary to the common criticisms, advertising is not a "know-nothing" medium. It is clear from both surveys and experiments that people learn politically relevant information, in the form of either issue positions or facts about performance in office, from campaign advertisements. Contrary to the findings of a generation of survey researchers, political advertisements, when isolated in the experimental setting, have strong persuasive effects on voters. A typical commercial increases the sponsoring candidate's lead by approximately seven and a half percentage points. This effect is larger than the congressional incumbency advantage (except in the mid-1980s), a subject that has attracted considerably more scholarly attention.

The electoral effects of campaign advertising, however, are not wholly beneficial. Perhaps the biggest development in political (and also commercial) advertising over the past decade is the rise of attack advertisements. Experimental research has been able to show rather conclusively that negative messages turn people off from politics and decrease intentions to participate in the political process, while positive ads stimulate people to vote. Not only should this finding raise the ire of most political reformers, but it should also raise doubts about the long-standing presumption among political scientists that campaigns necessarily raise people's interest and participation in elections.

These findings provide a solid foundation for understanding the electoral effects of political advertising. Other important questions, however, lack clear-cut answers. The persuasiveness of advertising content is not just a matter of issues versus images, but depends on the candidates' credibility on particular subjects. Also, the effectiveness of positive versus negative ads depends on the electoral context. In general elections, negative ads seem to be more persuasive; in primary elections, attacks are less persuasive. Finally, the public sees any one advertisement in a soup of other information about the campaign—messages from competing candidates, news about important issues, and even news about the campaign itself. All these factors may have significant effects on the receptivity of the voters to campaign advertising.

Understanding the conditions under which certain types of messages work is clearly the task of the next wave of advertising research. Current research consists of studies that were largely exploratory and not designed to determine which of several factors determines why advertisements work. Existing experimental and survey findings do, however, provide clues as to what those conditions may be. In the case of content, the focus of future research should be to determine how persuasive different kinds of candidates (e.g., incumbents and challengers, insiders and outsiders, Democrats, Republicans, and independents) are with different kinds of messages. In the case of negative campaigning, the onus is clearly on understanding why negative advertisements work in particular electoral contexts (e.g., general elections) but not in others (primaries). In examining questions of context, the avenues for further research are endless. We recommend that future research turn to the big events in the campaign season (conventions and debates) and also to understanding why news that is critical of candidates' advertisements seems to backfire and help the candidate.

To get at these increasingly subtle questions, however, requires that researchers raise the standards and quality of their methods. For too long, experimental standards have been lax and methodological anarchy has reigned. We have the following recommendations: (1) larger, representative samples (depending on the test, at least 250 or 375 nonstudents), (2) selection of and creation of materials based on information in surveys and actual campaign ads, (3) careful control of the experimental stimuli so that the only difference between treatments is the experimental factor (e.g., tone), (4) professionally produced, realistic (but not actual) campaign ads for stimuli, and (5) realistic treatments (e.g., ads shown during the news) and realistic experimental settings.

These are high standards, but so too are the stakes. Television advertising has become central to the way Americans choose their leaders. Carefully crafted research into its effects should hold great significance for campaign managers and reformers alike.

NOTES

The authors thank Richard Brody and Laurie Gould for their helpful comments.

Epigraph from V. O. Key, Jr., *The Responsible Electorate* (New York: Vintage Books, 1966), 2.

1. In *The Responsible Electorate*, Key mentions television just once, in reference to the Kennedy-Nixon debates of 1960. He himself seems skeptical about the ability of the medium as a forum for political discussion (112).

2. The only reasonably accurate measures of broadcast expenditures are the studies by the Federal Communication Commission in the 1960s, the proprietary and occasional studies done by the National Association of Broadcasters, and the aggregation of detailed Federal Elections Commission reports done by Sarah Fritz and Dwight Morris (1992) for the 1990 House and Senate elections.

3. In experiments, the effects of exposure to advertisements on voting intentions are not mediated by advertising recall.

4. The same criticism applies to experimenters who use actual campaign advertisements. It seems doubtful that subjects would be as attentive to commercials from past elections or from candidates in other states as they would be to commercials from ongoing races, involving actual candidates. What is more, when experimenters use commercials that the candidates have already aired and that may have received criticism from the media, the laboratory response measures past exposures to the ad as well as the experimental exposure.

5. Most recently, the Clean Campaign Act of 1985 and the Campaign Finance Act of 1990 have contained such incentives.

6. The same trend appears to have taken over in the commercial advertising world as well. In 1971, one in ten advertisements were comparative. In 1989, one in two were comparative (Muehling et al. 1989).

7. See Roger Ailes and Robert Squire's testimony before the House Subcommittee on Telecommunications and Finance of the Committee on Energy and Commerce (1991). For more on the opinions of consultants, see Johnson-Cartee and Copeland (1991, chap. 1), and Kern (1989, chap. 2). For a spirited academic defense of negative advertising, see William Mayer (1993).

8. Smaller experimental studies with poor experimental controls and small samples find mixed results. Basil, Schooler, and Reeves (1991) find demobilizing effects. Garramone et al. (1990), using fake ads for two fictitious Senate candidates shown to 372 students in a classroom, found no evidence of such an effect.

9. Also, the ads were shown in random order with candidate 1 going first half of the time and candidate 2 going first the other half.

REFERENCES

Achen, Christopher. 1986. *Statistical analysis of quasi-experiments*. Berkeley: University of California Press.
Ansolabehere, Stephen, and Shanto Iyengar. 1991a. The electoral effects of issues and attacks in campaign advertising. Paper presented at the annual meeting of the American Political Science Association, September, 1991, Washington, D.C.
Ansolabehere, Stephen, and Shanto Iyengar. 1991b. Television advertising as campaign strategy: Some experimental evidence. Paper presented at the annual meeting of the American Association for Public Opinion Research, March, 1991, Tempe, Ariz.
Ansolabehere, Stephen, and Shanto Iyengar. 1993a. How persuasive are political advertisements? Working paper, Department of Political Science, UCLA.
Ansolabehere, Stephen, and Shanto Iyengar. 1993b. Riding the wave and issue ownership: The interdependence between television news and campaign advertising. Working paper, Department of Political Science, UCLA.
Ansolabehere, Stephen, and Shanto Iyengar. 1993c. Can the press monitor campaign advertising: Some experimental evidence. Working paper, Department of Political Science, UCLA.
Ansolabehere, Stephen, and Shanto Iyengar. 1993d. Competing for votes: An experimental study of campaign advertising strategy. Working paper, Department of Political Science, UCLA.
Ansolabehere, Stephen, and Shanto Iyengar. 1993e. The effectiveness of negative political advertising. Working paper, Department of Political Science, UCLA.
Ansolabehere, Stephen, Shanto Iyengar, Adam Simon, and Nicolaus Valentino. 1993. Does attack advertising demobilize the electorate? Paper presented at the annual meeting of the American Political Science Association, September 2–5, Washington, D.C.
Bartels, Larry. 1993. Messages received: The political impact of media exposure. *American Political Science Review* 87:1–24.

Basil, Michael, Caroline Schooler, and Byron Reeves. 1991. Positive and negative political advertising: Effectiveness of ads and perceptions of candidates. In *Television and political advertising*. Vol.1, *Psychological processes,* ed. Frank Biocca. Hillsdale, N.J.: Lawrence Erlbaum Associates.

Berelson, Bernard, Paul Lazarsfeld, and William McPhee. 1954. *Voting: A study of public opinion formation in a presidential campaign.* Chicago: University of Chicago Press.

Biocca, Frank, ed. 1991. *Television and political advertising.* Vol. 2, *Signs, codes, and images.* Hillsdale, N.J.: Lawrence Erlbaum Associates.

Bode, Ken. 1992. Pull the plug: Empower the voters. *The Quill* 80:10–14.

Broder, David. 1990. Five ways to put some sanity back in elections. *Washington Post,* 14 January 1990, B1.

Campbell, Angus, Philip Converse, Warren Miller, and Donald Stokes. 1960. *The American voter.* Chicago: University of Chicago Press.

Campbell, Donald, and James Stanley. 1966. *Experimental and quasi-experimental designs for research.* New York: Rand-McNally.

Copeland, Gary, and Karen Johnson-Cartee. 1990. The acceptance of negative political advertising in the South and political efficacy and activity levels. Working paper, University of Oklahoma, Norman.

Crocker, Royce. 1989. Registration and turnout, 1948–1988. Congressional Research Service Report 89–179. Washington, D.C.: CRS.

Dennis, Everette E. 1992. *The media and Campaign 92.* New York: Freedom Forum Media Studies Center.

Diamond, Edwin, and Stephen Bates. 1992. *The spot: The rise of political advertising on television,* 3d ed. Cambridge: MIT Press.

Fiorina, Morris. 1981. *Retrospective voting in American national elections.* New Haven, Conn.: Yale University Press.

Franklin, Charles. 1991. Eschewing obfuscation? Campaigning and the perception of U.S. Senate incumbents. *American Political Science Review* 85:1193–1214.

Fritz, Sarah, and Dwight Morris. 1992. *The handbook of campaign spending.* Washington, D.C.: Congressional Quarterly Press.

Garramone, Gina. 1983. Issue versus image orientation and effects of political advertising. *Communication Research* 10:59–76.

Garramone, Gina. 1984. Voter response to negative political ads. *Journalism Quarterly* 61:250–59.

Garramone, Gina. 1985. Effects of negative political advertising: The roles of sponsor and rebuttal. *Journal of Broadcasting and Electronic Media* 29:147–59.

Garramone, Gina, Charles Atkin, Bruce Pinkleton, and Richard Cole. 1990. Effects of negative political advertising on the political process. *Journal of Broadcast and Electronic Media* 34:299–311.

Geiger, Seth, and Byron Reeves. 1991. The effects of visual structure and content emphasis on the evaluation and memory for political candidates. In *Television and political advertising,* Vol.1, *Psychological processes,* ed. Frank Biocca. Hillsdale, N.J.: Lawrence Erlbaum Associates.

Germond, Jack, and Jules Witcover. 1989. *Whose broad stripes and bright stars?* New York: Simon and Schuster.

Guskind, Robert, and Jerry Hagstrom. 1988. In the gutter. *National Journal* (5 November): 2782–90.

Hovland, Carl. 1959. Reconciling conflicting results from survey and experimental studies of attitude change. *American Psychologist* 14:8–17.

Iyengar, Shanto, and Donald Kinder. 1987. *News that matters.* Chicago: University of Chicago Press.

Jacobson, Gary C. 1990. The effect of campaign spending in House elections: New evidence for an old argument. *American Journal of Political Science* 34:334–62.

Jamieson, Kathleen Hall. 1992. *Dirty politics: Deception, distraction, and democracy.* New York: Oxford University Press.

Johnson-Cartee, Karen, and Gary Copeland. 1991. *Negative political advertising: Coming of age.* Hillsdale, N.J.: Lawrence Erlbaum Associates.

Kaid, Lynda. 1981. Political advertising. In *The handbook of political communication,* ed. Dan Nimmo and K. R. Sanders. Beverly Hills, Calif.: Sage.

Kaid, Lynda, and John Boydston. 1987. An experimental study of the effectiveness of negative political advertisements. *Communication Quarterly* 35:193–201.

Kern, Montague. 1989. *Thirty-second politics: Political advertising in the eighties.* New York: Praeger.

Kern, Montague, Darrell West, and Dean Alger. 1993. Adwatch journalism. Paper presented at the annual meeting of the American Political Science Association, September 2–5, Washington, D.C.

Key, V. O., Jr. 1966. *The responsible electorate.* New York: Vintage Books.

Kosterman, Richard. 1991. *Political spot advertising and routes to persuasion.* Ph.D. diss., Department of Psychology, UCLA.

Lazarsfeld, Paul, Bernard Berelson, and Hazel Gaudet. 1948. *The people's choice: How the voter makes up his mind in a presidential campaign.* New York: Columbia University Press.

Mayer, William. 1993. In defense of negative campaigning. Paper presented at the annual meeting of the American Political Science Association, September 2–5, Washington, D.C.

Muehling, Darrel, Donald Stem, and Peter Raven. 1989. Comparative advertising. *Journal of Advertising Research* (October-November), 38–48.

Neale, Thomas. 1991. Negative campaign in national politics: An overview. Congressional Research Service Report 91-775GOV, 18 September 1991. Washington, D.C.: CRS.

Patterson, Thomas E., and Robert D. McClure. 1973. *Political advertising: Voter reaction to televised political commercials.* New York: G. P. Putnam.

Patterson, Thomas E., and Robert D. McClure. 1976. *The unseeing eye.* New York: G. P. Putnam.

Petrocik, John. 1991. The theory of issue ownership. Working paper, Department of Political Science, UCLA.

Pfau, Michael, and Michael Burgoon. 1988. Inoculation in political campaign communication. *Human Communication Research* 15:91–111.

Pfau, Michael, and Henry Kenski. 1990. *Attack advertising: Strategy and defense.* New York: Praeger.

Price, Vincent, and John Zaller. 1992. Who gets the news? Predicting news reception and its impact. Working paper, Department of Political Science, University of Michigan.

Rosenstiel, Thomas. 1993. *Strange bedfellows: How television and the presidential candidates changed American politics, 1992.* New York: Hyperion Books.

Rosenstone, Steven. 1983. *Forecasting presidential elections.* New Haven, Conn.: Yale University Press.

Rothschild, Michael. 1978. Political advertising: A neglected policy issue in marketing. *Journal of Marketing Research* 15:58–71.

Sabato, Larry. 1981. *The rise of political consultants: New ways of winning elections.* New York: Basic Books.

Schleuder, Joan, Maxwell McCombs, and Wayne Wanta. 1991. Inside the agenda setting process: How political advertising and television news prime viewers to think about issues and candidates. In *Television and Political Advertising, Vol. 1, Psychological Processes,* ed. Frank Biocca. Hillsdale, N.J.: Lawrence Erlbaum Associates.

Schwartz, Tony. 1972. *The responsive chord.* Garden City, N.J.: Anchor.

Shyles, Thomas. 1986. Content of political spot ads. *Journalism Quarterly* 50:102–118.

Sniderman, Paul, Richard Brody, and Philip Tetlock. 1993. *Reasoning and choice: Explorations in political psychology.* New York: Cambridge University Press.

Tufte, Edward. 1978. *Political control of the economy.* Princeton, N.J.: Princeton University Press.

U.S. House. 1991. Committee on Energy and Commerce. Hearing on Campaign Advertising. 102nd Cong., 1st sess. 13 June.

Westlye, Mark. 1991. *Senate elections and campaign intensity.* Baltimore, Md.: Johns Hopkins University Press.

Part 2.
Persuasion by Political Elites

CHAPTER 5

It's a Matter of Interpretation

James H. Kuklinski and Norman L. Hurley

Political communication and attitude change are once again becoming active areas of research among students of public opinion, as this volume attests. One need not look far to find other telling indicators—Sniderman, Brody, and Tetlock's *Reasoning and Choice* (1991) and Zaller's *The Nature and Origins of Mass Opinion* (1992), for example. The reemergence of these topics represents more than a simple return to the research calendar of the 1950s. To be sure, the central query, how elite-generated information influences ordinary citizens' political judgments, has not changed. But contemporary researchers have begun to identify nuances and subtleties that their predecessors never even pondered.

Consider the closely related but nonetheless distinct aspects of the political communication process that scholars have recently brought under scrutiny. Reminiscent of Schattschneider (1960), some have explored how the presentation of issues and political conditions by elites influences citizens' evaluations of them (Iyengar 1991; Kinder and Sanders 1990; Sniderman et al. 1991). Others have asked whether elites, in emphasizing some issues over others, render the former more immediately consequential to the political decisions that citizens make (Iyengar and Kinder 1987; Krosnick and Kinder 1990). Preceding and following chapters in this volume illustrate the sophistication that researchers have brought to bear on these questions. The principal conclusion is that political elites—elected officials, activists, or members of the media—can define the dimensions of political issues (what psychologists call framing) and increase the salience of some issues vis-à-vis others (what psychologists call priming). In both instances, as long as ordinary citizens are listening and watching, the effects on mass judgments appear to be substantial.

Zaller (1992) takes yet a different tack and presents compelling evidence that the *configuration* of elite discourse sets a frame of reference for citizens. Using a combination of newspapers and magazines and National Election Study surveys, he finds that when elites uphold a clear picture of what should be done, the public tends to see events from that point of view, with the most politically attentive members of the public most likely to adopt the elite position. When elites divide, members of the public tend to follow the elites sharing their general ideological or partisan predisposition, with the most politically attentive members of the public mirroring most sharply the ideological divisions among the elite. (8–9)

Although his measure of elite discourse is self-admittedly crude (for the most part a dichotomous variable that indicates whether or not there is elite consensus) and his definition of *elites* a bit imprecise, Zaller presents numerous cross-sectional and longitudinal analyses to support his contention that the way elites line up on an issue sways people to prefer one position or another. And it is primarily political ideology, he argues, that facilitates this elite-mass connection.

That citizens form preferences on the basis of how elites are collectively configured, what they say, and how they say it has (inevitably?) generated an associated question: Just how real are mass preferences? This question has its roots in Converse's field-defining research on mass belief systems (1964, 1970); but the recurrent finding that people's preferences can be moved around, demonstrated most recently and most convincingly in experimental and experimental-survey settings, has once again thrust the issue to the fore of public opinion research.

We use this opportunity both to contribute to the growing literature on political communication and persuasion and to explore further the nature of mass attitudes. Beginning with the premise that political communications are inherently open to interpretation, we focus more heavily than other researchers have done on how citizens translate the elite cues that come their way. What most research implicitly assumes, that elite messages flow inexorably and unalterably into the auditory canals of a listening citizenry, we take as the focus of our inquiry.

The All-Pervasiveness of Interpretation

Interpretation pervades all aspects of life and occurs constantly. A student walks into a faculty member's office but receives no immediate recognition. The student concludes that the faculty member doesn't want to be interrupted right now; or that she failed to notice him; or that she dislikes students. Situations, events, and, most important to us, words often lack fixed meaning, which opens the door to interpretation.

In a series of groundbreaking experiments conducted more than 40 years ago, Asch (1952) demonstrated the influence of context on how people interpret even simple statements. The experimenter asked subjects to read and interpret a statement attributed to one author; immediately thereafter they reconsidered the same words as made by another. Asked if the statement's meaning had changed, a clear majority answered in the affirmative. For any particular source, moreover, different people interpreted the same statement differently. People, Asch concluded, attribute meaning to words and sentences as they arise in a specific situation. And this meaning will vary across individuals.

Why is it that a change in the source leads the same people to alter their interpretations of the same words; and why do different people interpret identical statements from the same source differently? The answer lies with two psychological processes even more fundamental than interpretation: categorization and attribution. Lakoff (1987, 6; the classic work is Rosch 1973, 1978) nicely captures the essence and importance of the former:

> There is nothing more basic than categorization to our thought, perception, action, and speech. Every time we see something as a *kind* of thing, for example, a tree, we are categorizing. Whenever we reason about *kinds* of things—chairs, nations, illnesses, emotions, any kind of thing at all—we are employing categories. . . . Without the ability to categorize, we could not function at all, either in the physical world or in our social and intellectual lives. An understanding of how we categorize is central to any understanding of how we think and how we function, and therefore central to an understanding of what makes us human.

People categorize along all kinds of lines—parent-child, student-teacher, lawyer-client, pretty-ugly. Largely cognitive, automatic, and unconscious, categorization often evokes affect. This occurs most frequently when people place themselves into a "we" and others into a "they" category. The classic example, racial classification, fosters stereotyping, which in turn colors intergroup perceptions and evokes negative feelings toward out-group members. Mental categorization necessarily and strongly influences what people see and hear.

Attribution research has found that people use causal analyses to understand events involving others' behavior (Heider 1958; Jones and Davis 1965; Kelley 1967). A key element of these sometimes implicit, sometimes explicit analyses is the attribution of motives; why did so-and-so act the way he did? In attributing motives to others' behavior, people gain stability in their understanding of the world and thus an enhanced feeling of control. Weiner's work (1979, 1982, 1985, 1986), especially, posits that specific emotional responses accompany the causal analyses that people make. Black people on welfare who attribute their plight to a white capitalist society will feel anger, those who blame themselves, guilt.

A simple example will demonstrate how categorization and attribution jointly influence one's interpretation. An environmentalist listening to a corporate executive contend that automobile manufacturers cannot meet a newly proposed emission standard without massive layoffs will (angrily) "hear" the plea as yet another effort to maintain high profit levels at the expense of the environment. An auto plant worker might (fearfully) "hear" the executive's statement as a bona fide attempt to save jobs. Both the environmentalist and the plant worker are categorizing, although along very different lines. For the former, the salient distinction is environmentalists versus corporate polluters; for the latter, employees of the organization versus enemies outside.

If categorization, attribution, and thus interpretation occur in everyday life, they most certainly must condition what ordinary citizens "hear" when elected officials make public statements. Suppose an inner-city black person, in this example a woman, hears the words, "we must get tough on inner-city crime." What she could *possibly* "hear" is: "they're sincerely trying to increase the safety of my neighborhood;" or "they're going after drug pushers;" or "they're putting more police in white neighborhoods;" or "they're declaring war on black teenagers;" or "they're blaming blacks for most or all of societal crime." What she *likely* will "hear" depends on a combination of who spoke the words and how our black resident divides up the world. Suppose she categorizes along racial lines, that is, she places people into an in-group (black people) and an out-group (white people). Then the first two interpretations would comport more, say, with Jesse Jackson's plea for reducing inner-city crime than Jesse Helms's, the latter three more with Helms's.

Political statements arise in a social context and concern real-world problems. It follows that people will focus on a statement's pragmatic meaning, that is, *why* it was said, and not its semantic meaning alone. The pragmatic meaning people assign depends on the interaction between their own outlooks and the characteristics and reputation of the political source.

An Empirical Example

Thus far we have asserted the obvious. Anyone who has listened to coworkers the morning after a presidential speech knows that people routinely interpret political events and statements; one sometimes wonders whether they all listened to the same president. When we began the study now to be summarized, we did not anticipate what we were to find: citizens can interpret elite cues in a way that renders them vulnerable to errors in judgment.

In the spring of 1992, we asked white and African-American subjects

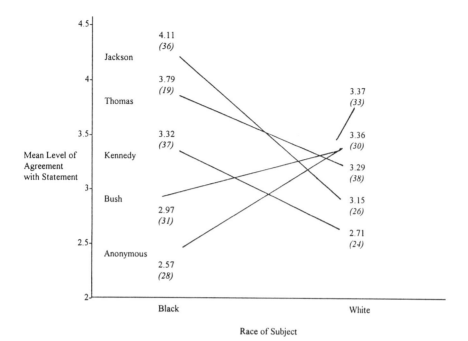

Fig. 1. Stance on black self-reliance by source of statement and race of subject (*N*s in parentheses).

chosen from the Chicago metropolitan area to complete a four-page questionnaire that included this item:[1]

> We would like to get your reaction to a statement that _____ recently made. He was quoted in *The New York Times* as saying that "African-Americans must stop making excuses and rely much more on themselves to get ahead in society." Please indicate how much you agree or disagree with _____'s statement.

The ostensible source of the assertion was either white conservative George Bush, black conservative Clarence Thomas, black liberal Jesse Jackson, or white liberal Ted Kennedy. Subjects were randomly assigned to one of the four sources, and a fifth group received the statement without attribution.

Figure 1 presents the findings that we initially found puzzling. Contrary to our expectations, black subjects displayed considerable elasticity in their attitudes on self-reliance; *who* purportedly advanced the idea strongly condi-

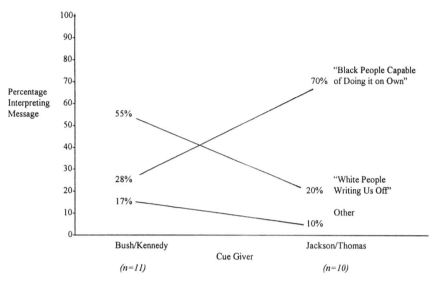

Fig. 2. Relationship between race of cue giver and interpretations of hypothetical *New York Times* statement.

tioned their agreement with it. Moreover, it was not Jackson and Kennedy, two of the most visible leaders of black civil rights during the 1970s and 1980s, who exerted positive influence, but Jackson and Thomas, who have been adversaries ever since Thomas's ascent. In other words, blacks deemed the *race* of the political figure, not his ideology, to be the relevant contextual information (Zaller 1992). In contrast, white subjects voiced the same level of support for black self-reliance irrespective of who proposed it.

So what's going on here, especially among African-Americans? How could they be equally persuaded by two black leaders who stand worlds apart on most issues that affect black citizens' lives? Upon further exploration, we identified two processes that help to explain the patterns. First, some black subjects appeared to hear the messenger but not the message. They based their judgments largely on whether they liked and trusted the political figure and, as measured by recall, paid scant attention to what he had said. Most black subjects expressed strong affection for both Thomas and Jackson, and this racially based bond led them unthinkingly to agree with the statement when it came from either of these black figures. Others, a larger number, did absorb the message, then interpreted it on the basis of the source's skin color (fig. 2). Specifically, when either Bush or Kennedy purportedly made the statement, black subjects overwhelmingly construed it to mean that "white people are writing us off." But when the call for black self-reliance allegedly came from

Thomas or Jackson, a striking 70 percent interpreted it as "we black people can do it on our own."

The following conclusions summarize our central findings:

1. On an issue as seemingly easy to understand and as relevant to African-Americans as black self-reliance, subjects did not show the kind of attitude stability we had predicted.
2. Their reactions to the statement varied widely as a function of which political leader advocated it.
3. The political figure's skin color, not his ideology and past civil rights record, explains this variance; statements emanating from Thomas or Jackson increased support for black self-reliance much more than those from Bush or Kennedy.
4. This influence occurred in one of two ways: (1) subjects agreed with the statement despite not absorbing it solely because they felt a strong affection toward the two black politicians; or, (2) they "heard" a plea for black pride and self-confidence from Thomas and Jackson and a harsh rejection from Bush and Kennedy.

At least among the African-Americans in our study, what they heard, when they heard the message at all, depended on the race of the messenger.

And therein lie the vulnerabilities. Strongly bonded to the two black leaders, our subjects did not always absorb or, if they did, effectively use both pieces of pertinent information: who conveyed the message and the content of the message itself. Some stopped attending once they knew the source. In other words, they acted as McGuire's "lazy organism" (1969, 198), who "tries to master the message contents only when it is absolutely necessary to make a decision. When the purported source is clearly positively or negatively valenced, he uses this information as a cue to accept or reject the message's conclusions without really absorbing the arguments used." When subjects did hear the message, they used skin color rather than political reputation as the relevant contextual information. Gut-level feelings for the political figure, steeped in demographic rather than ideological similarity, outweighed serious evaluation of the proposition's meaning in light of the source. What our black subjects "heard" does not comport with what we know about the ideological structure of national politics and the place of the four political figures in it.[2]

But it does comport with the psychological processes that we outlined earlier. Our black subjects obviously categorized the political officials along racial lines, which makes sense. Given the strong group identification among African-Americans, black-white is a natural and chronically accessible categorization scheme (Bargh 1984; Bargh, Lombardi, and Higgins 1988). It is a small step from black-white categorization to the kinds of attributions our subjects made.

Let us not be misunderstood. We are not suggesting, in the specific case of black citizens, that there is something inherently wrong in looking to political figures of the same race for relevant cues. Most of the time, we suspect, this heuristic serves the black community well. But uncovering even one (important) exception has led us to wonder how widespread the pitfalls of cue taking might be. Let us now turn to this question, after which we will consider what the presence of interpretation implies for the nature of mass attitudes.

Politics and Interpretation

Citizens function as effective cue takers when they make valid inferences from the communications that elites provide them. Skeptics might view our empirical results as weak support for the claim that people sometimes make *in*valid inferences; indeed, they might question our own inference. So perhaps two additional examples will help reveal further the potential pitfalls of cue taking. Whereas our original study focused narrowly on citizens' interpretations of a single statement, these examples look more broadly at the dynamics of the political system within which citizens take cues.

As we write, the nation is contemplating universal health coverage. Suppose that the American Medical Association (AMA) vociferously opposes such coverage, especially as President Clinton has proposed it. Joe Citizen, who believes the AMA to be motivated solely by greed and increased profits, therefore concludes that the Clinton plan cannot be all bad. When pollsters ask him whether he supports the plan, he answers yes. Of course, an initial proposal rarely remains intact; to garner sufficient support, the administration quietly adds, deletes, and amends provisions to render the concept increasingly palatable to the powerful medical profession. The latter, having gained major concessions, in turn quietly rescinds its strong opposition. Unaware of these dynamics, Joe Citizen continues to voice support, even though he would oppose the amended plan if he had better information.

Mary Citizen also follows the debate. A single mother, she would benefit from a provision to support child care for the children of single women. However, learning that the National Organization for Women (NOW) opposes the plan (in actuality, Clinton *did* include such a provision and NOW *did* appear to oppose the general proposal), she follows suit. Although generally supportive of the president's plan, NOW publicly opposes it solely for one reason: it fails to fund abortions. Given only two alternatives, accept the Clinton proposal or reject national health care, NOW would certainly choose the former. By publicly voicing opposition now, the organization hopes to gain additional concessions.

These examples drive home two ideas. First, elites often behave strategically rather than sincerely, sending signals that reveal more about the politics than the substance of a policy initiative. Members of Congress, interest groups, and other concerned actors convey not facts but their interpretations of them; and these interpretations vary as strategic goals vary. In other words, political elites' words characterize the world as the communicators want others to see it; they are not a logically derived and veridical expression of the facts.[3] Second, only the most astute observers of national politics will attend to and decipher all the relevant elite cues, and then only if they monitor continuously. To interject a personal note in this regard, one of us has closely followed Alain Enthoven's work on managed competition, a concept that the Clinton administration wholeheartedly endorsed during the presidential campaign. Lacking access to the news one day, he missed Enthoven's public denouncement of the administration's health plan and thus critical information that Clinton had slowly but deliberately replaced managed competition with cost ceilings.

This all goes to say that the world of mass politics is socially constructed, twice over, and therefore interpretation and all its potential pitfalls enter the representational equation twice. Citizens-as-cue-takers take elites' constructions, if they hear them at all, and then add their own by "hearing" one thing rather than another. Edelman puts it well (1988, 95, emphasis added):

> [i]nterpretation pervades every phase of news creation and dissemination. Officials, interest groups, and critics anticipate the interpretations of particular audiences, shaping their acts and language so as to elicit a desired response. The audiences for news are ultimate interpreters, paying attention to some stories, ignoring most, and fitting news accounts into a story plot that reflects their respective values. *For any audience, then, an account is an interpretation of an interpretation.*

In a public life where rhetoric and language reign supreme, elites strategically use words to convey a meaning that will garner support for their positions. Sometimes citizens don't hear the words, in which case the intended meaning is lost. When they do hear, they may interpret the words in any of a variety of ways. The interpretations they apply, in turn, influence the issue positions they take.

There is not always as much slippage in the cue taking process as we have portrayed here. Elites act strategically, but not without constraint. People interpret elites' statements, but not just randomly. Nonetheless, the mere existence of two layers of interpretation adds more noise to the elite-citizen linkage than advocates of cue taking have been wont to recognize. Ironically, while the focus on political interpretation led us to discover some heretofore unrecognized shortcomings of cue taking, so did it lead us to see the reality of political attitudes, a topic to which we now turn.

Are Mass Political Preferences Real?

Suppose social scientists discovered a new method that allowed them to probe into people's minds and directly observe political attitudes, just as a brain surgeon might see a patient's cerebral cortex. They could then say with certainty whether political attitudes exist, when they first become a mental reality, and what form they take. Lacking this option, researchers employ survey instruments that may create the very preferences they purportedly measure.

Unable to observe without intrusion, scholars have become embroiled in a debate about the nature of public opinion; are attitudes real or not? The controversy centers on what appears to be a lack of attitude stability. Survey research demonstrates that preferences change across time, experimental research that they change across conditions. But should political scientists take this apparent instability as evidencing an absence of real preferences? More to the point, what does an interpretation perspective add in the way of an answer to this question?

Those working in the survey tradition have equated nonattitudes with what they see as random change in preferences across time. The classic work, as we noted at the outset of this chapter, is Converse's (1964, 1970). In two of the most important pieces ever written on the subject, Converse uses his black-and-white model to estimate that less than 20 percent of the mass public hold real and stable political attitudes. Of the remaining 80 percent, Converse argues, a few confess to no opinion, while the great majority fabricate one on the spot. Scholars subsequently challenged Converse's assertion, but *not* his assumption that instability reflects nonattitudes. In an influential critique, for example, Achen (1975) takes the instability-equals-nonattitudes assumption as given and revisits Converse's panel study to show that much of the instability lies with unreliable questionnaire items. The remaining instability, he concludes, captures nonattitudes.

Although experimental studies have also identified shifts in attitudes, in this case across manipulations, the authors have not consistently or unanimously concluded that people lack real political attitudes. Consider Zaller's imaginative, two-wave study (1992), in which he examines what goes through people's minds immediately before or after they answer a typical National Election Studies (NES) issue question. He shows that people answer these items on the basis of what happens to be at the top of their minds at the moment; and these "considerations" change as a function of elite debate or the survey instrument itself. Zaller concludes (93–94) that "individuals do not typically possess 'true attitudes' on [political] issues. . . . [T]hey may be expressing real feelings . . . but the thrust of my argument [is] to deny the existence of any . . . true position. . . ."[4] His work draws heavily on an emerging psychological literature that views nearly all attitudes as temporary constructions (see Martin and Tesser 1992 for a summary).[5] Underlying this view is an assumption that people can tap into a large data base when forming attitudes, and what subset they use determines their preferences at any particular moment.

Demonstrating that political scientists are not immune to the very phenomenon he uncovered, Zaller himself apparently uses a different subset of considerations when he returns to the same data and reinterprets his results. In an important article that appeared later in the same year as his book, he and Feldman (1992, 611–12) now reach this verdict:

> We agree . . . that there is a great deal of uncertainty, tentativeness, and incomprehension in the typical mass survey response. The problem, we further agree, is much deeper than vague questions. And yet . . . we reject the premise . . . that most response fluctuation is due to essentially random guessing by people who have no meaningful opinions.
>
> Our claim is that even when people exhibit high levels of response instability, the opinions they express may still be based on real considerations. Even when these considerations turn out to be transitory, the opinion statements they generate are not, for that reason, necessarily lacking in authenticity.

Our objective here is not to characterize Zaller as ambivalent (though he may be) or inconsistent. It is to underline that even someone who has studied attitude change in the depth that he has cannot easily decide what inferences to draw from it. Perhaps attitude change implies nonattitudes, perhaps it does not. In any event, Zaller's revised position, especially, serves two valuable functions. It challenges the assumption that what looks like random change in panel surveys reflects a lack of real attitudes;[6] and it construes "public opinion" as a multilayered phenomenon, including people's directional preferences but also the considerations underlying them. Only by peeling off the top layer, the layer that NES-type issue questions measure, can one begin to see the reality of public opinion.

Sniderman, Tetlock, and Tyler (1993) go further. They contend that change often occurs *because* people possess attitudes. It is true, they say, that a person who says one thing in one circumstance and another thing in others may hold only superficial views. But it is also true that the shift may reflect a reaction to the changed situation. To support their proposition, they present evidence that when the researcher takes both individual dispositions and situational characteristics into account, the change in expressed preferences often makes sense. In one example, they present respondents with this situation: The police see two youths walking near a house where police know drugs are being sold. Respondents are told either that the youths are *well dressed and well behaved* or are *using foul language*. Sniderman et al. find that both the respondents' degree of conventionality (i.e., their support for order, obedience, and authority) and the characterization of the perpetrators help explain people's willingness to allow a police search of the youths. More important, even though attitudes change as the situation changes, the rank order remains intact: the stronger an individual's commitment to conventionality, the more likely that he or she will support a police search. What might be interpreted as evidence of fickle attitudes—after all, slight changes in question wording did shift expressed preferences—is in fact meaningful change.

Zaller (with and without Feldman) and Sniderman et al. make a significant contribution to the nonattitude literature. Rather than take change as evidence of nonattitudes, they try to uncover what lies behind it. They concur that it is the *presence* of attitudes that explains the change. These attitudes may not be the directional issue preferences that pollsters often ask about, but they are real, context dependent, and relevant to national politics. They also function as an important link between citizens and their elected officials.

We endorse this perspective. It would be easy to conclude, with respect to our own work, that the interpretation of elite messages and its concomitant effect on preferences demonstrate that people really do not hold true attitudes. It would be easy, but also wrong. Meaningful interpretation of political messages, that is, proper contextual interpretation, requires something akin to an attitude, "a mediating variable . . . [that] intervenes between an observable stimulus and an observable response, providing the necessary link" (Fiske and Taylor 1991, 462). Our black subjects, for example, clearly began with the premise that black politicians pursue their interests more faithfully than white politicians do. Whether accurate or not, this presumption functions as a critical linkage between what a particular politician says and what an individual citizen concludes. It remains constant, even though the preferences it generates vary as a function of political context.

We find it useful to think of premises as anchors or starting values (Tversky and Kahneman 1974); they are the stable component of political attitudes. There is also a movable component, which for some reflects nonattitudes and for others varies systematically as a function of contextual or situational factors.[7] In focusing on directional preferences, researchers see the movement but not the stability. Nor do they distinguish the two types of movement, that arising from nonattitudes versus that arising from reactions to context.

But, one might argue, the kinds of directional preferences that the National Election Studies and other national surveys measure are much closer to the meat of politics. Knowing where people stand on a guaranteed standard of living gives politicians more policy direction than knowing that black people overwhelmingly place their faith in black politicians. Moreover, when people know where they stand, they can more effectively evaluate proposed policies. Therefore, identifying people's directional preferences, and their consistency, must be the staple of scholarly research.

These arguments miss the mark. As we write, Congress is considering what the *New York Times* recently described as "bringing the communications laws into the digital age" (Andrews 1994). One can easily imagine a national poll asking people if Congress should encourage a national information infrastructure. Supposing that most people answer yes, what does the survey result tell members of Congress? While conveying general, ill-defined support for the idea, it communicates little policy-relevant information. Take the three proposals that Congress is now considering (see table 1). Nothing in "public opinion" as the survey measures it tells congressional members what course of action to pursue. If they are acting strategically, sponsors of all three bills will interpret majority sentiment as support for their positions. In this

TABLE 1. Pending Congressional Bills on Communications Networks

Brooks-Dingell Bill	Markey-Fields Bill	Hollings Bill
Bell companies could enter long-distance business upon approval of the Justice Department and the F.C.C. Bell companies could offer long-distance service inside their regions immediately, resell services from other carriers outside their own regions after 18 months, and build their own national networks after 5 years. Bell companies would be free to manufacture equipment.	Phone companies could provide cable TV over their networks but would be forced to open their networks to competing phone companies and video programmers. A joint federal-state regulatory board would make sure phone service remained affordable in remote areas.	Combines elements of two preceding bills. Phone companies could compete in long distance, but only if they convinced the F.C.C. that they faced "actual and demonstrable competition." Phone companies could enter the video market in exchange for letting other companies enter the local phone business. A new "universal service" fund would keep the price of basic phone service low. The F.C.C. would review restrictions on TV broadcasters, including rules that limit the number of stations a single company can own.

instance, as in many others (national health care or welfare reform, for example), mass affirmation of a policy direction falls short of a mandate for a specific policy decision.

Moreover, consider those citizens who express support for a communications infrastructure. It does not follow that they now can weigh the merits of one proposal vis-à-vis the others; chances are good that they cannot. Yet which proposal Congress adopts will affect people's lives for decades to come (let alone advantage some interests over others). Directional preferences, even if students of public opinion could agree they are real, do not straightforwardly function as validity checks on the policy action that really counts,[8] except to the extent that citizens effectively interpret elite cues and update their preferences as congressional deliberation proceeds. But this brings us right back to premises and considerations, the second and relatively neglected layer of public opinion.

With respect to individual attitudes, then, our conclusion goes something like this. Studies that uncover change in people's directional preferences and equate it with nonattitudes miss the mark. People hold real attitudes, even though typical survey questions indicate otherwise; this is so because these attitudes take the form of premises and considerations, not directional preferences. To those who argue that the former do not constitute public opinion, we would only point to the necessity of cue taking in large-scale political systems; people cannot function as informed citizens without it. Since premises and considerations form the basis for cue taking, they are a large part of public opinion. In a very real sense, people's political premises and considerations may be more closely linked to elites' policy decisions than their directional preferences are.

Interpretation and Collective Preferences

A recent and provocative theme in public opinion research is that while individual-level preferences lack meaning, collective public opinion is both meaningful and rational. "[R]eal, knowable, differentiated, patterned and coherent" (Page and Shapiro 1992, 381), it responds predictably, systematically, and understandably to events and other relevant stimuli. We have already argued that individual-level attitudes, when construed other than directionally, appear quite real. We now explore the possibility that collective preferences may be *less* real than students of macroanalysis believe.

In their influential and important work, Page and Shapiro (1992, 384–85) identify three factors that explain why there can be meaningful collective opinion despite the lack of true attitudes among individuals. First, random measurement errors cancel out across large numbers of respondents; second, temporary opinion changes by different individuals in different directions also cancel out; and third, people rely on trusted cue givers to compensate for a lack of political information. We find the first two explanations compelling (also see Converse 1990); but unlike Page and Shapiro, we now believe, contrary to what we believed earlier, that the existence of cue taking among average citizens can render collective preferences unintelligible, even though systematic patterns in directional preferences would suggest otherwise. The reason lies with what we have been arguing throughout this chapter: interpretation pervades the cue-taking process.

Recall our earlier discussion in which we proposed five plausible interpretations of the statement, "we must get tough on inner city crime." Suppose the distribution of these interpretations among African-Americans looks like that shown in table 2. Suppose further that the top two interpretations translate into a strong preference for government action, the bottom three into weak opposition, or at least skepticism. Then when pollsters ask black Americans their directional preferences on the desirability of government action, the distribution might look like that shown in the last column of the table. This distribution underestimates the desire among blacks to do something about inner-city crime. Even those who adhere to one of the last three interpretations deem crime a problem; it is just that their interpretations of elite actions and communications leads them to state a directional preference that suggests otherwise.

More generally, sometime during a major policy debate, pollsters ask people to express their directional preferences. Most do. The aggregate result is a tidy-looking and presumably self-explanatory distribution of preferences.

TABLE 2. Distribution of Collective Preferences as a Function of Distribution of Interpretations

Elite Statement	Interpretations		Distribution of Aggregate Directional Preferences	
	"They're sincerely trying to increase the safety of my neighborhood"	(30)	Strongly Favor	(50)
"Get tough on inner city crime"	"They're going after drug pushers"	(20)	Favor	(10)
	"They're putting more police in white neighborhoods"	(20)	Oppose	(30)
	"They're declaring war on black teenagers"	(20)		
	"They're blaming blacks for most or all of societal crime"	(10)	Strongly Oppose	(10)

In reality this distribution is an amalgamation of interpretations of interpretations that public opinion surveys mask.

Concluding Comments

Political scientists look for systematic patterns in their data. Until recently, they found little evidence of them when examining individual-level attitudes. To the contrary, randomness has been the central story line. On the other hand, the predictability and seeming reasonableness of collective opinion has engendered optimism, a sense that effective democratic governance exists despite the lack of real attitudes among individuals. Indeed, this newly found hope has a familiar ring, harking back to Berelson's closing chapter in *Voting*, where he asserts that (1954, 311–12, original emphasis)

> if the democratic system depended solely on the qualifications of the individual voter, then it seems remarkable that democracies have survived through the centuries. After examining the detailed data on how individuals misperceive political reality or respond to irrelevant social influences, one wonders how a democracy ever solves its political problems. But when one considers the data in a broader perspective—how huge segments of the society adapt to political conditions affecting them or how the political system adjusts itself to changing conditions over long periods of time—he cannot fail to be impressed with the total result. Where the rational citizen seems to abdicate, nevertheless angels seem to tread. . . .
>
> [This] is the paradox. *Individual voters* today seem unable to satisfy the requirements for a democratic system of government outlined by political theorists. But the *system of democracy* does meet certain requirements for a going political organization. The individual members may not meet all the standards, but the whole nonetheless survives and grows. This suggests that where the classic theory is defective is in its concentration on the *individual citizen*. What are undervalued are certain collective properties that reside in the electorate as a whole and in the political and social system in which it functions.

We do not dispute either set of findings, individual- or collective-level, when taken on their own terms. But we began from a very different perspective, one that neither starts nor ends with directional preferences; and from this perspective, we reached conclusions that run counter to conventional wisdom. On the one hand, individual-level attitudes look alive and real, which is not to say they are always well informed, or, when used in conjunction with elite cues, always render the right political judgment. On the other hand, noise may pervade collective preferences much more than it appears, which is not to say they are meaningless.

Given the extent to which our conclusions diverge from most of the nonattitudes literature, perhaps they are just wrong. It is a thought, we admit, that has entered our minds more than once. This said, we hope we have helped change the terms on which the nonattitude debate is carried on. Public opinion in all its complexity is more than directional preferences.

Finally, studies of the sort that we have taken as our starting point inevitably raise interesting and challenging normative questions about the effectiveness of a representative democracy in which its people presumably are to have a meaningful say. Not reticent to offer their evaluations, scholars for the most part have celebrated citizens' use of elite cues as a rational and valuable means by which to become informed about national politics (Mondak 1993; Page and Shapiro 1992; Popkin 1991; Sniderman, Brody, and Tetlock 1991; Zaller 1992). Echoing this theme, one of us concluded earlier, with more than a little enthusiasm, that "[given the] constraints that preclude an informed citizenry, [cue-taking is] a mechanism by which people can still make meaningful judgments" (Carmines and Kuklinski 1990, 241). While we do not reject this conclusion, we are less sanguine now than we were then.

Interpretation pervades the cue-taking process much more than we initially recognized. That reality renders the former more complex and problematic than we thought. Unraveling the complexity and thus discovering when cue taking does and does not work is a task that should challenge scholars for a few years.

NOTES

1. See Kuklinski and Hurley (1994) for a detailed description of the study.

2. The more politically sophisticated subjects, as measured by education, relied on skin color just about as heavily as the less sophisticated ones did.

3. Even the mass media, when trying objectively to understand presidential election results, construct explanations that best meet their definition of "good news." Hershey (1992) convincingly documents this process. See Vallone, Ross, and Lepper (1985) for some related ideas.

4. We have tried to distill what we see as his primary conclusion. Yet anyone who has read Zaller's important study knows that his argument is far more nuanced than we have suggested here.

5. If one fully accepts this perspective, there may be no need to ascertain the reality of political attitudes; *all* attitudes are constructions.

6. We can offer yet another perspective that questions the advisability of equating attitude change with nonattitudes. One of us is currently building a new house. During

the past three weeks, he has changed his mind about kitchen cabinets at least 10 times. Yet he doubts that he lacks true attitudes.

7. In fact, the story is more complex still. Some people use appropriate heuristics, others do not.

8. Directional preferences can preclude legislative action by working as a veto (Key 1961; Stimson 1991).

REFERENCES

Achen, Christopher H. 1975. Mass political attitudes and the survey response. *American Political Science Review* 69:1218–31.
Andrews, Edmund L. 1994. A free-for-all in communications. *New York Times,* 4 February 1994, C1.
Asch, Solomon E. 1952. *Social psychology.* New York: Prentice-Hall.
Bargh, John A. 1984. Automatic and conscious processing of social information. *Handbook of motivation and cognition,* vol. 3., ed. Robert. S. Wyer, Jr. and Thomas K. Srull. Hillsdale, N.J.: Lawrence Erlbaum Associates.
Bargh, John A., Wendy Lombardi, and E. Tory Higgins. 1988. Automaticity of chronically accessible constructs in Person X situation effects on person perception: It's just a matter of time. *Journal of Personality and Social Psychology* 55:599–605.
Berelson, Bernard R., Paul F. Lazarsfeld, and William N. McPhee. 1954. *Voting.* Chicago: University of Chicago Press.
Carmines, Edward G., and James H. Kuklinski. 1990. Incentives, opportunities, and the logic of public opinion in American representative democracy. In *Information and democratic processes,* ed. John A. Ferejohn and James H. Kuklinski. Urbana: University of Illinois Press.
Converse, Philip E. 1964. The nature of belief systems in mass publics. In *Ideology and discontent,* ed. David E. Apter. New York: Free Press.
Converse, Philip E. 1970. Attitudes and nonattitudes: Continuation of a dialogue. In *The quantitative analysis of social problems,* ed. Edward R. Tufte. Reading, Mass.: Addison-Wesley.
Converse, Philip E. 1990. Popular representation and the distribution of information. In *Information and democratic processes,* ed. John A. Ferejohn and James H. Kuklinski. Urbana: University of Illinois Press.
Edelman, Murray J. 1988. *Constructing the political spectacle.* Chicago: University of Chicago Press.
Fiske, Susan T., and Shelley E. Taylor. 1991. *Social cognition,* 2d ed. New York: McGraw-Hill.
Heider, Fritz. 1958. *The psychology of interpersonal relations.* New York: Wiley.
Hershey, Marjorie Randon. 1992. The constructed explanation: Interpreting election results in the 1984 presidential race. *Journal of Politics* 54:943–76.
Iyengar, Shanto. 1991. *Is anyone responsible?: How television frames political issues.* Chicago: University of Chicago Press.

Iyengar, Shanto, and Donald R. Kinder. 1987. *News that matters: Television and American opinion.* Chicago: University of Chicago Press.

Jones, Edward E., and Keith E. Davis. 1965. From acts to dispositions: The attribution process in person perception. In *Advances in experimental social psychology,* vol. 2, ed. Leonard Berkowitz. New York: Academic Press.

Kelley, Harold H. 1967. Attribution theory in social psychology. In *Nebraska symposium on motivation,* vol. 15, ed. D. Levine. Lincoln: University of Nebraska Press.

Key, V. O. 1961. *Public opinion and American democracy.* New York: Knopf.

Kinder, Donald R., and Lynn M. Sanders. 1990. Mimicking political debate with survey questions: The case of white opinion on affirmation action for blacks. *Social Cognition* 8:73–103.

Krosnick, Jon A., and Donald R. Kinder. 1990. Altering the foundations of support for the president through priming. *American Political Science Review* 84:497–512.

Kuklinski, James H., and Norman L. Hurley. 1994. On hearing and interpreting political messages: A cautionary tale of citizen cue-taking. *Journal of Politics* 56: 729–751.

Lakoff, George. 1987. *Women, fire, and dangerous things: What categories reveal about the mind.* Chicago: University of Chicago Press.

Martin, Leonard L., and Abraham Tesser. 1992. *The construction of social judgments.* Hillsdale, N.J.: Lawrence Erlbaum Associates.

McGuire, William J. 1969. Nature of attitudes and attitude change. In *The handbook of social psychology,* 2d ed., vol. 3, ed., Gardner Lindzey and Elliot Aronson. Reading, Mass.: Addison-Wesley.

Mondak, Jeffery J. 1993. Source cues and policy approval: The cognitive dynamics of public support for the Reagan agenda. *American Journal of Political Science* 37:186–212.

Page, Benjamin I., and Robert Y. Shapiro. 1992. *The rational public.* Chicago: University of Chicago Press.

Popkin, Samuel L. 1991. *The reasoning voter.* Cambridge: Harvard University Press.

Rosch, Eleanor. 1973. Natural categories. *Cognitive Psychology* 4:328–50.

Rosch, Eleanor. 1978. Principles of categorization. In *Cognition and categorization,* ed. Eleanor Rosch and Barbara B. Lloyd. Hillsdale, N.J.: Lawrence Erlbaum Associates.

Schattschneider, E. E. 1960. *The semi-sovereign people: A realist's view of democracy in America.* New York: Holt, Rinehart, and Winston.

Sniderman, Paul M., Richard A. Brody, and Philip E. Tetlock. 1991. *Reasoning and choice: Explorations in political psychology.* Cambridge: Cambridge University Press.

Sniderman, Paul M., Thomas Piazza, Philip E. Tetlock, and Ann Kendrick. 1991. The new racism. *American Journal of Political Science* 35:423–47.

Sniderman, Paul M., Philip E. Tetlock, and Anthony Tyler. 1993. The dynamics of public opinion in political behavior: The interaction of individual dispositions and situational characteristics in reasoning and choice. Paper presented at the Political Psychology Conference, University of Illinois at Urbana-Champaign.

Stimson, James A. 1991. *Public opinion in America: Moods, cycles, and swings.* Boulder: Westview Press.

Tversky, Amos, and Daniel Kahneman. 1974. Judgment under uncertainty: Heuristics and biases. *Science* 185:1124–31.

Vallone, Robert P., Lee Ross, and Mark R. Lepper. 1985. The hostile media phenomenon: Biased perception and perceptions of media bias in coverage of the Beirut massacre. *Journal of Personality and Social Psychology* 49:577–85.

Weiner, Bernard. 1982. The emotional consequences of causal attributions. In *Affect and cognition: The 17th annual Carnegie symposium on cognition,* ed. Margaret S. Clark and Susan T. Fiske. Hillsdale, N.J.: Lawrence Erlbaum Associates.

Weiner, Bernard. 1985. An attributional theory of achievement motivation and emotion. *Psychological Review* 92:548–73.

Weiner, Bernard. 1986. Attribution, emotion, and action. In *Handbook of motivation and cognition,* ed. Richard M. Sorrentino and E. Tory Higgins. New York: Guilford Press.

Zaller, John R. 1992. *The nature and origins of mass opinion.* Cambridge: Cambridge University Press.

Zaller, John, and Stanley Feldman. 1992. A simple theory of the survey response: Answering questions versus revealing preferences. *American Journal of Political Science* 36:579–616.

CHAPTER 6

Some of the People Some of the Time: Individual Differences in Acceptance of Political Accounts

Kathleen M. McGraw and Clark Hubbard

Successful democratic politicians . . . advance politically only as they placate, appease, bribe, seduce, bamboozle, or otherwise manage to manipulate the demanding and threatening elements in their constituencies.
— Walter Lippmann (1955)

Few would disagree with the assertion that success in the playing field of politics requires successful mastery of the art of persuasion—the strategies of placating, appeasement, bribery, seduction, bamboozlement, and manipulation to which Lippmann referred. Despite the patently obvious nature of this assertion, however, the systematic empirical study of persuasion has not had a great deal of influence in contemporary analyses of political behavior, a situation no doubt due in part to the conclusion of "minimal effects" attributed to the mass media in the 1960s (Klapper, 1960; see Kinder and Sears 1985 for a review). However, just as the study of the impact of the mass media is currently in a period of ascendancy and theoretical refinement (Iyengar and Kinder 1987; Iyengar 1991), so too should our more general understanding of political persuasion be systematically advanced.

Taking this prescription seriously has important implications for how we go about the science of politics. One of the oldest fields of academic inquiry, tracing its roots at least back to Aristotle, the study of persuasion has yielded a rich array of conceptual frameworks and an impressive body of scientific knowledge (see Perloff 1993; Pratkanis and Aronson 1992; and Zimbardo and Leippe 1991 for excellent and accessible overviews). As a result, the scholar interested in political persuasion has a well-established foundation upon which to build.

The serious study of political persuasion also holds promise for bridging two areas of scholarship that unfortunately tend to be treated as distinct: the study of the mass public and the study of elites.[1] This intellectual divide is artificial at best and substantively misleading at worst, because in reality, the links between elite discourse and mass political attitude formation and change are critical components of political behavior and democratic life. Conceptualization of the elite discourse—mass political attitude linkages within a persuasion theoretical framework forces us to take seriously the strategies elites use in formulating their communications, the processes by which the mass public is—and is not—persuaded, and the consequences for public opinion and electoral support. More generally, viewing elite discourse as persuasion provides a window into the complex dynamics and interplay between public officials and the constituents they serve (Graber 1976).

Our interest in elite discourse has been concerned with a particular type of communication: the explanations that public officials provide to account for their involvement in some sort of predicament— controversial roll call votes or scandalous or corrupt behavior—that results in criticism or disapproval from some valued audience (most obviously constituents, but also the media and colleagues). These explanations, or "blame-management strategies" (McGraw 1991) are a critical weapon in the strategic repertoire of politicians (Jacobson and Kernell 1983), aimed at containing the political fallout from the predicament. In other words, politicians are assumed to be concerned with maintaining the approval of their constituents because reelection is a dominant goal (Mayhew 1974), and explanations or accounts are instrumental in attaining that goal (see McGraw 1990, 1991, forthcoming; McGraw, Best, and Timpone 1995; McGraw, Timpone, and Bruck 1993, for further elaboration on these points).

Is it reasonable to conceptualize political accounts as a type of persuasive communication? Many definitions of persuasion exist, and Perloff's (1993, 14) synthesis is a good one: "Persuasion is an activity or process in which a communicator attempts to induce a change in the belief, attitude, or behavior of another person or group of persons through the transmission of a message in a context in which the persuadee has some degree of free choice." Political accounts map onto this definition nicely: they are verbal attempts by public officials to shape or change public opinion.

Officials have creative leeway in constructing accounts because a variety of different types of accounts exist. However, there is widespread agreement among account theorists that four types are fundamental (Cody and McLaughlin 1990; Gonzales et al. 1990, 1992; Schlenker 1980; Schlenker and Wiegold 1992; Schonbach 1990; Scott and Lyman 1968; Tedeschi and Reiss 1980; Tetlock 1985). *Concessions* involve an acknowledgment that the offense has occurred and implicit or explicit assumption of responsibility for the event; concessions often include expressions of regret and apologies. *Excuses* acknowledge that the offense occurred but involve a denial of full or partial responsibility. *Justifications,* in contrast, are characterized by an admission of responsibility but also an attempt to deny or minimize the undesirable nature of the act. Finally, *denials* or *refusals* involve a denial that the offense occurred and occasionally a condemnation of the other party's right to reproach. In our own work to date on accounting for controversial roll call votes, we have focused on the two types of accounts that occur most commonly, across a variety of domains, political and otherwise: excuses and justifications (Austin 1961; Bennett 1980; Cody and McLaughlin 1990). The studies we describe subsequently are similarly concerned with the effectiveness of excuses and justifications in accounting for controversial or unpopular policy votes.

Several theoretical frameworks for studying persuasion processes are available. McGuire's (1985) "input-output matrix" for the analysis of persuasive communication is a particularly useful framework for the study of political persuasion. McGuire's comprehensive and detailed model is a useful heuristic or "directive structure" (McGuire 1985) that points to the many critical aspects of persuasive communications that ought to be considered by any serious student of persuasion. The input component of the matrix points to the important factors that characterize any persuasive communication, organized along the classic view of communication as "who says what, via what medium, to whom, with what effect" (Lasswell 1948). In other words, five broad classes of variables are considered inputs: the source, the message, the channel, the receiver, and the targeted attitude.

The output component of the matrix consists of the chain of mediating responses that must occur if the communication is to have its desired impact. McGuire has provided shorter and longer lists of these output steps (McGuire 1966, 1978, 1985). For our purposes, the steps that are necessary for successful persuasion can be summarized as: (1) the recipients (constituents) must be *exposed* to the communication (the account); (2) they must pay *attention* to it; (3) they must *comprehend* it; and (4) they must *accept* the explanation as legitimate and credible.[2] If these four processes occur, attitude change should result. The fourth step, acceptance (or as it is frequently referred to, "yielding") is critical, because a citizen must be satisfied with a politician's explanation for it to have its desired ameliorative impact. Given the centrality of acceptance in effective persuasion, it is not surprising that our previous research has consistently shown that satisfaction with a provided account is the critical determinant of a variety of judgments about the political predicament, including global evaluations of the official, evaluations of the controversial policy, attributions of responsibility, and character perceptions (McGraw 1991, forthcoming; McGraw, Best and Timpone, 1995).

However, very little is known about the factors that are associated with acceptance of accounts. The "input components" of McGuire's matrix point to some likely candidates. For example, acceptance may depend heavily on an aspect of the account itself—a message variable. In line with this, we have found that accounts that subjects perceive to be more common in political rhetoric are also more acceptable (McGraw 1991), echoing Edelman's (1977) and Bennett's (1980) arguments that political rhetoric is banal.[3] Either public officials provide certain accounts more often because they believe them to be effective (a rational or instrumental explanation for the link), or accounts become effective because they are frequently used (a "mere exposure" explanation; Zajonc 1968), or as is likely, a combination of the two processes contribute to this "message" commonality effect.

Another promising line of inquiry, pursued here, considers the impact of recipient characteristics on account acceptance. The importance of individual differences seems obvious: people differ in their responses to persuasive communications. However, the ability to make precise predictions concerning which types of recipient characteristics mediate responses to persuasive communications has remained a rather elusive goal (Eagly 1981). The mixed history on this topic exists in part because the study of individual differences has had an uneven history in terms of intellectual legitimacy, eventually falling out of fashion (at least in psychology) during the 1960s (Eagly 1981; McGuire 1985). In addition, the relationships between predispositions and susceptibility to persuasion are much more complex than was initially assumed. Nevertheless, McGuire (1985, 285) predicted a revival of interest in the links between receiver predispositions and persuasion "as the Establishment consensus swings back toward the dispositional pole," and so bravely (foolhardily?) we have decided to explore the impact of individual differences on acceptance of political accounts. Many receiver characteristics have received attention in the persuasion literature, most prominently self-esteem, age, gender, self-monitoring, and intelligence (Eagly 1981; McGuire 1985; Perloff 1993). However, rather than investigating the impact of these likely suspects on account acceptance, we have chosen to focus on three characteristics that have particular relevance to *political* persuasion: trust in government, Machiavellianism, and political sophistication.

Trust in Government

"Trust" is a concept that carries multiple shades of meaning. As a personality characteristic, it is usually taken to mean an individual's view of human nature, tapping into expectations that other people are honest, moral, and reliable (Wrightsman 1991). Trust in government, a domain-specific version of a more generalized trust in human nature, can be thought of as a "basic evaluative or affective orientation toward government" (Miller 1974, 952). The expected impact of trust in government and account acceptance is fairly straightforward, namely, that people who are high in such trust should be more satisfied with political accounts because they are likely to view the source of the communication—the politician—as honest, sincere, and credible. In other words, "trusting citizens should be predisposed to give officials the benefit of the doubt" (Sigelman, Sigelman, and Walkosz 1992) when evaluating political predicaments.

That expectation, based upon the positive inferences trusting individuals are likely to make about the politician providing the account, raises an added complexity involving an ongoing debate concerning the meaning of "trust in government." Interpretation of the standard NES trust-in-government scale has suffered from a great deal of ambiguity, because it is unclear whether people respond to these items by expressing their attitudes toward government institutions more generally or incumbent authorities in particular (see the well-known controversy between Citrin and Miller 1974). The 1987 NES Pilot Study included items designed to differentiate between *incumbent-based trust* (evaluations of politicians and government officials) and *regime-based trust* (feelings of attachment to the system more generally, corresponding to Easton's 1965 notion of "diffuse system support"). Craig, Niemi, and Silver's (1990) analysis of these items provides some, although not compelling, support for the claim that these are distinct constructs. However, questions remain about whether the distinction between incumbent- and regime-based trust can and should be maintained. Evidence on differential predictive validity can serve as support for the claim that the distinction is an important one. If our logic is correct—that satisfaction with accounts is mediated in part by positive evaluations of the politician—incumbent-based, not regime-based, trust in government should be the critical factor in account acceptance. Accordingly, we examine the impact of both types of trust in government—incumbent- and regime-based—on the acceptance of political accounts.

Machiavellianism

The Italian writer Niccolò Machiavelli is one of the original masters of the art of political persuasion. In a collection of essays in *The Prince* (written in the early 1500s), Machiavelli presented a philosophy of interpersonal manipulation as well as a practical guide for politicians on how to use power and influence to manipulate the masses. More than 400 years later, Richard Christie, Florence Geis, and their associates developed a personality scale, based on items drawn from *The Prince* and aptly labeled "Machiavellianism," that measures the extent to which an individual believes that other people are manipulable, endorses the use of manipulative tactics, and (behaviorally) shows considerable skill in the art of manipulation (Christie and Geis 1970; Geis 1978). The scale is considered "a showcase example of successful attitude scale construction" (Wrightsman 1991, 374) and has been linked to many attitudinal and behavioral phenomena (Geis 1978; Snyder and Ickes 1985). Of particular relevance to our concerns is the conclusion that low Machs are "soft touches" (Geis and Christie 1970) who are easily influenced and persuadable, the "prototypic mark" (Snyder and Ickes 1985). This pattern of enhanced susceptibility to persuasion suggests that low Machs ought to be more accepting of political accounts than high Machs. But an alternate prediction is plausible. If high Machs can be characterized as the "prototypic con man" (Snyder and Ickes 1985), they may identify with what they perceive as the manipulative tactics used by a politician faced with a predicament, and so express greater satisfaction with the accounts than low Machs. We test these competing hypotheses in the studies described subsequently.

Political Sophistication

In contrast to trust and Machiavellianism, the third recipient characteristic we will explore—political sophistication—is more properly conceived of as a capability, rather than a personality characteristic. Political sophistication (also referred to as expertise or awareness) "deserves to rank alongside party identification and ideology as one of the central constructs in the public opinion field" (Zaller 1990, 125) because it has pervasive effects on many important attitudinal processes (see the special volume of *Social Cognition* [1990] devoted to the topic, as well as Sniderman, Tetlock, and Brody 1991, and Zaller 1992, for recent reviews and evidence). Sophistication can include several different components (such as attention to and interest in political affairs), but recent analysts have argued convincingly for the superiority of factual knowledge about politics as the most valid indicator (Fiske, Lau, and Smith 1990; Zaller 1990, 1992).

What role is sophistication likely to play in the processing of political accounts? Sophisticates are both motivated and able to carefully scrutinize a politician's explanation. Careful message scrutiny is frequently accompanied by cognitive responses of either a positive or a negative nature (Petty and Cacioppo 1986), the direction of which is critical to acceptance of persuasive messages and subsequent attitude change. In our experimental contexts, where the to-be-explained predicament is an unpopular policy, the context for the scrutiny of the politician's account is a negative one, suggesting that negative thoughts—counterarguments—are likely to prevail. According to this logic, then, sophisticates should be less satisfied with explanations accounting for an unpopular policy because they are better able to generate counterarguments in order to reject the account.

In sum, we set two goals for these analyses. The first is to explore the impact of these three predispositional factors—trust in government, Machiavellianism, and political knowledge—on acceptance of explanations provided to account for a controversial policy vote. We then examine the consequences for acceptance or rejection of the account on subsequent attitude change, the ultimate test of the success of a persuasive communication. We begin by describing the two studies that provide the data for exploring these issues.

Procedures and Measurement

The Initial Support Study

The subjects in this study were 860 undergraduates, each of whom received a randomly assigned booklet containing one of the versions of the stimulus materials. The instructions stated that the study concerned a hypothetical congressman, John Haywood, and his vote for a bill passed by the House of Representatives ("a complex deficit reduction plan that involves a number of economic measures, one of which is an increase in income taxes for most Americans"). The subjects were asked to imagine that they resided in Haywood's district and that the bill would affect them personally.

Two variables were manipulated in this study. The first was the *reputation* of the congressman, designed to vary the subjects' initial levels of support for him. Approximately one-third of the subjects were given information stating that he had a positive reputation among his constituents, another third information that he had a negative reputation, and the remaining third were not given any reputation information.[4] The second manipulated variable was the *account* that the congressman provided for his vote on the bill. The subjects were told that he had agreed to meet with a group of concerned citizens at a public meeting in his home district to explain his vote, with one of 12 different accounts provided as his response at this meeting (the accounts are listed in the appendix). The 12 accounts, including both excuses and justifications, parallel those used in earlier studies (McGraw 1990, 1991). A control group of subjects did not receive mention of the public meeting or of the subsequent account.

The Constituent Impact Study

The subjects in this study were 389 undergraduates. The procedure was nearly identical to the study just described. The subjects were told that the study involved a hypothetical congressman, John Sullivan, and his vote for a bill passed by the House of Representatives ("a complex multibillion-dollar education bill"). Two variables were manipulated in this study. The first was the *impact* of the bill on the subject. For approximately one-third of the subjects, the bill was described as one that would have a uniformly negative impact on residents of the district (negative sum outcome), another third of the subjects were told that it would have a negative impact on their school district, whereas others in the congressional district would benefit (zero sum/negative personal impact), and the remaining third were told that the bill would have a positive impact on their school district, whereas others in the congressional district would be hit hard (zero sum/positive personal impact; the details of this study are provided in McGraw, Best, and Timpone 1995).

The second manipulated variable was the *account* that the congressman provided for his vote. In this study, his response was to a challenger in a televised political debate. One of six accounts (listed in the appendix) was provided as his response. These accounts were selected because they represent a subset of the important accounts from our previous studies—claims of mitigating circumstances, benefits and normative justifications, and hypothetical comparisons—as well as two that were not previously considered: diffusion of responsibility to subordinates and a claim of party loyalty. As in the first study, a control group of subjects did not receive any information about the debate or an account.

Dependent Measures

Three variables are critical to the analyses. The first is acceptance of the account, operationalized as satisfaction. The subjects in both studies were asked, "How satisfied are you with Cong. _____'s explanation of his vote?", responding on a scale anchored "extremely dissatisfied" to "extremely satisfied." Evaluations of the controversial policy and the congressman himself were also measured via the 101-point feeling thermometer. The policy evaluated in the first study was increased income taxes as part of a deficit reduction plan; the policy evaluated in the second involved funding for education programs, the actual impact (positive or negative) dependent upon experimental condition.

Measurement of Personality Characteristics

Although these studies were not initially designed to examine the role that citizens' predispositions play in the blame-management process, as a standard rule we assess a variety of individual differences at the conclusion of experimental sessions. Fortunately, the four individual difference constructs discussed earlier were included in both of these studies. Four questions were included to measure *incumbent-based trust* (from Craig et al. 1990): "You can generally trust the people who run our government to do what is right"; "Unless we keep a close watch on them, many of our elected officials will look out for special interests rather than for all the people"; "When government leaders make statements to the American people on television or in newspapers, they are usually telling the truth"; and "Quite a few of the people running our government are not as honest as the voters have a right to expect." These items yielded reasonably reliable scales (alphas equal to .64 for the support study and .68 for the impact study, comparable to those evident in the NES data reported by Craig et al. 1990).

Regime-based trust, or diffuse system support, was also measured by four items from the Craig et al. (1990) study: "Whatever its faults might be, the American form of government is still the best for us"; "There is not much about our form of government to be proud of"; "It may be necessary to make some major changes in our form of government in order to solve the problems facing our country"; and "I would rather live under our system of government than any other that I can think of." The reliability of these scales is comparable to the incumbency-based trust scales, as well as to those reported by Craig et al. (1990) (alphas equal to .69 for the support study and .65 for the impact study). Not surprisingly, regime- and incumbent-based trust are positively correlated, but not excessively so, suggesting that they can be treated as independent, distinct constructs ($r = .36$ and .38 for the support and impact studies, respectively).

Machiavellianism was measured via two items in the support study: "The best way to handle people is to tell them what they want to hear" and "It is wise to flatter important people" ($r = .50$). Four additional items were included in the impact study: "Honesty is the best policy in all cases"; "There is no excuse for lying to someone else"; "Never tell anyone the real reason you did something unless it is useful to do so"; and, "Anyone who completely trusts other people is asking for trouble" (alpha for the six-item scale is .65). Machiavellianism and the two trust-in-government scales are for the most part independent in these samples; the only significant intercorrelation is a weak $-.11$ ($p < .05$) between Machiavellianism and incumbent-based trust in the impact study.[5]

Finally, a *political knowledge* scale was created by asking the subjects to identify the partisan identification of 10 prominent local and national public officials; the sum of the incorrect responses was subtracted from the sum of the correct responses. Political knowledge was very weakly related to the two trust measures, such that those with more knowledge tended to exhibit higher levels of regime-based trust ($rs = .10$, $p < .01$ and .07 for the support and impact studies, respectively), and lower levels of incumbent-based trust ($rs = -.06$ and $-.17$, $p < .01$). Political knowledge and Machiavellianism were independent in both samples.

Results

All the variables included in the analyses were recoded to range from 0 to 1, to facilitate comparisons within and between the two studies. Because the focus of this chapter is on the role individual differences play in the acceptance of political accounts, and the subsequent implications for attitude change, for the most part we do not consider the impact of the manipulated independent variables (the initial reputation from the first study and the impact from the second; detailed reports of these effects, as well as theoretical justifications for incorporating these particular manipulations, are available else-where; McGraw, Best, and Timpone 1995 and McGraw, Timpone, and Bruck 1991). Those manipulated variables were incorporated where appropriate in the statistical models to control for the impact of those effects.

Acceptance of the Accounts: The Impact of Predispositions

As Cody and McLaughlin (1990) note in their review, the evidence regarding the issue of whether different types of accounts are more or less effective is decidedly mixed, with seemingly all possible orderings of "effectiveness" resulting, depending in part on the nature of the domain (e.g., interpersonal, legal, and organizational). The average satisfaction ratings with the political accounts from these two studies are reported in the appendix. Clearly some accounts work better than others, and some fail miserably, at least in the context of explaining unpopular policy votes. Taken with the results of earlier studies (McGraw 1990, 1991), however, some patterns are consistently evi-dent. First, justifications appealing to normative principles—ethical standards such as fairness and the dictates of one's conscience—are generally among the more effective accounts. Second, among those justifications directly chal-lenging perceptions of the consequences of the policy, those pointing to addi-tional benefits are more acceptable than those involving more abstract compar-isons. Third, among the excuses, claims of mitigating circumstances are relatively effective, no doubt reflecting people's understandings that real polit-ical decisions are indeed constrained by external circumstances. And fourth, excuses involving diffusions of responsibility or pleas of ignorance are consis-tently poor accounts.

What are the relationships between the three predispositional factors and acceptance of the accounts? To explore these relationships, the following models were estimated, separately for each account condition in the two experiments:

$$Y = b_0 + b_1 \text{ Policy Evaluation} + b_2 \text{ Independent Variable}$$
$$+ b_3 \text{ Incumbent-Based Trust}$$
$$+ b_4 \text{ Regime-Based Trust} + b_5 \text{ Machiavellianism}$$
$$+ b_6 \text{ Political Knowledge} + e.$$

The dependent variable was satisfaction with the account. The thermometer ratings of the policy and the variables manipulated in each study—the con-gressman's reputation in the first and the impact of the policy in the second—

were also included in the models, to control for those effects. Thus, the effects due to the personality variables are those above and beyond the effects due to the manipulated variables and policy evaluations. The impact of the personality variables is summarized in table 1.[6]

Consider first the impact of incumbent-based trust. We expected that positive attitudes toward politicians and government officials would lead to greater satisfaction with accounts, because people who exhibit this kind of trust in government should accept these explanations as sincere and credible. The results were largely in line with this expectation. Out of the 18 tests reported in table 1, 14 yielded the predicted positive relationship; of the eight tests yielding statistically significant results, seven involved evidence of a positive trust-satisfaction relationship.

In contrast, we expected that regime-based trust—general feelings of loyalty to the political system—would have a much weaker relationship with

TABLE 1. Predicting Account Satisfaction

	Predictors			
	IB Trust	RB Trust	Machiavellianism	Knowledge
Account Type: Support Study				
1. Past mitigation	.31+	−.35**	−.01	.32+
2. Present mitigation	−.28	.19	.06	−.45**
3. Horizontal diffusion	.32+	−.17	−.12	−.34*
4. Vertical diffusion	.28+	−.17	.06	−.35*
5. Ignorance	.33**	−.03	.11+	−.21*
6. Present benefits	.27	−.42**	.14+	−.30+
7. Future benefits	.01	.04	.20*	.20
8. Past comparison	.24	−.09	.00	−.33+
9. Other comparison	−.14	.19	.20+	−.11
10. Hypothetical comp.	−.36+	.03	−.13	.07
11. Fairness	.23	−.04	.05	−.06
12. Conscience	.02	.15	.08	−.12
Account Type: Impact Study				
1. Mitigation	.08	.03	.27+	.19
2. Blaming staff	.34**	−.23*	.38***	.06
3. Party loyalty	.08	−.06	−.07	.06
4. Benefits	.23+	−.07	.07	.26+
5. Hypothetical comparison	−.33	.33*	.19	−.10
6. Normative justification	.35+	.16	−.19	−.35+

Note. The entries are unstandardized regression coefficients, with each row representing the results from a separate equation. All variables are coded to range from 0 to 1.

+$p < .20$
*$p < .1$
**$p < .05$
***$p < .01$

account satisfaction (in comparison to incumbent-based trust), and that expectation was largely borne out: only four of the 14 tests provided evidence of a significant relationship. What is surprising about the effects of regime-based trust is that its impact was just as often likely to be negative as positive (there is an equal number of positive and negative signs), and, more important, when its impact was substantial, it was more likely to be negative (e.g., for the claims of past mitigation and present benefits in the first study, and blaming of the subordinate in the second). That is, people with strong feelings of attachment to the system tended to be less satisfied with the accounts offered by specific representatives of that system. Perhaps they viewed the predicament generally and the explanation in particular as blemishes on the democratic ideals the system represents.

As we noted earlier, two contrasting predictions regarding the relationship between Machiavellianism and acceptance of the accounts can be posited. On the one hand, because Machiavellians tend to be less susceptible to persuasion, they may be less satisfied with the provided accounts, suggesting a negative relationship between Machiavellianism and satisfaction. In contrast, it is conceivable that Machiavellians may harbor some special appreciation for (what they view as manipulative) persuasion strategies public officials use to manage the fallout from political predicaments, suggesting a positive relationship. The data clearly supported the latter hypothesis. Thirteen of the 18 coefficients were positive; all six of those that reach an acceptable level of statistical significance were positive. Of particular interest is the substantial relationship between Machiavellianism and acceptance of "blaming subordinates," an excuse that ranks among the least acceptable of any we have ever included in our research. Perhaps because Machiavellians are characterized by a "cool detachment" that makes them less emotionally involved with other people (Geis and Christie 1970), they view this attempt to shift blame to one's subordinates as an acceptable, and even admirable, response.

Finally, we expected that political sophistication would be associated with lower levels of account acceptance, because people with more knowledge about politics are better able to reject—via counterarguing—an official's explanation for a controversial policy vote. The anticipated negative relationship was generally evident in table 1: 11 of the 18 coefficients were negative, and, more important, seven of the nine effects that reached an acceptable level of statistical significant were negative.

One of the important conceptual developments in the personality-persuasion literature was McGuire's (1968) argument that nonmonotonic associations—an inverted U—can prevail in some situations, with those in the middle of a personality distribution exhibiting the greatest amount of attitude change. The logic underlying the nonmonotonic prediction invokes the principle of countervailing mediating cognitive processes. That is, some individual difference variables (e.g., intelligence or self-esteem) tend to be positively related to reception (attention plus comprehension) of a message but negatively related to yielding to the message (see also Eagly 1981 and Zaller 1987, 1992 for extended discussions of these processes). We explored the possibility of such curvilinear effects among the individual difference variables in these studies. Although some scattered curvilinear effects were evident, there were no more than would be expected by chance (14 of the 72 effects, or 20 percent, were significant, which is exactly equivalent to the lenient alpha level we set in this portion of the analysis). Moreover, those curvilinear effects that were evident were neither consistent nor easily interpretable. In short, we are inclined to conclude that the predispositional relationships examined in these studies are monotonic, rather than nonmonotonic, in form. This conclusion is not surprising in a context where the persuasive "message"—the account—was easy to comprehend. In such a situation, linear effects are most likely to occur (McGuire 1968; Zaller 1987).

In sum, the data from these two experiments provide moderately reasonable support for three conclusions regarding the predispositional determinants of acceptance of political accounts: those who are more trusting of government officials, Machiavellians, and those who are less knowledgeable about politics are more likely to be satisfied with the explanations provided to account for an unpopular policy vote. Feelings of diffuse system support, on the other hand, had less of an impact on account acceptance, and to the extent that regime-based trust was associated with satisfaction, its effects were opposite in direction to incumbent-based trust. Two points deserve emphasis here (we will return to them at the chapter's conclusion). The first is that the links between these predispositions and satisfaction most likely are not reflections of a unitary psychological process but rather are due to different mediators: perceived credibility or sincerity of the politician by the trusting, "identification" with a fellow manipulator by the Machiavellians, and the inability or disinclination to counterargue by the less knowledgeable. The second important point is that these relationships are more evident with some accounts than others. That is, they are not inevitable, but appear to be determined by a complex matching of the citizen's predisposition, the account statement, and the characteristics of the politician and the predicament.

Attitude Change: Evaluations of the Policy

We move now to an examination of the consequences of account acceptance and rejection. One of the more robust results in our research program is that acceptance of an account, particularly a justification, results in a positive reevaluation of the controversial policy that is the basis of the predicament

(McGraw 1991; McGraw, Best, and Timpone 1995; McGraw, Timpone, and Bruck 1993). These revised policy opinions are contingent upon acceptance of the account, in line with the persuasive communication model. Moreover, they are properly conceived of as a *change* in attitude about the policy upon reception of the account, an inference that is warranted if a comparison can be made with a comparable group of subjects who were not provided with an explanation. The control groups in these studies, who did not receive an account for the policy vote, provide such a basis for comparison.[7]

We created two groups of subjects: those who were satisfied with the accounts and those who were dissatisfied with the accounts, based on their stated satisfaction judgments.[8] We then calculated the average ratings of the controversial policy for each satisfaction group and compared the resulting mean with that obtained by the control group of subjects who did not receive an explanation. The results are summarized in table 2.

In both studies, acceptance and rejection of the account resulted in an intriguing asymmetrical pattern of changes in opinions about the policy. In only one instance did rejection of the account—dissatisfaction—result in a "boomerang" effect such that evaluations of the policy actually became more negative (dissatisfaction with the hypothetical comparison in the impact study), and that effect was quite modest. Rather, acceptance of the account—satisfaction—consistently led to more positive reevaluations of the policy, averaging 13 degrees on the thermometer scale in the support study and 15 degrees in the impact study. Exploratory analyses—not reported here—showed that the same asymmetry was evident in the various experimental conditions, so the observed effects were not contingent upon such factors as the existing impression of the official or personal impact of the policy.

Attitude Change: Evaluations of the Official

Ultimately—from the perspective of the politician—the goal of an account is to limit the fallout from the predicament, in order to maintain the approval of valued constituent groups. Accordingly, an acceptable account should result in more positive opinions about the official, when compared to the impact of an unacceptable, or nonexistent, account. We conducted a set of analyses similar to those described earlier for evaluations of the policy, using the thermometer ratings of the hypothetical congressman as the dependent measure. Because the initial reputation information provided in the constituent support study had such a powerful impact on these global evaluation ratings (see the control group means in table 3), the impact of account satisfaction and dissatisfaction was examined separately for each reputation condition.[9] The results of those analyses are summarized in tables 3 and 4.

Two important conclusions can be drawn concerning the impact of account satisfaction on evaluations of the official providing the explanation. The first is that the asymmetrical pattern observed in the policy evaluation data was also evident here: the magnitude of change in opinions about the official was greater—in a positive direction—when the account was accepted than when the account was rejected. This pattern is evident in the impact study (table 4), where account satisfaction was associated with an average positive boost of 15 degrees in the thermometer ratings, whereas dissatisfaction resulted in an average drop of 8 degrees (an effect that is also statistically significant).

TABLE 2. Account Satisfaction and Attitude Change: Policy Evaluation

	Dissatisfied	Satisfied
Support Study		
1. Past mitigation	.39	.51**
2. Present mitigation	.37	.50**
3. Horizontal diffusion	.38	.53**
4. Vertical diffusion	.40	.41
5. Ignorance	.39	NA
6. Present benefits	.39	.49*
7. Future benefits	.33	.64***
8. Past comparison	.38	.52*
9. Other comparison	.44	.55***
10. Hypothetical comparison	.44	.51**
11. Fairness	.40	.47
12. Conscience	.41	.51**
Mean across all accounts	.39	.52***
Control group mean = .39		
Impact Study		
1. Mitigation	.30	.40
2. Blaming staff	.36	.53*
3. Party loyalty	.29	.54**
4. Benefits	.30	.48*
5. Hypothetical comparison	.30	.42
6. Normative justification	.25+	.53***
Mean across all accounts:	.30	.48***
Control group mean = .33		

Note. The entries are the mean evaluation of the target policy, on a scale ranging from 0 to 1, for those who are satisfied and dissatisfied with the provided account. NA = no available casees (none satisfied). Differences between the condition means and the control group mean assessed via *t*-tests.

+$p < .1$
*$p < .05$
**$p < .01$
***$p < .001$

The results from the initial support study (table 3) were a bit murkier, with conclusions hampered by much smaller cell sizes (for the account-specific comparisons). Examination of the aggregate means—collapsing across type of account—revealed a provocative twist on the positive impact of acceptance. Namely, although the same asymmetry in the impact of satisfaction and dissatisfaction is evident when the congressman had a negative or neutral reputation (satisfaction increasing those ratings by 13 and 12 degrees, respectively), the positive boost attributable to satisfaction disappeared when he had a positive reputation. Additional analyses of the determinants of these impressions (not reported here; see McGraw, Timpone, and Bruck 1991) suggest an explanation for this anomaly. In the positive reputation condition, impressions of the congressman were significantly more likely to be based on character perceptions (particularly empathy, the trait most relevant to the manipulation) than were the impressions in the other two conditions, with a corresponding drop in the impact of account satisfaction. In other words,

TABLE 3. Account Satisfaction and Attitude Change: Official Evaluations (Initial Support Study)

	Negative Reputation		No Reputation		Positive Reputation	
	Dissatisfied	Satisfied	Dissatisfied	Satisfied	Dissatisfied	Satisfied
1. Past mitigation	.34	.40*	.39	.58**	.55	.67
2. Present mitigation	.25	.39*	.49	.54*	.50	.62
3. Horizontal diffusion	.31	.27	.31**	.57*	.51	.51
4. Vertical diffusion	.28	.44**	.37*	NA	.58	NA
5. Ignorance	.27	NA	.32**	NA	.55	NA
6. Present benefits	.28	NA	.39	.55*	.57	.46
7. Future benefits	.28	.31	.44	.68***	.37	.68+
8. Past comparison	.18+	.46*	.45	.53	.54	.67
9. Other comparison	.28	NA	.41	.58+	.68	.71+
10. Hypothetical comparison	.37	NA	.41	.59	.60	.60
11. Fairness	.28	.44**	.42	.57	.60	.50
12. Conscience	.28	.46**	.43	.59**	.62	.66
Mean across accounts	.28	.39***	.40+	.58***	.56	.62
Control group mean	.26		.46		.60	

Note. The entries are the mean evaluations of the representative, on a scale ranging from 0 to 1. NA = no available cases (none satisfied). Differences between the condition and control group means assessed via t-tests.

$+p < .1$
$*p < .05$
$**p < .01$
$***p < .001$

TABLE 4. **Account Satisfaction and Attitude Change:
Official Evaluations (Constituent Support Study)**

	Dissatisfied	Satisfied
1. Mitigation	.36+	.53*
2. Blaming staff	.29***	NA
3. Party loyalty	.37	.60**
4. Benefits	.36*	.58**
5. Hypothetical comparison	.36*	.60***
6. Normative justification	.35*	.61***
Mean across all accounts:	.35**	.58***
Control group mean = .43		

Note. The entries are the mean evaluations of the representative, on a scale ranging from 0 to 1. Differences between the condition means and the control group mean assessed via *t*-tests.

+$p < .1$
*$p < .05$
**$p < .01$
***$p < .001$

those with a positive prior impression of the congressman were less likely to update their impressions on the basis of reactions—positive or negative—to the account.

Discussion

The results from these two studies provide reasonable support for the hypothesis that citizens' predispositions are an important determinant of acceptance of political accounts. Account acceptance, in turn, is the critical factor in subsequent attitude change. Thus, predispositions—receiver characteristics —play an important role in the dynamics contributing to successful persuasive accounts.

The predispositions examined in these studies were selected because they have important implications for understanding political behavior and include what are typically regarded as personality traits—trust in government and Machiavellianism—as well as a cognitive capability (political knowledge or sophistication). The divergence in the magnitude and direction of the effects of the two types of trust in government—incumbent- and regime-based— suggests that this distinction is one that is well worth maintaining in future research (Craig et al. 1990). The positive relationship between Machiavellianism and acceptance is an important one, because it is contrary to the robust finding from the social psychology literature that low Machs are more susceptible to persuasion than are high Machs (Geis and Christie 1970; Snyder and Ickes 1985). It is reasonable to assume that satisfaction with explanations provided by a fellow manipulator—a politician—is driven in this situation by an appreciation of a "master's" techniques. This is reminiscent of the "communicator similarity" effect that is widely evident in the persuasion literature, in which a source perceived as similar to the recipient tends to be more effective in changing attitudes (Petty and Cacioppo 1982). Finally, the impact of political sophistication is consistent with the recent trend to view this construct as the most important source of individual heterogeneity in political information processing (e.g., Sniderman, Tetlock, and Brody 1991; Zaller 1992; but see Rahn, Aldrich, Borgida, and Sullivan 1990 and Rahn 1995 for dissenting views).

It is possible that, in the long run, the causal arrow between predispositions and acceptance of accounts may also move in the other direction, such that political accounts may have an impact on citizens' predispositions, particularly views about government legitimacy (which includes trust; Weatherford 1992). In an important paper, Bennett (1980) suggested a provocative hypothesis concerning the impact of political accounts on basic orientations toward government: "The analysis of patterns in the use of political accounts can provide new understandings about the everyday bases of political stability and legitimacy. . . . Accounts can be approached both as specific variables in conflict situations and in more general terms as important sources of information about the pragmatics of potential conflicts and the workings of political institutions" (817). In other words, not only may accounts have an impact on attitudes about the event and official in question, but also on citizens' more basic views of government. Fenno (1978) suggests a similar process. If explanations, as part of the representative's "home style" repertoire, contribute to constituents' level of trust in that particular official (as Fenno argues), then it is plausible that trust in that representative may contribute to more general feelings of incumbent-based, and even regime-based, trust. Although the impact of accounts—and by extension, communications from elected officials in general—on views about the legitimacy of government have yet to be examined, such a line of inquiry holds great promise for examining how citizens' predispositions are shaped by ongoing political dramas.

We view our work as a preliminary, and primarily illustrative, exploration of the workings of predispositions in the political persuasion process. An important next step is to clarify the cognitive mediators that underlie the observed effects. We have suggested that the observed predisposition-acceptance links are due to a variety of psychological processes: positive evaluations of the official (particularly regarding sincerity) among those with high levels of incumbent-based trust; identification with a fellow "con man" on the part of Machiavellians, and counterarguing among the politically knowledgeable. Analyses of cognitive responses (Petty and Cacioppo 1986) as well as measurement of relevant variables would provide a valuable addition to the analyses we have presented here.

Our data also suggest that the impact of the predispositions tended to be account-specific. This specificity is no doubt due in part to chance variability, but also likely due to more systematic forces inherent to the accounts themselves, such as commonality (McGraw 1991), credibility, complexity, and the attributional dimensions critical to Weiner's framework (internality, intentionality, and controllability; e.g., Weiner et al. 1987). An important direction for future research is the scaling of the structural characteristics of common political accounts, as well as consideration of their interaction with citizens' predispositions in the acceptance process.

Finally, the data clearly show that acceptance of accounts results in a change in attitudes not only about the official providing the account, but also of the controversial policy itself, replicating previous work. Thus, not only do successful accounts serve the politician's goal of shoring up public support, but they also can have an impact on how constituents ultimately view specific policies and issues. Whether viewed positively as the representative educating an attentive constituency (Fenno 1978) or negatively as the self-serving manipulation of an ill-informed public, it is clear that political explanations can be used strategically to structure public opinion (Stone 1989).

The asymmetry in the relative impact of acceptance and rejection of accounts—such that acceptance resulted in positive attitude change, but a corresponding negative attitude change attributable to rejection was weaker or nonexistent—deserves comment, because this asymmetry is inconsistent with one research tradition but consistent with another. Specifically, the impression formation literature suggests that negative information has a more powerful impact on impressions of other people than does positive information (Sears and Whitney 1973; Skowronski and Carlston 1989). But we found virtually no support for negativity effects of this sort: a negative evaluation of the account—dissatisfaction—had little impact on attitudes about the politician. On the other hand, the attitude change literature suggests that, *given acceptance,* attitude change most often occurs in the direction of the message and that this kind of positive attitude change is more prevalent than a "boomerang" effect, or negative attitude change given rejection (it is our impression that the prevalence of "boomeranging" is not a well-documented phenomenon). Our results are obviously more consistent with this latter interpretation.

In conclusion, our hope is that the issues we have discussed in this chapter as well as the analyses we have reported serve to encourage further empirical work on the mechanisms underlying successful and unsuccessful political persuasion. Citizens' predispositions are just one factor—albeit an important one (Sigelman et al. 1992)—in this process. Exploration of the vast number of other important persuasion "input" factors together with consideration of the cognitive mechanisms underlying attitude change—largely uncharted territory in political science—will enrich our discipline's understanding of the complex and dynamic relationship that exists between elites and the mass public.

Initial Support Study

Excuses

1. *Past Mitigating Circumstances:* "I had to vote for the income tax bill because the previous administration's policies crippled our nation's economy; drastic measures had to be taken." (mean = .48)
2. *Present Mitigating Circumstances:* "I had to vote for the income tax bill because of the poor shape of the nation's economy; drastic measures had to be taken." (mean = .46)
3. *Horizontal Diffusion of Responsibility:* "Although I voted for the income tax bill, I think that it is important to remember that it was a group decision; the bill was passed by a majority of the House of Representatives." (mean = .33)
4. *Vertical Diffusion of Responsibility:* "Although I voted for the income tax bill, I think that it is important to remember that its ultimate passage will be due to the President signing it into law." (mean = .26)
5. *Plea of ignorance:* "I voted for the income tax bill, but it was complicated and I did not foresee that it would result in increased income taxes for so many residents of this district." (mean = .21)

Justifications

6. *Present Benefits:* "Although the bill will result in increased income taxes, I think it is important to remember that the increased revenue brings important benefits to this district." (mean = .39)
7. *Future Benefits:* "Although the bill will result in increased income taxes, in the long run the increased revenue will result in greater economic efficiency that will help this community and the entire nation." (mean = .48)
8. *Comparison to Past Circumstances:* "Although the bill will result in increased income taxes, I think it is important to remember that the tax rates are generally still lower than what they have been in the past." (mean = .39)
9. *Comparison to Others:* "Although the bill will result in increased taxes, I think it is important to remember that the bill had even more serious consequences in other districts in the nation." (mean = .36)
10. *"Worse-case" Comparison:* "Although the bill will result in increased income taxes, it could have been a lot worse. Other proposals would have raised taxes even more." (mean = .41)
11. *Fairness:* "I voted for the income tax bill because I believe the distribution of

the tax burden is fairer for all of this nation's citizens than under the current tax scheme." (mean = .41)

12. *Conscience:* "I had to follow my conscience in voting for the income tax bill, and therefore I did what I thought was in the best interests of the community and the nation." (mean = .38)

Constituent Impact Study

Excuses

1. *Mitigating Circumstances:* "I didn't feel that I had a choice on this one because a change was necessary. The failure of this nation's previous education policies requires drastic solutions such as those included in the education bill." (mean = .40)
2. *Diffusion of Responsibility to Staff:* ". . . and very complicated. Unfortunately, my staff failed to provide me with complete information about the likely consequences of the bill and therefore I wasn't made fully aware of all of its possible ramifications." (mean = .22)

Justifications

3. *Party Loyalty:* "I agree with the leaders of my party that the passage of this bill is in the nation's best interests, and I voted accordingly." (mean = .35)
4. *Benefits:* "I voted for the education bill because I think that it also brings with it real benefits for this district. For example, as part of the same package of legislation, funds have been set aside for research on improving science education and reducing dropout rates." (mean = .43)
5. *"Worse-case" comparison:* "This education bill could have been a lot worse. For example, other versions of the bill were considered that would have resulted in much more serious cuts in funding for this district." (mean = .33)
6. *Normative Justification:* "I voted for the education bill because I believe that under the new allocation criteria the distribution of education funds is fairer, going to those who need the funding the most. I followed my conscience and did what I thought was the right thing to do." (mean = .42)

Note: The means reported in parentheses are the mean satisfaction ratings for each account, collapsing across the manipulated independent variables in each study, where higher values reflect more satisfaction.

NOTES

1. As Rahn and Sullivan (forthcoming) have noted, a number of recent books have placed elites at the center of theories of mass political attitudes (e.g., Brody 1991, Page and Shapiro 1992; Carmines and Stimson 1989; Zaller 1992), indicating that elite-mass public links are increasingly the subject of serious scholarship.

2. McGuire's model includes a number of additional output steps for a persuasive communication to have a subsequent impact on a behavior, such as voting. These include: storing the changed attitude in memory; at decision time, retrieving the changed attitude from memory; deciding to act on the retrieved attitude; and finally, acting in accord with this decision. Our research to this point has been concerned with the judgmental rather than behavioral consequences of accounts, so these latter steps—although important and provocative in their implications regarding the on-line versus memory-based processing of persuasive messages (Hastie and Park 1986; Lodge, McGraw, and Stroh 1989)—have been reserved for the future.

3. More specifically, Bennett (1980, 798) argued, "accounts are so often over-worked they dull the sense with their repetition. A close inspection of a sample of ordinary political accounts would not doubt reveal that the same limited and redundant themes are attached mechanically to the ongoing diversity of political action."

4. The reputation information was operationalized as responsiveness to one's constituents. The positive information read: "During this time in office, he has developed a reputation for being responsive to the needs and interests of the 34th District. He makes frequent trips back home to keep in touch and better serve his constituency." The negative information read: "During this time in office, he has developed a reputation for being aloof and unresponsive to the needs and interests of the 34th District. He rarely comes back home to keep in touch with his constituency."

5. In contrast to the independence between Machiavellianism and trust in government evident in these samples, Machiavellianism and a more generalized trust in human nature are typically highly negatively correlated (Wrightsman 1991).

6. For the sake of brevity, only the personality variable effects are reported in table 1. The effects due to the manipulated reputation information in the constituent impact study were for the most part significant, indicating that our subjects were more satisfied with accounts provided by an official they liked than one they disliked (collapsing across the different accounts, mean satisfaction ratings are equal to .34, .37, and .44 for the negative, no, and positive reputation conditions respectively). This is evidence of the impact of another input factor—source characteristics—on account acceptance. The impact of evaluations of the policy was also consistently significant in both studies, suggesting that reactions to the "to-be-explained" event provide an anchor for subsequent judgments. However, as will be seen, this policy evaluation–account satisfaction link is a reflection of a nonrecursive relationship, with the causal arrow going in both directions. Finally, the direct effect of the manipulated impact information (in the second study) on satisfaction was quite weak; the direct effect of the manipulation was largely on evaluations of the policy itself, not the account.

7. This is an example of a *posttest only control group de*sign, which is frequently used in attitude change research (Petty and Cacioppo 1981). Attitude change in this kind of design is defined as the aggregate difference between the posttest attitudes of the experimental and control groups. The alternative design is a pretest-posttest design, where attitude change is measured at the individual level. The design of these two studies does not permit a determination of attitude change at this level.

8. In contrast to a similar analysis reported in an earlier paper utilizing a different data set (McGraw 1991), these groups are based on the objective satisfaction ratings,

not within-condition median splits. The latter technique results in a relative conceptualization of satisfaction (and the troublesome classification of some as "satisfied" even if they expressed "moderate dissatisfaction"). Although justifiable in the earlier study because of sample size problems, the objective classification used in the present analyses is preferable.

9. In contrast, the influence of the personal impact information on evaluations of the congressman in the second study was not significant, so the results from that study are collapsed across that variable.

REFERENCES

Bennett, W. Lance. 1980. The paradox of public discourse: A framework for the analysis of political accounts. *Journal of Politics* 42:792–817.

Brody, Richard A. 1991. *Assessing the president.* Stanford: University of California Press.

Carmines, Edward G., and James A. Stimson. 1989. *Issue evolution: Race and the transformation of American politics.* Princeton: Princeton University Press.

Christie, Richard, and Florence L. Geis. 1970. *Studies in Machiavellianism.* New York: Academic Press.

Citrin, Jack. 1974. Comment: The political relevance of trust in government. *American Political Science Review* 68:973–88.

Craig, Stephen C., Richard G. Niemi, and Glenn E. Silver. 1990. Political efficacy and trust: A report on the NES pilot study items. *Political Behavior* 12:289–314.

Cody, Michael J., and Margaret L. McLaughlin. 1990. Interpersonal accounting. In *Handbook of language and social psychology,* ed. Howard Giles and Peter Robinson. New York: Wiley.

Eagly, Alice H. 1981. Recipient characteristics as determinants of responses to persuasion. In *Cognitive responses to persuasion,* ed. Richard E. Petty, Thomas M. Ostrom, and Timothy C. Brock. Hillsdale, N.J.: Lawrence Erlbaum Associates.

Edelman, Murray. 1977. *Political language: Words that succeed and policies that fail.* New York: Academic.

Fenno, Richard. 1978. *Home style: House members in their districts.* Boston: Little, Brown.

Fiske, Susan T., Richard R. Lau, and Richard A. Smith. 1990. On the varieties and utilities of political expertise. *Social Cognition* 8:31–48.

Geis, Florence L. 1978. Machiavellianism. In *Dimensions of personality,* ed. Harvey London and John E. Exner. New York: Wiley.

Geis, Florence, and Richard Christie. 1970. Overview of experimental research. In *Studies in Machiavellianism,* ed. Richard Christie and Florence L. Geis. New York: Academic Press.

Gonzales, Marti Hope, Debra J. Manning, and Julie A. Haugen. 1992. Explaining our sins: Factors influencing offender accounts and anticipated victim responses. *Journal of Personality and Social Psychology* 62:958–71.

Gonzales, Marti Hope, Julie Haugen Pederson, Debra J. Manning, and David W. Wetter. 1990. Pardon my gaffe: Effects of sex, status, and consequence severity on accounts. *Journal of Personality and Social Psychology* 58:610–21.

Graber, Doris A. 1976. *Verbal behavior and politics.* Urbana: University of Illinois Press.

Hastie, Reid, and Bernadette Park. 1986. The relationship between memory and judgment depends on whether the task is memory-based or on-line. *Psychological Review* 93:258–68.

Iyengar, Shanto, and Donald R. Kinder. 1987. *News that matters.* Chicago: University of Chicago Press.

Iyengar, Shanto. 1991. *Is anyone responsible? How television frames political issues.* Chicago: University of Chicago Press.

Jacobson, Gary C., and Samuel Kernell. 1983. *Strategy and choice in congressional elections.* New Haven, Conn.: Yale University Press.

Kinder, Donald R., and David O. Sears. 1985. Public opinion and political action. In *The handbook of social psychology,* Vol. 2, ed. Gardner Lindzey and Eliot Aronson. New York: Random House.

Klapper, J. T. 1960. *The effects of mass communications.* Glencoe, Ill.: Free Press.

Lippman, Walter. 1955. *Public opinion.* New York: Free Press.

Lodge, Milton, Kathleen M. McGraw, and Patrick Stroh. 1989. An impression-driven model of candidate evaluation. *American Political Science Review* 83:399–419.

Mayhew, David. 1974. *Congress: The electoral connection.* New Haven, Conn.: Yale University Press.

McGraw, Kathleen M. 1990. Avoiding blame: An experimental investigation of political excuses and justifications. *British Journal of Political Science* 20:119–42.

McGraw, Kathleen M. 1991. Managing blame: An experimental investigation into the effectiveness of political accounts. *American Political Science Review* 85:1133–58.

McGraw, Kathleen M. Forthcoming. Political accounts and attribution processes. In *Political psychology,* ed. James Kuklinski. New York: Cambridge University Press.

McGraw, Kathleen M., Samuel Best, and Richard Timpone. 1995. What they say or what they do? The impact of elite explanation and policy outcomes on public opinion. *American Journal of Political Science* 39:53–74.

McGraw, Kathleen M., Richard Timpone, and Gabor Bruck. 1991. Managing blame with a cushion of support. Paper presented at the annual meeting of the American Political Science Association, Washington, D.C.

McGraw, Kathleen M., Richart Timpone, and Gabor Bruck. 1993. Justifying controversial political decisions: *Home style* in the laboratory. *Political Behavior* 15:289–308.

McGuire, William J. 1966. Attitudes and opinions. *Annual Review of Psychology* 17:475–514.

McGuire, William J. 1968. Personality and susceptibility to social influence. In *Handbook of personality theory and research,* ed. Edgar F. Borgatta and William W. Lambert. Chicago: Rand McNally.

McGuire, William J. 1978. The communication/persuasion matrix. In *Evaluating advertising: A bibliography of the communication process,* ed. B. Lipstein and William J. McGuire. New York: Advertising Research Foundation.

McGuire, William J. 1985. Attitudes and attitude change. In *The handbook of social psychology,* 3d ed., ed. Gardner Lindzey and Elliot Aronson. New York: Random House.

Miller, Arthur H. 1974. Political issues and trust in government: 1964–1970. *American Political Science Review* 68:951–72.

Page, Benjamin I., and Robert Y. Shapiro. 1992. *The rational public.* Chicago: University of Chicago Press.

Perloff, Richard M. 1993. *The dynamics of persuasion.* Hillsdale, N.J.: Lawrence Erlbaum Associates.

Petty, Richard E., and John T. Cacioppo. 1981. *Attitudes and persuasion: Classic and contemporary approaches.* Dubuque, Iowa: William C. Brown.

Petty, Richard E., and John T. Cacioppo. 1986. *Communication and persuasion: Central and peripheral routes to attitude change.* New York: Springer Verlag.

Pratkanis, Anthony, and Elliot Aronson. 1992. *Age of propaganda: The everyday use and abuse of persuasion.* New York: W. H. Freeman and Co.

Rahn, Wendy. 1995. Candidate evaluation in complex information environments: Cognitive organization and comparative processes. In *Political judgment: Structure and process,* ed. Milton Lodge and Kathleen M. McGraw. Ann Arbor: University of Michigan Press.

Rahn, Wendy, John H. Aldrich, Eugene Borgida, and John L. Sullivan. 1991. A social-cognitive model of candidate appraisal. In *Information and democratic processes,* ed. John A. Ferejohn and James H. Kuklinski. Urbana: University of Illinois Press.

Rahn, Wendy and John L. Sullivan. Forthcoming. Political psychology: The role of politics and psychology. In *Political psychology,* ed. James Kuklinski. New York: Cambridge University Press.

Schlenker, Barry R. 1980. *Impression management.* Monterey, Calif.: Brooks/Cole.

Schlenker, Barry R., and Michael F. Weigold. 1992. Interpersonal processes involving impression regulation and management. *Annual Review of Psychology* 43:133–68.

Schonbach, Peter. 1990. *Account episodes: The management or escalation of conflict.* Cambridge: Cambridge University Press.

Scott, Marvin B., and Stanford M. Lyman. 1968. Accounts. *American Sociological Review,* 33:46–62.

Sears, David O., and Richard E. Whitney. 1973. Political persuasion. In *Handbook of communication,* ed. Ithiel de Sola Pool, Frederick W. Frey, Wilbur Schramm, Nathan Maccoby, and Edwin Parker. Chicago: Rand McNally.

Sigelman, Lee, Carol K. Sigelman, and Barbara Walkosz. 1992. The public and the paradox of leadership: An experimental analysis. *American Journal of Political Science* 36:366–85.

Skowronski, John J., and Donal E. Carlston. 1989. Negativity and extremity biases in impression formation: A review of explanations. *Psychological Bulletin* 105:131–42.

Sniderman, Paul M., Philip Tetlock, and Richard Brody. 1991. *Reasoning and choice.* New York: Cambridge University Press.

Snyder, Mark, and William Ickes. 1985. Personality and social behavior. In *The handbook of social psychology,* 3d ed., ed. Gardner Lindzey and Elliot Aronson. New York: Random House.

Stone, Deborah. 1989. Causal stories and the formation of policy agendas. *Political Science Quarterly* 104:23–35.

Sullivan, John L., John H. Aldrich, Eugene Borgida, and Wendy Rahn. 1990. Candidate appraisal and human nature: Man and superman in the 1984 election. *Political Psychology* 11:459–84.

Sykes, G. M., and D. Matza. 1957. Techniques of neutralization: A theory of delinquency. *American Sociological Review* 22:664–70.

Tedeschi, James T. and Harry Reiss. 1980. Predicaments and verbal tactics of impression management. In *Ordinary language explanations of social behavior,* ed. Charles Antaki. London: Academic Press.

Tetlock, Philip E. 1985. Toward an intuitive politician model of attribution processes. In *The self and social life,* ed. Barry Schlenker. New York: McGraw-Hill.

Weatherford, M. Stephen. 1992. Measuring political legitimacy. *American Political Science Review* 86:49–168.

Weiner, Bernard, James Amirkhan, Valerie S. Folkes, and Julie A. Verette. 1987. An attributional analysis of excuse giving: Studies of a naive theory of emotion. *Journal of Personality and Social Psychology* 52:316–24.

Wrightsman, Lawrence S. 1991. Interpersonal trust and attitudes toward human nature. In *Measures of personality and social psychological attitudes,* ed. John P. Robinson, Phillip R. Shaver, and Lawrence S. Wrightsman. New York: Academic Press.

Zajonc, Robert B. 1968. Attitudinal effects of mere exposure. *Journal of Personality and Social Psychology Monographs* 9:1–27.

Zaller, John. 1987. The diffusion of political attitudes. *Journal of Personality and Social Psychology* 53:821–33.

Zaller, John. 1990. Political awareness, elite opinion leadership, and the mass survey response. *Social Cognition* 8:125–53.

Zaller, John R. 1992. *The nature and origins of mass opinion.* New York: Cambridge University Press.

Zimbardo, Philip G., and Michael R. Leippe. 1991. *The psychology of attitude change and social influence.* New York: McGraw-Hill.

CHAPTER 7

Methodological Considerations in the Analysis of Presidential Persuasion

Lee Sigelman and Alan Rosenblatt

I sit here all day trying to persuade people to do the things they ought to have sense enough to do without my persuading them, Harry S Truman is said to have lamented about the presidency. That's all the powers of the president amount to.

—Neustadt (1960, 9–10)

Persuasion is the essence of presidential power. The Constitution endows the presidency with broad formal authority, but the positive powers of the office hinge on the president's ability to persuade others to change their minds or to alter their behavior.

Persuasion and the Concept of Power

It is not just the president's power that consists of persuading others to change their minds or their behavior. Political power, in Robert Dahl's (1957) classic formulation, consists of the ability of A to get B to do something that B would not otherwise have done. A is not powerful simply because B does what A wants, which B might have done without even knowing of A's wishes. For example, if A "commands" a bus to arrive within two minutes just before one actually does, we cannot say A caused the bus driver, B, to pull up to the curb.

Drawing on Dahl's formulation, we can denote the president's degree of success in exerting persuasion in a given situation as

$$M = p_2 - p_1,$$

where M (for the German word *Macht*) designates A's power, p_1 designates the baseline probability that B will do something in the absence of an influence attempt by A, and p_2 designates the probability that B will do something given an influence attempt by A. A's attempt to influence B succeeds to the extent that p_2 exceeds p_1, is inconsequential if p_2 equals p_1, or backfires to the extent that p_1 exceeds p_2.

This understanding of power is simple conceptually but can be extremely complex operationally. The basic problem is that it requires one to assume a counterfactual. That is, one must know not only what A was trying to get B to do and what B actually did, but also what B would have done in the absence of any influence attempt by A. In the bus stop example, we know that A wanted B to stop within two minutes and that B did so, but we might also be confident that B would have done so even if A had not so desired. However, because we often lack the equivalent of a bus schedule—a guide to B's baseline behavior—it is difficult to determine whether A has exercised power over B or B has simply done what B was going to do anyway. What we require, then, is a reliable estimate of p_1, a benchmark against which to gauge A's wishes and B's actions. Without such a standard, any attempt to gauge A's power over B will be speculative at best and futile at worst. In laboratory settings, experimenters can create such benchmarks by devising various treatments and by maintaining a control group. In analyzing the real world of presidential politics, the best that one can ordinarily hope for is a natural experiment, but even in that case the tight control that is possible in the experimental laboratory is simply impossible.

Consider the contrast many pundits drew during the early days of the Clinton administration between presidents Bill Clinton and Ronald Reagan as leaders of public opinion. In the early 1980s Reagan, the "Great Communicator," won widespread public support for his economic program, but a decade later Clinton was roundly criticized when a large portion of the public turned thumbs down on his economic program. The conventional wisdom held that Reagan's use of his persuasive powers had been masterful and Clinton's inept. However, those who drew this contrast failed to take into account the fundamental difference between the persuasive task Reagan undertook in 1981 and the one Clinton set for himself 12 years later. Reagan only had to convince people to endorse a major tax cut—hardly a daunting task. Clinton, on the other hand, had to win public support for a tax increase of historic proportions and a reduction in federal services—a bitter pill for many people to swallow. The acid test of the president's persuasive power is how many people he can bring around to his point of view, not how popular his point of view is. Reagan may have been more effective than Clinton as a persuader, but this cannot be established simply by comparing levels of public support for their very different programs.

Designs for the Analysis of Presidential Persuasion

It is one thing to understand the president's power of persuasion at a broad, conceptual level, but it is something else again to apply one's conceptual understanding of presidential persuasion to concrete circumstances. Like so many methodological issues, this one is subject to being dismissed as narrow, technical, and even boring—as a distraction from interesting matters of substance. However, matters of substance cannot be divorced from questions of method: one gets answers that warrant varying levels of confidence depending on the method one uses to address the questions of substance. This is hardly unique to the study of presidential persuasion. For example, Ansolabehere and Iyengar, in chapter 4 of this book, show how methodological considerations affect our understanding of the political impact of advertising.

In what follows, we consider various methods of gauging the president's persuasive power, using prior studies (including several of our own) as examples of these methods and, in some cases, their shortcomings.

The After-Only Design

We begin by considering a historic attempt by one former president, Harry Truman, to shape public opinion: the March 12, 1947, "Truman Doctrine" speech. In that speech, Truman posed the specter of worldwide communist threat and aggression and appealed for U.S. economic and military aid to Greece and Turkey to counter Soviet initiatives in the region. According to a Gallup poll, two weeks after the speech, 57 percent of those who had an opinion were in favor of aid to Greece and 46 percent supported aid for Turkey. Based on these figures, one might well conclude, as did political scientist Samuel Kernell, that:

> Although perhaps short of a mandate, Truman succeeded in quickly generating substantial public enthusiasm for his internationalist policy. If contemporaneous informal readings of public opinion were correct in portraying a pervasive isolationist mood throughout the country, these percentages represent a sizable turnaround in public opinion. (Kernell 1986, 158)

But what hard evidence exists that Truman's speech actually occasioned "a sizable turnaround in public opinion"? Applying Dahl's definition of power, we would need a reasonable estimate of what public opinion about aid would have been had Truman not delivered his speech; that is, we would need an estimate of p_1. Kernell bowed toward this requirement when he referred to the "pervasive isolationist mood throughout the country." However, neither Kernell nor anyone else has any way of knowing how a random sample of people in the United States would have answered if, before March 12, they had been asked whether they would support or oppose U.S. aid to Greece and Turkey. The methodological problem is simple: the only available evidence comes from a Gallup poll that was conducted after Truman's speech. If a poll had been conducted on the same issues shortly before March 12, then we could compare levels of public support for U.S. aid before and after the speech. Even though (as we shall shortly see) any differences in before-and-after support levels would fall short of being proof positive of presidential influence or the lack thereof, they would constitute a firmer basis than after-only data for inferring presidential influence.

From this example we can derive two methodological lessons. First, we cannot directly observe the president persuading the public. We can observe presidential activities intended to persuade the public, but we can only infer whether these activities have borne fruit. In the case of Truman's speech, evidence from an opinion poll conducted after the speech does not provide a very firm basis for inferring that public support for aid was higher afterward than it had been beforehand. But even if before-and-after evidence had been available, we would still have to select presidential persuasion from all the possible sources of an opinion shift as the most plausible explanation for the observed shift. Second, the after-only design in particular is not a compelling basis for drawing inferences about presidential persuasion, because it leaves p_1 unmeasured. A before-and-after design would constitute a step forward, but as we are about to see, it too falls well short of being foolproof.

The Simple Before-and-After Design

Dahl's definition of power seems to suggest a simple before-and-after design for gauging the extent to which a president influences those he seeks to persuade. All one needs to activate this design is a measure of the attitudes or behavior of the president's intended target before the president's attempt at persuasion and a comparable measure afterward. To the extent that the before-and-after measures differ, one infers that the president has been persuasive.

Consider, for example, a major presidential address delivered two decades after the Truman Doctrine speech: President Lyndon Johnson's March 31, 1968, announcement of a halt in U.S. bombing of North Vietnam. Until then, the United States had been aiming for a military victory in Southeast Asia—trying, in the language of the day, to "bomb Hanoi to the peace table." But in "one of history's most dramatic speeches" (Cottam 1977, 133), President Johnson announced that he had ordered a limited bombing halt as the "first step" toward de-escalation and negotiation. Did this announcement spark a shift from support for escalation to de-escalation? That is exactly what application of a simple before-and-after design seems to suggest. In the last national survey conducted before Johnson announced the bombing halt, a mid-March Gallup poll, only 40 percent opposed the bombing of North Vietnam, while 50 percent favored a continuation of bombing. By contrast, in the first national survey conducted after the address, an early-April Gallup poll, 64 percent approved of the decision. Mueller (1973, 71) describes this gap between 40 percent opposition to bombing before President Johnson announced a change in U.S. strategy and 64 percent approval of the bombing halt as "striking," even "spectacular," evidence that the president converted a large portion of the public to his point of view.

At first blush, this before-and-after evidence seems compelling, but closer scrutiny reveals numerous problems (Sigelman 1979), the most serious of which stems from the occurrence during the early months of 1968 of several significant events besides Johnson's March 31 address. Of these, the most notable was the Tet Offensive, a series of North Vietnamese and Vietcong attacks on major population centers in South Vietnam at the end of January. The scope and vigor of these attacks far exceeded the American public's expectations of North Vietnamese capabilities. Is it possible that what appeared, from a simple before-and-after perspective, to have been the effects of Johnson's address were instead aftereffects of the Tet Offensive? Figure 1 presents a longer series of responses to survey questions about support for a bombing halt. Public support for a bombing halt was higher just after Johnson's address than it had been in mid-March; this is the simple before-and-after difference we just noted. However, public support for a bombing halt was already sharply on the rise well before the president's March 31 address. Between early February and mid-March, in the wake of the Tet Offensive, support for a bombing halt mushroomed from 16 percent to 40 percent. If Johnson had not given his March 31 address and if support for a bombing halt had continued to gather momentum at its February–March pace, then by early April public approval of a bombing halt would have reached almost exactly the level it actually did reach after Johnson's speech. Of course, this is only speculation, for we are imagining what might have taken place if the address had not been delivered. However, it is certain that a substantial shift in favor of a bombing halt was already under way by mid-March, and it seems very likely that this shift continued for the rest of March.

How much of the March–April increase in public support for a bombing halt can be attributed to the president's address? Perhaps all of it, perhaps only some of it, or perhaps none of it at all. The "spectacular" before-and-after evidence of the president's powers of persuasion turns out, on closer inspection, to be inconclusive. Indeed, because Johnson's address was preceded by a large-scale change in public opinion, a strong case can even be made that the bombing halt was more an effect than a cause of the change in public opinion.

The basic lesson of this example is that the simple before-and-after design is too simple. To be sure, it is a significant improvement over the even simpler after-only design, for it involves an attempt to estimate p_1. But in many real-world situations, circumstances are not nearly as uncomplicated as the simple before-and-after design assumes. In particular, the simple before-and-after design leaves us ill equipped to rule out other plausible explanations of the $p_2 - p_1$ difference because it fails to consider events other than the president's attempt at persuasion; it does not isolate the effects of the president's actions—a problem that students of research design will recognize as the "history" threat to internal validity. Thus, by treating the "before" measure as p_1 and the "after" measure as p_2, it falls easy prey to invalid causal inferences.

The Interrupted Time-Series Design

One way to sidestep some of the problems associated with the simple before-and-after design is to extend the "before" and "after" observations in either direction from the president's attempt at persuasion. In contrast to the simple before-and-after design, which takes a snapshot of public opinion shortly before a presidential action and another snapshot shortly afterward, the interrupted time-series design takes a sequence of snapshots before and after. If we designate a presidential action as X and a measurement of public opinion as O, we can represent the simple before-and-after design as OXO and the interrupted time-series design as . . . OOOXOOO . . . The interrupted time-series approach has many advantages normally associated with experimental designs. However, it does not allow for random assignment to groups, so it is more appropriately considered a quasi-experimental design (Lewis-Beck 1986).

As we saw in figure 1, lengthening a time series can lead to an entirely different inference about the impact of the address. Alternatively, it might yield the same inference, but in a manner that enhances confidence that the inference is correct. For example, shortly before the Truman Doctrine speech, only 22 percent of the respondents in a nationwide survey cited anything in the realm of foreign affairs as the nation's "most important problem," but just after the speech, foreign affairs issues were named by 54 percent (Kernell 1986, 157). It might seem, then, that Truman's speech increased the salience of foreign affairs, but the lesson of figure 1 is that we should be extremely reluctant to draw such an inference from simple before-and-after data.

Figure 2, based on additional data presented by Kernell, extends this time series and thereby provides a sounder basis for assessing the impact of Truman's address. During the months preceding the speech, the salience of foreign affairs never rose above 23 percent. No trend is visible that would have led anyone to forecast a sharp turn upward around the time one actually occurred.

The passage of three months between the last prespeech and the first postspeech measurements of opinion poses a potential threat to any inference about the impact of the speech; just as in the spring of 1968, there was ample time in early 1947 for events other than Truman's speech to affect the salience

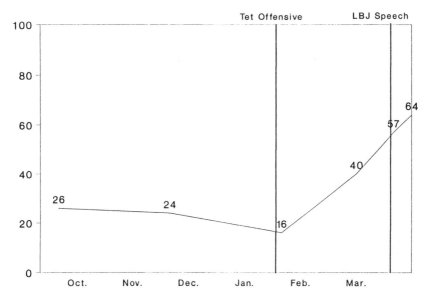

Fig. 1. Percentage of public support for a bombing halt, 1967–68. (Data from Sigelman 1979.)

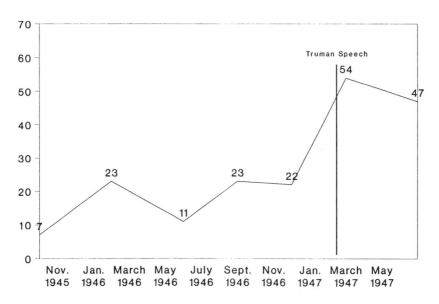

Fig. 2. Percentage of public concern over foreign policy, 1945–47. (Data from Kernell 1986.)

of foreign affairs. However, historical accounts of the period suggest no plausible rival explanation for the sharp December–March rise in the salience of foreign affairs. Because no trend toward greater salience for international affairs was under way before Truman's address and because no other events occurred that could have produced the observed change, the interrupted time-series design provides a reasonable basis for inferring that by delivering the speech, Truman redirected the public's attention toward foreign affairs.

By now, the superiority of the interrupted time-series design over the simple before-and-after design should be clear. However, this design may prove challenging to implement in an acceptable manner. Unless each observation in the series is measured via the same question wording and unless the sampling process underlying each observation in the series is identical, comparison of such observations runs the risk of producing misleading conclusions. Naturally, these requirements make it even more difficult to locate appropriate data for this type of design. Moreover, valid application of the interrupted time-series design is predicated on the availability of a dense and more-or-less continuous series of observations—the longer the series and the higher the ratio of observations to time points, the better. The problem of a relatively sparse time series is precisely the one we just noted in figure 2: the longer the time that elapses between observations, the greater the opportunity for phenomena other than the presidential action to have a substantial, yet undetected, impact on the observations in the series; and a long gap is problematic when the observations consist of the last one before the president's action and the first one thereafter.

How long a gap between observations is too long? There is no generally applicable answer to this question. Based on our knowledge of events during 1946 and 1947, we are relatively satisfied even with the sparse time series in figure 2, but we would obviously be more comfortable if the readings were more closely spaced.

Unfortunately, even when the gap between observations is short, it is easy to go wrong. Suppose that one night the president goes on prime-time television to deliver a speech that ends at 11:00 p.m. How soon should one begin assessing the public's response to the speech? In light of the lateness of the hour, the best one will probably be able to do is to begin polling the next day. But even by then it may be too late.

To see why this is so, consider the second debate of the 1976 presidential campaign, which took place on the evening of October 6. That debate lives on in memory because in the middle of it, the Republican candidate, Gerald Ford, asserted that the nations of Eastern Europe were not under Soviet domination. Ford's Democratic opponent, Jimmy Carter, briefly criticized Ford's comments, but the debate quickly turned to other subjects.

Contacted between 5:00 p.m. and midnight on October 7, the night after the debate, a national sample called Carter the winner of the debate by a 42-percentage-point margin (Steeper 1978). Taken at face value, this reading of public opinion, taken within 24 hours of the debate, suggests that most people, responding to the performance of the two candidates, concluded that Carter had been the more impressive of the two candidates. In this case, though, appearances are deceiving, as becomes clear when we take into account the evolution of public opinion during the 24 hours following the debate. The survey we cited in the beginning of this paragraph actually started as soon as the debate ended and continued throughout the next day. Of those contacted between 11:00 p.m. and 1:00 a.m. on the night of the debate, 44 percent perceived Ford as the winner, as against only 35 percent for Carter. During that immediate postdebate period, 54 percent said they intended to vote for Ford, as against only 36 percent for Carter; 52 percent considered Ford's answers to questions during the debate more credible, as against only 27 percent for Carter; 48 percent found themselves agreeing more with Ford during the debate, as against only 36 percent for Carter; and virtually no one viewed the disagreement about Eastern Europe as one of the main areas in which either candidate had done either well or poorly (Steeper 1978).

Unfortunately for Ford, public responses to the debate were influenced by more than viewers' own evaluations of the performance of the candidates. Throughout the day after the debate, media coverage focused intensively on Ford's remarks about Eastern Europe, which were generally treated as a blunder. As figure 3 shows, as the barrage of criticism continued throughout the day of October 7, public assessments of Ford and his performance in the debate steadily declined. Thus, for example, whereas Ford initially enjoyed a 9-percentage-point edge over Carter as the perceived winner of the debate, by the next night Carter was seen as the winner by a 42 percentage-point-margin—a truly remarkable turnaround. There were concomitant swings in voting intentions (which changed from an 18-percentage-point lead for Ford to a 17-percentage-point lead for Carter) and in agreement with the two candidates and perceptions of their credibility. Drawing on these data, Steeper (1978) concludes that by the morning after the debate, what the public was responding to was less and less the performance of the two debaters, and more and more a feeding frenzy of media commentary about the performance of one debater.

One lesson we can learn from this episode is that in a period of fast-breaking events, an extremely dense series of observations is likely to be required to isolate the impact of an event. Continuous monitoring of opinions on a daily or even weekly basis is rare, and yet even it may provide an insufficient basis for drawing valid inferences about the president's persuasive powers. Second, it is crucial but extremely difficult to distinguish between direct and mediated public responses to a presidential action. Within hours of

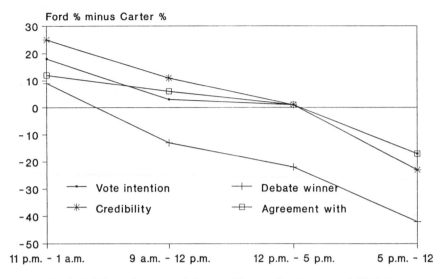

Fig. 3. Public evaluations of the candidates after the second 1976 debate. (Data from Steeper 1978.)

such an action, most people may have talked about it with family members, read about it in the newspaper, seen television coverage of it, listened to radio reports of it on their way to or from work, and discussed it with coworkers. To make matters even worse, in recent years the opposition party has often broadcast an immediate reply to presidential speeches; this may be a smart move politically, but it is certainly no boon to causal inference. Because of all the "noise" that surrounds presidential actions, even if they have had a certain effect, this effect can be overridden by the postevent brouhaha. The final lesson, and the most general one, stems from the similar logic that underlies the after-only, before-and-after, and interrupted time-series designs, each of which is premised on the serial occurrence of events. Before we can treat one event as a cause of another, we must know that it preceded its presumed effect. But temporal priority is only one basis for inferring causality, and it is not a sufficient basis. Accordingly, each of these designs, being based on temporal sequencing, is subject to the post hoc, ergo propter hoc fallacy. What is needed is a design that goes beyond temporal sequencing to eliminate other plausible causes of an observed change in public opinion.

The Control Group Design

An obvious alternative to these temporal sequence-based designs is to approach the problem as an experimentalist would: by employing a control group. Here, rather than focusing on the difference between one reading of public opinion taken shortly before a presidential action and another shortly thereafter, one conceives of a presidential action as a stimulus administered to a group of experimental subjects, but not to a control group. Provided that membership in the treatment and control groups is randomly assigned or that the two groups are otherwise equivalent, a significant intergroup difference in opinions on the subject of the president's action constitutes evidence that the president's action has influenced opinions.

How can the control group design be used to gauge the president's persuasive power? Rosen (1972) asked survey respondents to evaluate a Nixon administration proposal to guarantee $1,600 per year to each low-income family. For a randomly selected half of the respondents, Rosen identified President Richard Nixon as the source of this plan, but the remaining respondents assessed the same plan with no knowledge of its source. In this latter, control condition, 48 percent favored the plan, 40 percent opposed it, and 12 percent were undecided. When Nixon was identified as the plan's sponsor, it evoked 50 percent support, 25 percent opposition, and 24 percent indecision. As Rosen interpreted these findings:

> The president, for most respondents, is an expert and trusted source of communications. To oppose his plan, for many, would create an un-wanted tension between their opinion on the issue and their opinion of the chief executive. Since the latter opinion appears to be more important than the former, there is a tendency for respondents to move toward the president's position, generally by avoiding taking any stance at all. (Rosen 1972, 285–86)

Rosen reached this conclusion before the events of the 1970s and 1980s eroded public trust in government institutions. Could public support for presidential initiatives have grown less "automatic" since then? This question motivated a follow-up study during the latter days of the Carter administration (Sigelman and Sigelman 1981). Figure 4, which summarizes the results, indicates that the respondents gave the same family income plan higher ratings when it was presented to them unattributed than when it was labeled (inaccurately) as President Carter's proposal. That is, being presented as President Carter's proposal proved to be something of a "kiss of death" for the proposal. This effect was a product of the tendency of those who disapproved of Carter's performance in office to downgrade "his" plan, combined with the failure of Carter's supporters to rally behind an idea they, too, thought was his.

This pair of studies involved simple applications of the control group design. More complex extensions of this design are also possible. Sigelman and Sigelman (1986), for example, probed the public response to "out-of-

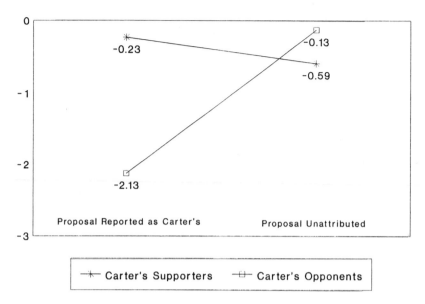

Fig. 4. Evaluations of a family assistance plan. (Data from Sigelman and Sigelman 1981.)

character" presidential actions (defined as actions that deviate sharply from positions with which a president has previously been closely identified). Several competing predictions guided the analysis. One was that in international affairs the public would give the president a "blank check"; another was that people who are predisposed in a certain policy direction would respond positively when the president moved in that direction, negatively when he moved in the opposite direction; a third was that the president would be downgraded if he appeared to be "waffling"; and a fourth, which contradicted the third, was that if the president acted in a manner sharply incongruent with his established record, he would disarm the very people who would normally oppose such an action.

To test these interpretations, Sigelman and Sigelman began by categorizing each respondent as either a "hawk" or a "dove" in international affairs. Respondents then read about Benjamin Warren, a hypothetical president, who was described to a randomly selected half of them as a foreign policy hawk and to the other half as a dove. Next, they were briefed about a crisis in Angola. A randomly selected half of those for whom Warren was described as a hawk and half of those for whom he was described as a dove were told that he had decided to send American troops to Angola to quell the crisis; the others were told that he had refused to commit American troops.

Two results of the experiment stood out. First, respondents did not display anything approaching blanket approval of Warren's actions, as predicted by the "blank check" hypothesis. Rather, evaluations of these actions were strongly influenced by respondents' foreign policy predispositions; doves in particular were especially supportive when the president was described as handling the crisis in a manner consistent with their foreign policy predispositions. Second, contrary to the idea that "wafflers" would be downgraded, an out-of-character presidential action (commitment of troops by a dovish president or refusal to commit troops by a hawkish president) was evaluated more positively than the same action when it was committed by a president for whom it was in character. Thus, many people who might otherwise have been expected to oppose a presidential action tolerated it when the president himself would normally have been expected to oppose it. This tendency bore out the "perverse" proposition that:

> We judge politicians' preferences and political characters from their past records and pronouncements. We rationally come to trust those who seem steadfastly to share our own values and sentiments. If such politicians then suddenly start advocating a policy which they—and we— have always found objectionable, saying that they have reluctantly concluded that it is now necessary or desirable, we would be much more willing to believe this coming from them than had it come from one of our long-standing opponents. (Goodin 1983, 421–42)

The Self-Control Group Design

In a variant of the control group design, respondents are not assigned to either the treatment or the control group, or to one of several treatment groups. Rather, in what we call the "self-control group" design, respondents establish an initial or baseline tendency and then are given a stimulus designed to test their susceptibility to presidential persuasion. Thus, the logic of the self-control group design directly parallels that of the simple before-and-after design, for input from the president intervenes between the "before" and "after" measurements. However, by maintaining control of the stimulus, the researcher is able to avoid the inferential problems that beset the simple before-and-after design.

The self-control group design is essentially identical to the "counterargument technique" described by Piazza et al. (1989), the point of which is to determine how readily people who have staked out a position can be talked out of it—and thus how malleable their opinions are. To see this design in action, let us turn first to Conover and Sigelman's (1982) assessment of President Carter's ability to influence public views about the appropriate response to the

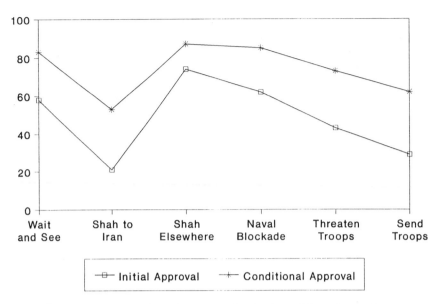

Fig. 5. Percentage of public support for Iranian crisis policy options. (Data from Conover and Sigelman 1982.)

seizure of American hostages in Iran in 1979. Shortly after the hostage crisis began, respondents in an opinion poll were asked whether the United States should take any or all of the following actions: (1) wait to see if the situation resolves itself; (2) send the deposed shah back to Iran, per Iranian demands; (3) send the shah to a country other than Iran; (4) impose an American naval blockade on Iran; (5) threaten to send U.S. troops into Iran; and (6) actually send U.S. troops into Iran. Of these actions, Carter was implicitly following the first while taking preliminary actions to facilitate the third; he had forsworn the second and had rejected the sixth for the time being; and he was considering the fourth and fifth.

Support for these alternative strategies varied widely, as the "initial approval" line in figure 5 indicates. At one extreme, only 21 percent approved of capitulating to Iranian demands by returning the shah to Iran. At the other extreme, 74 percent wanted to send the shah to a third country. More generally, the pattern of support for and opposition to the six policy alternatives was congruent with the Carter administration's actions to that point. However, as we noted earlier, congruence between the course of action the public favors and the course of action the president follows is not necessarily indicative of presidential leadership of public opinion. Perhaps President Carter was simply doing what he and his advisors thought the public wanted, or perhaps the president was avoiding actions the public seemed unlikely to tolerate.

To get a firmer grip on this issue, Conover and Sigelman followed up the initial round of questions by asking those who expressed disapproval of or uncertainty about a given course of action whether they would approve or disapprove of the same policy "if President Carter considered it necessary." Thus, any change from initial lack of support for a policy to support for the same policy in response to the follow-up question could only reflect respondents' self-estimates of their willingness to follow the president's lead. The "conditional approval" line in figure 5 shows the extra support for each course of action associated with the "if President Carter considered it necessary" proviso. In every instance but one, approval rose by at least 20 percentage points on the basis of a hypothetical endorsement by President Carter; in the one exceptional instance, support for the policy was already so high that Carter's endorsement could not elevate it much farther. "This high degree of [public] followership is particularly impressive," Conover and Sigelman (1982, 255) concluded, "when it is remembered that seconds before giving their conditional approval to an action each respondent had refused to endorse the same policy."

Hurwitz (1989) improved on Conover and Sigelman's method of measuring conditional approval. In the Conover-Sigelman study, those who had initially been opposed to or undecided about a particular course of action were asked whether they would support it if the president deemed it necessary, but no follow-up questions were asked of those who had initially expressed support for a policy. However, Hurwitz recognized that the president's ability to turn supporters of a policy he opposes into opponents of the policy should also be taken into account. Accordingly, Hurwitz asked those who were initially opposed to or uncertain about "sending U.S. troops to stop the spread of Communism in Central America" to reconsider on the assumption that "President Reagan felt it was necessary to send U.S. troops there," and he asked those who initially expressed support for sending U.S. troops to reconsider on the assumption that "President Reagan opposed the use of U.S. troops there"; furthermore, he devised parallel questions about "restricting foreign imports to protect American jobs" and "cutting government services in such areas as health and education to reduce government spending."

The willingness to reposition oneself on an issue to match the president's position, Hurwitz found, varied markedly from issue to issue (see table 1). Respondents were least susceptible to presidential influence on imposing domestic spending cuts and were most pliable on committing military forces abroad.

By providing a reliable estimate of p_1, these two control group designs provide a firmer basis for drawing causal inferences. However, the internal validity of the (self-) control group design is likely to come at a high price, for the use of such hypothetical situations immediately raises questions about external validity. Can reactions in pencil-and-paper experiments safely be extrapolated to public responses to actions undertaken by a real president in an actual foreign policy crisis?

In part, these are questions about whether an experimental scenario is realistic enough to capture the complexities of a real-world situation. Experimental scenarios simplify in order to highlight certain features of a situation while holding all other features constant. The question is whether they oversimplify, and to this question there can be no blanket answer. A well-designed experiment obviously can shed light on real-world issues. However, it cannot simply be assumed that experimental findings are generalizable to nonexperimental settings, and the burden of proof rests squarely on the shoulders of the experimenter. Here again, then, we are operating in the shadowy realm of inference—in this case, an inference that phenomena observed under controlled conditions map into situations that arise in the real world.

In responding to an experimental scenario, many people might say that they would oppose a certain presidential action if such an action ran counter to a value they had just identified as their own. In actual practice, though, they might find themselves being carried along with the president on a tidal wave of patriotism induced by the "rally-around-the-flag" effect (Mueller 1973). More generally, people are notoriously inaccurate reporters of their own mental processes, not so much because they deliberately lie as because they simply do not know their own minds (Nisbett and Wilson 1977). For example, when social psychologist Stanley Milgram (1974) asked people whether they would obey an experimenter's instructions to administer electrical shocks to another person, virtually every one of them said they would stop at low voltage levels. But when Milgram actually placed people in precisely this

TABLE 1. Initial and Reconsidered Policy Positions

		Initial Position	
Reconsidered Position		Favor	Oppose
Troop Use in Central America			
Favor		55%	35%
Oppose		45	65
	Change: 40%		
Import Restrictions			
Favor		65%	29%
Oppose		35	71
	Change: 32%		
Domestic Service Cuts			
Favor		70%	9%
Oppose		30	91
	Change: 12%		

Source: Hurwitz 1989.

situation, he found that two-thirds of the people he tested followed instructions all the way to the end. Clearly, verbal reports of how one thinks one would react in a particular situation are subject to a vast array of response biases and cannot be taken at face value as behavioral data.

Composite Designs

To this point, we have considered designs in which researchers attempt to infer from the temporal sequence of actual events how successful presidents have been in leading the public toward a new position, and designs in which researchers devise controlled, hypothetical situations as a basis for inferences. The primary strength of each is the primary weakness of the other. Time sequence–based designs focus on actual episodes of attempted presidential influence, but in a way that leaves causal inferences in doubt. Experimental designs permit solid conclusions about causal processes, but these conclusions may be only indirectly related to the phenomena of genuine interest.

Is there a way to achieve a satisfactory blend of external and internal validity? A composite design that melds the strengths of the designs considered to this point offers researchers an unmatched ability to reach trustworthy conclusions about actual episodes of attempted presidential persuasion.

To see how a composite design works, consider another major speech: President Reagan's October 27, 1983, televised address about recent events in Lebanon and Grenada. On October 23, 241 U.S. service personnel were blown up by a "kamikaze" explosives-filled van driven by Arab terrorists into the U.S. military base in Beirut. On October 26, the United States attacked Cubans who were building an airfield in Grenada. On October 27, Reagan went on nationwide television to explain the commitment of noncombat troops to Lebanon and the invasion of Grenada.

Drawing on national surveys conducted on October 26, after the invasion of Grenada, and October 27, immediately following the president's speech, Rosenblatt (1992) gauged the impact of the speech on public appraisals of U.S. actions in Lebanon and Grenada. According to the October 26 survey, 54 percent approved of the decision to send the U.S. Marines into Lebanon, 38 percent thought the marines could keep the peace, and 41 percent said the marines should be withdrawn. However, just after Reagan's speech on October 27, 67 percent of those who had heard it expressed approval of the decision to send the marines into Lebanon, 54 percent saw the marines as capable of keeping the peace, and only 30 percent called for withdrawal (see also Gilboa 1990).

These are differences of impressive magnitude over the course of a single day, but they are no more impressive than those that emerged when the questioning turned to Grenada. On October 26, 65 percent viewed the new government in Grenada as a threat to its neighbors, 60 percent perceived it as a threat to U.S. citizens in Grenada, and 54 percent endorsed the deployment of troops there, but only 33 percent thought that sending troops was the best policy for the United States to have pursued. But the next day, those who had heard President Reagan's address took a much more positive view: 76 percent accepted the premise that the new Grenadan government posed a threat to neighboring countries, agreed that the new government jeopardized U.S. citizens in Grenada, and approved of the deployment of U.S. troops; and 50 percent said sending troops was the best policy.

In sum, support for the administration's actions in both Lebanon and Grenada was considerably higher among those who had just heard President Reagan's explanation of these actions than it had been among a cross section of the public just the day before. However, in light of our criticisms of the before-and-after and interrupted time-series designs, we cannot accept these data as convincing evidence that opinion moved in response to the president's address. Support for the two military actions might have already been trending upwards before the president spoke, or the public might have been responding to other events that occurred on October 27.

This is where the composite character of Rosenblatt's design comes into play. Respondents in the October 27 survey were of two types—those who had heard President Reagan's speech and those who had not—though to this point we have considered only the former. The latter in effect constitute a control group, for, like those who listened to the speech, they experienced the "history" of October 26 and 27, but they did not receive the stimulus of the presidential address. If their evaluations of U.S. actions in Lebanon and Grenada closely resemble those of the October 27 respondents who listened to Reagan's address, we would have strong reason to disregard the address as an influence on public opinion. On the other hand, if the opinions of those who did not listen to the president's speech closely resemble those of the October 26 interviewees, then we would have a strong basis for inferring that the speech did swing opinion toward greater support for the administration's actions.

The full set of comparisons is given in table 2. There we see, in six cases out of seven, that the opinions of those polled on October 27 who had not heard President Reagan's speech were very similar to the opinions of those polled on October 26. We also see, in six cases out of seven, that the opinions of those polled on October 27 who had listened to the speech stood out perceptibly from those polled on October 26 and the other October 27 respondents.

Are we therefore ready to infer that it was President Reagan's speech that made the difference? Not quite. If assignment to the October 27 treatment or control group had been randomly determined, that would be a reasonable inference. However, the October 27 interviewees assigned themselves to the treatment or control group by listening or not listening to the president's speech. Accordingly, selection bias looms as a potential alternative explanation of the response patterns summarized in table 2. Perhaps those who listened to the speech were disproportionately predisposed to support the president. Rosenblatt (1992), however, shows that the demographic and, more important, the political differences between the October 27 interviewees who listened to the speech and those who did not were far too minor to account for the observed differences in evaluations of U.S. actions in Lebanon and Grenada. Of course, as John Zaller argues elsewhere in this volume, self-reports that one watched or listened to a particular television or radio program cannot be taken at face value. Nonetheless, Rosenblatt's comparisons of those who heard the speech and those who did not do much to allay concern about selection bias.

Thus, by combining a simple before-and-after design with a control group design, Rosenblatt could speak more authoritatively to the issue of presidential persuasion than could researchers who have used only one type of design. Random assignment of respondents to the treatment or control group would have been preferable to establishing the equivalence of the two groups after the fact. However, the sorts of demands that experimenters routinely make upon subjects in tightly controlled laboratory settings often cannot be imposed in nonlaboratory settings; in this case, the polling firm could hardly insist that some respondents watch the president's address and that others not do so. Thus, even though the best way to constitute a control group is via

TABLE 2.   Public Opinion after President Reagan's Lebanon-Grenada Speech

		October 27	
Item	October 26	Did not hear speech	Heard speech
Approve of U.S. having troops in Lebanon	54%	48%	67%
Marines can keep peace in Lebanon	38	39	54
U.S. should withdraw marines from Lebanon	40	47	30
The new government in Grenada threatened its neighbors	65	66	76
The new government in Grenada endangered Americans in Grenada	60	72	76
Approve of sending troops to Grenada	54	57	76
Sending troops was best policy in Grenada	33	36	50

Source: Rosenblatt 1992.

random assignment, and even though establishing equivalence after the fact is a second-best measure, in situations like this one, second-best may realistically be the best that one can do.

Conclusion

Although we have considered a number of different designs for the analysis of presidential persuasion, we have not exhausted the possibilities. We have not, for example, considered multivariate statistical designs in which researchers try to resolve inferential problems by accumulating a large number of cases rather than focusing on only one or two and by imposing statistical rather than experimental controls. Some of these designs encounter the same problems as the simple before-and-after design, though they come a step closer to resolving these problems by statistically controlling for potential sources of change in public opinion other than presidential activities (see, e.g., Page et al. 1987). Other designs of the time-series regression type raise methodological and technical issues too far-ranging to be considered here (see, e.g., Brace and Hinckley 1993; Ragsdale 1984; Simon and Ostrom 1989).

We have also restricted our focus to designs for gauging the immediate or short-term impact of presidential actions. It is extraordinarily difficult to get reliable answers to questions like how long an effect persists or whether a short-term effect of a certain type is transformed into a medium- or long-term effect of another type (as in "sleeper" and "boomerang" effects). "History," we saw earlier, is a threat to the validity of inferences about short-term opinion change, but it is a threat-writ-large to the validity of inferences about long-term opinion change, for in the long term so much more occurs that could account for the observed change.

Even with these caveats in mind, the key to understanding presidential influence and to conducting research on presidential persuasion lies in the conceptualization and operationalization of power. Dahl's conceptualization distinguishes between leadership and followership in a way that lends itself to empirical observation and systematic measurement by comparing responses to a presidential action to our expectations of what would have occurred had no action been taken. Most of the designs considered here have significant shortcomings insofar as our ability to draw trustworthy inferences about the effectiveness of a presidential attempt at persuasion is concerned. The problem is not that a weak research design predetermines one's conclusions about presidential persuasion, for there is no direct correspondence between methods and findings. Rather, the problem is that a weak research design undermines confidence in whatever conclusions one draws. A composite approach, the most versatile of the designs we have considered, weds the external validity of sequence-based observational designs with the internal validity of control group–based designs and thereby holds out the greatest potential for understanding presidential persuasion.

REFERENCES

Brace, Paul, and Barbara Hinckley. 1993. Presidential activities from Truman through Reagan: Timing and impact. *Journal of Politics* 55:382–98.

Campbell, Donald T., and Julian C. Stanley. 1966. *Experimental and quasi-experimental designs for research.* Chicago: Rand McNally.

Conover, Pamela J., and Lee Sigelman. 1982. Presidential influence and public opinion: The case of the Iran hostage crisis. *Social Science Quarterly* 63:249–64.

Cottam, Richard W. 1977. *Foreign policy motivation: A general theory and a case study.* Pittsburgh: University of Pittsburgh Press.

Dahl, Robert A. 1957. The concept of power. *Behavioral Science* 2:201–15.

Gilboa, Eytan. 1990. Effects of televised presidential addresses on public opinion: President Reagan and terrorism in the Middle East. *Presidential Studies Quarterly* 20:43–53.

Goodin, Robert E. 1983. Voting through the looking glass. *American Political Science Review* 77:420–34.

Hurwitz, Jon. 1989. Presidential leadership and public followership. In *Manipulating public opinion: Essays on public opinion as a dependent variable,* ed. Michael Margolis and Gary A. Mauser, 222–49. Pacific Grove, Calif.: Brooks/Cole.

Kernell, Samuel. 1986. *Going public: New strategies of presidential leadership.* Washington, D.C.: Congressional Quarterly Press.

Lewis-Beck, Michael S. 1986. Interrupted time series. In *New tools for social scientists: Advances and applications in research methods,* ed. William D. Berry and Michael S. Lewis Beck. Beverly Hills, Calif.: Sage.

Milgram, Stanley. 1974. *Obedience to authority: An experimental view.* New York: Harper and Row.

Mueller, John. 1973. *War, presidents, and public opinion.* New York: Wiley.

Neustadt, Richard E. 1960. *Presidential power: The politics of leadership.* New York: Wiley.

Nisbett, Robert E., and Timothy D. Wilson. 1977. Telling more than we can know: Verbal reports on mental processes. *Psychological Review* 84:231–59.

Page, Benjamin I., Robert Y. Shapiro, and Glenn R. Dempsey. 1987. What moves public opinion? *American Political Science Review* 81:23–44.

Piazza, Thomas, Paul M. Sniderman, and Philip E. Tetlock. 1989. Analysis of the dynamics of political reasoning: A general-purpose computer-assisted methodology. In *Political analysis,* vol. 1, ed. James A. Stimson, 99–119. Ann Arbor: University of Michigan Press.

Ragsdale, Lyn. 1984. The politics of presidential speechmaking, 1949–1980. *American Political Science Review* 78:971–84.

Rosen, Corey M. 1973. A test of presidential leadership of public opinion: The split-ballot technique. *Polity* 6:282–90.

Rosenblatt, Alan. 1992. We interrupt our regularly scheduled program . . . : The president, the public, and the selling of foreign policy in the age of television. Ph.D. diss., American University.

Sigelman, Lee. 1979. Rallying to the president's support: A reappraisal of the evidence. *Polity* 11:542–61.

Sigelman, Lee, and Carol K. Sigelman. 1981. Presidential leadership of public opinion: From "benevolent leader" to "kiss of death"? *Experimental Study of Politics* 7 (3): 1–22.

Sigelman, Lee, and Carol K. Sigelman. 1986. Shattered expectations: Public responses to "out-of-character" presidential actions. *Political Behavior* 8 (3): 262–86.

Simon, Dennis M., and Charles W. Ostrom, Jr. 1989. The impact of televised speeches and foreign travel on presidential approval. *Public Opinion Quarterly* 53:58–82.

Steeper, Frederick T. 1978. Public response to Gerald Ford's statements on Eastern Europe in the second debate. In *The presidential debates: Media, electoral, and policy perspectives,* ed. George F. Bishop, Robert G. Meadow, and Marilyn Jackson-Beeck, 81–101. New York: Praeger.

Part 3.
Individual
Control of the Political
Persuasion Process

CHAPTER 8

Creating Common Frames of Reference on Political Issues

Dennis Chong

Current thinking about public opinion is warming to the idea that political attitudes are expressions of underlying arguments or "considerations" that are recalled from memory (Kelley 1983; Zaller 1992; Chong 1993). Considerations are feelings and beliefs that originate from information acquired through discussion, personal experience, and the media. Individuals choose to accept some of the arguments that they encounter and reject others, depending upon their general ideological predispositions, which results in a reservoir of considerations that are available for use in evaluating an issue.

Usually, a person will not bring to bear all the considerations that are in mind when offering an opinion on an issue. Instead, he or she selects a subset of one or a few considerations using some kind of sampling procedure. Most people seem to give answers off the tops of their heads—meaning that they sample whatever considerations are readily available in memory. The vacillation that is commonly observed in survey responses therefore occurs for two reasons: (1) the responses are not based each time on the same subset of considerations and (2) not all the arguments considered point to the same conclusion—to take the simplest case, for example, some may lead to a conservative opinion, while others support a liberal view.

This model sheds light on survey response effects, attitude instability, and the process of attitude change. Response effects are a general category of influences on opinions that stem from manipulations in the administration of the survey (e.g., Schuman and Presser 1981). The most common response effect occurs when a slightly reworded question alters the distribution of opinion even though the original and reworded questions ostensibly address the same topic. Other response effects result from changing the order or context of questions; they can even be due to the kind of person asking the questions. An African-American interviewer, for example, might incline a respondent to evaluate issues along racial lines (Sussman 1986). All such effects can be traced to how the manipulation of the survey instrument affects the arguments people factor into their answers.

Instability of opinion, however, is commonplace even when survey conditions are not altered. It occurs when the identical question asked in the same context prompts sampling of different considerations at different times. Thus, sampling variation is inherent even when there has been no manipulation of the survey instrument. As long as there is a mixture of considerations sampled, there will be a certain amount of ambivalence in the attitude expressed. Only those individuals with entirely consistent considerations will display high attitude stability. For example, if one has accepted only liberal arguments on an issue, then no matter which are sampled, a liberal opinion will follow.

Attitude change, from this perspective, occurs when there is a change in the overall balance of liberal and conservative considerations stored in a person's memory. When the proportion of each type of consideration is altered as a result of persuasive communications, personal experiences, or other events, there is a corresponding change in the likelihood of a liberal or conservative opinion.

A shortcoming in the present formulation of the theory, however, is that it treats considerations with too much equanimity. All considerations about an issue in one's memory are available for sampling; and each consideration, if sampled, has an equal effect on an individual's opinion. This assumption overlooks systematic factors (aside from the kinds of response effects mentioned earlier) that often cause people to give priority to certain considerations over others. Someone who believes, for example, that women should be free to make reproductive choices may well concede many arguments that highlight the unpleasant realities of abortions, yet not be persuaded by those factors. Although such contrary considerations have not been purged from one's mind, neither do they constitute relevant considerations that undermine confidence in one's position. Similarly, many people with firm opinions on the death penalty will acknowledge that both supporters and opponents of capital punishment have plausible arguments; still, they take a consistent stand on one side or the other because they have decided that certain considerations override others.

An important aspect of public opinion formation is the development of common frames of reference on political issues. A common frame of reference is an interpretation of an issue that has been popularized through discussion. When an issue has a common frame of reference, people learn to base their opinion on certain considerations rather than others. One kind of common frame of reference that I will explore in this chapter is a norm or principle. When people hold to a principle, they set aside arguments that may recommend decisions that are inconsistent with the principle—even though they may agree with these arguments in isolation.

For example, in an earlier analysis of how people evaluate civil liberties issues (Chong 1993), I found individuals who let their opinions be guided by their understanding of the relevant legal norm rather than by competing considerations that came to mind. Norms pertaining to individual rights were the common frames of reference in this instance. The same type of framing effect occurs widely. A key part of the electoral process is deciding on the agenda of issues that deserve special consideration and attention (Riker 1986). Since voters' preferences can change as they shift their focus from one issue to another, candidates for public office have reason to emphasize those issues that play to their strengths and qualifications.

Efforts to change attitudes therefore do not depend exclusively on changing the balance of considerations that people hold about a person or issue.[1] Instead, they can rely on manipulating the priority that people give to different arguments or considerations. In such cases, people are "primed" (Iyengar and Kinder 1987; Kinder and Sanders 1990; Krosnick and Kinder 1990) or persuaded to focus attention on certain beliefs rather than to add new beliefs or change existing ones. It may indeed often be easier to change frames of reference than the beliefs underlying one's attitude.

In arguing for the importance of subjective considerations on individual choice, Simon (1985) notes that we need models that delineate "*what* considerations, out of a host of possible ones, will actually influence the deliberations that precede action." We have to locate "where the frame of reference for the actors' thinking comes from—how it is evoked. An important component of the frame of reference is the set of alternatives that are given consideration in the choice process. We need to understand not only how people reason about alternatives, but where the alternatives come from in the first place. The process whereby alternatives are generated has been somewhat ignored as an object of research" (302).

I take up this agenda in this chapter by offering a theory of how people select their frames of reference and how they arrive at common frames of reference. The two questions that I address are: How do people choose from the set of possible frames of reference on a political issue? And how do they learn to connect or associate that frame of reference to a preference, choice, or opinion? The insight for the theory is discussed in the following section. Then I outline a mathematical model of how people sort through multiple interpretations and develop particular frames of reference to evaluate political issues. The framing model serves up numerous deductions about the process of attitude formation and change and the susceptibility of different individuals to framing effects and persuasion. Next, I provide survey evidence for one of the major deductions of the model about how people assign priority to different frames of reference. Finally, I discuss the advantages of the framing model and offer some comments about the direction of research on political attitudes and public opinion.

Evidence from In-Depth Interviews

My insight into how considerations are sorted and ordered stems from my analysis of open-ended interviews with 30 ordinary citizens from the San Francisco Bay Area. The interviews served as a pretest for a mass national survey (reported in McClosky and Brill 1983). Each interview was carried out in a single session generally lasting just under two hours. Subjects were given ample opportunity to think aloud and speak freely on such topics as crime, human rights, abortion, freedom of expression, privacy, prostitution, homosexuality, prisoners' rights, censorship, and other important controversies involving individual rights and liberties.

I discovered in these open-ended interviews that legal norms supporting a tolerant opinion had a grip on the mind in the sense that the norm rarely was completely overridden and frequently prevailed over other considerations that suggested a different opinion. All considerations that came to mind therefore were not treated equally by the respondent. People's understanding of how the courts had reasoned through these issues—which may have come from secondary sources rather than directly from the courts themselves—influenced how they themselves interpreted and deliberated over them. There was variation, however, in the way that different people reasoned through competing arguments on an issue. Analysis of these differences revealed a systematic process behind the sorting of alternative interpretations of a topic that has important implications for models of the survey response.

On a variety of subjects, some respondents simply reacted to the most salient frames of reference suggested by the question; they laid out two or three competing arguments without being able to resolve them in any convincing fashion. Respondents who gave off-the-top-of-the-head responses based on a single consideration often gave a different response upon contemplating a second consideration. Similarly, respondents who were conflicted over several considerations typically vacillated from one side of the issue to the other over the brief course of their answer. In both cases, it was as if they were answering the same question a number of times as they thought out loud; sometimes, their answer would favor one position; at other times, they would come out for the contrary position as we would expect in a probabilistic process. (See figure 1.)

These interviews also revealed, however, that those who knew more about politics more easily sifted through the various positions on an issue to

$$F_1 \longrightarrow F_2 \longrightarrow F_3 \longrightarrow F_4$$

Fig. 1. Shifting frames of reference.

arrive at some kind of overall conclusion. Indeed, they seemed to be able to reach their opinions sometimes without considering in any detail the underlying arguments. In such cases, the off-the-top-of-the-head response may be highly reliable. I am not suggesting that those who are more knowledgeable have a superior ability to reason through the issues on the spot (although this may also be true). Rather, more knowledgeable respondents appear to frame issues more quickly and confidently because they already have some familiarity with them. They are aware of the common frames of reference or interpretations used in public discussions of these issues. Less knowledgeable respondents, on the other hand, have to improvise by responding to the most salient cues in the question.

In discussions about rights and liberties, less knowledgeable respondents often focus on who the issue involves (e.g., what groups—criminals, communists, racists, feminists, homosexuals?) and how the matter affects them, in addition to being influenced by their comprehension of legal norms. They are susceptible, in other words, to a variety of frames of reference, and much depends on which frame happens to be chosen. On the other hand, those who are more attuned to politics are more likely to ignore consideration of the specific groups involved in favor of a more general interpretation of the issue. They conform to public discourse on civil liberties matters, which typically centers on democratic values and the abstract rights of individuals. I call this a framing or winnowing process, referring to how an individual learns to focus on certain considerations on the issue (symbolized by **F** in figure 2) and to disregard others.

Therefore, although there are two principal classes of considerations driving responses to civil liberties issues, they are not accorded equal weight by everyone. Group-based considerations are generally more salient to those with little experience in these matters. In contrast, those with greater political acumen are more likely to frame the issues in terms of the underlying norms and principles and to downplay or compartmentalize their feelings about the groups that wish to exercise their rights.

The ability to ignore certain considerations, to treat them as "irrelevant," is a trained capacity (cf. Restle, 1955).[2] The essence of *public* opinion formation—as opposed to *private* opinion—is that there are systematic influ-

Fig. 2. Winnowing of frames of reference.

ences that cause people to pay attention to particular features of the issue and to ignore others. Primary among these influences are the arguments and messages regarding political issues that are conveyed through the mass media by politicians, courts, policy experts, journalists, editors, academics, interest groups, and other opinion leaders. Through these messages, the public learns to think about political issues using certain common frames of reference. In more formal terms, we might say that, of the total number of possible interpretations of an issue, some proportion is ruled out, or winnowed, by public debate and discussion as public opinion leaders establish the parameters of debate. Political discourse, in other words, determines what the issue is and is not about. People gradually learn, through exposure to public discussion on the issue, to base their opinions on certain pertinent aspects of the issue, and at the same time they learn *not* to pay attention to other features of the issue deemed to be irrelevant. Exposure to information therefore narrows one's focus on an issue to a smaller number of relevant interpretations when there is general agreement among opinion leaders about how to think about the issue. Such agreement exists, for example, on many (but by no means all) civil liberties issues. The terms *relevant* and *irrelevant,* I hasten to add, have nothing to do with whether any consideration is more valuable, worthy, or persuasive than others. They are simply analytical designations for the arguments that opinion leaders tend either to use or to set aside in their discussions of the issue.

The Framing Model

In this section, I outline a formal model of how the public arrives at its evaluations of political issues and how common frames of reference are developed.

The basic assumptions of the framing model are as follows:

1. An issue can be interpreted using any of a number of frames of reference or dimensions. Frames of reference or dimensions encompass or group together sets of considerations or arguments. For instance, if a person's frame of reference for the election is the state of the economy, then that person's evaluation of the economy is based on the various arguments that she or he has heard and perhaps same firsthand observations.
2. Different frames of reference predispose one to take different positions on the issue; that is, if the issue is evaluated along one dimension, a person is likely to draw a different conclusion than if he or she considers it according to another dimension. Obviously, without this second assumption, the frame of reference concept has no leverage.

3. A person's preference on the issue is based on the frames of reference chosen and the associations between those frames and the set of possible responses. Both the frames of reference chosen and their associations are the product of a learning process in which one relies on information and cues provided by opinion leaders.
4. A common frame of reference is a particular interpretation of an issue that has been popularized through political discussion.

The phrasing of the question is undoubtedly the biggest factor that affects which considerations come to mind. Take, for example, the question, "Can the majority vote to ban the expression of certain unpopular political opinions?" A number of possible frames of reference might be used to evaluate this question: the focus might be placed on the notion of majority rule, the principle of free speech, the ideas of unpopular political groups, or some other aspect of the issue. As stated in assumption two, I assume that the frame or frames used to interpret the question affect the position taken. If you think about the unpopular group, you will tend to adopt a different position than if the issue brings to mind the Bill of Rights. According to the third assumption of the model, the response depends on which of these (one or more) frames of reference are sampled, and then, once accessed, how these frames dispose the respondent to answer the question.

Two Main Processes

There are thus two main processes that need to be modeled. First, how does one learn to associate any particular frame of reference to a position on an issue? Second, out of the possible frames of reference, which are used to evaluate the issue? There is no necessary order between the two processes, although we can tell a story that gives priority to one process over the other. I will forgo such a story. Start with a set of frames of reference or dimensions that may be used to judge an issue. Political discussion partitions or winnows this set of frames by suggesting how to interpret the issue. As a result, some frames become relevant while others become irrelevant. It is not automatic, however, that everyone will learn to adopt the relevant frame of reference. The weight that people attach to the two subsets of frames—relevant and irrelevant—is a product of the information that they gather on the issue. I assume that on issues with a focus, there is a stream of messages that persuade the recipient to pay greater attention to certain dimensions of the issue rather than others. These messages either tell the recipient directly how to assign his or her priorities ("the elections about the economy") or they guide the recipient, through constant repetition of a theme, to conceptualize the issue in the manner in which it is being discussed. If, for example, the only subject that politicians and commentators will talk about is the state of the economy, then it is reasonable for one to infer that economic policy is the key issue in the campaign.

The Framing Process

The framing mechanism is represented as a dynamic process in equation 1. Messages are assumed to be of two types—those that focus on the relevant frames of reference and those that focus on the irrelevant frames. The probability of receiving each type of framing message in any given period is represented, respectively, by π_{1f} and π_{2f}. The probability of not receiving any framing message in a given period is represented by

$$\pi_{3f} = 1 - \pi_{1f} - \pi_{2f}$$

Clearly, if there is little distinction between the sizes of π_{1f} and π_{2f}, then there is not much of a case to be made for any consensual frame of reference. The interesting cases, from the point of the model, are those issues on which discussion seems to point to certain interpretations at the expense of others. Some of the civil liberties issues that I will analyze later have this characteristic. When there are clear public messages reinforcing and legitimizing one perspective or rationale on an issue, then π_{1f} is large relative to π_{2f}. It is not automatic, however, that people will yield to these messages. Two additional parameters in the model, q_1 and q_2, index the receptiveness of the individual to messages that emphasize, respectively, the relevant and irrelevant dimensions.

$$w_{\text{rel},n+1} = [(1 - q_1) w_{\text{rel},n} + q_1] \pi_{1f} + [(1 - q_2) w_{\text{rel},n}] \pi_{2f}$$
$$+ (1 - \pi_{1f} - \pi_{2f}) w_{\text{rel},n} \tag{1}$$

Knowing only the distribution of framing messages, the receptivity of individuals, and the initial value of w_{rel} (at time zero), we can calculate w_{rel} for any period n using the following solution to equation 1:

$$w_{\text{rel},n} = (1 - \pi_{1f} q_1 - \pi_{2f} q_2)^n (w_{\text{rel},0} - w_{\text{rel}}^*) + w_{\text{rel}}^* \tag{2}$$

where

$$w_{\text{rel}}^* = (\pi_{1f} q_1) / (\pi_{1f} q_1 + \pi_{2f} q_2) \tag{3}$$

The value w_{rel}^* constitutes the equilibrium state of the framing process; in other words, w_{rel}^* is the end state toward which the process will converge in the long run.

The efficiency of the framing process, as reflected in the weight given to the relevant frame of reference in any given period n, $w_{rel,n}$, therefore depends on the characteristics of discussion surrounding the issue and on the characteristics of individual members of the public. The size of π_{1f} is directly related to (1) the loudness and clarity of messages favoring a particular frame of reference and (2) the attentiveness of the audience. First, if there is a consensus among opinion leaders about the interpretation of the issue, then framing will occur more rapidly as people recognize and conform to the way the issue is being evaluated. On the other hand, if you ask the public about issues that, from its perspective, are remote and esoteric and have not been clarified by political discussion or are rife with many competing interpretations, then you are likely to uncover more idiosyncratic interpretations.

Second, as a rule, the more informed one is about a subject, the more likely one will be attuned to the common interpretations of the issue established by public opinion and reference group leaders. Individuals who do not actively follow politics will experience greater difficulty providing focused responses to questions because they will tend to be affected by a greater number of competing interpretations.

The receptiveness of the individual to messages favoring a particular frame of reference, q_1, will depend on the degree of consensus or ideological agreement over how the issue should be interpreted. If there is a bipartisan consensus on how to think about an issue, then we would expect that both liberals and conservatives would yield to this interpretation. But if there is ideological division, then liberals and conservatives would be expected to favor the interpretations being promoted by the opinion leaders in their respective ideological camps. Furthermore, within each ideological camp, more informed individuals will be more likely to adopt ideologically consistent interpretations and to reject inconsistent frames of reference that they encounter.

The interpretation of an issue can change over time. Attention can be redirected to a new frame of reference through persuasive communications—the same way that the old frame of reference gained priority in the first place. If, for example, political leaders and the media alter their messages during the campaign by giving greater emphasis to foreign policy rather than the economy, then the weight given to that policy dimension will increase over time relative to the weight given to economic matters. The previously irrelevant frame of reference would become the relevant frame.

The Association Process

The accompanying belief formation or association process of the model explains how any given frame of reference activates beliefs that trigger one's response to an issue. Some frames of reference (e.g., Saddam Hussein as another Hitler) may be so symbolically loaded that everyone who adopts them will draw the same liberal or conservative conclusion on the issue. On the other hand, some frames of reference are more dimensional or bipolar in nature. For example, if you are persuaded by the candidates and media commentators that the election should be a referendum on the economy rather than on the candidates' characters, then it is less of a foregone conclusion which candidate you will prefer. How the candidates will be evaluated using this dimension will depend on a learning process in which individuals gather and process information about the relative merits of the candidates' economic policies. Here we would expect Democrats and Republicans, and liberals and conservatives, to gather and accept different types of information according to their partisan biases. Also, we would expect that information gathering and acceptance would vary according to the political interest levels of individuals. More sophisticated individuals gather more information, but they are likely to be more selective about what arguments they will accept; less sophisticated individuals receive less information and are generally more easily persuaded by the messages they encounter.

These assumptions are embodied in equation 4, representing how one learns to evaluate any particular frame of reference, F_i. (To reduce clutter, I have omitted the subscript i throughout equations 4–6.) In any time period, a person receives a liberal argument or a conservative argument or no argument whatsoever; the likelihood of each event is indexed, respectively, by π_{1a}, π_{2a}, and π_{3a}, which depend, as in the case of framing messages, on the prominence of the argument and the interest levels in the general public. (The a subscript differentiates the probability of receiving these arguments from the probability of receiving framing messages.) The person's receptivity to liberal arguments is represented by a, while receptivity to conservative arguments is represented by b.

$$F_{n+1} = p_{\text{lib},n+1} = [(1 - a)\, p_{\text{lib},n} + a]\, \pi_{1a}$$

$$+ [(1 - b)\, p_{\text{lib},n}]\, \pi_{2a} + (1 - \pi_{1a} - \pi_{2a})\, p_{\text{lib},n} \tag{4}$$

Note that if $\pi_{1a} = \pi_{2a} = 0$, then $p_{\text{lib},n+1} = p_{\text{lib},n}$. There is no change, in other words.

The solution to equation 4 for any period n equals:

$$F_n = p_{\text{lib},n} = (1 - \pi_{1a}a - \pi_{2a}b)^n\, (p_{\text{lib},0} - p_{\text{lib}}^*) + p_{\text{lib}}^*, \tag{5}$$

where

$$p_{\text{lib}}^* = (\pi_{1a}a)/(\pi_{1a}a + \pi_{2a}b) \tag{6}$$

The value p_{lib}^* represents the equilibrium state of the association process, given assumptions about the stream of messages that are circulating and the receptivity of different types of individuals to those messages. If the process reaches this state at any time, it will remain there in all subsequent periods.

Combining the Association and Framing Processes

On a given issue then—more specifically, on a given question about an issue—there is a set of frames of reference prompted by the way the question is worded, each of which is probabilistically associated with the possible responses on the issue, but these frames are not equally weighted. In order to deduce an individual's response to a particular question at time n, we need to ascertain (1) the weights attached to the relevant, $\mathbf{F}$, and irrelevant, F, frames of reference and (2) the ideological dispositions (i.e., $p_{\text{lib},n}$) of those frames of reference. This calculation is represented in equation 7 in the simplest case of one relevant and one irrelevant frame of reference.[3]

$$P_{\text{lib},n} = \mathbf{F}_n \times w_{\text{rel},n} + F_n \times (1 - w_{\text{rel},n}) \tag{7}$$

Equation 7 combines the framing and association processes represented in equations 2 and 5, respectively. It states that the overall probability of providing a liberal response on the question is a weighted sum of the probabilities of giving a liberal response associated with each relevant and irrelevant frame of reference used to interpret the question. According to the model, on issues with a common frame of reference, political discussion increasingly focuses attention on the relevant frame. Therefore, the weight given to the relevant frame increases at the expense of the weight given to irrelevant frames.

Deductions from the Framing Model

If we set aside the framing process for a moment, the belief formation process represented in equation 4 reproduces the main deductions of the exposure-acceptance models developed in the 1960s by McGuire (1968) and Converse (1962) and elaborated upon recently by Zaller (1992). A common feature of these models—which I will call single-process models because they do not incorporate framing effects—is that attitude change depends on reception of a message ("exposure") and yielding to that message ("acceptance"). The parameters of equation 4 permit a similar interpretation. This simple model produces a number of interesting deductions. For example:

The development of consensus on political issues. When there is a uniform stream of messages supporting one side of an issue—say the liberal view—support for that position increases with exposure to those messages (the speed of learning is directly related to π_{1a}). In the absence of bipartisan divisions, neither liberals nor conservatives reject the message (a is large and b is small across the board, meaning there is little resistance to the message). Therefore, any recipient characteristic that increases the probability of receiving that information—such as education, interest in politics, attention to the mass media, membership in political organizations—will promote support for the consensual position.

Polarization of public opinion. Ideological contrasts will sharpen on issues that are unsettled or sharply debated. When liberal and conservative opinion leaders send out conflicting messages (π_{1a} and π_{2a} are comparable in size), rank-and-file liberals and conservatives will tend to be polarized because they accept messages that are consistent with their partisan beliefs and reject inconsistent messages (a is large while b is small for liberals; the reverse holds for conservatives).

Curvilinear pattern of support for a policy. Support for liberal (conservative) policy proposals among conservatives (liberals) will be curvilinearly related to information levels. This is a standard finding in the literature on who is most susceptible to persuasion. Conservatives of middling sophistication will be more likely than the least sophisticated to hear an ideologically contrary message (i.e., π_{1a} will be greater in the middle group) and they will be more likely than the most sophisticated to be susceptible to persuasion (i.e., a will be greater in the middle group than in the group of sophisticates). A parallel deduction can be drawn about liberals. The stability of the extremes therefore stems from the failure of the least aware to encounter dissonant messages and the refusal of the most aware to entertain them.

The addition of a second process represented by equation 1—a framing mechanism—to the model generates a variety of new deductions:

Considerations receive varying weights. Some considerations will have little or no effect on one's attitude on an issue. As w increases in size, attention shifts to a common frame of reference. This proposition is tricky to test, however, because we have to demonstrate that although one holds a particular belief about an issue, that consideration does not affect one's opinion on it. But an irrelevant consideration is less likely to be revealed in the first place. People tend to answer questions by referring to those factors that explain their position, not to those they regard as being peripheral. What we need to show, then, is that people learn to give more priority to some considerations than to others as they follow discussion of the issue. An ideal test, therefore, would be conducted across time on an issue that became increasingly well defined by opinion leaders. Alternatively, in a cross-sectional survey, irrelevant dimensions will have their greatest impact on the attitudes of the least informed, since the size of *w* is directly related to the information level of the respondent. This is an important result that gives a theoretical interpretation for specified relationships in cross-sectional analysis. I will elaborate on this deduction in the next section when I test it.

Value and normative consistency. On a set of issues that is united by a common frame of reference such as a norm or value, those who are better informed are more likely to employ that frame of reference consistently because they are less likely to be affected by competing considerations. This explains, for example, why those who are better educated are more likely to support consistently a democratic principle on general questions calling for abstract support of the value as well as in concrete cases involving unpopular groups and dangerous ideas (Prothro and Grigg 1960). Both better and less informed individuals respond to the honorific principle on the general questions because alternative frames of reference are not brought to mind (*w* approaches 1 for all respondents), but only the better informed focus on the applicable norm on the concrete issues and ignore alternative considerations made salient by the question (*w* approaches 1 for only the better informed respondents).

Specification of relationships over time. On consensual issues with a common frame of reference, the relationship between measures of awareness and one's attitude will depend on whether the analysis is made early or late in the opinion formation process. Early in the process, only the most attentive conform to the common frame of reference on the issue. In time, however— as the opinion formation process approaches equilibrium—the less attentive members of the public gradually learn what the issue is about and, in the process, to adopt the common frame of reference.

Explanation of survey response effects. Response effects can also be interpreted using the two processes described by the framing model. These effects result from modifying the respondent's reservoir of beliefs (changing the value of $p_{\text{lib},n}$ in equation 4 by providing novel arguments) and from shifting attention to some beliefs rather than others (changing the frame of reference used by changing the relative values of π_{1f} and π_{2f} and thereby changing *w*). The survey question, from this perspective, is simply another message or set of messages to the respondent, not unlike the messages he or she receives from the news or in conversations with his friends or family. A survey question posing two contrasting alternatives, for example, in effect sends two competing messages to the respondent, which he or she can accept or reject by evaluating them on the spot. The phenomenon of "acquiescence," in this regard, is simply a readiness to agree to the arguments raised by questionnaire items. Moreover, because the mind is not brainwashed between questions, a survey sometimes has to be evaluated in its entirety rather than as a set of discrete questions. For example, a series of questions on the state of the economy is like a series of messages emphasizing the importance of that frame of reference. Consequently, the economy will be on the respondent's mind when he or she interprets subsequent questions.

Response effects are commonplace, I think, because people tend to have a small reservoir of beliefs related to political subjects. Many surveys, moreover, raise themes that do not coincide precisely with recent political discussions. Therefore, the questions contained in these surveys have to be interpreted extemporaneously. People often have to build their opinions by allowing the cues in the question to guide their thinking and reasoning. Consequently, a telltale test would be to evaluate response effects on topics familiar to respondents to see if they are just as likely to be affected by survey manipulations when contemplating proximate issues.

Resistance to response effects. Cues in survey questions that raise, from the respondent's perspective, irrelevant arguments or considerations will not affect the opinion expressed. Consequently, people who adhere to a particular frame of reference and who apply it consistently should be more resilient against attempts to deflect them from their position through manipulations in wording and framing. In general, a frame of reference that is made salient by the question format will have an impact to the extent that it has not been winnowed by previous contemplation.

Immunity to persuasion. Why is it the case that people who are familiar with both sides of the issue will be more likely to resist persuasive communications arguing against their point of view? The framing model views inoculation against opposing ideas to be the result of winnowing. Arguments on both sides are considered; opposing arguments, even if they possess some merit, are discounted in the process. When people know the arguments on both sides, they have been thoroughly briefed about the scope of the issue; the issue has, in effect, been completely framed for them. Knowledge of opposing arguments implies awareness of the counterpoints that should be discounted in arriving at one's opinion. If completely new arguments are pressed on someone, the possibility exists that the issue will be reframed along lines more favorable to those taking the opposite side of the issue. New arguments open up the debate to new interpretations. For instance, as long as pornography is seen in free-speech terms, liberals are comfortable defending the rights of pornographers; but if instead the issue is restated to take consideration of the harm that the existence of pornography in society inflicts upon women in general, then the issue cannot be so patly resolved. An analogy can be made to immunization—someone who has heard the opposing viewpoint is also likely to have rehearsed the reasons why those views do not carry the argument and why contrary arguments should be accorded precedence (Pratkanis and Aronson 1992).

Testing for Framing Effects

A central deduction from the framing model is that better-informed respondents will give higher priority to those considerations that have been highlighted in public discussion of an issue. The evidence that I cited earlier from the in-depth interviews about civil liberties controversies showed that more knowledgeable subjects ignored certain considerations in taking their positions even though they mentioned them in the course of responding; instead, they were more likely to address issues by applying the relevant democratic norm. In terms of the formal model, as w increases in size, the influence of irrelevant frames of reference diminishes. How much this occurs depends on the extent to which political discussion has focused attention on specific frames of reference as well as the amount of attention an individual pays to these discussions.

The following series of tests is based on the idea that certain considerations about civil liberties controversies are ignored (although not forgotten) as one learns to conceptualize the issues along conventional lines. People learn to interpret these issues by applying the relevant legal norm as they understand it. This prediction differs from that of current models, which hold that all considerations will be factored into the attitude.

Therefore, on issues that have been largely settled in elite discussions through the application of a principle or norm, the tendency to evaluate the issue by using that principle should increase with the information level of the respondent, while the tendency to respond to the issue using other arguments and considerations should decrease. More informed individuals will learn to base their views on certain commonly defined considerations rather than others.

This proposition is tested by examining opinions expressed on a variety of civil liberties controversies in a 1977–78 national survey of opinion leaders and the general public (McClosky and Brill 1983). Since these issues are often given an authoritative judicial interpretation that guides how they are discussed, they probably represent some of the clearest illustrations of the development of a common frame of reference. Each issue is controversial insofar as there are readily apparent reasons why one might choose one side rather than another on the matter. The questions are typically worded to raise concern for both sides: references to the need to protect individual rights are commingled with allusions to the potential dangers of political, social, or criminal nonconformity and the importance of maintaining social order and protecting certain social groups or individuals who are the targets of nonconformists. Yet, despite the ostensible conflicts of values embodied in these issues, they can have at the same time a more settled legal standing if they have been the subject of political debate and litigation.

According to the theory I have outlined, even though people may share common beliefs about a matter, they cannot be assumed to apply those beliefs in an identical fashion. They may have similar evaluations of specific arguments, yet not assess the overall issue in the same way. On civil liberties issues, which are commonly understood and discussed by public opinion leaders in terms of general principles, those who are more familiar with the abstract arguments on these matters are predicted to be less likely than people who are not as well informed to be influenced by their beliefs about the groups involved, their feelings about law and order, and other concerns that typically incline them to be less tolerant. The reason is not that information causes people to cease to believe those things that might make them more intolerant (although this may occur to some extent also); rather, the acquisition of information leads to the development of a particular frame of reference that gives less weight to these other dimensions on the issue. Therefore, the underlying beliefs still reside in memory, but they are not applied in the same manner by those who have acquired a particular interpretation of the issue.

For example, the first group of items in table 1 deal with the rights of criminal defendants. Given how the items are phrased, I assume that they prompt the respondent to think (even if only fleetingly) about one or more of the following conflicting ideas: due process, legal protections for those accused, the right to have one's day in court, the effectiveness of the criminal justice system, the prevalence of crime in society, the lack of safety in one's neighborhood. One's overall attitude on the issue is likely to be a product of some combination of these beliefs. A person who believes that a fair trial should be given to everyone who has been accused of a felony, but who also thinks that too many criminals are escaping punishment due to so-called technicalities or rights violations, may show more ambivalence on the issue than someone who believes that criminals are the unfortunate victims of unfair social circumstances.

If people gave equal weight to all considerations that were conjured in reaction to the question, then we would expect that people who held similar beliefs about crime, criminals, and equal protection under the law would have roughly—subject to sampling variation—the same opinions on the issue. But to the extent that there exists a common normative frame of reference so that alternative considerations are ignored or winnowed, we should find some individuals who hold the attitude that those accused of a crime should be given the right to remain silent, the right to an attorney, a fair trial, and other protections *despite* their antipathy toward those who break the law.

How to measure the effect, or lack thereof, of a particular consideration? The most straightforward way to establish the effect of various beliefs on attitudes is to develop separate measures of these beliefs and then to estimate the contribution each belief makes to the overall attitude expressed on the

TABLE 1. Effect of Competing Considerations on Support for the Rights of the Accused

If someone is caught red-handed beating and robbing an older person on the street: (b) it's just a waste of taxpayers' money to bother with the usual expensive trial, or (a) the suspect should still be entitled to a jury trial and all the usual legal protections.

% Tolerant among Respondents Claiming
Strong Abstract Support for the Right to a Trial

| | Attitude toward Lawbreakers[a] | | | |
	Sympathetic	Moderate	Punitive	Δ
Less Informed[b]	80[c]	64	48	32
Mass Public	86	78	63	23
More Informed	88	84	71	17
Lawyers and Judges	99	97	99	0

Should rapists or child molesters be given the same sort of "fair trial" as other criminals? (a) Yes, because the right to a fair trial should not depend on the nature of the crime, or (b) No, because their crimes are so inhuman that they do not deserve the usual legal protections.

% Tolerant among Respondents Claiming
Strong Abstract Support for the Right to a Trial

| | Attitude toward Lawbreakers | | | |
	Sympathetic	Moderate	Punitive	Δ
Less Informed	70	62	45	25
Mass Public	84	78	69	15
More Informed	90	86	81	9
Lawyers and Judges	99	99	98	1

Once an arrested person says he wishes to remain silent, the authorities: (a) should stop all further questioning at once, or (b) should keep asking questions to try to get the suspect to admit his crimes.

% Tolerant among Respondents Claiming
Strong Abstract Support for the Right to Remain Silent

| | Attitude toward Lawbreakers | | | |
	Sympathetic	Moderate	Punitive	Δ
Less Informed	57	46	40	17
Mass Public	66	54	49	17
More Informed	70	59	54	16
Lawyers and Judges	97	94	88	9

The "right to remain silent": (a) is needed to protect individuals from the "third degree" and forced confessions, or (b) has harmed the country by giving the criminals too much protection.

% Tolerant among Respondents Claiming
Strong Abstract Support for the Right to Remain Silent

| | Attitude toward Lawbreakers | | | |
	Sympathetic	Moderate	Punitive	Δ
Less Informed	69	57	38	31
Mass Public	80	71	56	24
More Informed	85	78	66	19
Lawyers and Judges	98	95	92	6

(*continued*)

TABLE 1. *Continued*

Forcing people to testify against themselves in court: (b) may be necessary when they are accused of very brutal crimes, or (a) is never justified, no matter how terrible the crime.

% Tolerant among Respondents Claiming
Strong Abstract Support for the Right to Remain Silent

	Attitude toward Lawbreakers			
	Sympathetic	Moderate	Punitive	Δ
Less Informed	32	23	20	12
Mass Public	53	46	43	10
More Informed	62	58	54	8
Lawyers and Judges	98	99	100	−2

If a police officer stops a car for a traffic violation, he should: (b) be allowed to search the car if he suspects it contains narcotics or stolen goods, or (a) be limited to dealing with the traffic violation and nothing else.

% Tolerant among Respondents Claiming
Strong Abstract Support for the Right to Privacy

	Attitude toward Lawbreakers			
	Sympathetic	Moderate	Punitive	Δ
Less Informed	42	28	25	17
Mass Public	46	31	26	20
More Informed	48	33	27	21
Lawyers and Judges	76	44	32	44

Source: Data are from a 1977–78 national survey of judges and lawyers ($N = 486$) and the mass public ($N = 1,993$). For details and a report of the results, see McClosky and Brill (1983).

[a]See footnote 4 for a description of the scale used to measure attitude toward lawbreakers.

[b]Based on scores on a 20-item test of constitutional and political knowledge. "Less Informed" respondents in the mass public obtained 10 or fewer correct answers. "More Informed" respondents obtained 11 or more correct answers.

[c]Cell entry is the probability of giving a tolerant response (alternative "a" of each question).

issue. On questions about the rights of suspects, for example, we can measure people's feelings about the right to a fair trial and the right to remain silent, and we can also measure separately their attitude toward lawbreakers (by asking their views on punishment versus rehabilitation, the death penalty, how to reduce crime rates, and so on).[4] The effect of various law-and-order considerations, then, is the observed difference in attitude on the issue between those who take a consistently hard line toward lawbreakers and those who are more sympathetic toward them. On issues that fall under clear legal norms protecting the rights of those accused, we should find that as the political awareness of subjects increases, these other beliefs will exert less influence on their attitudes.

This prediction is confirmed in a variety of ways by the data in tables 1–4, which report the effect of a competing consideration among those who profess strong support for the civil libertarian principle that is being tested on the question. Each row in these tables should be read, going from left to right, as the change in probability of giving a tolerant response depending on one's attitude toward a competing consideration. For example, the first item in table 1 asks whether a mugger who has been caught red-handed should be given a trial or punished summarily. By holding constant people's attitudes toward the rights of criminal suspects, we can calculate how much their opinions are influenced by their attitudes toward lawbreakers. We find that, as respondents become better informed, they pay less and less attention to their attitude toward lawbreakers. Among those in the general public scoring in the bottom half of an information test based on knowledge of constitutional rights and political facts, the probability of being tolerant on this item decreases .32 if one is punitive rather than sympathetic toward criminals. In the general public as a whole, the change in probability is .23. Among those in the upper half of the information scale, the drop in probability is only .16. Finally, in a well-trained sample of lawyers and judges, where considerations about the nature of the crime and attitudes toward criminals are forecast to have the least weight, there is 0 change in probability according to one's attitude toward lawbreakers. The same pattern is observed in a second question about whether rapists and child molesters deserve a trial and in three other items testing support for a suspect's right to remain silent.

For comparison, I included the last item in table 1 to demonstrate that, on a search-and-seizure issue with a debatable legal interpretation, law-and-order considerations sway attitudes markedly. Across all information levels, there is a sharp difference of opinion about the proper bounds of a police search of a car, the driver of which has been stopped for a traffic violation. Those who take an uncompromising view of criminal offenders are much more likely to feel that a search is permissible if the officer suspects that the car contains contraband.

The second set of items in table 2 raises issues about the right of various nonconformists to exercise freedom of expression. These groups are disliked by the general public in varying degrees.[5] Some of the groups, such as Nazis, racists, and the Ku Klux Klan are almost universally disliked, although a meaningful distinction can be drawn between those who believe such groups are a threat to society and those who find them to be obnoxious but not especially threatening or harmful. Other groups, such as feminists, student protesters, and atheists elicit divided reactions from the public. Some describe these groups as being beneficial to society, others are irritated but not threatened by them, while still others feel that they pose a danger to society. The question for our purposes is whether the weight of these considerations about the groups on people's attitudes varies inversely with the information level of the respondent.

The data in table 2 accord with the framing model's prediction. The attitude that one has toward the group involved in the controversy has a much

TABLE 2. Effect of Competing Considerations on Support for Freedom of Expression

If some students at a college want to form a "Campus Nazi Club": (a) they should be allowed to do so, or (b) college officials should ban such clubs from campus.

% Tolerant among Respondents Claiming
Strong Abstract Support for the Right to Free Speech

	Attitude toward Nazis[a]		
	Not Dangerous	Dangerous	Δ
Less Informed[b]	29[c]	7	22
Mass Public	54	22	32
More Informed	60	28	32
Lawyers and Judges	90	77	13

Should groups like the Nazis and Ku Klux Klan be allowed to appear on public television to state their views? (b) No, because they would offend certain racial or religious groups, or (a) Yes, no matter who is offended.

% Tolerant among Respondents Claiming
Strong Abstract Support for the Right to Free Speech

	Attitude toward Nazis		
	Not Dangerous	Dangerous	Δ
Less Informed	54	16	38
Mass Public	63	40	23
More Informed	65	50	15
Lawyers and Judges	94	81	13

	Attitude toward the KKK		
	Not Dangerous	Dangerous	Δ
Less Informed	36	17	19
Mass Public	54	42	12
More Informed	60	51	9
Lawyers and Judges	91	83	8

A humor magazine which ridicules or makes fun of blacks, women, or other minority groups: (b) should lose its mailing privileges, or (a) should have the same right as any other magazine to print what it wants.

% Tolerant among Respondents Claiming
Strong Abstract Support for Freedom of the Press

	Attitude toward Racists		
	Not Dangerous	Dangerous	Δ
Less Informed	72	50	22
Mass Public	73	68	5
More Informed	74	75	−1
Lawyers and Judges	97	96	1

(*continued*)

TABLE 2. *Continued*

The freedom of atheists to make fun of God and religion: (b) should not be allowed in a public place where religious groups gather, or (a) should be legally protected no matter who might be offended.

% Tolerant among Respondents Claiming
Strong Abstract Support for the Right to Free Speech

	Attitude toward Atheists		
	Not Dangerous	Dangerous	Δ
Less Informed	d	d	d
Mass Public	86	32	54
More Informed	89	41	48
Lawyers and Judges	96	84	12

Should a community allow its civic auditorium to be used by atheists who want to preach against God and religion? (a) Yes, or (b) No

% Tolerant among Respondents Claiming
Strong Abstract Support for the Right to Free Speech

	Attitude toward Atheists		
	Not Dangerous	Dangerous	Δ
Less Informed	d	d	d
Mass Public	82	21	61
More Informed	86	25	61
Lawyers and Judges	94	73	21

Should a community allow its civic auditorium to be used by feminists to organize a march for the Equal Rights Amendment? (a) Yes, or (b) No

% Tolerant among Respondents Claiming
Strong Abstract Support for the Right to Free Speech

	Attitude toward Feminists		
	Not Dangerous	Dangerous	Δ
Less Informed	75	30	45
Mass Public	88	49	39
More Informed	91	59	32
Lawyers and Judges	98	90	8

Mass student protest demonstrations: (b) have no place on a college campus and the participating students should be punished, or (a) should be allowed by college officials as long as they are non-violent.

% Tolerant among Respondents Claiming
Strong Abstract Support for the Right to Free Speech

	Attitude toward Student Protesters		
	Not Dangerous	Dangerous	Δ
Less Informed	86	58	28
Mass Public	97	70	27
More Informed	100	75	25
Lawyers and Judges	98	90	8

(*continued*)

TABLE 2. *Continued*

Freedom to worship as one pleases: (a) applies to all religious groups, regardless of how extreme their beliefs are, or (b) was never meant to apply to religious cults that the majority of people consider "strange," fanatical, or "weird."

% Tolerant among Respondents Claiming
Strong Abstract Support for Religious Freedom

| | Attitude toward the Unification Church | | |
	Not Dangerous	Dangerous	Δ
Less Informed	72	65	7
Mass Public	84	74	10
More Informed	88	77	11
Lawyers and Judges	94	82	12

Source: Data are from a 1977–78 national survey of judges and lawyers (*N* = 486) and the mass public (*N* = 1,993). For details and a report of the results, see McClosky and Brill (1983).

[a]See footnote 5 for a description of items used to measure attitudes toward various groups.

[b]Based on scores on a 20-item test of constitutional and political knowledge. "Less Informed" respondents in the mass public obtained 10 or fewer correct answers. "More Informed" respondents obtained 11 or more correct answers.

[c]Cell entry is the probability of giving a tolerant response (alternative "a" of each question).

[d]Insufficient cases in one or more categories.

greater impact on those who are less knowledgeable than on those who are well informed. I have arranged these items according to whether the issue deals with the promotion of progressive or reactionary ideas. On issues involving the propagation of right-wing extremism—through a campus Nazi club, public television appearances by Nazis and the Ku Klux Klan, and humor magazines that target blacks, women, and minorities—the effect of one's feelings toward Nazis, the KKK, and racists is greatest among the least knowledgeable. The impact of one's attitude toward these groups diminishes steadily with greater information.

The identical pattern emerges on issues dealing with the rights of liberal and left-wing activists. Feelings toward student protesters, feminists, and atheists have the most marked impact on those who are less informed. For example, in response to whether feminists should be allowed to use a community auditorium to conduct a rally promoting women's rights, 75 percent of the least informed who believe that feminists benefit society would permit such a rally, compared to only 30 percent of those who think that feminists are harmful. In the more informed stratum of the general public, there is a somewhat reduced 32 percent difference according to whether one likes or dislikes feminists. In the legal elite sample, this contrast shrinks to 8 percent. These patterns repeat themselves across all but the last item in this grouping.

The final item testing support for religious freedom shows that competing considerations make little difference when the common normative frame of reference is apparent to virtually all respondents. In this case, large majorities at all information levels respond favorably to the tolerant principle that the right to worship applies to all religious groups, even if they promote unusual beliefs. The alternative option—that religious cults are not entitled to the same protection—is not strongly endorsed even by those who feel that the Unification Church is a danger to society.

The two questions included in table 3 pose conflicts between majority

TABLE 3.   Free Speech Versus Majority Rule

If the majority in a referendum votes to stop publication of newspapers that preach race hatred: (b) such newspapers should be closed down, or (a) no one, not even the majority of voters, should have the right to close down a newspaper.

% Tolerant among Respondents Claiming
Strong Abstract Support for Freedom of the Press

| | Attitude toward Majority Rule[a] | | |
	Less Important	Extremely Important	Δ
Less Informed[b]	c	c	c
Mass Public	64[d]	46	18
More Informed	69	50	19
Lawyers and Judges	100	91	9

If the majority votes in a referendum to ban the public expression of certain opinions, should the majority opinion be followed? (a) No, because free speech is a more fundamental right than majority rule, or (b) Yes, because no group has a greater right than the majority to decide which opinions can or cannot be expressed.

% Tolerant among Respondents Claiming
Strong Abstract Support for the Right to Free Speech

| | Attitude toward Majority Rule | | |
	Less Important	Extremely Important	Δ
Less Informed	67	32	35
Mass Public	80	55	25
More Informed	88	63	25
Lawyers and Judges	100	83	17

Source: Data are from a 1977–78 national survey of judges and lawyers ($N = 486$) and the mass public ($N = 1,993$). For details and a report of the results, see McClosky and Brill (1983).

[a]See footnote 6 for a description of the item used to measure attitude toward majority rule.

[b]Based on scores on a 20-item test of constitutional and political knowledge. "Less Informed" respondents in the mass public obtained 10 or fewer correct answers. "More Informed" respondents obtained 11 or more correct answers.

[c]Insufficient cases in one or more categories.

[d]Cell entry is the probability of giving a tolerant response (alternative "a" of each question).

rule and freedom of expression—can the majority vote to suppress unpopular forms of expression, or ban racist publications? Although two democratic principles are in conflict, there is a clear legal norm on each issue that restricts the majority's prerogative to interfere with free speech. Therefore, the effect of attitudes toward majority rule should be specified by the respondent's level of knowledge.[6] This prediction is confirmed in table 3, which shows that those who are more informed are more willing to discount the priority that they assign to majority rule than those who are less informed.

Finally, the set of items in table 4 includes several issues involving censorship that do not enjoy a consensual interpretation among political elites. Although these issues fall within the realm of individual rights, the specific controversies have not been placed squarely under the umbrella of the First Amendment. As I discussed earlier in conjunction with the search-and-seizure item, on issues that lack a common normative frame of reference, the theory predicts that competing considerations will exercise a strong influence on attitudes. Opinion should be polarized according to the respondent's ideological leaning.

This last hypothesis is also confirmed by the data. Opinions about whether pornographic materials should be regulated or censored and whether explicit sex should be shown on television are strongly related to the respondent's feelings about sexual freedom and the effects of pornography.[7] In addition, the magnitude of these relationships is consistent across all information levels. Those in the bottom quartile of the information scale are affected by these considerations no more than those in the top quartile, nor any more than lawyers and judges who are well versed on individual rights.

Final Comments and Future Directions

Virtue of the Framing Model

This model makes explicit the process by which individuals are primed to choose among alternative frames of reference in arriving at their opinions on political issues. To the extent they have been discussed at all, the factors that determine which frame of reference will be given priority by the subject have heretofore been poorly understood in public opinion research and have not been given formal treatment in a model. This choice mechanism is combined with a two-message model of persuasion that is similar to the McGuire-Zaller model of attitude change. The mathematics of the framing model offered here are more streamlined, however, and the model can account for the same patterns of opinion formation, as well as explain additional empirical findings, because it takes account of competing frames of reference. If all frames of reference are identical—that is, if debates employing any of them have the

TABLE 4. Effect of Competing Considerations on Censorship Issues

Closing down magazines that print obscene or "dirty" pictures: (a) is a bad idea because it might easily lead to other restrictions on freedom of publication, or (b) is necessary to protect children from being exposed to unhealthy influences.

% Tolerant among Respondents Claiming
Strong Abstract Support for the Right to Free Speech

	Attitude toward Sex and Pornography[a]		
	Liberal	Conservative	Δ
Less Informed[b]	63[c]	4	59
Mass Public	77	12	65
More Informed	81	16	65
Lawyers and Judges	89	18	71

Selling pornographic films, books, and magazines: (a) is really a victimless crime and should therefore be left unregulated, or (b) lowers the community's moral standards and therefore victimizes everyone.

% Tolerant among Respondents Claiming
Strong Abstract Support for the Right to Free Speech

	Attitude toward Sex and Pornography		
	Liberal	Conservative	Δ
Less Informed	38	11	27
Mass Public	51	1	50
More Informed	63	0	63
Lawyers and Judges	71	0	71

When it comes to pornographic films about sex: (a) people should be allowed to see anything they want to, no matter how "filthy" it is, or (b) the community should set the standards for what people are allowed to see.

% Tolerant among Respondents Claiming
Strong Abstract Support for the Right to Free Speech

	Attitude toward Sex and Pornography		
	Liberal	Conservative	Δ
Less Informed	84	6	78
Mass Public	79	7	72
More Informed	77	8	69
Lawyers and Judges	80	9	71

(*continued*)

TABLE 4. *Continued*

Television programs that show people actually making love:
(a) should be permitted as long as they are shown in the late
evening, during adult viewing hours, or (b) should not be
allowed on TV at all.

% Tolerant among Respondents Claiming
Strong Abstract Support for the Right to Free Speech

| | Attitude toward Sex and Pornography | | |
	Liberal	Conservative	Δ
Less Informed	66	10	56
Mass Public	52	7	45
More Informed	59	6	53
Lawyers and Judges	58	0	58

Source: Data are from a 1977–78 national survey of judges and lawyers ($N = 486$) and the mass public ($N = 1,993$). For details and a report of the results, see McClosky and Brill (1983).

[a]See footnote 7 for a description of the scale used to measure attitude toward sex and pornography.

[b]Based on scores on a 20-item test of constitutional and political knowledge. "Less Informed" respondents in the mass public obtained 10 or fewer correct answers. "More Informed" respondents obtained 11 or more correct answers.

[c]Cell entry is the probability of giving a tolerant response (alternative "a" of each question).

same impact on liberals and conservatives, so that one frame of reference cannot be strategically more important as a means to persuasion—then the model reduces mathematically to one frame of reference or dimension for an issue. Opinion on the issue depends simply on degrees of exposure to and acceptance of the stream of liberal and conservative messages pertaining to this aspect of the issue; and patterns of opinion formation can be derived from equation 4 alone.

However, the evidence presented here shows that all frames of reference do not lead to the same response. On many civil liberties issues, whether one thinks in terms of abstract democratic principles or concrete dangers that could result from upholding those principles bears crucially on the likelihood of being tolerant. A vital aspect of political tolerance is the ability to hold in abeyance ideas and thoughts that recommend repressing nonconformists. When political discussion suggests a common normative frame of reference, people learn to give more weight to that aspect than to others. Consequently, people may hold conflicting considerations, yet still provide consistent answers if they have decided that the contrary considerations are irrelevant. Such contrary considerations remain part of the person's belief system, and may even be expressed in open-ended interviews, but ultimately they do not affect one's position on the topic. In contrast, models such as Zaller's assume that consistently expressed views imply a homogeneous set of underlying considerations.

The framing model presented here also has the advantage of being explicitly dynamic. Change over time is incorporated into the model using difference equations, permitting analyses of equilibrium and stability conditions. The dynamic model provides a more literal representation of the stream of messages that an individual receives over time and the changes of opinion that occur in response to new information. This process approaches equilibrium in the long haul, but the model also represents the distribution of opinion in intermediate periods before equilibrium is attained. Therefore, we have a running tally of the distribution of opinion over the life of an issue rather than a single-point representation of opinion as in earlier models. This difference is important because a message that is constantly repeated can be expected to diffuse eventually to virtually the entire population. The difference in the views of more and less informed individuals will therefore depend on when we survey them—early on, when the message has just been introduced, or later on, when the diffusion process is near completion. Before the process reaches equilibrium, there will be sharp contrasts by information level, but these differences will be negligible at equilibrium.

The Universe of Issues

In my research on attitudes toward civil liberties controversies, laws and court decisions are compelling coordinators of opinion. Consequently, there may be greater consensus on the frame of reference on these issues than on other matters, including many contentious, unsettled civil liberties controversies, where there may be many contending interpretations rather than a common frame of reference. It is worth exploring the development of public opinion when there are competing frames of reference offered by contending factions, such as liberals and conservatives and Democrats and Republicans.

Which Frames Are Possible?

Much public opinion formation is a strategic process in which opinion leaders are trying to persuade the public to think about political issues along particular lines, to activate existing values, prejudices, and ideas (Edelman 1964), and to draw obvious conclusions from those chosen frames of reference. Given the processes of opinion and value formation described by the model, the next step is to study what strategies politicians employ to build winning coalitions and how they try to mobilize their constituencies by framing political issues to their advantage (see, e.g., Jacobs and Shapiro 1994).

At the same time, it is implausible that political elites can arbitrarily designate any dimension to guide public discussion of an issue. Models of information transmission imply that the ideological faction that expends sufficient resources on propaganda and manipulation, and that sends sufficiently loud signals, can always prevail in defining the terms of debate. In practice, opinion leaders have less influence than this implication suggests. Consequently, such models need to be balanced with further specification about what frames of reference the public is inclined or willing to accept in considering an issue of importance to it. Arrival at common frames of reference must be the product of interaction between opinion leaders (who can be regarded as entrepreneurs in this regard) and the public. Certain frames of reference are easier to promote because the public is already predisposed to give priority to some dimensions over others. Presumably, opinion leaders anticipate popular reactions to their messages and choose frames of reference that take into consideration the interests of their constituents.

NOTES

This chapter was originally prepared for delivery as a paper at the annual meeting of the American Political Science Association, Washington, D.C., September 2–5, 1993.

1. Zaller (1992) discusses framing effects, but he explains attitude change as "a change in the balance of positive and negative considerations relating to a given issue. To model it, one must represent the process by which new considerations are added to the pool of existing considerations in the person's mind, thereby permanently altering long-term response probabilities on the issue." His mathematical model of attitude change therefore does not include framing effects.

2. Schauer (1989, 397) writes, for example, that only through abstraction can "Nazis become political speakers, profit maximizing purveyors of sexually explicit material become proponents of an alternative vision of social existence, [and] glorifiers of sexual violence against women become advocates of a point of view. . . . [T]he law of the First Amendment mandates that some otherwise relevant considerations, most obviously and most frequently the harmlessness, worthlessness or falseness of classes of utterances, be excluded from governmental decision-making."

3. In the case of multiple relevant and irrelevant frames, the weights are applied to the average values of each subset. Of course, there is likely to be variation in the probability values of the individual frames in each subset.

4. Attitude toward lawbreakers was measured using a scale composed of the following items: (1) Which of these policies do you think would be more effective in reducing crime? (b) Giving longer and tougher prison sentences to hardened criminals, or (a) treating prisoners more humanely so they will gain self-respect and become law-abiding citizens. (2) In dealing with people imprisoned for crime, it is better to: (a) try to rehabilitate them and return them to normal life, or (b) punish them for the wrongs they have done. (3) Which do you believe? (a) All but the most hardened criminals could be rehabilitated if society would only make the effort, or (b) Very few criminals

can be turned into good citizens no matter what we do. (4) The death penalty is: (b) a proper and necessary punishment for criminals who have committed horrible crimes, such as premeditated murder, or (a) morally wrong, doesn't really prevent crime, and should be abolished. (5) When riots break out, the police: (b) are usually too easy on the rioters, or (a) often use too much force and cause more violence than might otherwise have occurred. (6) Improving the treatment of prisoners: (a) would probably reduce crime, or (b) would probably increase crime.

5. Attitude toward each group was measured following this introduction: "Americans differ in their views about whether certain controversial groups are, or are not, harmful to the country. How would you describe your own feelings about each of the following groups? Do you consider them: MOSTLY HARMFUL, OBNOXIOUS BUT NOT REALLY HARMFUL, or MOSTLY BENEFICIAL AND GOOD FOR THE COUNTRY?" In coding responses to these questions, the "obnoxious" and "mostly beneficial" categories were combined.

6. Attitude toward the principle of majority rule was measured following this introduction: "One way of describing a country is by the values its people hold. Americans share many values, but disagree about how important certain of these values are compared to the others. The following questions address a number of such values. How would you rate each of these values? Which values, in other words, do you consider EXTREMELY IMPORTANT, which do you consider IMPORTANT, SOMEWHAT IMPORTANT, or LESS IMPORTANT? How would you rate majority rule?" In coding responses to this question, the "extremely important" and "important" categories were combined, as were the "somewhat important" and "less important" categories.

7. Attitude toward sex and pornography was measured using a scale composed of the following items: (1) In dealing with prostitution, the government should (a) license and regulate it, or (b) arrest or fine the people who have anything to do with it. (2) Birth control devices: (a) should be available to teenagers if they want them, or (b) should be kept from teenagers since they are too young to handle sexual matters sensibly. (3) These days: (b) there is too much sexual freedom and loose living, or (a) people have healthier and more relaxed ideas about sex. (4) Sex education of children: (a) should be taught in school, or (b) is a matter for the parents to handle. (5) Pornographic films: (b) can easily lead unbalanced people to commit violent sex crimes, or (a) are mostly harmless, even if some people find them distasteful.

REFERENCES

Chong, Dennis. 1993. How people think, reason, and feel about rights and liberties. *American Journal of Political Science* 37:867–99.
Converse, Philip E. 1962. Information flow and the stability of partisan attitudes. *Public Opinion Quarterly* 26:578–99.
Edelman, Murray. 1964. *The symbolic uses of politics.* Urbana: University of Illinois Press.
Iyengar, Shanto, and Donald R. Kinder. 1987. *News that matters.* Chicago: University of Chicago Press.

Jacobs, Lawrence R., and Robert Y. Shapiro. 1994. Issues, candidate image, and priming: The use of private polls in Kennedy's 1960 presidential campaign. *American Political Science Review* 88:527–40.

Kelley, Stanley, Jr. 1983. *Interpreting elections.* Princeton, N.J.: Princeton University Press.

Kinder, Donald R., and Lynn M. Sanders. 1990. Mimicking political debate with survey questions: The case of white opinion on affirmative action for blacks. *Social Cognition* 8:73–103.

Krosnick, Jon, and Donald Kinder. 1990. Altering the foundations of support for the president through priming. *American Political Science Review* 84:497–512.

McClosky, Herbert, and Alida Brill. 1983. *Dimensions of tolerance.* New York: Russell Sage Foundation.

McGuire, William J. 1968. Personality and susceptibility to social influence. In *Handbook of personality theory and research,* ed. E. F. Borgatta and W. W. Lambert. Chicago: Rand-McNally.

Pratkanis, Anthony, and Elliot Aronson. 1992. *The age of propaganda.* San Francisco: Freeman.

Prothro, James W., and Charles W. Grigg. 1960. Fundamental principles of democracy: Bases of agreement and disagreement. *Journal of Politics* 22:276–94.

Restle, Frank. 1955. A theory of discrimination learning. *Psychological Review* 62:11–19.

Riker, William. 1986. *The art of political manipulation.* New Haven, Conn.: Yale University Press.

Schauer, Frederick. 1989. Harry Kalven and the perils of particularism. *University of Chicago Law Review* 56:397–414.

Schuman, Howard, and Stanley Presser. 1981. *Questions and answers in attitude surveys.* New York: Wiley.

Simon, Herbert. 1985. Human nature in politics: The dialogue of psychology with political science. *American Political Science Review* 79:293–304.

Sussman, Barry. 1986. Do blacks approve of Reagan? It depends on who's asking. *Washington Post,* weekly edition, February 10.

Zaller, John R. 1992. *The nature and origins of mass opinion.* Cambridge: Cambridge University Press.

CHAPTER 9

The Candidate as Catastrophe: Latitude Theory and the Problems of Political Persuasion

Gregory Andrade Diamond and Michael D. Cobb

What we mean by *persuasion* depends in part upon our structural model of attitudes. Public opinion researchers usually define a person's *attitude* on a given political issue as her or his most favored (or *ideal*) point on a conceptual or ideological dimension along which the range of all possible policies may be arrayed. Populations may be similarly characterized by the mean or median of these optimal points. This model of attitude structure is so pervasive that it's generally unnamed; we call it the *point placement* model.

Scholars have relied upon an implicit model of persuasion that suits this model of attitude structure: persuasion as an act of *conversion*. *Persuasion* is defined as convincing others, changing their views, shifting their ideal points along the imagined line. This notion alters the meaning of the word's Latin root, *suadere,* which means only "to advise, or urge." Advising others need not entail seeking their conversion. One may advise tolerance, tentativeness, open-mindedness, or obstinacy, even without changing a person's ideal points. Similarly, construing political persuasion only as conversion ignores the opening of political opportunities by *neutralization* of political opposition. This term's sinister connotation is ironic: it literally denotes impelling one's opponents to become neutral (for example, by broadening the range of alternatives they will accept), a *milder* goal than prodding them to endorse the contrary of what they did before. This fits well with the representation of politics as the "art of the possible."

The point placement model has at least one historical alternative in the *social judgment* theory of Muzafer Sherif and Carl Hovland (1961). This theory comprises (1) a model of attitude *structure* and (2) a model of attitude *change* based on assimilation of and contrasts between persuasive communications and people's own positions. Since our interest is in Sherif and Hovland's model of attitude structure, and not their assimilation and contrast model of attitude change, we will specify the former as *latitude theory.*

Latitude theory shares with point placement models the assumption that a given dimension (or dimensions) underlies the policy choices that people make. It breaks from traditional models, however, in placing little or no emphasis on a person's *optimally preferred point* on those dimensions.[1] Instead, it introduces three theoretical constructs: the *latitude of acceptance,* the *latitude of noncommitment,* and the *latitude of rejection.* The boundary between the first two of these demarcates what one affirmatively likes from what one is indifferent toward, and the boundary between the latter two separates what one is indifferent toward from what one actively dislikes. When issue positions are measured on dimensions broad enough to include extreme options at both ends of the continuum, most people will have a latitude of acceptance at some intermediate point on the dimension, bounded by a latitude of noncommitment and then a latitude of rejection on both sides.

Assessing the relative benefits and detriments of these two models forms the bulk of this chapter. Our principal argument is simple. To the extent that the most important thing to know about a person's (or, by metaphorical extension, a population's) attitude on a given issue is the optimally preferred point alone, the standard model is quite apt. But, to the extent that more important information is conveyed by the shifting boundaries between the desirable and the tolerable, and between the tolerable and the intolerable, then public opinion researchers have been seeking mass attitudes in the wrong place, and often concluding that they don't exist.

Latitude Theory: Old Wine in Old Wineskins?

Latitude theory has had limited, and declining, influence in the study of opinion, so in suggesting its reclamation for political science we have encountered questions as to why we seek to "rouse the dead." The moment and justification of a theory's departure are never as clear as those of its appearance, but we have attempted to respond to such questions by reviewing why it was that latitude theory was originally discredited. Our conclusion is that it never truly *was.* Almost all of the intellectual debate over social judgment theory in major psychological journals during the 1960s and early 1970s addressed predictions of the assimilation and contrast model of attitude change, and it is this theory that was found wanting in part. (See Diamond and Cobb 1994 for a review of the major research findings that undermined the model.) The *structural* portion of the theory received generally friendly commentary (e.g., Oskamp 1977). Far from being discredited, latitude theory remains a viable challenge to point prediction models. Even if it were not useful as a tool for opinion assessment, we believe it would be vital to a sound conceptual understanding of attitudes. We will show, however, that a methodological approach that builds on the foundation of latitude theory can actually outperform the standard point prediction model at explaining candidate preferences. Before turning to the advantages of latitude theory, however, we will catalog the problems of the point placement approach.

Theoretical Problems with the Point Placement Model

The Optimality Assumption

Use of the point placement model is epitomized by the *spatial modeling* assessment procedure (Downs 1957; Enelow and Hinich 1984), in which attitudes are treated as *points* on *lines* representing *dimensions* of opinion, and rational voters support candidates to whom their opinions are *closest* in a multidimensional space. The researcher must determine two points on the underlying dimension: that representing the voter's opinion and that representing the voter's perception of the candidate's position (a *placement*). This is a daunting task for both researcher and voter.

Cognitive psychology suggests, however, that respondents' seeking of optimal placements of self and others would be a poor strategy. Simon's (1955) classic conception of *satisficing* suggests that the marginal benefit from determining optimal choices (or positions) is not usually worth the added costs of information acquisition and analysis. This should be especially true in domains that are relatively unimportant to people, as are most questions of national politics (Berelson, Lazarsfeld, and McPhee 1954; Downs 1957). In addition, research on heuristics (Kahneman, Slovic, and Tversky 1982; Dawes 1988; Sniderman, Brody, and Tetlock 1991) suggests that people dispose of great amounts of information available for decision making as a matter of course and that most of the information normally required to make optimal decisions is commonly distorted along the course of the decision-making process, if not at its outset. Given a range of possible options, or even of affective responses to a given option, for most people in most situations distinguishing between the precisely right response and the sufficiently right response is hardly worthwhile.

Previous authors have weakened the optimality assumption of the point placement model in a variety of ways. Proponents of *attitude centrality* (Converse 1970; Judd and Krosnick 1982) have argued that certain attitudes will be more (even preemptively) powerful in determining subjective closeness of opinion. Yet, these disproportionately influential attitudes are still conceived of as optimal points on lines. Zaller and Feldman (1992; also Zaller 1992) have argued that preference points on issues are not fixed, but rather reflect an ad hoc, stochastic sample of considerations that might impel one toward various positions on that issue. In criticizing "true attitudes," however, the authors dispose not only of the importance of optimal points, but of all *other* enduring features of individual opinion on an issue, *including* judgments of what positions on that issue may be threatening, which we believe are less likely to be constructed arbitrarily and ad hoc.

This is a critical distinction between our approach and Zaller and Feldman's. We are not surprised that optimal preference points should vary from instance to instance, but we would be very surprised if judgments that certain policies were abhorrent did so as well. Since consistency over time requires stability not only of an underlying construct but also of the means of assessing it, testing this proposition demands reliable techniques of placing the inner borders of respondents' personal latitudes of rejection and, in turn, reliable techniques of generating the policy dimensions on which they might be scaled.

Lodge and colleagues (Lodge, McGraw, and Stroh 1989; Lodge 1994) have argued that differences in issue positions do not directly determine candidate evaluations at all, except insofar as the affect generated from such incongruity is recorded in a continually updated affective marker for a candidate, which renders retention of the specific basis of such discrepancies in memory unnecessary. This on-line processing model leaves the question of why only certain political differences yield certain affective consequences unanswered, however, and this is part of what our theory will address.

One reason for the success of these challenges to spatial modeling is that they fit nicely with the notion that people conserve cognitive resources (Simon 1955, 1985; sometimes called the "cognitive miser" assumption). Cognitive conservation also may underlie the central thesis of Converse's (1964) classic article on mass public opinion: most people never develop much in the way of coherent ideology (certainly not enough from which to derive issue positions), and their expressed positions on individual issues are often entirely ad hoc. Why, if people find political conceptualization so hard or unappealing, do they *bother* trying to determine the *optimal* placement of their opinion on an ideological dimension? In dismissing the opinions of the nonideological as "nonattitudes," however, Converse's "black-and-white" model of mass public opinion implies a "black-and-white" model of the utility of political preferences. If people cannot determine the *optimal position* they hold on an issue, Converse assumes that they bring *no* useful information to bear in evaluating it. Latitude theory will suggest otherwise.

Subsequent challenges to Converse (e.g., Hochschild 1981) have suggested that in analyzing political issues, people can use ideological dimensions that don't match those of political elites, but still afford some derivation of issue positions from general principles. Again, this seems like a step in the right direction, but one must wonder why people, even using idiosyncratic dimensions of analysis, should try to determine *optimal* positions on issues. People do not like politics any more than they like politicians. That the emotion and energy devoted to understanding politics is inferior in kind and degree to that given to understanding sports, entertainment, and interpersonal domination and attraction is well accepted (Popkin 1991). For most scholars of politics, politics is an intricate and (one hopes) fascinating exercise, and a model that assumed that we really wanted to maximize the degree to which our opinions were the ones that ran the world might perform well. But we are a minority. For most people, political cognition is more simple. If it weren't, it might not happen at all.

The Positivity Assumption

A second and related problem is that people appear to be especially sensitive to *negative* information about political candidates (Lau 1982). The optimality assumption suggests that the most important distinctions people make are *positive* ones, between optimal preference points and near neighbors. This is essential to rationality from a utility-maximization perspective, such as one might use in evaluating major purchases. Yet, psychologists have challenged this assumption as well. Tversky's (1972) "elimination by aspects" heuristic for consumer decision making depends primarily on sensitivity to strong negative information. So does *coping theory,* developed by clinical researchers to explain how people address potentially threatening environments (Lazarus and Folkman 1984). Coping theorists assume that people monitor their environment, which consists largely of things that are good or indifferent, for signs of threat; this process is known as *primary appraisal.* Identification of a threat leads to a *secondary appraisal* of what should be done about it. This is sometimes known as a *threat appraisal* model.

Revising the Assumptions:
Political Attitudes as Latitudes

Our contention is that political cognition has less in common with the process of careful placement of self and other in meticulously fashioned, logically determined policy dimensions than with trying to walk through a parking lot at night without getting mugged or run over. That is, what we look for in representatives is less the optimal mix of wisdom and fidelity to our views than the reassurance that the person in question is simply not so mad as to (depending on our inclinations) outlaw abortion, allow homosexuals to teach in the schools, raise taxes, cut services. It is the rare candidate these days who is generally seen as a savior, but many of them may represent potential catastrophes, and warding off disaster may be a better reason to exercise one's franchise than most.

In contrast to the standard model, latitude theory depicts a preference not as an optimal point on a dimension of opinion, but as a line segment, within which all points may be roughly equivalent in attractiveness. (This assumption is not an absolutely necessary feature of the model; see note 1.) In such a model, the point within the line segment that represents the most favored response—possibly but not necessarily the midpoint or mean value—is of relatively little theoretical interest. (In fact, the greatest utility the mean may have is heuristic, in that it may represent the midpoint of the acceptable range of responses.) From a threat appraisal viewpoint, the "action" is at the outer borders of people's preferences, at the points where others' positions become actively threatening. Adopting this perspective, latitude theory suggests that across various situations, people exert influence on the political system itself in a negative way, that is, by ruling out what they do not like rather than by pulling for precisely what they do.

Threat appraisal models accord well with both latitude theory and with the cognitive miser hypothesis, since the presence of a candidate's issue position in one's latitude of rejection should lead readily and spontaneously (Lodge 1994; Uleman 1989) to negative affect marked against that candidate. Furthermore, we believe that such judgments will tend to be more stable over time than optimal point preferences. This idea underlies our disagreement with the Zaller and Feldman approach. Even if our reported most-preferred position on an issue is the erratic result of a stochastic process, the *general contours* of our opinion on that issue may be fairly stable. Not even the most skewed mental samplings of considerations on the issue of alcohol use would prompt many people to say that drunkards should be summarily shot or that wine should be served in high school cafeterias.

We also see this insight as a necessary complement to the approach of Lodge (1994) and his colleagues. The distinction between the tolerable and the unbearable is likely to be more salient in and retrievable from memory than the distinction between the best and the next-best, and a candidate's endorsement of an entirely unacceptable proposal should be less likely to disappear into the affective blender along with the faint cognitive traces of bland stances on other issues. A threatening policy stance is more likely to be consequential than other campaign-related information studied by Lodge.

Practical Problems of the Point Placement Model

The dominant approach to assessing public opinion relies upon two kinds of Likert scales, one measuring *intensity of affect* and the other *optimal policy placement*. This first kind of Likert scale, exemplified by the National Election Studies (NES) thermometer scale items, asks respondents to consider a solitary attitude object (usually a proposal, person or group) and indicate how much they like or dislike (or approve or disapprove of) that object. If one views opinion as a histogram in which the height of columns represents extent of support for various horizontally arrayed policy options, this type of item holds the horizontal point on the policy dimension fixed (only one object is asked about at a time) while the researcher seeks variance across respondents in degree of affect. The respondent's task is to figure out a way to represent internal affect on an interval scale and map her or his feelings toward the object onto that scale. Sometimes a single item will be considered sufficient to "place" a respondent; in other cases a battery of questions will be asked on a common topic, and responses to all questions will be summed, with answers to all questions usually receiving equal weight. A combination of positively weighted responses to positively worded items and negatively weighted responses to negatively worded items will generate a score for each subject that places them along an implicit dimension of support for that issue.

The second kind of Likert scale is exemplified by the NES seven-point policy scales, which present two different policy options as anchors to an implicit dimension of opinion on an issue and ask each respondent to indicate his or her most preferred option on that dimension. In other words, the point on the vertical dimension of liking is fixed (at least relative to other points, in the sense that the researcher is seeking the maximum positive feeling) while the researcher seeks population variance along the horizontal policy dimension. This approach allows subjects to place themselves directly on a policy dimension, but it makes the strong assumption that subjects have sufficient knowledge not only to generate a coherent dimension along which opinion might be arrayed on each issue, but to arrange different points along that dimension so as to form an interval scale. (While the Likert approach is sufficiently robust that many of these assumptions can be violated to some degree, it is unclear whether the degree to which they *are* commonly violated exceeds tolerance levels.)

Problems in Responding to Likert Scales

Psychological studies give little reason to hope that average citizens, operating in a novel (and imposed) dimensional space, are capable of the mental athleticism required by this second kind of scale. Several problems arise:

Lack of cogent, coherent dimensions. It is unclear that people generate cogent dimensions on which to represent policy options for political issues. Not only do various people construe political issues differently, but they are more likely to have a much better sense of what they mean by one pole of a dimension than by the other (Kelly 1955).

Placement and meaning of endpoints. Even if people can generate mental dimensions, it is not clear that they will be anchored where the researcher expects. This is a problem for the simpler "intensity of affect" as well as for the "optimal policy preference" types of Likert scales; while researchers assume that subjects respond in terms of an interval scale of affect, subjects may respond in terms of their *certainty* of agreement or disagreement. Particularly when a judgment of a political person or actor is negative, strong responses may indicate that respondents are sure that this is something they don't like, rather than that they don't like it strongly. "I'm a '7' on taxes and he's a '1'" may mean nothing more than "I'm absolutely sure that we disagree." Not even responses at the endpoints of opinion scales afford clear interpretation, since people differ in the characteristic ways they respond to the question-answering situation. (Blacks, for example, have been found to use the endpoints of the scale much more frequently than do whites, which probably does not represent differences in internal equivocation but rather different learned norms of expression; Bachman and O'Malley 1984.)

Abstractness of intermediate points. People do not think in terms of a politician's being a "2" on a seven-point Likert scale, which either does (or does not) strongly conflict with their own "4." Instead, people think in terms of concrete examples, which may be broad, as with "I oppose Clinton because I think he'll raise taxes." The intermediate response options on policy items are abstract rather than concrete; a response of "3" on a seven-point scale, for example, means that respondents must mentally traverse one-third of the way from the "1" to the "7" endpoint. Since respondents' ability to do so is impeded even by these intermediate points being left unlabeled (Krosnick 1991), they cannot likely do so readily with complicated policy dimensions.

The center cannot hold. The problems associated with Likert scales can most clearly be demonstrated by considering the ambiguities associated with responses placed at the middle point of scales (say, "4" on a seven-point scale). In some cases, such a response will indicate true moderation—what may in fact be a strong commitment to a position at the middle of a policy-related distribution. More commonly, however, the "4" response may indicate uncertainty, lack of any strong belief, or unwillingness to commit to a position in the face of others' presumed expertise. In still other cases, the "4" response may indicate strong attraction (or repulsion) to aspects of both poles of the distribution; here the response may indicate a willingness to jump to either far end of the distribution depending on what aspect or frame of the issue at hand becomes the individual's temporary focus of concern. Or, it may indicate that the respondent construes a particular issue in some way orthogonal (or nearly so) to the dimension the researcher assumes; we may see this when libertarians attempt to place themselves on the traditional "liberal to conservative" dimension of opinion. Each of these different possibilities has different implications for how an individual should be expected to respond to that political issue. And, while the problems we face may be most clear at the midpoint of opinion scales, they in fact muddy the interpretation of *every* intermediate point.

Toward a Latitude-Based Assessment Procedure

We have argued earlier, following Converse, that point placement of self and other on either type of Likert scale is largely arbitrary. Of course, this is a matter of degree. It is petty to complain about imprecision of a few points in a 101-point thermometer scale, but it is obdurate to claim that the sorts of failures commonly pointed out in the methodological literature (e.g., Krosnick 1991) are not alarming. We believe that researchers still cling to Likert policy measures mainly due to the sense that they do retain gross validity. If a respondent rates a politician at "70" on a thermometer scale, we are not surprised if the "true" rating (as if we could know) should have been "60" or "50," but if the true rating should have been a "10," we might think that she or he was being deliberately perverse, or had misunderstood the instructions. Intuitively, we recognize that even if these types of scales do not give us reliable information about the *optimal* placement of subject positions, they are far from useless.

The basis for this intuition may be that we recognize that there is *some* level of psychological discrimination that it makes *sense* for people to be able to do: the distinctions between what we *like* enough to approach intentionally and what we neither approach nor avoid, and between what we neither approach or avoid and what we *dislike* enough to avoid intentionally. Such simple affective judgments are primitive (Zajonc 1980) and critical to adaptation to our environment (Toda 1982). It is possible and desirable to build a theory of political cognition based on people's ability to make these two plausible distinctions rather than on the untenable assumption that people distinguish between optimal points and near neighbors.

Sherif and Hovland's latitude-based assessment procedure addresses the theoretical problem of optimality by simultaneously assessing attitudes along both the vertical (intensity) and horizontal (placement) dimensions. On the vertical dimension, the respondent's task is simplified by asking people to perform the simple, primitive task of classifying objects only as good, bad, or indifferent. On the horizontal dimension, respondents are asked about *specific* attitude objects whose relative placement have been previously determined by the researcher, so as to gauge the expansion and contraction of latitudes of acceptance and rejection. Since decisions about concrete objects require less cognitive effort, they should generate more meaningful responses.

Readers may have noticed superficial similarities between the latitude-based approach and old-style Thurstone scaling, and it is important to note the distinctions. Though both latitude and Thurstone scaling assess responses to objects set out at various points on an underlying dimension, Thurstone scaling represents respondents by the mean value of the responses they endorse: each person is still presumed to be best represented by a point on a line. The latitude approach is fundamentally different. The person is represented most tellingly by the range of items that he or she favors (or at least tolerates). Rather than visualizing respondents as trying to push policy toward a desired optimal goal, we may visualize them as trying to pull policy away from rejected outcomes while remaining quite unsure of precisely where they want to end up. Unlike hoi polloi in Converse's "black-and-white" model, respondents in the model we propose can have *something* important to say politically without knowing *precisely* what it is they want to say.

To summarize, what matters to people is not the attainment of optimal satisfaction, but the avoidance of *dis*satisfaction (Key 1966). Model an attitude not as a point on a line, but as a *segment* of a line, and attention shifts from the central point to the *border* areas—the ends of the line segments where one's attitudes shift from advocacy to tolerance to rejection. Line segments do not afford the sort of mathematical manipulation—the adding, averaging, multiplying, and matrix algebra—that points do, and conceiving of attitudes as line segments may demand different mathematical approaches from those now in use. Even so, we will ultimately be better served by focusing on the vital borders of attitudes rather than on their inert centers.

Advantages of a Latitude-Based Approach

Wedding Attitude Strength to Attitude Placement

One underappreciated weakness of survey scales is precisely that they separate strength and placement of opinion, as in the types of Likert scales discussed earlier. Researchers often flow freely between them in interpreting extremity as commitment and vice versa; as a result, public opinion has had scant space available either for committed moderates or for those who tentatively endorse "extreme" positions (if a scale's endpoints can be considered extreme). We know that *important* attitudes will affect choice and other behaviors in ways that unimportant ones will not—and yet "importance" itself is commonly defined *both* (at various times) as attitude strength and extremity and assessed by asking respondents, in effect, which of their many responses they think should really "count" (Berent and Krosnick 1995).

Latitude theory suggests a clear, novel operationalization of attitude strength or centrality; strong and central attitudes have wide latitudes of rejection and minimal latitudes of noncommitment (Sherif, Sherif, and Nebergall 1965.) Rather than switching between two sets of measures to study strength and placement, the latitude model integrates them. It clearly and immediately distinguishes the person who strongly endorses a given position *and will accept nothing else* from the person whose optimal position may be at the same point on the line, but who will tolerate a wide variety of other options. It explicitly recognizes that some people at the middle of an ideological spectrum will be as set on their policies as those on either end.

Additional implications of latitude theory for other aspects of politics would take us beyond the space allotted to the present chapter. Implications for theories of representation and political debate are discussed in Diamond (in press.)

A Study of Threat Appraisal in Candidate Evaluation

While we emphasize the value of latitude theory as a conceptual tool, we recognize the need to buttress it with empirical findings. We sought to demonstrate that a survey derived from threat appraisal and latitude theories could explain vote choice as well as or better than one designed along the point placement lines of the NES. We report here our attempts to explain vote choice on the basis of respondents' attitudes on three issues—health care, trade policy and affirmative action—and on a summary measure of whichever each identified as the most important of the three. Some details regarding survey design and procedures, sample composition, and variable and model construction may be found in the appendix. A comprehensive report on the survey may be found in Diamond and Cobb (1994).

The latitude-based scales assessed whether respondents placed candidate positions on each of a variety of policy options into their own latitudes of rejection; we equate doing so with appraisal of threat. First, seven concrete policy options for each issue were chosen, reflecting a range of ideological positions as determined by pilot testing. Respondents indicated whether they *supported, opposed,* or were *neutral* toward each policy option. Respondents then indicated whether they felt that each policy option was *very likely, somewhat likely, not very likely,* or *not at all likely* given the election of each of the three major presidential candidates. As described in the appendix, dummy variables indicating the presence of threat—operationalized as a prospective candidate behavior being located in a respondent's latitude of rejection—were then constructed along the lines of table 1. Where respondents were neutral, their judgments of the likelihood of candidates' enacting policy options were assumed not to affect candidate evaluations.

Threats were coded as being of two types: (1) *likely* prospects for policies that the respondent *opposed* (cell *e,* and to a lesser extent cell *f* in table 1), and (2) *unlikely* prospects for policies that the respondent *supported* (cell *d,* and to a lesser extent cell *c.*) We will call these threats of *commission* and *omission,*

TABLE 1.   Presence and Types of Threat Regarding Candidate Position on Issues

Do you approve of a given proposal?	How likely is this proposal to be enacted if a given candidate is elected?			
	Very	Somewhat	Not Very	Not at All
Approve	a	b	c	d
Disapprove	e	f	g	h
Neutral	w	x	y	z

Note: Threat of omission is equal to $c + d$ (or CD). threat of commission is equal to $e + f$ (or EF). The threats of omission and commission can be summed to equal the presence of a threat, which can be stated as $CD + EF$ (or $C - F$).

respectively. In our analyses, we can distinguish between these two types of threat, set different threshold levels for judging whether these threats exist, and create composite variables detailing the total number of threats for each candidate-issue pair.

We tested two NES-style and three latitude-based models of candidate preference, as indicated in table 2. The NES measures reflect differences in candidate and self-placements; the latitude measures reflect presence of threats. All three latitude-based models are properly thought of as analogs of the absolute-difference NES-style model; we can create analogs of the signed-difference model but do not do so here.

Results

Threateningness of candidates. We first examined how threatened subjects were by each candidate's prospective threats of omission and commission on

TABLE 2.   Models of Candidate Preference Tested

Label	Class	Name	Variable Range	Note
DIF	NES	Signed difference	−6 to 6	Positive numbers reflect conservatism; negative reflect liberalism.
ABS	NES	Absolute difference	0 to 6	Does not account for ideological direction of disagreement.
OMIT	LAT	Threats of omission	0 to 7	Policy enaction desired but unlikely.
COMMIT	LAT	Threats of commission	0 to 7	Policy enaction opposed but likely.
BOTH	LAT	Sum of OMIT and COMMIT.	0 to 7	No single policy can be both a threat of omission and of commission.

TABLE 3. Mean Number OMIT, COMMIT, and BOTH Threats for Candidate-Issue Pairs

	Health Care			Trade Policy			Affirmative Action			Most Important Issue		
	OMIT	COMMIT	BOTH	OMIT	COMMIT	BOTH	OMIT	COMMIT	BOTH	OMIT	COMMIT	BOTH
Bush	1.65	1.40	3.01	1.19	.96	2.16	1.57	1.23	2.80	1.66	1.30	2.95
Clinton	.77	1.26	1.96	.78	1.34	2.12	.87	1.39	2.07	.80	1.17	1.92
Perot	1.07	1.17	2.16	.73	1.34	2.07	1.25	1.05	2.30	1.10	1.17	2.26

Note: A maximum of seven threats were possible for each candidate-issue pair.

each issue. The results are found in table 3. First, we found foreseeable discrepancies in what scares voters about each candidate. People were much more afraid of Bush's inaction than of the prospect that he would actively do something wrong. The opposite was the case for Clinton. For Perot, threats of omission and commission were fairly balanced, with the exception of the issue of trade, where there was little fear of Perot's failure to enact policies. Voters were much more threatened by policy prospects under Bush than those of the other candidates, the discrepancy being almost entirely due to fears of his inaction. This fact suggests (as did both of his opponents) that the election was indeed about "change"—more so involving the issues of health care and affirmative action policy than trade. For example, respondents were twice as threatened by the prospect of Bush's failure to act on health care as by the prospect of Clinton's failure to act. We find this information more useful than the simple, standard identification of health care as an important problem for voters. Most striking are the results for the single issue each respondent felt was most important. Bush tallied a mean of 1.66 threats of omission, compared to Clinton's .80 and Perot's 1.10 threats of omission.

Readers may note that while Perot was less threatening on these issues than was Bush, the latter got more votes. While this may be due to our limited choice of issues examined here, it may also be a function of Perot's problem being less a matter of his positions on issues than concerns about his temperament and fitness to be president. These are concerns for which voters will also have latitudes of acceptance—we suspect narrower ones than on policy issues—but that lend themselves less readily to the sort of analysis we have conducted here due to the problems of generating a scale of temperament. (But see Diamond, in press.) This disadvantage is apart from whatever others inhere in running an independent presidential campaign.

Explaining vote choice. It is possible, though not very interesting, to tote up the number of statistically significant regression coefficients at each level of significance for the NES-style models and compare them to the number obtained for the latitude-based models, or to compare the best models (ABS and OMIT) overall, or to create a "best ball" comparison of significant loadings in each equation. By any of these standards, the latitude/threat models explain vote choice at least slightly better than the NES ones. Yet while this may (or may not) be a useful heuristic, the models should best be compared on the grounds of how *useful, interpretable, sensible,* and *consistent* their results are. We turn to a discussion on these grounds.

The two NES-style models results yielded varied indications of which candidates' variables explained vote choice significantly in which equations. In explaining the intention of voting for Clinton on the basis of health care policy (table 4), for example, respondents' absolute distance from Clinton policies predicted significantly, as did their signed distance from Bush policies. It isn't clear, though, why the opposite (Clinton voters displaying large absolute distance from Bush, and being less signed difference from Clinton) should not have held true as well (or instead). The combination of the two significant and two nonsignificant loadings is not very telling as to why voters supported Clinton, other than indicating that Clinton voters liked his health care policies and thought Bush was too conservative on the issue.

Explaining the intention to vote for Clinton on the basis of health care was the strongest of all candidate-issue pairs examined using the NES-style

TABLE 4. Explaining Vote Choice for Bush, Clinton, and Perot According to Health Care

Health Care		Dummy Variable: Vote for Bush				
		Respondent Reaction to				
	[Model]	{Bush	Clinton	Perot}	Party ID	χ^2
NES	*ABS*	−2.25+	.06	−.22	6.32***	51.3
	DIF	8.25**	−1.78	−3.10	5.79***	60.3
	OMIT	−8.34*	−.16	3.99	7.58***	68.6
LAT	*COMMIT*	−6.22*	.45	1.35	7.78***	54.9
	BOTH	−11.89**	−3.39	4.73	8.12***	66.7

Health Care		Dummy Variable: Vote for Clinton				
		Respondent Reaction to				
	[Model]	{Bush	Clinton	Perot}	Party ID	χ^2
NES	*ABS*	1.97	−3.71*	−.38	−4.85***	62.1
	DIF	−5.31*	2.44	−1.56	−4.77***	60.4
	OMIT	−.97	−2.63	2.55	−4.29***	45.3
LAT	*COMMIT*	2.09	−2.02	.91	−3.74***	35.5
	BOTH	.48	−2.07	2.23	−3.63***	36.4

Health Care		Dummy Variable: Vote for Perot				
		Respondent Reaction to				
	[Model]	{Bush	Clinton	Perot}		χ^2
NES	*ABS*	.63	1.93*	−.62		4.3
	DIF	−.22	−1.81	1.52		1.5
	OMIT	5.62**	4.99*	−8.07**		18.3
LAT	*COMMIT*	.40	3.38	−1.64		3.3
	BOTH	3.86**	5.09**	−4.75*		14.1

Note: Coefficients, significance levels of predictor variables, and chi-square statistics for equations are reported above. Party was included as a covariate for prediction of votes for Bush and Clinton but did not significantly predict votes for Perot, so it was excluded from those equations. Higher scores for respondents indicate (for ABS) maximal distance from the candidate, (for DIF) being located to the right of the candidate on the relevant ideological dimension, and (for OMIT, COMMIT, or BOTH) presence of the according judged threat for that candidate on that issue.

+$p < .10$
*$p < .05$
**$p < .01$
***$p < .001$

model, yet the story it tells is somewhat muddled and banal. Looking across all candidate-issue pairs is not much better. For health care, Bush supporters were much closer to Bush's position and far more conservative on the issue than those opposing him. Perot supporters were also farther away from Clinton than were opponents. For affirmative action (table 5), Bush voters were relatively more conservative—and Clinton voters more liberal—than other voters in relation to their placements of Bush's position. Clinton votes could

TABLE 5. Explaining Vote Choice for Bush, Clinton, and Perot According to Affirmative Action

Affirmative Action		Dummy Variable: Vote for Bush				
		Respondent Reaction to				
	[Model]	{Bush	Clinton	Perot}	Party ID	χ^2
NES	ABS	−.59	.95	−1.07	6.54***	65.5
	DIF	6.43*	−3.64	2.10	7.86***	74.8
	OMIT	−10.63*	−1.29	10.60*	12.83***	87.6
LAT	COMMIT	−.94	.32	5.38*	10.68***	81.3
	BOTH	−3.86*	−.26	7.49**	13.39***	88.9

Affirmative Action		Dummy Variable: Vote for Clinton				
		Respondent Reaction to				
	[Model]	{Bush	Clinton	Perot}	Party ID	χ^2
NES	ABS	1.57	−1.88+	.13	−6.62***	78.0
	DIF	−5.92*	1.52	−.84	−7.64***	87.3
	OMIT	2.22	−4.07+	−1.62	−4.75***	67.1
LAT	COMMIT	2.37+	−1.58	−1.84	−5.18***	62.9
	BOTH	3.10*	−2.46+	−2.48+	−4.74***	68.9

Affirmative Action		Dummy Variable: Vote for Perot				
		Respondent Reaction to				
	[Model]	{Bush	Clinton	Perot}		χ^2
NES	ABS	−.84	1.06	−.04		2.5
	DIF	1.39	−2.08	4.67+		8.7
	OMIT	1.07	3.71+	−1.29		4.8
LAT	COMMIT	−1.20	.70	−4.58*		7.8
	BOTH	.04	1.55	−2.13		2.7

Note: Coefficients, significance levels of predictor variables, and chi-square statistics for equations are reported above. Party was included as a covariate for prediction of votes for Bush and Clinton but did not significantly predict votes for Perot, so it was excluded from those equations. Higher scores for respondents indicate (for ABS) maximal distance from the candidate, (for DIF) being located to the right of the candidate on the relevant ideological dimension, and (for OMIT, COMMIT, or BOTH) presence of the according judged threat for that candidate on that issue.

+$p < .10$
*$p < .05$
**$p < .01$
***$p < .001$

be explained by lower absolute distance from Clinton, and Perot voters saw themselves as significantly less liberal in comparison to Perot than did his opponents. None of this is very surprising; nor, while giving us some indication of whose issue stances may have been more pivotal than others in the election, is it all that useful. The frequent switches—for a given issue absolute (but not signed) differences from one candidate matter, but the reverse for someone else—muddy the response pattern's interpretability.

The latitude-based models prove more useful. We found initially that the intention to vote for Bush was affected independently by judgments that he would support the wrong policies on health care reform (table 4), and would fail to support the right policies. Perot supporters, meanwhile, were highly threatened by the prospect of what Clinton and Bush would fail to do on health care and were much more confident than other respondents that Perot would not fail to act appropriately. Naturally, we are faced with the question of whether our survey results match reality—we have no reason to believe that they do not—but even at this point we can conclude that the threat questions suggest hypotheses about the role of issue positions in the presidential campaign that the NES method does not.

On the issue of affirmative action (table 5), respondents intending to vote for Bush are less afraid of what their candidate will fail to do, but highly afraid of Perot—both of what he won't do, and of what he *will* do that they oppose. We find this interesting if true. Clinton supporters are less afraid of their candidate's inaction, and more afraid of Bush taking actions they oppose, than are his opponents. Perot backers are afraid of what Clinton will fail to do. (Analyses not reported here identify this as a fear that he will not adopt more conservative policies.)

Certain themes emerge from this analysis. As might be expected of an election featuring a distressed incumbent, Bush was the issue in the election more so than Clinton or Perot. Judged threats of omission were more powerful predictors of support than were threats of commission: the election was about the government's not doing what it ought rather than about its doing what it ought not. This was especially true for Perot voters. Supporters of all three candidates often indicated that their man would not fail to act; this was the most commonly significant variable across all equations. We find that, even without coding for the ideology of the various proposals that elicited fear, this methodology provides us with a more consistent, interpretable, and useful set of findings, and one that (not incidentally) comports with much of the consensual expert analysis of the 1992 presidential campaign.

Implications and Conclusions

We would be happy if the sole effect of reclaiming latitude theory for political science were to impel researchers to question the predominant, automatic use of point placement models. Methodologically, we believe our assessment approach holds substantial promise. While more time-consuming than NES scales—a deficiency we acknowledge—the threat-appraisal model affords a much richer analysis. Seeing which threats voters perceive on which issues—rash action or do-nothingism—may help clarify the roles of such issues in elections, as with our finding of disproportionate fear of Bush's failure to act on these policy issues. Coding variables for responses in cells *a* and *b*, and *g* and *h*, from table 1 (as we have not yet done) may provide a sounder basis for measuring feelings of hope and satisfaction, respectively, than eliciting retrospective judgments of emotional experience (Kinder 1994), and contrasts of these responses with expressions of fear and disappointment may aid the integration of cognitive and affective political research. We recognize that the latitude approach requires asking more questions than does NES, which both requires more time and increases the cumulative problem of missing data. The lower amount of missing data *per question* using our model, though, suggests that responding to a given proposal and judging its broad likelihood if candidates win is an easier task, about which respondents feel more confident, than placing candidates' positions on policy dimensions (especially when one of them lacks a party affiliation as a cue).

Moreover, we believe that our approach dumps the by-now thoroughly soiled bathwater (the notion that individuals have lasting, retrievable, consequential stands on the issues of the day) without discarding the baby: issues still do matter in our political system. Citizens are not entirely at the mercy of elites; rather, by rejecting abhorrent policies, they shape action in a given year and across time (Key 1966).

In terms of political persuasion, we conclude that the battle is not to convince citizens that one's policy is *right*, but simply that it is *not unreasonable:* that a favored candidate's election (or incumbent's policy proposal) does not portend catastrophe. This suggests that governments have more leeway in policy implementation than most theories of public opinion suggest. Many periods of active change in government policy (1965, 1981, 1993) bear out this suspicion. If addressing social problems requires approaches that won't garner general public support in advance (e.g., tax increases, benefit cuts), our message is a hopeful one: Citizens need not be "converted" before change can occur, but need only be willing to reserve judgment. Craven "government by poll," of which both the Bush and Clinton administrations have been accused, is less necessary than commonly supposed; politicans may safely take a longer view without panicking at every jag of public opinion. And, claims that even powerful electoral victories imply a "persuaded" electorate are dubious.

Politicians may already recognize this, even if theorists don't. A more important implication for students of mass behavior is that governments *need* persuade citizens on issues less than is generally supposed. This argument is often made by elite theorists who imply that mass opinion is therefore not worth studying; that is emphatically not our message. Masses can and do constrain elite initiatives—but only when they have the ability and motivation to do so.

Political actors may successfully further desired policies not only by convincing people, but by widening their latitudes of noncommitment through fostering feelings of resignation, impotence, confusion, or cynicism (Diamond, in press.) Latitude theory says that the question of how regimes manipulate the ability and will of masses to engage given issues—indicated in part by measures of political efficacy and motivation—is central to the study of political persuasion. By contrast, perpetual assessment of citizens' shifting optimal preferences on complex issues is, fortunately (and ironically), beside the point.

APPENDIX

Some technical aspects of the survey described in this chapter are detailed here. More complete details may be found in Diamond and Cobb (1994).

Procedures. Between October 28 and November 2, 1992, we conducted a survey of 1,030 respondents from the Champaign-Urbana local calling area whose phone numbers had been generated randomly and who were registered to vote in the November 3 general election. In exchange for credit for an election-related assignment, 115 students worked from one to 10 hours interviewing up to 10 people by phone. Approximately 3,000 eligible respondents were called at least once, yielding a minimum response rate of 34 percent. This figure may be deceptively low: students were to limit how many numbers they were actively trying at any given time, but many tried as many as 50 numbers at a time to reach their quota. Approximately 900 numbers received only one call. Excluding these numbers yields a response rate of about 48 percent. We are more concerned with the internal validity of our cross-form experiment than the external validity of our entire survey, and so are roughly satisfied either way.[2]

Survey design. Respondents were randomly assigned to one of four types of survey form. We asked respondents questions about six issues: health care, trade policy, affirmative action, abortion, tax policy, and unemployment. To keep the average duration of interviews below 15 minutes, we split the six issues across two forms apiece. Only those 486 respondents who answered questions about the first three issues are included in the present analysis, 231 using the NES-style form and 255 using the latitude-based form.

Sample demographics. To ensure that differences between the two NES and LAT methodologies were not due to random differences in the *obtained* samples of respondents, we verified their comparability. The NES-form sample was 48.5 percent female and 93.5 percent white; the latitude-form sample was 52 percent female and 91 percent white. Of the NES-form sample, 29 percent were liberal, 28 percent conservative, and 36 percent moderate, and 31 percent registered Democrats, 25 percent Republicans, and 39 percent Independents. Of the latitude-form sample, 31 percent were liberal, 33 percent conservative, and 38 percent moderate, and 31 percent Democratic, 28 percent Republican, and 34 percent Independent. Of the NES-form sample, 29 percent intended to vote for Bush, 50 percent for Clinton, and 10 percent for Perot, while 28 percent of the latitude-form sample intended to vote for Bush, 56 percent for Clinton, and 12 percent for Perot. Comparable voting figures for Champaign-Urbana area precincts, adjusting for the exclusion of dormitory telephone numbers from our sample, were 31 percent for Bush, 54 percent for Clinton, and 15 percent for Perot.

Variable construction. The NES-style survey asked subjects to place their own attitudes on policy dimensions by first endorsing one of two opposing statements (or neutrality) and then indicating their intensity of feeling (strong, somewhat, or slight); these were then used to construct seven-point scales.[3] Respondents then likewise placed the issue stances assigned to candidates on the same dimension, using the same two-part method. Each candidate placement for each issue was then subtracted from each self-placement to determine discrepancies between respondent and candidate.

In the LAT form, six dummy variables representing presence of threat were created for each issues; variously counting threats in cells d, e, $d + e$, $c + d$, $e + f$, and $c + d + e + f$ from table 1. (No cell is included in more than one dummy variable in a given equation. Thus, $c + d + e + f$ and $e + f$ are not simultaneously used in any policy equation.) We report only on analyses involving the latter three dummy variables in this chapter.

Model construction. We tested a variety of NES and latitude models. Equations explained the intention to vote for a candidate based on judgments of that candidate alone, or of all three candidates; with full, partial, and no control for demographics; and by considering information in one issue domain, two issue domains, or all three issue domains. In the interests of space, we present only the most general results, which well represent the entire set. This general logit model treated each issue separately. A dummy variable representing the intention to vote for each candidate was explained by how much voters differed from (using the NES model) or were threatened by (using the latitude model) each of the three candidates. Party identification served as a control for Bush and Clinton equations, but not for those of Perot. (Party ID predicted votes for Perot very poorly). Other controls for race, gender, and education level were tried, but not found to predict significantly in most cases, and were removed from the general model.[4] For the most important problem domain described in Diamond and Cobb (1994), scores for respondents indicating ties in issue importance were assigned fractional weights summing to 1.0 across issues.

As noted in table 2, the latitude/threat approach was represented by three models. One, *threats of commission,* considered the total number of policies for each candidate-issue pair that the respondent opposed, but thought were somewhat or very likely to be enacted given a candidate's victory. This corresponds to respondent placement in cells e and f from table 1. The *threats of omission* model considered the number of policies for each candidate-issue pair that the respondent supported, but thought were not very or not at all likely to be enacted given a candidate's victory. This corresponds to respondent placement in cells *c* and *d* from table 1. The final model was a simple summation of the first two, and also ranged from zero to seven (since a respondent could not simultaneously fear a threat of commission and omission for a given policy.) All three variables were then rescaled on a zero-one interval. For each of the latitude variables, a positive coefficient value indicates a judgment of more threats for a given candidate on a given issue, while a negative coefficient value represents fewer judged threats.

NOTES

Thanks to Mark Giamalva and Steven Kukulka for completing the yeoman's task of entering data from 1,030 questionnaires, and to Jim Kuklinski and the editors for helpful comments on earlier drafts of this chapter.

1. Sherif and Hovland did have people indicate their most and least preferred points on dimensions, but this played no important part in their structural theory. Our model exaggerates theirs slightly, to highlight the differences between the latitude and point placement approaches. Our most severe assumptions, however, can be relaxed without compromising our argument.

2. Data from questionnaires were then transcribed onto coding sheets and then into a computer file; random verification of 10 percent of the data lines indicated that fewer than 2 percent of these had one or more error per data line, and almost none had more than one error. All errors involved mistaken entry of a number rather than the more serious displacement of a data column.

3. We chose this approach to give the NES method fair treatment in our comparison by maximizing the comparability between the NES and latitude measures and to avoid the difficulties associated with novice interviewers administering a seven-point scale survey. Moreover, the use of separate questions to indicate direction and intensity of opinion has been found to produce more reliable results than asking respondents to place their preference directly on a seven-point scale.

4. Demographic variables—gender for Clinton, education for Perot, race in affirmative action items—occasionally loaded significantly in the latitude models, but not for NES-style equations. These demographic variables, though not independently significant, infrequently brought issue-difference explanations into significance for the NES-style equations.

REFERENCES

Bachman, J., and P. O'Malley. 1984. Yea-saying, nay-saying, and going to extremes: Black-white differences in response styles. *Public Opinion Quarterly* 48:491–509.

Berelson, B., P. Lazarsfeld, and J. McPhee. 1957. *Voting*. New York: Free Press.

Berent, M., and J. Krosnick. 1995. The relation between political attitude importance and knowledge structure. In *Political judgment: Structure and process,* ed. M. Lodge and K. McGraw. Ann Arbor: University of Michigan Press.

Converse, P. 1964. The nature of belief systems in mass publics. In *Ideology and discontent,* ed. D. Apter. New York: Free Press.

Converse, P. 1970. Attitudes and non-attitudes: Continuation of a dialogue. In *The quantitative analysis of social problems,* ed. E. R. Tufte. Reading, Mass.: Addison-Wesley.

Diamond, G. (In press) Latitude theory, representation, and political debate. In *Political psychology and public opinion,* ed. J. Kuklinski. Cambridge: Cambridge University Press.

Diamond, G., and M. Cobb. 1994. The candidate as catastrophe: Threat perception and issue voting in the 1992 presidential election. Paper presented at the annual Midwestern Political Science Association conference, Chicago.

Downs, A. 1957. *An economic theory of democracy.* New York: Harper and Row.

Enelow, J., and M. Hinich. 1984. *The spatial theory of voting: An introduction.* New York: Cambridge University Press.

Hochschild, J. 1981. *What's fair?: American beliefs about distributive justice.* Cambridge: Harvard University Press.

Judd, C., and J. Krosnick. 1982. Attitude centrality, organization, and measurement. *Journal of Personality and Social Psychology* 42:436–47.

Kahneman, D., P. Slovic, and A. Tversky. 1982. *Judgments under uncertainty: Heuristics and biases.* New York: Cambridge University Press.

Kelly, G. 1955. *The psychology of personal constructs.* New York: Norton.

Key, V. O., Jr., with M. C. Cummings, Jr. 1966. *The responsible electorate: Rationality in presidential voting.* Cambridge: Harvard University Press.

Kinder, D. 1994. Reason and emotion in American political life. In *Beliefs, reasoning, and decision making: Psycho-logic in honor of Bob Abelson,* ed. R. Abelson, R. Schank, and E. Langer. Hillsdale, N.J.: Lawrence Erlbaum Associates.

Krosnick, J. 1991. The stability of political preferences: Comparisons of symbolic and non-symbolic attitudes. *American Journal of Political Science* 35(2): 547–76.

Lau, R. 1982. Negativity in political perceptions. *Political behavior* 4:353–78.

Lazarus, R., and S. Folkman. 1984. *Stress, appraisal, and coping.* New York: Springer.

Lodge, M. 1994. Towards a procedural model of candidate evaluation. In *Political judgment: Structure and process,* ed. M. Lodge and K. McGraw. Ann Arbor: University of Michigan Press.

Lodge, M., K. McGraw, and P. Stroh. 1989. An impression-driven model of candidate evaluation. *American Political Science Review* 83:399–419.

Oskamp, S. 1977. *Attitudes and opinion.* Englewood Cliffs, N.J.: Prentice-Hall.

Popkin, S. 1991. *The reasoning voter: Communication and persuasion in presidential campaigns.* Chicago: University of Chicago Press.

Sherif, M., and C. Hovland. 1961. *Social judgment: Assimilation and contrast effects in communication and attitude change.* New Haven, Conn.: Yale University Press.

Simon, H. 1955. A behavioral model of rational choice. *Quarterly Journal of Economics* 69:99–118.

Simon, H. 1985. Human nature in politics: The dialogue of psychology with political science. *American Political Science Review,* 79:293–304.

Sniderman, P., R. Brody, and P. Tetlock. 1991. *Reasoning and choice: Explorations in political psychology.* Cambridge: Cambridge University Press.

Toda, M. 1982. Emotional fungus-eaters. In *Man, robot and society: Models and situations,* ed. M. Toda. Boston: Mastinus Nijhof.

Tversky, A. 1972. Elimination by aspects: A theory of choice. *Psychological Review* 79:281–99.

Uleman, J. 1989. A framework for thinking intentionally about unintended thought. In *Unintended thought,* ed. J. Bargh and J. Uleman. New York: Guilford.

Zajonc, R. 1980. Feeling and thinking: Preferences need no inferences. *American Psychologist* 35(2): 151–75.

Zaller, J. 1992. *The nature and origins of mass opinion.* Cambridge: Cambridge University Press.

Zaller, J., and S. Feldman. 1992. A simple theory of the survey response: Answering questions versus revealing preferences. *American Journal of Political Science* 36(3): 579–616.

CHAPTER 10

Persuasion in Context: The Multilevel Structure of Economic Evaluations

Jeffery J. Mondak, Diana C. Mutz, and Robert Huckfeldt

The idea that social context influences political attitudes is now widely accepted in studies of political persuasion (e.g., Eulau 1986). However, since individuals are each part of numerous different social contexts, this seemingly straightforward maxim often tells us very little. Will people rely on the social environment comprised of their immediate families, their neighborhoods, their states, or their nation as a whole in making political judgments? In this chapter we use the multilevel structure of economic evaluations to examine which social environments are most important to political judgments; in addition, we look at how the basis of these judgments is altered by the presence of high levels of information.

In the United States, citizens tend to hold presidents responsible for the economic state of their nation. But at the same time, people tend not to attribute responsibility for their personal problems to national political leaders (see Sniderman and Brody 1977; Brody and Sniderman 1977). Although there are notable exceptions to this generalization (e.g., Sears and Citrin 1982; Tufte 1978), on balance the accumulation of findings suggests that sociotropic judgments, that is, perceptions of the state of the nation as a whole, are far more important to people's political views (e.g., Schlozman and Verba 1979; Kiewiet 1983; see Sears and Funk 1990, for a review).

Nowhere has this counterintuitive pattern in the formation of political attitudes been as thoroughly established as in the economic realm. Neither declining family financial conditions nor even loss of a job has been found to have much of an impact on judgments of national political leaders. As Kinder and Kiewiet (1979, 523) summarized, "Private economic experience is important, but not for politics. Economic discontents and political judgments inhabit separate domains." Despite the immediacy and obvious personal relevance of economic experiences within the immediate family, they are apparently less persuasive when it comes to political attitudes because it is quite difficult for people to connect this social context with judgments of national political leaders.

At the same time, it has been well established that judgments of national economic conditions significantly and consistently enter into political evaluations. While personal experiences are "morselized" (Lane 1962) and rarely connected to political judgments, perceptions of national economic conditions are quite readily connected to judgments about political leaders at both presidential and congressional levels (e.g., Kiewiet 1983; Kinder and Kiewiet 1979). As a result, national political leaders tend to be held accountable for retrospective perceptions of national economic performance.

But personal experience and perceptions of national economic well-being are only two points along a broad continuum; in between an individual's immediate life space and his or her perceptions of national conditions is a broad middle ground consisting of perceptions of successively larger collectives with whom people may interact either through interpersonal or mass mediated communication (e.g., Conover 1985; Weatherford 1983; Mutz 1994). What remains unclear is what kind of role these intermediate-level collectives play in the process of evaluating political leaders. For example, are perceptions of community economic well-being insulated from political consequences as are personal economic experiences? Or are they processed more like collective, national-level information and readily connected to judgments of political leaders?

The reason for the neglect of intermediate-level collectives does not rest in past null findings or in a theoretical rationale predicting that these collectives should be less persuasive politically or inherently less important. Instead, it results largely from a lack of available data corresponding to judgments about the economic conditions of more local entities.

The purpose of this chapter is to examine the processing of economic information from an intermediate collective, in this case, one's own neighborhood. The neighborhood is of potential political significance simply due to the ready availability of socially transmitted information—information that may complement or counter economic perceptions premised solely on personal or national conditions. We do not assume the neighborhood to be a self-contained community in which the resident conducts all of life's daily activities. For a few rare individuals this may be the case, but for most it is surely not. Our assumption, instead, is that social relations are inescapable within any geographically based collectivity. When we look out the front window or walk around the corner, we are exposed to information about the neighborhood, and that information ultimately may contribute to our political judgments. Further, perceptions regarding the neighborhood's economic fortunes can be formed without attention to either one's own economic situation or national economic developments. Hence, neighborhood-level perceptions may influence political judgments independent of the familiar family-level and national-level effects.[1]

We begin this exploration by reviewing the bits and pieces of evidence currently available on the politicization of subnational economic perceptions. Next we simultaneously examine the politicization of family economic experience, perceived neighborhood economic experience, and perceived national economic experience. By comparing the politicization of different social contexts among those with varying levels of exposure to outside sources of economic information, we gain further insight into differences in how information from various social contexts is processed and how this information ultimately influences judgments about presidential economic policies.

Politicizing Subnational Collective Economic Judgments

Each individual lives within a unique social environment. Residence in a neighborhood, membership in a church, and employment in a workplace expose the individual to a unique blend of information that conditions political behavior (Huckfeldt 1986). For example, a neighborhood context conveys social information that affects individual-level electoral choice (Huckfeldt and Sprague 1987, 1995). Similar contextual effects may operate on other aspects of political behavior, including the evaluation of political leaders.

The debate over what type of information people use to evaluate economic performance has led to some consideration of collectives other than the nation as a whole. It is generally agreed that state and local community economic contexts have the potential to influence assessments of political leaders, but there has been little empirical research establishing the contributions of these perceptions. As Weatherford (1983, 870) argues, "The evaluation of economic conditions is a natural situation for contextual effects to operate through interpersonal contact; individuals are readily aware of co-workers and acquaintances who are unemployed, and shoppers in markets as diverse as food and real estate commonly compare their experiences with inflation" (see also Kinder, Rosenstone, and Hansen 1983).

While there are studies that have looked at economic influences in other than congressional and presidential elections, the measures of economic conditions usually have been at the national level (e.g., Klorman 1978). In one exception, Piereson (1977) examined congressional elections and changes in economic conditions within congressional districts but found voting to be largely independent of district economic conditions. On the other hand, Chubb (1988) found state economic conditions to be significantly related to gubernatorial election outcomes. However, for purposes of this study, we are interested in the extent to which people hold presidents accountable for economic conditions closer to home than perceived national conditions, yet less parochial than one's own personal experiences.

The few studies that meet these criteria generally do not address perceptions of economic conditions within clearly circumscribed communities that are defined by boundaries such as state or city borders (cf. Pollard 1978). Instead, they involve measures of researcher-defined groups such as classes or Labor Market Areas (e.g., Weatherford 1983, 1978). Typically, they relate aggregate, objective measures of how a group is faring economically with individual political attitudes. Although subjective perceptions of local economic conditions are probably closely related to objective measures of local economic conditions (e.g., Weatherford 1983), they do not easily lend themselves to comparisons with the predictive power of family finances or subjective perceptions of national conditions.

In a study directly examining the effects of perceptions of group economic well-being, Conover (1985) found that perceptions of group economic interests were perceived to overlap very little with personal financial interests, and even less with perceptions of change in national conditions.[2] Moreover, she found that perceptions of group economic interests had significant independent effects on presidential performance evaluations (see also Kinder, Rosenstone, and Hansen 1983; Kinder, Adams, and Gronke 1989). Mutz (1993) found that hearing about unemployment problems interpersonally contributed to less favorable attitudes toward the president as well as to less favorable assessments of national economic conditions (see also Mutz 1992).

Processing Economic Information

Although the results of studies examining perceptions of group economic conditions confirm their potential for influence, they are inconclusive with regard to theoretical rationale. For example, why should people be influenced by group interests when they are seldom swayed politically by personal ones? Personal experiences originally recommended themselves as readily available, low-cost sources of economic information. Since this type of information is accessible without much effort, it seems a natural referent for a notoriously poorly informed, weakly motivated public. But as Downs (1957) reminds us, procurement costs are only one of several types of costs required to become informed.

In addition to the time and effort required to gain access to information, it is particularly important to take into consideration the costs of evaluation, that is, the costs of relating that information to political judgments. When it comes to family economic experience, these costs are extremely high. Such highly personal events are not seen as immediately relevant to political judgments. And although the strengths and weaknesses of personal experiences and perceived national conditions—in terms of ease of access and evaluation—might logically balance out to a stalemate, they typically do not. Past research suggests that the low cost of obtaining personal-level information is over-shadowed by the high costs of its interpretation (Mutz 1994).

Nonetheless, the immediate personal experience of those who live to-gether has long been considered a social context with tremendous potential for political influence (Chaffee and Mutz 1988). The high personal relevance of this social context and its close physical proximity make it difficult to ignore. Moreover, the vividness and immediacy of one's own immediate surround-ings should have tremendous political potential if the evaluative costs can be overcome and those perceptions can be connected to political consequences. Groups may be in an ideal position to capitalize on both immediacy and collectivity. Information about groups will have more personal relevance than information about the nation as a whole; but at the same time, perceptions of group well-being should have more obvious political relevance (Conover 1985).

The idea that groups might serve as a middle ground, facilitating the connection of the personal and political, is reinforced by analyses suggesting that, from the perspective of most citizens, both family economic experiences and perceptions of national conditions have serious drawbacks as sources of information on which to base political judgments. The most logical and effi-cient way for people to decide which of their many social environments to use in framing a response to a policy question is to judge that source of informa-tion against the dual criteria of trustworthiness and relevance to the evaluative situation at hand (Weatherford 1983). One can be fairly certain that percep-tions of one's own family finances are based on complete and accurate infor-mation, but the logical relationship between family finances and how the president is doing is far more of a leap. In other words, trustworthiness is high, but relevance is low. On the other hand, perceptions of national eco-nomic conditions are clearly relevant to evaluating the president, but macro-economic information is extremely difficult to understand (e.g., McCloskey 1990); in this case, the trade-off is in favor of relevance, but it minimizes trustworthiness. The efficiency of procuring highly trustworthy information through personal and highly parochial experiences consistently clashes with the ease of interpreting its political relevance. Again, groups may serve as an important middle ground combining moderately trustworthy information with perceptions of a collective that has more obvious political relevance than personal economic problems.

Effects of Information Levels on the Processing of Economic Judgments

Much of what we know about why some types of information are more easily connected to political judgments than others comes from studies that have examined differences in how these judgments are connected to political views among subgroups in the population. For example, several studies have shown that personal experiences are more likely to be connected to political judgments among the less politically informed. Weatherford (1983) and Conover et al. (1986) both found that personal experiences were more politically influential among those unknowledgeable about national economic conditions. Mutz (1992) also found that high levels of exposure to news about the economy decreased the importance of personal concerns to political judgments.

Studies along these lines are generally interpreted as indicating that personal experience serves as a default source of political information, to be relied upon only in the absence of more abstract, national-level information. Comparisons of the predictive power of national economic judgments seem to confirm this idea. Weatherford (1983), for example, found that high levels of information primed the importance of collective, national-level perceptions to political evaluations, while people with low levels of information relied instead on personal economic experience.

All else being equal, people will rely on the social context most relevant to the judgment they are making (in this case, national-level conditions), even if it means some sacrifice in the trustworthiness of that information. But in forming impressions of the national economic climate, individuals will strive to balance efficiency and reliability (Mondak 1994a). Simple default judgments may be efficient, but they will be of little utility if these judgments are of uncertain reliability. Consequently, reliance on default information should decrease when substantive information relevant to an evaluation becomes available (Chaiken, Lieberman, and Eagly 1989; Mondak 1994b). As Weatherford (1983, 162) argues, "The dilemma of choosing between personal and national referents for economic voting is more apparent than actual. Realistically, neither extreme is likely to be represented, but the population can be conceptualized as distributed between the two poles. Along this continuum, the balance will shift from personal to national conditions as the dominant basis for assessing government economic policy."

The idea that people will default to less relevant criteria for judging presidential economic performance only in the absence of more appropriate, collective-level information has received considerable support in recent research. But this perspective contradicts an equally theoretically compelling argument suggesting precisely the opposite. Mill ([1861] 1962), for example, argued that political discussion promoted the awareness of connections between the personal and political: "It is a school in which people learn the impact of remote events on their and other people's political interests" (944). Formal and informal channels of political communication could enhance the extent to which people politicize their immediate social contexts by helping them connect this information to politicians and policies (e.g., Mutz 1994).

Although this argument makes intuitive sense, evidence suggests that some types of information or ways of framing issues may aid people in politicizing their personal experiences, while others may discourage people from doing so (e.g., Iyengar 1991). But in general, information that comes to us from outside the life space provides a more relevant, if somewhat less reliable, basis for assessing a national leader. Thus, the general tendency will be to rely on the larger social context, but in a pinch, people will extrapolate from their more immediate social context.

Overall, then, we expect external information to decrease the importance of personal financial assessments to political judgments and simultaneously to increase the importance of national-level perceptions of economic trends. To the extent that perceptions of neighborhood conditions represent a middle ground between the immediacy of personal experiences and the political relevance of national conditions, the neighborhood context may help people connect a highly immediate, yet still collective, problem to government officials. On the other hand, to the extent that perceptions of neighborhood economic well-being serve merely as default sources of economic news, outside information may decrease the importance of perceptions of neighborhood economic well-being.

In addition to these hypothesized interactions, we expect the three perceptions of economic conditions to each have independent main effects on perceptions of how the president is handling the economy. As in so many other studies, we expect a small effect from personal experiences, and a much stronger effect from perceived national economic conditions. Perceptions of trends in neighborhood economic well-being should fall somewhere in between the two since they represent moderate levels of accessibility and relevance. While people clearly do not feel comfortable concluding based on their own family economic experiences that government is to blame, a somewhat larger sample of experiences will make them more confident of the relevance of that judgment. In short, it should convince them that the problem is not simply yours or mine, but rather one that is shared by many others.

Methods

The data used in this study are drawn from the first wave of a larger project focusing on contextual effects on political behavior. Fifteen hundred residents of South Bend, Indiana, were interviewed at three points in time during the 1984 election campaign. The interview from which the data in this study are derived took place after the Indiana primary but before the national party conventions. All data collection was done by the Center for Survey Research at Indiana University using computer-assisted telephone interviewing.

Neighborhoods served as the primary sampling units in this sampling frame. As Huckfeldt and Sprague (1995) explain, neighborhoods were not chosen because the investigators attributed any particular epistemological status to them as groups, but rather because they structure proximity and exposure—two important elements of involuntary social interaction (Huckfeldt 1983): "Where we live determines the churches that are nearby, where we do our shopping, the bumper stickers and yard signs that surround us. Moreover, neighborhoods serve as staging grounds for a variety of voluntary social activities" (see Huckfeldt and Sprague 1995, chap. 2, for sampling details).

The specific items used to compare the predictive power of personal and collective referents were a series of questions asking for retrospective assessments of economic conditions in the nation as a whole, the neighborhood, and in the immediate family.[3] These questions were asked using a retrospective one-year time frame. Previous studies suggest that memory even for family economic experiences is too poor to provide reliable estimates when asked about a longer time period (see Kernell 1978; Fair 1978), and there is little difference in the predictive validity of the item when it is asked using a more recent, six-month time frame. The dependent variable was the commonly asked question regarding how well the respondent approves or disapproves of the way the president is handling the economy.[4] In order to avoid artificially inducing self-interested political attitudes in the context of the survey itself, questions concerning economic perceptions were asked after the questions about Reagan approval and were separated by a large number and variety of other questions (see Sears and Lau 1983).

An additive index of the amount of outside information reaching individual respondents was constructed by combining responses to four different questions. These questions included attention to campaign news, frequency of reading political news in newspapers and listening to it on the radio or television, and the frequency with which respondents discussed politics with others.[5] In order to test the hypothesized interactions between economic judgments and information levels, the scale was dichotomized into those with high and low levels of outside information. These measures of mass and interpersonal political communication are all indicative of contact with social contexts outside the immediate life space. They are not designed to tap the reception or storage of specific messages as they might well be if they were designed to assess the influence of exposure on perceptions of the nation's economic wellbeing or some other form of attitude change (see Zaller, this volume). Nor are we concerned with the accuracy or directionality of the economic information respondents have encountered. Instead, our goal is simply to characterize each respondent's information environment in terms of the extent of exposure to information outside of his or her immediate life experiences and to evaluate how such exposure alters the standards people use in assessing the president's handling of the economy.

In order to establish a baseline against which to assess the relationships between economic perceptions and presidential approval, a battery of demographic variables were also included in the logit regression equations predicting attitudes toward Reagan's handling of the economy; these included age, gender, family income, and education.[6] Even more important for purposes of eliminating potential reciprocal relationships and establishing people's long-term political predispositions, the equations include measures of party identification and ideology. Ideology was measured using the traditional seven-point scale.[7] Since people sometimes adjust the strength of their party identification in response to short-term economic changes (see Kiewiet 1983), we used two dummy variables to represent Republican or Democratic party identification, but did not incorporate the strength of partisanship in these measures in order to avoid reactivity problems.[8] These controls, in combination with the fact that the dependent variable is a dichotomous measure of support, further decreased the likelihood of reciprocal causation.

Findings

The logit equation in table 1 presents results that are consistent with previous findings on sociotropic voting. First there was predictable rationalization of

TABLE 1. The Influence of Personal, National, and Subnational Economic Conditions on Evaluation of Presidential Performance

	Coefficient	*t*-value
Constant	−0.22	−0.32
Sex	−0.33#	−1.92
Republican	1.07**	4.28
Democrat	−0.86**	−4.59
Education	0.01	0.28
Age	−0.01	−1.46
Income	0.09	1.54
Ideology	0.15*	3.28
Family	0.44**	3.76
Nation	0.79**	7.08
Neighborhood	0.57**	3.44
Model chi-square $=$ 442.18		
$N = 952$		

Source: 1984 South Bend study.

Note: The dependent variable is support for Reagan's handling of the economy (1 = approve; 0 = disapprove). Probability of approval $= e^f / 1 + e^f$ where $f = a + b_1 x_1 + b_2 x_2 + \ldots$

**$p < .001$
*$p < .01$
#$p < .10$

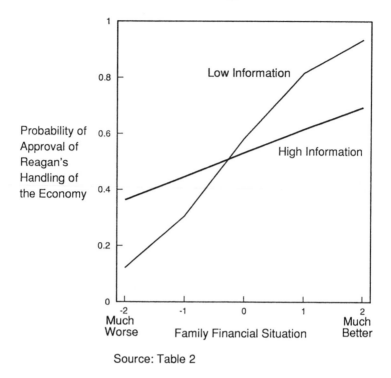

Source: Table 2

Fig. 1. Influence of perceptions of family financial situation, by level of information.

Reagan's handling of the economy according to partisan and ideological leanings. More conservative respondents were more likely to approve of Reagan's handling of the economy, as were Republicans, while Democrats were negatively predisposed in their assessment of his performance.

As in so many previous studies of economic influences on voting, retrospective perceptions of national economic conditions had a strong impact on support for the president's handling of the economy. The coefficient corresponding to perceptions of national economic conditions was nearly twice the size of the coefficient corresponding to family finances, though both achieved statistical significance in the equation. Most important, the size of the coefficient corresponding to perceptions of neighborhood economic conditions fell in between the family and national coefficients, as predicted. While all three effects were significant, perceptions of national conditions mattered most and family finances the least. Although the three economic perception measures were fairly strongly correlated (mean $r = .49$), they each made significant independent contributions to the chi-square value of the equation. Table 2

summarizes the results for the equation incorporating the hypothesized interactions with levels of outside information. Level of information alone made
no difference to people's evaluations of the president, but it clearly mediated
the effects of the economic variables. As illustrated in figure 1, perceptions of
family finances were indeed stronger predictors of approval of Reagan's handling of the economy among those with low information (in all figures values
for control variables are held at their means). As the negative coefficient in
table 2 indicates, those with high levels of information were less likely to rely
on family finances to inform their judgments about Reagan's handling of the
economy. Although family finances also maintained a significant direct effect
on Reagan approval, the negative interaction coefficient meant that this effect
was quite small for those with high levels of external information.

**TABLE 2. Economic Conditions and Evaluation
of Presidential Performance, by Level
of Information**

	Coefficient	t-value
Constant	−0.13	−0.18
Sex	−0.34#	−1.95
Republican	1.04***	4.14
Democrat	−0.84***	−4.40
Education	0.02	0.36
Age	−0.01	−1.45
Income	0.09	1.51
Ideology	0.16***	3.40
Family	1.16**	3.20
Nation	0.24	0.84
Neighborhood	−0.23	−0.49
Information	−0.21	−0.84
Information × Family	−0.81*	−2.13
Information × Nation	0.65*	2.08
Information × Neighborhood	0.90#	1.80
Model chi-square = 453.97		
$N = 952$		

Source: 1984 South Bend study.

Note: The dependent variable is support for Reagan's handling of
the economy (1 = approve; 0 = disapprove). Probability of approval
= $e^f / 1 + e^f$ where $f = a + b_1 x_1 + b_2 x_2 + \ldots$

***$p < .001$
**$p < .01$
*$p < .05$
#$p < .10$

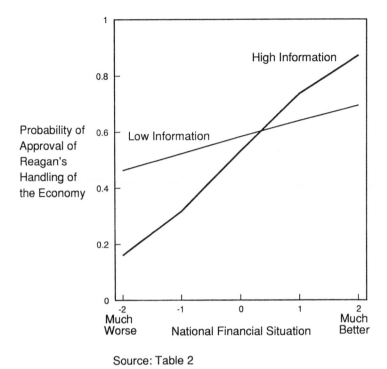

Source: Table 2

Fig. 2. Influence of perceptions of national financial situation, by level of information.

The coefficients in table 2 suggest that the main effect of national economic conditions in table 1 was driven primarily by respondents high in external information. The main effect of perceived national conditions was weak and statistically insignificant, but the interaction indicated that the effect was strong and significant among the high information subgroup. As figure 2 illustrates, if national conditions were perceived to be much worse than in the previous year, low information respondents were less likely to punish the president for this downturn, but they were also less likely to reward him if they perceived conditions to have improved.

Finally, figure 3 summarizes this same relationship for perceptions of neighborhood economic conditions. The main effect of neighborhood perceptions disappeared when the interaction was included in the equation, but the interaction coefficient itself was large, and approached statistical significance. In general, the pattern in figure 3 is very similar to figure 2, although the interaction is more pronounced in figure 3.

The findings for neighborhood context are largely consistent with our

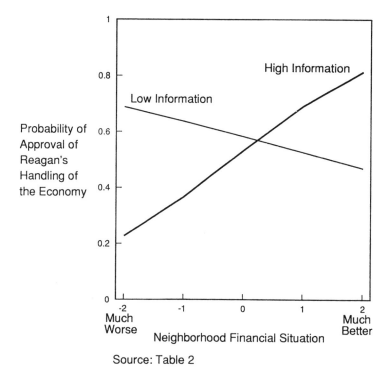

Source: Table 2

Fig. 3. Influence of perceptions of neighborhood financial situation, by level of information.

earlier discussion. Although information of this kind may be more costly to acquire than information on family finances, once obtained it is, in fact, easier to connect to judgments of political leaders than personal experiences. At the same time, it is not seen as equally relevant to presidential evaluations as are judgments of national conditions. The predicted impacts of relevance and accessibility are as anticipated.

But the pattern of responses to these questions is particularly telling with respect to the ease with which people make judgments about the economic state of their neighborhoods. The distribution of responses to the family finances question indicates that only a very small number of people were unable to assess change in their family financial situation—a mere 12 in all. But there were nine times as many "don't know/no response" answers to the neighborhood question, virtually the same number as for the question on national economic conditions. This pattern suggests that one does not, by default, have readily available information on neighborhood economic conditions. Moreover, the nonrespondents to the neighborhood question were not the same as those who did not respond to the national question; only 27 respondents fell into this category in both instances. Not surprisingly, the type of information gathering that gives one impressions of national conditions appears to be different from the type of information gathering that gives one an impression of what the neighborhood is like.

Discussion

First and foremost, the results of this study suggest that judgments drawn from a variety of social contexts may enter into the formation of attitudes toward presidential policies. People are most likely to utilize the social context most relevant to presidential evaluations, that is, the state of the nation as a whole, and, in descending order of importance, the neighborhood economic context, followed by the immediate family financial situation. However, since information about these contexts is not equally accessible or efficient to gather, people who are not heavily exposed to outside sources of information are more likely to utilize less relevant, but more accessible, social contexts in framing their response to a policy question. The context within which issues are evaluated may be altered by the amount of mass and interpersonal information reaching a given individual.

Clearly, structuring the question of what kind of economic information matters most as a competition between personal economic experience and perceived national conditions ignores a wide range of intermediate collectives with substantial potential for influence (Weatherford 1983). Neighborhoods are only one example of an intermediary collective of this kind; they are probably neither the most nor the least influential type of intermediary collective. On one hand, neighborhoods provide substantial opportunities for obtaining impressions of neighborhood economic conditions; in addition to many opportunities for interpersonal exchange of information, neighborhoods make it possible to indirectly observe changes in economic well-being. New cars in the driveway, home improvements and expansions, as well as obvious signs of neglect all contribute to neighborhood economic impressions without requiring interpersonal contact. On the other hand, from the perspective of group identification, they are probably not the most salient groups in many people's minds. The fact that they, nonetheless, have a substantial impact on assessments of the president, suggests that intermediary collectives are well worth incorporating into models of economic influences on the evaluation of political leaders. These results also suggest that people utilize information about neighborhoods in much the same way they do national judgments. There is a natural tendency to see information concerning more proximate collectives as easier to obtain. One might assume, therefore, that ease of access combined with greater confidence in the reliability of the information would make it a natural "default" if one lacks national-level economic information. However, our results suggest that neighborhood judgments are no easier to obtain than national economic judgments. Moreover, people with low levels of information default to personal experiences and *not* to neighborhood perceptions. It is precisely the same individuals with ample access to information about those outside of their personal life space who are most likely to utilize both neighborhood economic evaluations and national ones.

Mass media coverage focused on national-level economic phenomena may make it far easier to come by reliable impressions of national economic trends than impressions of more proximate groups with which one has limited interpersonal contact. In any case, the quality of communication networks within groups may be a better predictor of their political import than their size, proximity to the individual, or geopolitical significance.

Although the nation may serve as the most important social context for purposes of forming attitudes toward presidential policies, it remains to be seen whether forming attitudes toward more local political leaders prompts people to frame similar judgments in terms of more local social contexts. While this might be the general tendency, it seems likely that again, those who are limited in the amount of information on that particular collective may be forced to default to a less relevant, yet more easily accessible social context. The persuasive power of social context is not inherent in the immediacy or vividness of a particular social realm, but is, in itself, a function of the political context in which the judgment is made.

NOTES

1. We recognize that countless other collectivities exist. We do not claim that the neighborhood is any more important than these other groups, but only that the neighborhood constitutes a viable context for our purposes.

2. In this case, respondents each individually designated the group they felt closest to.

3. *Family finances:* "In general, would you say that you and your family are better off, worse off, or about the same financially compared with a year ago? Much or somewhat better/worse?" Coded as a five-point scale from much worse (-2) to much better ($+2$). *Neighborhood conditions:* "How about your neighborhood, would you say that most families in your neighborhood are better off, worse off, or about the same financially compared with a year ago? Much or somewhat better/worse?" Coded as a five-point scale from much worse (-2) to much better ($+2$). *National conditions:* "Now let's talk about the country as a whole. Would you say that most families in the country are better off, worse off, or about the same financially compared with a year ago? Much or somewhat better/worse?" Coded as a five-point scale from much worse (-2) to much better ($+2$).

4. "Do you approve or disapprove of the way Ronald Reagan is handling the economy?" Coded as approve (1) or disapprove (0).

5. To form the information index, four questions were combined to form a 14-point scale. To designate high and low levels of information, the scale was divided so that scores of 0 through 6 indicated low information, and 7 through 13 high information. "How much attention do you pay to news reports about the campaign for president—a great deal, quite a bit, some, very little, or none?" Coded as a five-point scale from none (0) to a great deal (4). "Some people are more involved in politics than others, and we would like to find out about your involvement. I'm going to read you a list of things that some people do in politics. Could you tell me whether you do these things regularly, sometimes, rarely, or never: Discuss politics? Read political stories in newspapers? Listen to political reports on radio or tv?" Coded as four-point scales from never (0) to regularly (3).

6. *Gender:* Recorded by the interviewer: Male (0), Female (1). *Education:* "What is the highest grade of school or year of college you have completed?" Coded as 18-point scale indicating actual number of years. *Age:* "In what year were you born?" Year number was subtracted from 1984. *Family Income:* "Last year, before taxes, was your total family income: Under 5,000 dollars; 5 to 10,000 dollars; 10 to 15,000 dollars; 15 to 20,000 dollars; 20 to 30,000 dollars; 30 to 40,000 dollars; 40 to 50,000 dollars? 50,000 dollars and over?" Coded as eight-point scale from 0 to 7.

7. *Ideology:* "When it comes to politics, do you usually think of yourself as a liberal, a conservative, a moderate, or what?" If liberal or conservative: "Do you think of yourself as a strong liberal/conservative or a not-very-strong liberal/conservative?" If neither liberal nor conservative: "Do you think of yourself as closer to liberal or closer to conservative?" Coded as a seven-point scale from strong liberal (0) to strong conservative (6).

8. *Party identification:* "Generally speaking, do you usually think of yourself as a Republican, a Democrat, an independent, or what?" Coded as two dummy variables, Republican (1) or not (0), and Democrat (1) or not (0).

REFERENCES

Brody, R. A., and P. M. Sniderman. 1977. From life space to polling place: The relevance of personal concerns for voting behavior. *British Journal of Political Science* 7:337–60.

Chaffee, S. H., and D. C. Mutz. 1988. Comparing mediated and interpersonal communication data. In *Advancing communication science: Merging mass and interpersonal,* ed. R. P. Hawkins, J. M. Wiemann, and S. Pingree. Newbury Park, Calif.: Sage.

Chaiken, S., A. Lieberman, and A. Eagly. 1989. Heuristic and systematic processing within and beyond the persuasion context. In *Unintended thought: Limits of awareness, intention, and control,* ed. J. S. Uleman and J. A. Bargh. New York: Guilford.

Chubb, J. E. 1988. Institutions, the economy, and the dynamics of state elections. *American Political Science Review* 82:133–54.

Conover, P. J. 1985. The impact of group economic interests on political evaluations. *American Politics Quarterly* 13:139–66.

Conover, P. J., and S. Feldman. 1986. Emotional reactions to the economy: I'm mad as hell and I'm not going to take it anymore. *American Journal of Political Science* 30:50–78.

Conover, P. J., S. Feldman, and K. Knight. 1986. Judging inflation and unemployment: The origins of retrospective evaluations. *Journal of Politics* 48:565–88.

Downs, A. 1957. *An economic theory of democracy.* New York: Harper and Row.

Eulau, H. 1986. Life space and social networks as political contexts. In *Politics, self, and society.* Cambridge: Harvard University Press.

Fair, R. C. 1978. The effect of economic events on votes for president. *Review of Economics and Statistics* 60:159–73.

Huckfeldt, R. 1983. The social context of political change: Durability, volatility, and social influence. *American Political Science Review* 77:929–44.

Huckfeldt, R. 1986. *Politics in context: Assimilation and conflict in urban neighborhoods.* New York: Agathon.

Huckfeldt, R., and J. Sprague. 1987. Networks in context: The social flow of political information. *American Political Science Review* 81:1197–216.

Huckfeldt, R. and J. Sprague. 1995. *Citizens, politics, and social communication: Information and influence in an election campaign.* New York: Cambridge University Press.

Iyengar, S. 1991. *Is anyone responsible? How television frames political issues.* Chicago: University of Chicago Press.

Kernell, S. 1978. Explaining presidential popularity. *American Political Science Review* 72:506–22.

Kiewiet, D. R. 1983. *Macroeconomics and micropolitics: The electoral effects of economic issues.* Chicago: University of Chicago Press.

Kinder, D. R., G. S. Adams, and P. W. Gronke. 1989. Economics and politics in the 1984 American presidential election. *American Journal of Political Science* 33:491–515.

Kinder, D. R., and D. R. Kiewiet. 1979. Economic discontent and political behavior: The role of personal grievances and collective economic judgments in congressional voting. *American Journal of Political Science* 23:495–527.

Kinder, D. R., S. J. Rosenstone, and J. M. Hansen. 1983. Group economic well-being and political choice. Pilot Study Report to the 1984 NES Planning Committee and NES Board, October 1983.

Klorman, R. 1978. Trend in personal finances and the vote. *Public Opinion Quarterly* 42:31–48.

Lane, R. E. 1962. *Political ideology.* New York: Free Press.

McCloskey, D. N. 1990. *If you're so smart: The narrative of economic expertise.* Chicago: University of Chicago Press.

Mill, J. S. [1861] 1962. *Considerations on representative government.* Chicago: Henry Regnery.

Mondak, J. J. 1994a. Cognitive heuristics, heuristic processing, and efficiency in political decision making. In *Research in micropolitics,* Vol. 4, ed. M. X. Delli-Carpini, L. Huddy, and R. Y. Shapiro. Greenwich, Conn.: JAI Press.

Mondak, J. J. 1994b. Question wording and mass policy preferences: The comparative impact of substantive information and peripheral cues. *Political Communication* 11:165–83.

Mutz, D. C. 1992. Mass media and the depoliticization of personal experience. *American Journal of Political Science* 36:483–508.

Mutz, D. C. 1993. Direct and indirect routes to politicizing personal experience: Does knowledge make a difference? *Public Opinion Quraterly* 57:483–502.

Mutz, D. C. 1994. Contextualizing personal experience: The role of the mass media. *Journal of Politics* 56:689–714.

Piereson, J. E. 1977. District economic conditions and congressional elections. Paper presented to the Midwest Political Science Association, Chicago, Ill.

Pollard, W. 1978. Effects of economic conditions on elections—A study controlling for political variables. Paper presented at the annual meeting of the Public Choice Society, New Orleans.

Schlozman, K. L., and S. Verba. 1979. *Injury to insult.* Cambridge: Harvard University Press.

Sears, D. O., and J. Citrin. 1982. *Tax revolt: Something for nothing in California.* Cambridge: Harvard University Press.

Sears, D. O., and C. L. Funk. 1990. Self-interest in Americans' political opinions. In *Beyond self-interest,* ed. J. J. Mansbridge. Chicago: University of Chicago Press.

Sears, D. O., and R. R. Lau. 1983. Inducing apparently self-interested political preferences. *American Journal of Political Science* 27:223–52.

Sniderman, P. M., and R. A. Brody. 1977. Coping: The ethic of self-reliance. *American Journal of Political Science* 21:501–21.

Tufte, E. R. 1978. *Political control of the economy.* Princeton: Princeton University Press.

Weatherford, M. S. 1978. Economic conditions and electoral outcome: Class differences in the political response to recession. *American Journal of Political Science* 22:917–38.

Weatherford, M. S. 1983. Economic voting and the "symbolic politics" argument: A reinterpretation and synthesis. *American Political Science Review* 77:158–74.

CHAPTER 11

Time of Vote Decision
and Openness to Persuasion

Steven H. Chaffee and Rajiv Nath Rimal

The search for voters who are susceptible to persuasion in a U.S. election campaign has often employed time of decision as a locator. From the 1940s until the 1970s, the predominant view was that few voters could be affected by campaigning. Most people knew which way they would vote early on, and were not thereafter open to change; the remainder did not decide until the end of the campaign because it had in effect not reached them.

Since that era, a number of studies have rejected this "limited effects" conclusion, seeking to identify which voters might be affected, and how. While some of this shift in theoretical emphasis grows out of historical changes in the electorate and the media, it can be traced also to different operationalizations and interpretations of the concept of time of decision, the topic of this chapter.

The dichotomous model. Two conditions are, almost by definition, necessary for a vote decision to be influenced by campaign communication. First, the voter must be *undecided* in some degree; otherwise there is no decision to be made. Second, the voter must pay at least some *attention* to campaign messages. Early voting researchers linked these two requirements to a dualistic model of the electorate, dividing it theoretically into two ideal types: (1) the predecided majority, who were deeply partisan and thus unaffectable despite paying close attention to the campaign; and (2) a late-deciding residuum that was uninterested, unexposed, inattentive, unguided, and unpredictable (Lazarsfeld, Berelson, and Gaudet 1944; Berelson, Lazarsfeld, and McPhee 1954). The Michigan group implicitly accepted this model after further testing in the elections of the 1950s (Campbell, Gurin, and Miller 1954; Campbell et al. 1960; Benham 1965).

Campaign deciders. Noting that increasing numbers of voters are interested and attentive yet not highly partisan, recent scholars have amended the dualistic early-late model. The rise of television as the principal medium of campaigning (Arterton 1978) has been accompanied by a diminution of political parties as communication channels and as psychological referents (Ranney 1983). Because party identification has become less stable, and has declined as a correlate of the vote, fewer predetermined decisions exist in advance of an election campaign. And because the campaign is brought to virtually every citizen's home via television, fewer voters ignore it than was the case when newspapers and radio were the main channels. Appreciable numbers of vote decisions are being made during and in response to the campaign. These cases are commonly called "campaign deciders," although that rubric covers several distinct patterns of voter behavior.

The time span available for within-campaign decision making has lengthened, due to the rise of primaries in the nominating process (Matthews 1978). To occur "precampaign," a decision must be made a good deal earlier in today's election year than was the case in the 1940s and 1950s. For example, when Lazarsfeld's group began interviewing in Erie County, Ohio, in the spring of 1940, they asked vote-intention questions about parties rather than candidates, because the nominees would not be named until the conventions.[1] In more recent decades, delegates won in primaries have usually reduced the convention nomination procedure to a formality. Because the schedule of events in an election year has changed, the same survey procedure, across election years, is not measuring the same thing. The historical record (Miller and Traugott 1989) shows no long-term trend in median time of decision, as reported in postelection national surveys. The variances around this central tendency are unfortunately not comparable, because the timescale of the campaign has shifted historically.

Spacing out of the election year affords researchers more opportunity to trace the evolution of vote decisions across time. Scholars have suggested that those who decide during the campaign base their votes on different factors from those who wait until the last minute. In terms of communication behaviors at least, the campaign-decision group may be as distinct from the partisan predecided voters and the casual last-minute deciders as the latter two groups are from one another (Chaffee and Choe 1980).

Both campaign deciders and last-minute deciders may be open to persuasion, but for different reasons and in different ways. Decisions that are made at the very end of a normal (i.e., bipartisan) campaign tend to be flimsy and unpredictable, easily influenced by such familiar devices as attack ads (Bowen 1994). But decisions that evolve during the campaign, and that (unless there is a serious third candidate) occur well in advance of the final days before the election, are of a different character. If campaign deciders follow media news, know a good deal about the candidates and the issues, and vote on the basis of this information, they may be open to persuasion, but not in the easy manner that typifies the classical last-minute decision maker. Voter uncertainty coupled with heavy information processing indicates a different persuasional strategy from uncertainty in the absence of information.

Hierarchies-of-effects. In marketing theory terms (Ray 1973), campaign deciders hypothetically match the "learning hierarchy-of-effects" model, whereas last-minute voters are better described by the "low-involvement" hierarchy. Low-involvement consumers process little information and can be persuaded directly by a single message, such as a single advertisement; in this interpretation, a last-minute decision is often a "snap" decision by a voter who cares little and knows less. In the learning hierarchy, by contrast, a good deal of information is processed and evaluated over time before a decision is reached.

The learning hierarchy can be capsulized as a cognition-affect-conation sequence, whereas the low involvement hiearchy is simply cognition-conation (Ray 1973). As Krugman (1965) suggested, television advertising works well for products that people purchase casually, without caring much about them; the last-minute vote decision may be characterized in a similar way. Rothschild and Ray (1974) demonstrated that the learning model is typical of vote decisions for major offices, while the low-involvement model is more applicable to minor offices.[2] For even a major office such as president, however, last-minute decisions may be the norm if the voter feels little involvement in the election outcome or campaign issues.

Methodological issues. Time of decision raises methodological as well as theoretical problems. It is an empirically ambiguous concept, although at first blush it may seem straightforward to measure. In a postelection survey, it usually involves only a single question; in a panel study, a variable can be constructed easily by asking the same voters their intentions at several points throughout an election year. But these alternative operationalizations produce different marginal results. A continuing issue is the comparative validity of these two indicators, for explaining how different voters respond to campaign messages.

Scholars disagree on even so basic an issue as the proper unit of analysis: Should time of decision be considered an attribute of voters, or of decisions? That is, does the measure indicate an individual difference trait, or a complex set of responses to situational conditions? Does it vary from election to election, and between offices in the same election year, or can voters be classified as if each holds an enduring predisposition to decide at some characteristic point during the campaign? Part of our data analysis will deal with these measurement issues.

Research Background

When time of decision entered the research literature, the goal of social science was framed as "theories of the middle range" (e.g., Berelson and Steiner 1964). It was assumed that relationships between variables are generally stable, so that observed correlations indicate approximate regularities in human behavior; this has proven not to be the case with time of decision. Apart from the unsurprising finding that early deciders are more partisan, time of decision has not generated consistent findings. The marginal percentages who decide in various time periods shift with electoral circumstances, and the empirical correlates of time of decision vary from one study to the next.

The first studies. In dichotomizing their 1940 Erie County sample into "early" and "late" deciders, Lazarsfeld, Berelson, and Gaudet (1944) tacitly conceived of time of decision as a general linear variable. They treated it as a stable trait that would be monotonically related to other attributes of voters, such as partisanship and interest. People were "cross-pressured" if they belonged to politically conflicting social categories (e.g., low education but white collar); these voters "delayed their final vote decisions because they were waiting for events to resolve the conflicting pressures." So a seemingly dynamic variable, time of decision, was treated as a stable individual trait determined by one's position in the social structure. Time-of-decision patterns that did not match one of their two polar types were treated as theoretically anomalous, and generally ignored in summaries of results. In their 1948 Elmira study, Berelson, Lazarsfeld, and McPhee (1954) reemphasized the stability of vote intention, which is to say predecided voters. People who expressed indecision in any within-campaign interview were simply omitted from their key table on this point (16).

The University of Michigan's National Election Studies (NES) have included a postelection recall question on time of decision since 1952 (Campbell, Gurin, and Miller 1954). *The American Voter* (Campbell et al. 1960, 78) noted that the 1952 and 1956 postelection surveys "confirm the judgment that the psychological forces guiding behavior arise before the campaign opens." Like Lazarsfeld, the authors emphasized precampaign decision making. *The American Voter* reported a particularly low multiple correlation between attitudes and the vote of last-minute deciders (Campbell et al. 1960, fig. 4-3, 79). This result is often replicated; both precampaign and within-campaign deciders tend to be much more predictable, when issue and candidate perceptions are included in the model (Gopoian and Hadjiharalambous 1994). In the 1960s, though, this finding was described as if it were characteristic only of the precampaign deciders, for whom party identification provided a very strong independent variable.

Communication effects. Only one discursive paragraph of *The American Voter* concerned mass media, a feature of the campaign that was classified as a weak form of participation rather than a source of potential influence (Campbell et al. 1960, 92). But one of the authors (Converse 1962) reopened the question of media effects, ushering in an era of attempts to characterize decision-making voters who might be influenced by an election campaign. Daudt (1961) noted that "floating voters" were heavy media users; so were "ticket splitters" (de Vries and Tarrance 1972).

Still, the prevailing view in the 1960s and early 1970s was that only "minimal consequences" should be expected of an election campaign (Buchanan 1977). Benham (1965) stressed early decision making in his interpretation of the 1960 and 1964 campaigns. Katz (1973) maintained a front-loaded dualistic model: "Typically about 80 percent, or more, of the voters have made up their minds about the vote before the campaign begins." Voters who shift *during* the campaign, he added, are "relatively uninterested in the election and its outcome" (306).

The conceptual choice of whether to emphasize predecided voters or to analyze within-campaign decision-making processes among the remaining voters is largely a matter of seeing the glass as half full versus half empty. By the 1960 and 1964 NES surveys, some 20 to 25 percent of all voters were saying they had decided during the main campaign period (Miller and Traugott 1989), not before it and not near the very end. But the dichotomous formulation persisted.

A reformulated model. Panel measures began to yield a revised picture, beginning with Mendelsohn and O'Keefe (1976). In 1972, they found that within-campaign "switchers" (mostly Democrats who considered voting for George Wallace) were active—and not especially selective—consumers of campaign communication. They were, then, presumably open to persuasion. But switchers numbered "only one panel respondent in ten," so Mendelsohn and O'Keefe's (1976) conclusions mainly reiterated the dichotomous model. In a follow-up survey, though, O'Keefe, Mendelsohn, and Liu (1976) found that the early deciders of 1972 were two years later (i.e., post-Watergate) about equally likely to be early or late deciders. This cast doubt on the traditional characterization of time of decision as a stable personality trait, suggesting instead that decisions are situational. The authors concluded (328) that, contrary to almost all prior literature, the unit of analysis should *not be* thought of in terms of individual differences: "Difficulty of voter decision making appears primarily to be a function of circumstances of a particular campaign rather than a characteristic of certain voters *per se.*"

In a panel study of Wisconsin voters in fall 1976, Chaffee and Choe (1980) found that only 30 percent of a statewide panel had been predecided as late as mid-September. Some 40 percent decided during the Ford-Carter debates period, while the other 30 percent remained undecided a week before the election. In two important respects, the campaign deciders were *not intermediate* between the early and last-minute deciders: They were the lowest of the three groups in partisanship and the highest in attention to the campaign (especially on television). The predecided group was, as in most studies, distinguished primarily by high partisanship. Last-minute deciders were very low on campaign communication measures—and ended up casting votes consistent with their party leanings, which, though weak, were apparently undisturbed by the campaign. The authors suggested that the promise of candidate

debates, which had not been held since 1960, induced many voters to with-
hold their final decisions until they had watched Ford and Carter in direct
competition.

In 1980, Whitney and Goldman (1985) attempted literally to replicate the
Chaffee and Choe (1980) study. They asked the same questions at about the
same times as in the 1976 Wisconsin panel, but with some unavoidable
deviations in design—and almost a complete contradiction in terms of findings. Whitney and Goldman's study was a local one, in the area surrounding
the University of Illinois at Urbana-Champaign. This constituency was notably attracted to a third candidate of 1980, Illinois Republican congressman
John Anderson, who in their estimation offered an erudite alternative to the
arch-conservative Ronald Reagan and the failed presidency of Jimmy Carter.
Many voters in the university community debated whether to cast a "message"
vote for the attractive but unelectable Anderson or to stick with one of the
major party alternatives. The result was a survey in which the 1980 "last-
minute deciders" looked much more like the "campaign deciders" of 1976,
and vice versa. Where Chaffee and Choe had found campaign deciders highly
attentive and focused on campaign-specific issues and candidates, Whitney
and Goldman discovered these behaviors in the late deciders. They concluded
that findings for one campaign, at one time and in one place, should not be
routinely generalized to all times and places; voter decision making is a
situational process. Although their result was probably due in part to the local
sampling frame, the 1980 NES survey also indicated an unusually high incidence of last-minute decision making nationally (Miller and Traugott 1989).
The notion of a theory of the middle range regarding time of decision receded
as empirical findings accumulated.

Evidence of persuasibility. New data and concepts enhanced the empirical study of persuasion and time of decision in the 1970s and 1980s. Beginning in 1974, the NES added media use measures, and a preelection panel
design, so that this archive became considerably richer in relevant evidence.
Several new concepts also appeared in the literature in the next few years to
suggest that many voters were indeed busy making decisions throughout the
campaign season. Phenomena of "voter volatility," including abstention,
ticket splitting, and weakened party loyalty, were analyzed by Bybee et al.
(1981). Voters' party identification underwent thorough review. Noting a rise
in calling oneself "independent" (Weisberg 1980; Kamieniecki 1985), Dennis
(1983) suggested that identification as independent is orthogonal to the partisan dimension. Brody and Rothenberg (1988) showed that fewer than half of
the 1980 voters were stable throughout the campaign year in their self-
descriptions on the NES party identification question. Such findings encour-
aged scholars to conceive of the electorate as more open to persuasion.

The 1980 NES panel enabled Plumb (1986) to compare the two methods of estimating time of decision: panel measurement based on answers given to the same question at different times versus the retrospective postelection question. The panel method classified more cases as campaign deciders; the retrospective measure produced the U-shaped distribution of decisions across time that had informed theories of the middle range in earlier decades. Only 40 percent of the 1980 NES sample fell into the same time categories by both methods. Clearly, these were different measures.

Short-term fluctuations in vote intentions began to be noted in nonpresidential elections, too (Tedin and Murray 1981; Latimer 1987). Using exit polls following a U.S. Senate election, Bowen (1994) related a retrospective time-of-decision measure to open-ended responses about information sources that had been helpful in reaching the voting decision. News accounts were cited most often by voters who said they had been predecided, and TV debates by those who decided during the main body of the campaign. Bowen was, however, mostly concerned with advertisements and last-minute decisions—which were strongly associated phenomena. TV ads were mentioned, for example, by only 18 percent of those who decided "in the last week," but by 79 percent of those who decided "the night before" the election. Most of the last-minute commercials in these exit polls were negative "attack" ads. Conversely, voters' mentions of news as a factor declined precipitously with later decision times (Bowen 1994, table 2).

Bowen emphasized the strategic importance to campaigners of time of decision, a research application that dates back to the Erie County study—but reached a strikingly different conclusion. Whereas Lazarsfeld, Berelson, and Gaudet (1944) suggested that late deciders would be susceptible to seemingly random last-minute influences, Bowen demonstrated how to reach those voters: highly salient attack ads on television, very late in the campaign. His advice seems to coincide with practices of recent candidates.

Bowen's exit poll results also suggest some amendment to the inferences of Plumb and others regarding the greater validity of the panel method versus the retrospective postelection question about time of decision. One valuable feature of the panel survey is that questions about vote intention can be asked while the voter is actively thinking about the election and how to vote. Retrospective questions typically come a week or more after the vote has been cast; they ask the person to recall (after the election result is known) an entire decision-making process that the person had no reason to keep track of during the preceding months. Exit polls, however, do not share these features of removal in time and contamination by the election outcome. The exit poll question is retrospective, but immediately so. It is asked at a time when the decision itself is likely to be uppermost in the voter's mind: the moment just after that vote was finally cast. The reliability of this measure is suggested by the large differences Bowen found regarding the final days of the campaign.

On the other hand, exit poll data are probably no better than any other postelection method for discriminating accurately between those who made their decisions in, say, May or June and those who did not decide until August or September.

Time of decision has, then, been a useful fulcrum for analysis, in a long-term refashioning of the image of the electorate during a political campaign. There is considerable room for persuasion, based on varying kinds of appeals, throughout an election year. Party identification, once considered the foundation of a predominantly predecided vote, is now viewed as tentative and multidimensional. Mass communication has become prominent in research and theory, although demonstration of specific directional effects on undecided voters remains elusive.[3] Circumstantial evidence, of at least the potential for persuasion, has become fairly strong.

The 1992 Election Study

The empirical analysis of time of decision we report here is based on a four-wave panel survey of registered voters in four counties of southern and northern California during the election year of 1992. Three major races were followed: president and two open U.S. Senate seats, one for a two-year term and the other for a six-year term. Voters were sampled randomly from county registration lists in January. The first wave of interviews was completed in early March, just before the first primary election (New Hampshire). Wave 2 took place in late June and early July; it was conducted after the California primary and before the party conventions, which meant also that it was completed just before Ross Perot announced that he was dropping out of the race. Wave 3 began October 12, just after Perot's reentry TV debate, and was completed the weekend before Election Day. The final wave of interviews began immediately after the election and was completed within two weeks.[4] The postelection interview included a retrospective question on time of decision for each of the three races, to complement the panel method of categorizing decision time.[5]

Comparing measures. Table 1 is a cross-tabulation between the two time-of-decision measures (panel reconstruction and retrospective self-report) for each of the three elections. While there is some tendency for decisions in the three-way presidential race to be delayed longer than in the two U.S. Senate races, the findings as between the two methods are consistently the same: The retrospective measure yields higher estimates of decisions that occur either very early or very late, while the panel method identifies more voters as campaign deciders. This result parallels Plumb's (1986) findings, and a comparison of 1976 panel data (from Chaffee and Choe 1980) with the 1976 NES retrospective measure (from Miller and Traugott 1989).

Each measure admits its own characteristic bias into one's research. The marginal results for the two bipartisan U.S. Senate races are similar within method and between contests; in both cases, the estimate of predecided votes is about 60 percent. Of the remainder, though, the percentage of campaign deciders for the Senate seats is nearly twice as high when the panel method is used rather than a retrospective item.

Overall, 58 percent of decisions are classified the same by both methods in table 1. (Chance agreement would be 33 percent.) Most of this consistency, though, is due to the predecided group; 70 percent of those who were classified as precampaign deciders by one measure were by the other as well, across the three races. Between the later two categories, campaign deciders and last-minute deciders, consistent classification was just 55 percent—little better than chance coincidence, which would be 50 percent. Clearly the measures are more interchangeable for identifying predecided voters than when making discriminations between decision times within the campaign.

In the following analyses we use the panel classification rather than the retrospective method. The panel measure offers the advantage of differentiating between those who were merely undecided at various times and those who said they supported different candidates at different times. We also consider the retrospective measure more contaminated by faulty memory and by inter-

TABLE 1. Time of Decision Groups, as Measured by Retrospective vs. Panel Methods

	Panel Method					
Retrospective Method	PD (%)	CD (%)	LM (%)	Row Total[a] (%)	(N)	%
	Presidential Election					
Predecided (PD)	74	22	4	100	(129)	39
Campaign Deciders (CD)	46	42	12	100	(85)	26
Last-minute Deciders (LM)	28	27	45	100	(119)	36
Total	51	29	21		(333)	101
	Two-year Senate Election					
Predecided (PD)	76	15	8	99	(202)	63
Campaign Deciders (CD)	47	25	28	100	(32)	10
Last-minute Deciders (LM)	29	25	46	100	(85)	27
Total	61	19	20		(319)	100
	Six-year Senate Election					
Predecided (PD)	68	18	13	99	(196)	61
Campaign Deciders (CD)	50	28	22	100	(36)	11
Last-minute Deciders (LM)	33	31	36	100	(87)	27
Total	57	23	20		(319)	99

[a]Not all rows total 100 percent, due to rounding.

vening events such as the election outcome. The results we report here should not be compared directly with analyses based only on the retrospective item.

Unit of analysis. Table 2 examines the issue of consistency between races, cross-tabulating the three election races by estimated time of decision. The question at stake is conceptual: Is a given person likely to make decisions for several offices at about the same time, or is timing not a consistent individual trait? That is, should the unit of analysis for time of decision be considered the person or the decision?

The answer seems to be the latter, except that early deciders do tend to be the same people more often than not. In table 2, we display the cross-tabulation between the two Senate races (for which the results are quite similar) and the presidential race. There is very little predictability of decision time from presidential to senatorial races, if we ignore the 32 percent who had made all three decisions by the time of our first interview. This suggests strongly that we should not think of time of decision as an attribute of voters, but of decisions or of the situations in which they occur. This conclusion is quite contrary to what Lazarsfeld, Berelson, and Gaudet (1944) implied, when they explained their time-of-decision groups in terms of individual differences and group cross pressures. It is more consistent with the conclusion of O'Keefe, Mendelsohn, and Liu (1976) that time of decision groupings should not be assumed to represent types of voters.

While time of decision may locate factors that bear on a given choice for a given office in a given campaign, then, it is not a variable likely to produce

TABLE 2. Time of Decision Categorization, Presidential vs. Senate Elections, 1992

	Senate Elections			Row Total[a]		
Presidential Election	PD (%)	CD (%)	LM (%)	(%)	(N)	%
	Two-year Senate Election					
Predecided (PD)[b]	64	16	20	100	(166)	51
Campaign Deciders (CD)	58	22	20	100	(93)	29
Last-minute Deciders (LM)	57	19	24	100	(67)	21
Total	61	18	21		(326)	101
	Six-year Senate Election					
Predecided (PD)	64	19	17	100	(162)	50
Campaign Deciders (CD)	45	25	31	101	(94)	29
Last-minute Deciders (LM)	57	28	16	101	(69)	21
Total	57	23	21		(325)	100

[a]Not all rows total 100 percent, due to rounding.
[b]Panel method was used to classify time of decision groups for this and subsequent tables.

widely applicable generalizations that describe voters' stable dispositions. With regard to influenceability, a voter may be fully predecided on one electoral choice, and yet quite open to persuasion for another office. The determining factors are likely to arise from specific circumstances, such as the number of candidates, availability of key information, and campaign tactics.

Voting consistency. In table 3 we examine consistency, across the three major California elections of 1992, in the voting behavior of four decision groups: the predecided; the campaign deciders (who were undecided in wave 1, but had decided by wave 2 or 3); "switchers," who changed from an early decision to vote for one candidate, expressing a different intention in a later wave; and the last-minute deciders, who expressed no firm preference even in wave 3. The small "switchers" group is distinguished from other campaign deciders here because Mendelsohn and O'Keefe (1976) found them to be active and open-minded media users. Consistency is summarized, in line with deVries and Tarrance (1972), in two categories: those who voted a straight Republican, or straight Democratic, ticket across the three offices versus those who did not. The latter group includes all who voted for Ross Perot, plus those who split their votes between candidates on the Republican and Democratic tickets or did not vote for all three offices. Straight-ticket voting predominates by about 60–40; nearly one-half of these straight-ticket voters were not predecided, but apparently many voted for a party rather than deciding on each candidacy separately.

Table 3 can be summarized simply: split-ticket voting becomes more

TABLE 3. Ticket-Splitting by Time of Decision across Three Elections

Voting Pattern	Predecided (%)	Campaign Deciders (%)	Switchers (%)	Last-minute Deciders (%)	Row Total[a] (%)	(N)	%
		Presidential Election					
Straight ticket voters	57	31	4	9	101	(199)	60
Split ticket voters	41	25	15	19	100	(135)	40
Total	50	29	8	13		(334)	100
		Two-year Senate Election					
Straight ticket voters	73	15	5	8	101	(199)	61
Split ticket voters	42	24	8	26	100	(127)	39
Total	61	18	6	15		(326)	100
		Six-year Senate Election					
Straight ticket voters	66	19	7	9	101	(199)	61
Split ticket voters	41	29	6	24	100	(128)	39
Total	56	23	6	15		(327)	100

[a]Not all rows total 100 percent, due to rounding.

probable the later the voter makes a decision for any one office. Aggregating the data for all 987 decisions represented in this table, 71 percent of the time a decision existed before the campaign started, the person ended up voting for the same party in all three races. This straight-ticket voting figure falls to 56 percent for campaign decisions and 35 percent in the last-minute decision condition. The "switcher" decision-making pattern was intermediate; 44 percent of decisions that got reconsidered involved people who finally voted a straight party ticket.

The monotonic pattern of table 3 is consistent with prior studies, which have mostly considered only the extremes of the time-of-decision distribution. Predecided voters are clearly party oriented, and last-minute decisions are the least predictable of any category. The other two categories—decisions made during the campaign and those in which a voter vacillated to the extent of declaring once in favor of one candidate and later for another—are simply intermediate. This result would not in itself surprise anyone schooled in the dichotomous model of the 1940–1970 era. But we have not yet considered differences between these four groups in their communication behaviors, and other functional variables that might indicate differential persuasibility.

Discriminant analysis. To assess the utility of time-of-decision categories as a clue to persuasibility, we performed a multiple discriminant analysis on the four time-of-decision groups from table 3. We entered, as possible discriminating variables, partisanship[6] (a folded-over party identification scale); tests of knowledge of partisan issue differences[7] (a 20-item index) and of personal information about the presidential candidates[8] (a 10-item index); and self-report measures of attention to the campaign in each of the major mass media channels: television news, television ads, and newspapers.[9] Each of these variables is manifestly related to persuasion, and there is some reason in the research literature to expect each of them to vary by time of decision as well. Table 4 displays the results of the discriminant analysis. Although with four groups there could be three discriminant functions, only two were significant and are reported here.

The first (i.e., the more powerful) function discriminates almost exclusively between the two intermediate decision groups, which are indistinguishable in terms of split-ticket voting behavior in table 3. The campaign decision group is very low on function 1 in table 4, and the "switcher" group is at the opposite extreme. Indices most strongly correlated with this function indicate that voters who switched between favored candidates during the campaign tended to be quite high in attention to television news of the campaign and in knowledge about party differences on issues. The less mercurial voters, who gradually moved from "undecided" to a vote decision during the main campaign period, were neither closely attentive to TV news nor well informed regarding party politics.

Television news attention and political issue knowledge are, we might note, rarely associated with one another in empirical studies or critical writings about mass media effects. More often, scholars conclude that there is little of substance to learn from TV news (e.g., Patterson and McClure 1976) or that little is learned from exposure to it (e.g., Becker and Whitney 1980). We have not here tested the informative power of television news directly; table 4 shows only that it is located on the same function with both knowledge measures, in discriminating among time of decision groups. Other studies do, however, suggest positive political learning effects of attention (as distinct from simple exposure) to TV news (e.g., Chaffee and Schleuder 1986; Zhao and Chaffee 1995).

Function 1 in table 4 is perhaps even more surprising for what it says about the campaign deciders, when we distinguish them from those whose stated intentions switched between candidates. Voters who merely changed from "undecided" to a candidate preference at either wave 2 or wave 3 are less knowledgeable and less attentive to television news about the campaign. This finding on its surface contradicts the results of Chaffee and Choe (1980) regarding campaign deciders. More precisely, though, it refines that earlier finding, by distinguishing the "switching" pattern of decision making from gradual decision making. Those who switch back and forth are much more involved and knowledgeable than are other voters who also come to their decisions during the campaign.

TABLE 4. Multiple Discriminant Analysis of Time of Decision Groups

		Function 1	Function 2
Discriminating Variable[a]			
Issue knowledge		.39	.26
Attention to campaign on television		.37	−.13
Candidate knowledge		.23	.20
Partisanship		−.18	.81
Attention to political ads		−.26	−.27
Attention to campaign in newspapers		.14	.15
Chi-square		50.50***	23.20*
Time of Decision Group Centroids[b]			
Predecided	($N = 168$)	.09	.22
Campaign deciders	($N = 96$)	−.37	−.20
Switchers	($N = 27$)	.72	−.54
Last-minute deciders	($N = 43$)	.01	−.05

[a]Cell entries are correlations between each discriminating variable and the canonical discriminant functions.
[b]Cell entries are group means on the canonical discriminant functions. Groups are defined by time of decision for presidential vote only.
  *$p < .05$
***$p < .001$

Pragmatically, approaches to persuasion should be quite different, in terms of both channel and anticipated sophistication, for these two types of voters. Although both groups made their decisions during the same period in 1992, they did so in quite different ways. The distinction between these two groups, which is the dominant finding of table 4, may be peculiar to three-cornered races such as 1992. But such campaigns have occurred often enough in recent elections (e.g., 1968, 1980), and multicandidate races are common enough in other countries, that the three-way situation ought to be incorporated into theorizing about electoral behavior in general.

The second discriminant function in table 4 holds fewer surprises. It is dominated by the single-measure partisanship item, and as expected from table 3, this function differentiates the predecided group from all the other decision-time categories. This is wholly consistent with prior research, which emphasizes the partisan predecided voter. Indeed, we had expected that function 2 would be the first, and dominant, factor in our discriminant analysis.

A second feature of function 2 is, however, contrary to expectations based on most prior studies. Members of the group at the opposite extreme in time of decision, that is, the last-minute decision makers, were not the lowest in partisanship. Indeed, they were the second highest on function 2. Instead it is the two intermediate time of decision groups, which were so sharply differentiated on function 1, that lie at the opposite extreme from the predecided voters on function 2. This is reminiscent of Chaffee and Choe's (1980) finding that last-minute decisions included consideration of party identification almost as much as did precampaign decisions, even though the last-minute group did not feel strong party ties. In table 4, too, the last-minute deciders for president are not notably deficient in political information, as the literature would predict; their location on the knowledge-dominated function 1 is almost exactly intermediate. This result is more like the findings of Whitney and Goldman (1985) in the three-candidate 1980 race.

Attention to candidate advertising, one key channel of persuasion, does not load cleanly on either discriminant function. It may be worth noting, though, that campaign deciders and attention to ads are positively associated in this multivariate analysis, in that each of these attributes is negatively related to both discriminant functions; both knowledge measures, on the other hand, load positively on both functions. While some of the coefficients in question are weak, this could mean those who finally reached a decision during the main campaign period did so in the absence of much information other than what they were getting from TV ads. Newspaper reading, another major information source, also loads (weakly) in the direction opposite to campaign deciders and attention to ads, on both functions. Reaching the more complex "switchers," on the other hand, would call for an entirely different strategy, one that assumes the high-involvement learning hierarchy of effects

(Ray 1973). Last-minute decision makers are, in this study as in many others dating back to *The American Voter,* rather nondescript; that is, they do not load strongly in either direction on each discriminant function, and there was no significant third function in this analysis. We should recall, though, Bowen's (1994) evidence that senatorial decisions made very late in the campaign were heavily influenced by advertising and very little by news.

Predicting the vote. The standard procedure for evaluating the theoretical import of attributes of vote decisions is to examine them as correlates of the choice itself, in the context of traditional predictors such as party and issue factors. Communication behaviors, which involve contradictory messages that mostly cancel one another out, do not as a rule account for the direction of voting, and we therefore omit them from this analysis. In table 5 we model separately the predictors of support for each of the three major presidential candidates, Bush, Clinton, and Perot, and also of the two winning senatorial candidates, Democrats Barbara Boxer and Dianne Feinstein; the results for the two losing senatorial candidates (not shown) were essentially mirror images of the findings for the two victors. The dependent measure of support for each candidate is measured on a three-point scale; voting for the candidate is the high end, and "considered, but did not vote for" is the intermediate level on this scale.

The first equation in table 5 involves party identification. To accommodate the presence of Ross Perot in the 1994 presidential race, we have added to the model a measure of degree of partisanship, which consists simply of folding over the party identification continuum so that strong Republicans and strong Democrats have the same (high) score. Not surprisingly, this partisanship scale is in table 5 the strongest predictor of support for Perot, who was in effect the antiparty candidate. For the four partisan candidates, party identification is, as usual, a very strong predictor, and the first equations account for 35 to 40 percent of the variance in support. In Perot's case, we account for only 10 percent of the variance by these two independent variables.

The second equation in table 5 adds measures on issue closeness and the perceived influence of news about the economy to the predictive model. These issue-related variables add considerably to the predictive power of the presidential equations, beyond the party factors. Clinton, whose campaign staff's motto was, "It's the economy, stupid," clearly benefited from concern over the depressed economy, as to a lesser extent did Perot and the two Democratic candidates for the Senate. (We do not have an issue closeness measure for the Senate races, and Perot was omitted from this set of questions in wave 3.) Issues are to some extent redundant to party identification, but these measures preserve a traditional distinction that is made in the voting literature. So it is important that in equation 2, issues, especially the economic bad news that prevailed through most of 1992, had a separate

TABLE 5. Predictors of the Vote in Presidential and Senatorial Races

| | Presidential Support[a] | | | | | | Senatorial Support[b] | | | |
| | Bush | | Clinton | | Perot | | Boxer | | Feinstein | |
Predictors[c]	r[d]	Beta[e]	r	Beta	r	Beta	r	Beta	r	Beta
Equation 1. Party factors										
Party ID (Democrat)[f]	−.58***	−.60***	.65***	.66***	−.14**	−.16**	.61***	.62***	.58***	.59***
Partisanship[g]	.15**	.14**	.03	.04	−.26***	−.27***	.00	−.02	−.05	−.09
R-square, Eq. 1	(.376***)		(.435***)		(.098***)		(.383***)		(.359***)	
Equation 2. Issue factors										
Economic news influence (EC)[h]	−.49***	−.13***	.44***	.15***	.13*	.15**	.39***	.20***	.36***	.16**
Closeness on issues[i]	.80***	.70***	.71***	.46***	.45***	.42***				
R-sq change, Issues	(.316***)		(.160***)		(.207***)		(.035***)		(.021**)	
R-square, Eq. 2	(.692***)		(.595***)		(.305***)		(.418***)		(.380***)	
Equation 3. Time of decision (dummy variables)[j]										
Precampaign Decider (PD)	−.08		.12*		.25***		−.12*		−.12*	
Campaign Decider (CD)	−.19**	.07	.27***	.19***	.05	.04	−.12*	−.03	−.14*	−.04
Last-minute Decider (LM)	.11*	.09**	−.16**	.03	.25***	.16**	−.03	−.02	−.02	.05
R-square change, decision time	(.007*)		(.033***)		(.022**)		(.001)		(.005)	
R-square, Eq. 3	(.699***)		(.628***)		(.327***)		(.419***)		(.385***)	

Equation 4a. Interaction with party ID[k]										
Party × PD	-.53***		.57***		-.16**		.54***		.50***	
Party × CD	-.27**	-.01	.28**	-.05	-.04	.03	.25***	-.09	.21***	-.11*
Party × LM	-.16**	.05	.17**	-.09*	-.16**	-.05	.17***	-.13*	.11*	-.19***
R-square change	(.001)		(.006**)		(.003)		(.013*)		(.028***)	
Equation 4b. Interaction with economic news influence										
EC × PD	-.32***		.32***		.25***		.12*		.10	
EC × CD	-.23***	-.15	.29***	-.02	.07	-.16	-.08	-.19	-.10	-.11
EC × LM	.06	-.12	-.11	.22	.25***	-.39*	.02	.03	.01	-.13
R-square change	(.001)		(.003)		(.009)		(.002)		(.001)	

*$p < .05$
**$p < .01$
***$p < .001$

a Dependent variable: 3 = voted for candidate; 2 = considered, but did not vote for; 1 = did not consider.

b Senatorial results are shown for winning candidates only. Results for their opponents are virtually identical, in the opposite direction.

c Predictors entered as blocks in hierarchical regression.

d Entries are zero-order Pearson correlations between each predictor and support for the listed candidate.

e Entries are standardized regression coefficients from the first equation in which the variable is entered.

f Range from −5 (Strong Republican) to +5 (Strong Democrat).

g Folded-over party identification scale, range from 0 up to 5 for strong identification with either major party.

h This measure was a single post-election five-point agree-disagree item. "News about the economy influenced my votes a lot."

i This measure was based on six questions asked in waves 2 and 3 of the panel survey. In June-July, respondents were asked, "Which one do you think is closest to your own views on domestic issues, Bush, Clinton, or Perot?" and, "Which one is furthest from your views on domestic issues?" These questions were repeated for "your views on foreign policy?" In October, when it was unclear whether Perot had resumed his candidacy, a two-candidate format was used: "Next, on domestic issues, would you say George Bush, or Bill Clinton, is closer to your own views?" and, "Which one is closer to your own views on foreign policy, Bush or Clinton?" Indices of favorability toward each of the three candidates were constructed, adding points when the respondent said a candidate was close, and subtracting them if "further" or "furthest." These questions were not asked regarding the Senate candidates.

j Coefficients for all three time of decision groups are shown, for information. Only two dummy variables (CD and LM) were entered in equation 3.

k Each set of interaction terms was tested in a separate equation (4a and 4b). Correlation and beta coefficients are shown to indicate direction of effect only; differences of these coefficients from zero are not interpreted statistically due to high correlations between each interaction term and its two constituent measures. Statistical significance is evaluated by increment to *R*-square.

impact on vote decisions as evidenced by significant increments to the variance explained.

Time of decision is added to the predictive model in equation 3. Because of the small size of the "switchers" group (see table 3), we have grouped them here with the campaign deciders; viewed strictly in terms of time, these two sets of decisions were made within the same, intermediate time frame, although as we have noted (table 4) the two groups differed in knowledge and communication behaviors. The incremental effects of adding time of decision in equation 3 are significant for all three presidential candidates. Clinton received a disproportionate amount of his support from people whose decisions were made during the campaign period. Both Bush and Perot did better among voters whose decisions were made at the last minute. Perot also gained support early on, which in the context of this panel study means prior to wave 2, or early summer. Time of decision does not, however, relate significantly to voter support in either senatorial race.

It is not surprising that Perot did not fare well in decisions made during the main campaign period, June through October, since that was the time in which he announced that he was pulling out of the race, and then only gradually seemed to reenter. Some voters considering Clinton seem to have waited at first, perhaps to see how the economy was doing; support flowed to Clinton primarily when, by late summer, there had been no apparent economic turnaround. Bush's support, which was based on strong identification with the Republican party (equation 1), did not manifest itself strongly until very late, suggesting that a lot of Republicans delayed because they were tempted to support Perot instead—as many did.

The final set of equations in table 5 involves interactions between time of decision and the two major predictors of the vote, which were party identification and economic news. The purpose of these interaction tests is to look for clues to differential bases of voting in different time periods. Overall, neither of these factors interacts strongly with campaign decision time, after these factors are separately controlled in Equations 1, 2, and 3 of the hierarchical regression procedure. The only significant increment to variance in support for a presidential candidate involves Clinton, who lost some last-minute Democrats relative to his holding power in the earlier decision time periods (equation 4a). The same pattern is seen for the senatorial races (equation 4a), where the interaction of party identification and time of decision is clearly significant. In general, both Boxer and Feinstein did less well than expected, on the basis of party loyalties, among last-minute deciders.

The interactions of time with party in equation 4a are consistent with our earlier findings of more split-ticket voting among the last-minute deciders. They are contrary to Chaffee and Choe's (1980) finding that party identification was a major predictor of the votes of last-minute deciders.

The time-by-issue interactions (equation 4b) are nonsignificant in all five tests. If we were to delete the predecided cases from the analyses, however, there is a clear contrast between the campaign deciders and the last-minute deciders, which can be seen in a comparison of the raw correlations reported along with the overall results for equation 4b. Economic issues seem to have affected support for each of the three presidential candidates in decisions reached in a specific time period. Clinton benefited, and Bush suffered, from campaign-period decisions that were influenced by economic news, a finding that accords with Chaffee and Choe's (1980) evidence that campaign deciders were affected strongly by campaign-specific information. Last-minute presidential choices between the two major-party candidates were significantly correlated with party identification (see correlations for equation 4a) but not with economic news. In general, support for major-party candidates is much less predictable, from both party and issue factors, among the last-minute deciders, a result that echoes findings from Campbell et al. (1960) through Chaffee and Choe (1980).

While the time-specific influences of economic news are overall nonsignificant (equation 4b), it may be noteworthy that the direction of prediction reverses slightly at the end. Perhaps at least some last-minute decisions were affected by indicators, which came late in the campaign, of an upturn in the economy. The main beneficiary of this shift, though, was not the incumbent Bush, but Ross Perot. If we ignore predecided voters and simply compare campaign deciders with those who decided at the last minute, support for Perot, especially support associated with economic news influence, accounts for the strongest entries in all of table 5 that involve last-minute decision-making. Doubtless the comings and goings of Ross Perot in the 1992 election race influenced many voters and created results regarding time of decision that differ from what is found in two-party campaigns. This is similar to our general explanation for the wide differences in findings between the 1976 Ford-Carter campaign (Chaffee and Choe 1980) and the 1980 Carter-Reagan-Anderson study (Whitney and Goldman 1985). The presence of a strong third candidate induces many voters who would otherwise reach decisions during the campaign to delay. This situation creates a mixed bag of last-minute decisions, a category that would otherwise probably continue to be as they have been traditionally characterized: apathetic, uninformed, and easily persuaded by attack ads (Bowen 1994).

Conclusions

The original formulaic approach to time of vote decision has been superseded by a more situational conception. In the 1940s and 1950s, time of decision was assumed to be a general variable whose linear correlates were to be ascertained through replications and elaborations of the dualistic paradigm laid down by the Columbia and Michigan groups. By the 1970s, this assumption had clearly failed; time of decision is today seen as a much lumpier piece of business. Sometimes its correlates are curvilinear, and their properties shift from study to study.

What accounts for these irregularities, and do general patterns lie beneath them? It is difficult to tell, due to the particular procedures of each study. Syntheses of findings tend to overlook differences in sampling frame, measurement, category boundaries, and interview timing. Such operational contingencies greatly affect one's evidence, starting with the marginal percentages of early deciders. Each researcher tends to present a new study as the latest (and hopefully the best) answer to long-standing questions, rather than as a limited set of data to be added to a larger picture.

There have been important related changes in the electorate, and in the political process. The present study is one of very few analyses in which party identification has not overshadowed all other factors (see table 4). A window of opportunity for greater campaign influence is opening up as party identification recedes in its importance for voters. Third-party candidacies become more likely when party identification is shifting, and, as we have noted here, a third candidate encourages many thoughtful voters to defer their final decisions until all the campaign evidence is in—in contradiction to the traditional image of last-minute deciders as apathetic know-nothings.

As for communication, the dominant fact of recent American political history has been the arrival, and currently the dominance, of television in election campaigns. Television reaches virtually every voter, but purposeful attention to TV varies—with time of decision, among other factors. Easy availability of campaign information enables voters to make decisions throughout the campaign, rather than in advance of it *or* at the last minute. The campaign via TV has rendered the early dichotomous model obsolete. But if a sizable number of attentive voters are still undecided late in the campaign, they can be influenced by news such as a late shift in economic conditions. The timing of their final decisions is not a particularly sound indicator of the bases on which votes are decided, although in the usual two-party race, last-minute decisions involve less political information and are more likely to be influenced by attack ads than by current news.

Many studies of time of decision make suggestions for campaign planning. The most common recommendation is to disseminate messages on behalf of one's candidacy during the period when most decisions are being made. In the era when partisan early deciders were considered the predominant case, for example, it was suggested that campaign efforts should begin much earlier than the election year (e.g., Benham 1965). Late deciders were largely dismissed as random in their behavior (Gopoian and Hadjiharalambous 1994). Some within-campaign switchers, and some voters seriously pondering a three-way choice, may be more active and sophisticated than other voters who also make their decisions in the same phase of the campaign. Research rarely indicates just how to approach these types of decision making, but it does illuminate the process enough that a careful student of electoral behavior can make informed judgments in campaign planning.

Our most general conclusions about time of decision are that it does not represent a single concept, and it is not a unidimensional variable. The factors it might locate vary from one election situation to another. Our 1992 research did not particularly replicate earlier studies with similar panel designs. Like so many variables that are easy to measure (one thinks of education, gender, and age), time of decision's theoretical implications are ambiguous. Still, it has proven itself a useful method of sorting out voters and their decisions.

For campaign strategists, being able to estimate how many decisions remain to be made at any given time, and the kinds of communication channels that might affect them, is invaluable information. For journalists, some appreciation of the different character of vote decisions that are being made at different times might enlighten coverage of an otherwise lengthy, plodding campaign year. For scholars, time of decision has not been the surest guide to new conceptions of voter behavior, but it continues to help in the search. Whether decision time itself is changing historically or not, its relationship to such factors as candidate prominence, third-candidate alternatives, and the meaning of self-reports about party identification certainly merits continued investigation in future elections. For those who study mass communication effects, time of decision was for many years a discouraging organizing theme, used to explain why the media and the campaign in general were of trivial importance to an election outcome. Scholars no longer believe that, no more than do candidates, nor do the professional communicators who manage their campaigns.

NOTES

1. In 1940, President Franklin D. Roosevelt was widely expected to, and did, run for reelection. But because a third term was unprecedented, there was some doubt and a good deal of opposition in principle prior to the Democratic convention. The Republican convention produced a surprise nominee, Wendell Willkie. Despite not knowing the identity of either candidate, however, many respondents interviewed prior to the conventions stated which party they expected to vote for—and later reported that this was indeed the way they eventually voted.

2. Rothschild and Ray (1974) experimented with commercials that simply presented the candidate's name repetitively. This variable influenced vote intentions for offices like the state assembly, but had no effect on gubernatorial vote decisions, for example.

3. Zaller's chapter in this book indicates that the total effect of media messages in a campaign can be massive, even though the net effect is usually small because the competing sides tend to neutralize one another's impact.

4. The California voter sample contains a strong upward bias (especially in education), due to two features of the design. First, the sampling frame of registered voters (as of January 1992) omitted many eventual voters who had not been registered at the start of the election year. Further, attrition from the panel was nonrandom, due to the study's nature (politics) and sponsorship (universities) and to differential residential mobility. Both these factors tended to select older, more established voters. In other respects, such as family income or the percentage voting Republican, the sample was close to U.S. Census and aggregate voting figures for the counties in which the interviews were conducted (Sue and Chaffee 1993).

5. The panel measure of time of decision was constructed from comparing the successive responses each voter gave to the following series of questions: (Wave 2) "If the general election for President were held today, do you think you would vote for George Bush, Bill Clinton, Ross Perot, or someone else?" "Next, for the two-year Senate seat, do you think you would vote for Dianne Feinstein, John Seymour, or someone else? (If asked: If the election were held today.)" "For the six-year Senate seat, do you think you would vote for Barbara Boxer, Bruce Herschensohn, or someone else? (If asked: If the election were held today.)" (Wave 3) "In the presidential election, do you think you will vote for George Bush, Bill Clinton, Ross Perot, or someone else?" "There are also two U.S. Senate seats open in California this year. For the six-year seat, do you think you will voter for Barbara Boxer, Bruce Herschensohn, or someone else?" "For the two-year Senate seat, do you think you will vote for Dianne Feinstein, John Seymour, or someone else?" (Wave 4) "Did you vote in the November election?" (If yes) "Who did you vote for, for President?" "Who did you vote for in the U.S. Senate race between Dianne Feinstein and John Seymour?" "And who did you vote for in the U.S. Senate election for the six-year seat, between Barbara Boxer and Bruce Herschensohn?" A retrospective question was asked (Wave 4) immediately after respondents had been asked how they had voted for each office: "When would you say you finally decided for sure which way you were going to vote, for [President/in the Feinstein-Seymour race/in the Boxer-Herschensohn race]? For instance, had you already decided in January, or did you decide after the California primary election in June, or during the campaign in September, or didn't you decide for sure until the very end, in November?" All three contests were won by Democrats—Clinton, Feinstein, and Boxer.

6. The question, asked in waves 2 and 3, was, "In politics do you think of yourself as a Republican, a Democrat, or something else?" (If Republican or Democrat) "Do you consider yourself a strong Republican/Democrat, or not a strong Republican/Democrat?" (If neither) "Well, do you you feel closer to the Republican party, or to the Democratic party?"

7. Asked in wave 2: "Now, some political issues. On a scale of 1 to 5, which party is more in favor of these positions? A 5 means the Republicans are strongly in favor, a 1 means the Democrats. Answer 3 if you don't think there is any difference between the parties. First, affirmative action for minorities. A 5 would mean the Republican

party, and a 1 would mean the Democratic party, is more in favor of affirmative action for minorities. Aid to families with dependent children? Building more prisons? Federal grants to cities? Federal vouchers for private school students? Less regulation of business? Protection of endangered species? Prayer in public schools? Reduce military spending? Restrictions on abortion?" Asked in wave 3: "Now, some questions about the political parties. On a scale of 1 to 5, which party is more in favor of these positions? A 5 would mean the Republicans are strongly in favor, a 1 means the Democrats. Answer 3 if you don't think there is any difference between the parties. And if you don't know, just say so. Cutting capital gains taxes: Which party is more in favor, the Republicans or the Democrats? Equal rights for women? Federal vouchers for parochial school students? Free trade with other countries? Gun control? Letting the market decide? Protection of civil rights? Reducing the deficit by raising taxes? Strict environmental protection? Tougher anti-drug laws?"

8. Asked in wave 2: "The next few questions ask some personal facts about Bush, Clinton, and Perot. If you don't know the answer, just say so. Do you know who is the oldest, Bush, Clinton, or Perot? Who is the shortest? Which one says he dislikes broccoli? Which one was a successful computer salesman? Who has Mexican-American grandchildren? Which one was a star first baseman on his college baseball team? Which one plays the tenor saxophone? Which one was a Rhodes scholar? Who has been endorsed by Arnold Schwarzenegger? Which one was head of the CIA?"

9. Asked in waves 1, 2, and 3: "Now I'm going to ask you about news on television. On a scale of 1 to 5 where 1 is *not at all* and 5 is *a lot,* how much attention are you paying to TV news about the election campaign?" "Next, newspapers. On the scale of 1 to 5, how much attention are you paying to the campaign in the newspapers?" "Now think about television advertisments for the candidates. On the scale of 1 to 5, how much attention do you pay to TV ads for the candidates?"

REFERENCES

Arterton, F. Christopher. 1978. The media politics of presidential campaigns: A study of the Carter nomination drive. In *Race for the presidency: The media and the nominating process,* ed. James David Barber, 25–54. Englewood Cliffs, N.J.: Prentice-Hall.

Becker, Lee B., and D. Charles Whitney. 1980. Effects of media dependencies: Audience assessment of government. *Communication Research* 7:95–120.

Benham, Thomas W. 1965. Polling for a presidential candidate: Some observations on the 1964 campaign. *Public Opinion Quarterly* 29:185–99.

Berelson, Bernard, and Gary Steiner. 1964. *Human behavior: An inventory of scientific findings.* New York: Harcourt, Brace and World.

Berelson, Bernard, Paul F. Lazarsfeld, and William N. McPhee. 1954. *Voting.* Chicago: University of Chicago Press.

Bowen, Lawrence. 1994. Time of voting decision and use of political advertising: The Slade Gorton–Brock Adams senatorial campaign. *Journalism Quarterly* 71:665–75.

Brody, Richard A., and Lawrence Rothenberg. 1988. The instability of partisanship: An analysis of the 1980 presidential election. *British Journal of Political Science* 18:445–65.

Buchanan, William. 1977. American institutions and political behavior. In *Foundation of political science,* ed. Donald M. Freeman, 84–122. New York: Free Press.

Bybee, Carl R., Jack M. McLeod, William D. Luetscher, and Gina Garramone. 1981. Mass communication and voter volatility. *Public Opinion Quarterly* 45:69–90.

Campbell, Angus, Gerald Gurin, and Warren E. Miller. 1954. *The voter decides.* Chicago: Row, Peterson.

Campbell, Angus, Philip E. Converse, Warren E. Miller, and Donald E. Stokes. 1960. *The American voter.* New York: John Wiley.

Chaffee, Steven H., and Sun Yuel Choe. 1980. Time of decision and media use in the Ford-Carter campaign. *Public Opinion Quarterly* 44:53–69.

Chaffee, Steven H., and Joan Schleuder. 1986. Measurement and effects of attention to media news. *Human Communication Research* 13:76–107.

Converse, Philip E. 1962. Information flow and the stability of partisan attitudes. *Public Opinion Quarterly* 26:578–99.

Daudt, H. 1961. *Floating voters and the floating vote: A critical analysis of American and English election studies.* Leiden: H. E. Stenfert Kroese.

Dennis, Jack. 1983. Toward a theory of political independence. Paper presented at the annual meeting of the American Political Science Association, Chicago.

de Vries, Walter, and Lance Tarrance, Jr. 1972. *The ticket-splitter: A new force in American politics.* Grand Rapids, Mich.: William B. Eerdmans.

Dreyer, Edward C. 1971. Media use and electoral choices: Some political consequences of information exposure. *Public Opinion Quarterly* 35:544–53.

Gopoian, J. David, and Sissie Hadjiharalambous. 1994. Late deciding voters in presidential elections. *Political Behavior* 16:55–78.

Kamieniecki, Sheldon. 1985. *Party identification, political behavior, and the American electorate.* Westport, Conn.: Greenwood Press.

Katz, Elihu. 1973. Platforms and windows: Broadcasting's role in election campaigns. *Journalism Quarterly* 48:304–14.

Krugman, Herbert E. 1965. The impact of television advertising: Learning without involvement. *Public Opinion Quarterly* 29:349–56.

Latimer, Margaret K. 1987. The floating voter and the media. *Journalism Quarterly* 64:805–12.

Lazarsfeld, Paul F., Bernard Berelson, and Hazel Gaudet. 1944. *The people's choice.* New York: Columbia University Press.

Matthews, Donald R. 1978. 'Winnowing': The news media and the 1976 presidential nominations. In *Race for the presidency: The media and the nominating process,* ed. James David Barber, 55–78. Englewood Cliffs, N.J.: Prentice-Hall.

Mendelsohn, Harold, and Garrett J. O'Keefe. 1976. *The people choose a president: Influences on voter decision making.* New York: Praeger.

Miller, Warren E., and Santa A. Traugott. 1989. *American National Election Studies data sourcebook—1952–1986.* Cambridge: Harvard University Press.

Nie, Norman, Sidney Verba, and John Petrocik. 1979. *The changing American voter.* Cambridge: Harvard University Press.

O'Keefe, Garrett J., Harold Mendelsohn, and Jenny Liu. 1976. Voter decision making 1972 and 1974. *Public Opinion Quarterly* 40:320–30.

Patterson, Thomas E., and Robert McClure. 1976. *The unseeing eye: The myth of television power in political campaign.* New York: Putnam.

Plumb, Elizabeth. 1986. Validation of voter recall: Time of electoral decision making. *Political Behavior* 8:302–12.

Ranney, Austin. 1983. *Channels of power: The impact of television on American politics.* New York: Basic Books.

Ray, Michael L. 1973. Marketing communication and the hierarchy-of-effects. In *New models for communication research,* ed. Peter Clarke. Beverly Hills, Calif.: Sage.

Rothschild, Michael L., and Michael L. Ray. 1974. Involvement and political advertising effect: An exploratory experiment. *Communication Research* 1:264–85.

Sue, Valerie, and Steven H. Chaffee. 1993. *Sample characteristics of the Stanford 1992 California panel.* Stanford, Calif.: Stanford University Institute for Communication Research.

Tedin, Kent L., and Richard W. Murray. 1981. Dynamics of candidate choice in a state election. *Journal of Politics* 43:435–55.

Weisberg, Herbert F. 1980. A multidimensional conceptualization of party identification. *Political Behavior* 2:33–60.

Whitney, D. Charles, and Steven B. Goldman. 1985. Media use and time of vote decision: A study of the 1980 presidential election. *Communication Research* 12:511–29.

Zhao, Xinshu, and Steven H. Chaffee. 1995. Campaign advertisements versus television news as sources of political issue information. *Public Opinion Quarterly* 59:41–65.

Contributors

Stephen Ansolabehere is Associate Professor of Political Science at the Massachusetts Institute of Technology. He is coauthor, with Shanto Iyengar, of *Going Negative: How Attack Ads Polarize and Shrink the Electorate.*

Richard A. Brody is Emeritus Professor of Political Science and Communication at Stanford University. He is the author of *Assessing the President,* coauthor of *Reasoning and Choice: Explorations in Political Psychology,* and serves as editor of *Political Behavior.* He is also a Fellow of the American Academy of Arts and Sciences.

Steven H. Chaffee (Ph.D., Stanford University, 1965) is Janet M. Peck Professor of International Communication, and Professor (by courtesy) of Political Science, at Stanford University. He was formerly Vilas Research Professor of Journalism and Mass Communication at the University of Wisconsin-Madison. He is editor of the monograph series *Communication Concepts.*

Dennis Chong is Associate Professor of Political Science at Northwestern University. He has written on collective action, public opinion formation, and political behavior and is coeditor of the Cambridge University Press book series on *Public Opinion, Political Psychology, and Communications.*

Michael D. Cobb is a Ph.D. candidate in Political Science at the University of Illinois, Urbana-Champaign, where his primary research area is race and politics.

Gregory Andrade Diamond is Assistant Professor of Psychology at St. Joseph's College in Indiana, moving there from Lyon College. His research interests include the application of latitude theory to the problem of interpersonal attraction. He has previously taught political science at the University of Illinois, Urbana-Champaign, and as an adjunct at George Washington University.

Clark Hubbard is Assistant Professor of Political Science at the University of New Hampshire. He earned his Ph.D. from SUNY, Stony Brook, and has taught in the Department of Communication at the University of Michigan.

Robert Huckfeldt is Professor of Political Science at Indiana University in Bloomington. His most recent book, coauthored with John Sprague, is *Citizens, Politics, and Social Communication,* and he is currently engaged in a study of opinion dynamics in the 1996 presidential election campaign.

Norman L. Hurley is a Ph.D. candidate in the Department of Political Science at the University of Illinois at Urbana-Champaign and an instructor in the Department of Political Science at the University of North Carolina at Chapel Hill.

Shanto Iyengar is Professor of Political Science at the University of California, Los Angeles. His research on the effects of mass media on political attitudes has been published in *News That Matters, Is Anyone Responsible?* and most recently, *Going Negative: How Attack Ads Polarize and Shrink the Electorate.*

Jon A. Krosnick is Associate Professor of Psychology and Political Science at Ohio State University. His research interests include the role of attitude strength in regulating political cognition and action, agenda-setting and priming by the news media, and the cognitive processes underlying people's responses to survey questionnaires. In 1995, he was awarded the Eric H. Erikson Award for Distinguished Early Career Contribution to Political Psychology by the International Society for Political Psychology.

James H. Kuklinski is Professor of Political Science and a member of the Institute of Government and Public Affairs at the University of Illinois, Urbana-Champaign.

Kathleen M. McGraw is Professor of Political Science and Psychology at SUNY, Stony Brook. Her research interests are in the areas of political psychology, political communication, and public opinion.

Joanne M. Miller is a Ph.D. candidate in social psychology at Ohio State University. Her research interests include the effects of the mass media on political attitudes and the roles that perceptions of threat and efficacy play in motivating public membership and political participation. She has been an instructor in the OSU Summer Institute in Political Psychology and a fellow in the OSU Research/Training Group on the Role of Cognition in Collective Political Decision-Making.

Jeffery J. Mondak is Associate Professor of Political Science at the University of Pittsburgh. He is the author of *Nothing to Read: Newspapers and*

Elections in a Social Experiment. His articles appear in such journals as the *American Journal of Political Science, Journal of Politics, Political Research Quarterly,* and *Public Opinion Quarterly.*

Diana C. Mutz is Associate Professor of Political Science at the University of Wisconsin-Madison. Her research interests involve the effects of mass media on political behavior, public opinion, and political psychology. Her research has appeared in journals including the *American Journal of Political Science, Journal of Politics,* and *Public Opinion Quarterly.*

Rajiv Nath Rimal (Ph.D., Stanford University, 1995) is Assistant Professor of Speech Communication at Texas A&M University. His research focuses on persuasion, primarily in health promotion through behavioral change.

Alan Rosenblatt is Assistant Professor in the Department of Public and International Affairs at George Mason University. A specialist in research methods, electoral behavior, and public opinion, his research has focused on public opinion on foreign policy issues.

Lee Sigelman is Professor and Chair of the Department of Political Science at George Washington University. He has written extensively on issues pertaining to public opinion and mass communication, including presidential leadership of public opinion.

Paul M. Sniderman is Professor of Political Science at Stanford University and Research Scientist at the Survey Research Center, University of California, Berkeley. His latest book is *The Clash of Rights: Liberty Equality and Legitimacy in Pluralist Democracies.*

John Zaller is Professor of Political Science at the University of California, Los Angeles. His most recent book is *The Nature and Origins of Mass Opinion.*

DATE DUE

HIGHSMITH #45115